"This series has it all: a love story over millennia,
intrigue, a

"*Resurrectionists* is supe acked
punch. Fred Van

—Jim Zub (*Samurai Jack, Wayward*)

RESURRECTIONISTS™

People are trapped in history and history is trapped in them.

"Fred Van Lente is a treasure in our industry. Every word from his pen reinvents what comics are capable of."
—Joshua Hale Fialkov (*The Bunker, The Life After, I, Vampire*)

"This is a fun concept that clearly leaves the reader with many questions and possibilities."
—Comic Book Resources

"The story is clever and exciting."
—Comic Bastards

"Overall, *Resurrectionists* #1 is an action packed adventure that promises heists and intrigue for the future. Van Lente can deliver a script and Rosenzweig and company can bring the artistic goods to help create one of the most unique books on the shelf today."
—Comicosity

"An excellent blend of action, suspense, romance, and drama."
—Adventures in Poor Taste

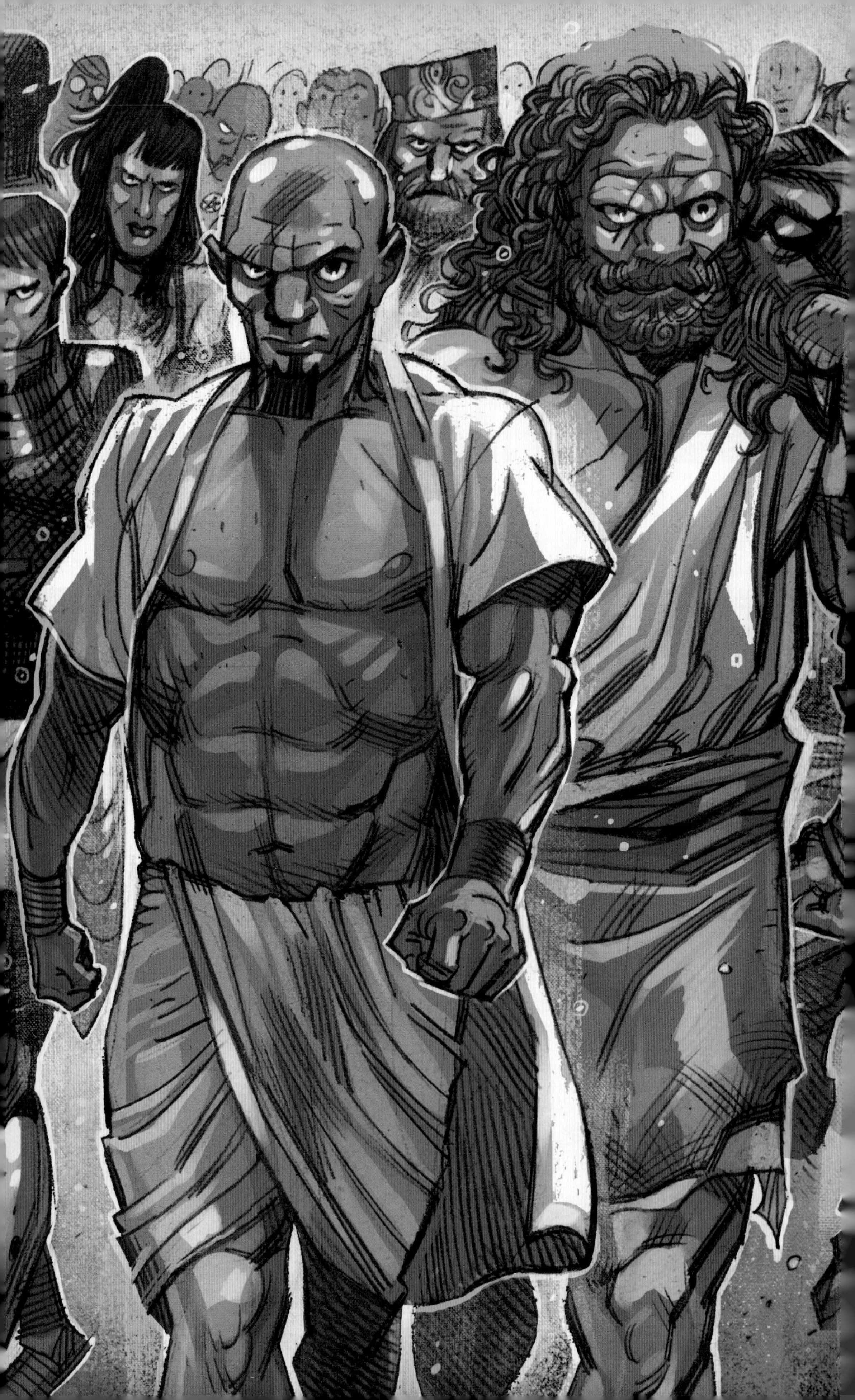

RESURRECTIONISTS

People are trapped in history

and history is trapped in them.

Story by **FRED VAN LENTE**

Pencils by **MAURIZIO ROSENZWEIG**

Inks and colors by **MORENO DINISIO**

Letters by **NATE PIEKOS OF BLAMBOT®**

Cover and chapter break art by **JUAN DOE**

DARK HORSE BOOKS

President and Publisher
MIKE RICHARDSON

Editor
JIM GIBBONS

Assistant Editor
SPENCER CUSHING

Digital Production
RYAN JORGENSEN

Collection Designer
DAVID NESTELLE

To Crystal, in this and all the other lifetimes.—Fred
To Dr. Dania, my goddess of thunder.—Maurizio

Neil Hankerson Executive Vice President • Tom Weddle Chief Financial
Officer • Randy Stradley Vice President of Publishing • Michael
Martens Vice President of Book Trade Sales • Scott Allie Editor in Chief
• Matt Parkinson Vice President of Marketing • David Scroggy Vice
President of Product Development • Dale LaFountain Vice President
of Information Technology • Darlene Vogel Senior Director of Print,
Design, and Production • Ken Lizzi General Counsel • Davey Estrada
Editorial Director • Chris Warner Senior Books Editor • Diana Schutz
Executive Editor • Cary Grazzini Director of Print and Development •
Lia Ribacchi Art Director • Cara Niece Director of Scheduling • Mark
Bernardi Director of Digital Publishing

Published by Dark Horse Books
A division of Dark Horse Comics, Inc.
10956 SE Main Street
Milwaukie, OR 97222

First edition: August 2015
ISBN 978-1-61655-760-7

10 9 8 7 6 5 4 3 2 1
Printed in China

International Licensing: (503) 905-2377
Comic Shop Locator Service: (888) 266-4226

Library of Congress Cataloging-in-Publication Data

Van Lente, Fred.
  Resurrectionists : near-death experienced / story by Fred Van Lente ; pencils by Maurizio
Rosenzweig ; inks and colors by Moreno Dinisio : letters by Nate Piekos of BLAMBOT ; cover and
chapter break art by Juan Doe. -- First edition.
     pages cm.
  Summary: "People are trapped in history, and history is trapped in them. Resurrectionists are
a select group of people who can not only remember their past lives, but also become them.
Framed architect-turned-thief Jericho Way and his crew of modern-day tomb robbers aren't
born knowing they've been trying to pull off the same heist for three millennia. First, they have
to wake up. But with enlightenment comes grave danger--the eternally antagonistic Sojourn
Corporation is now hot on their heels! To fight their future, they'll have to steal the past. Res
urrectionists: Near-Death Experienced collects New York Times best-selling author Fred Van
Lente's original, gripping heist thriller with a twist!"-- Provided by publisher.
  Summary: "Jericho Way, framed-architect turned thief, discovers he is a Resurrectionist, a
member of an elite group that can awaken to remember and utilize the skills of every one
of his past lives. He's about to help pull off a heist 3000 years in the making"-- Provided by
publisher.
  ISBN 978-1-61655-760-7 (paperback)
  1. Thieves--Comic books, strips, etc. 2. Graphic novels. I. Rosenzweig, Maurizio, illustrator. II.
Dinisio, Moreno, colorist. III. Piekos, Nate, letterer. IV. Doe, Juan, illustrator. V. Title. VI. Title: Near-
death experienced.

  PN6727.V354R47 2015
  741.5'973--dc23

                         2015009984

This volume collects Resurrectionists #1–#6, published by Dark Horse Comics.

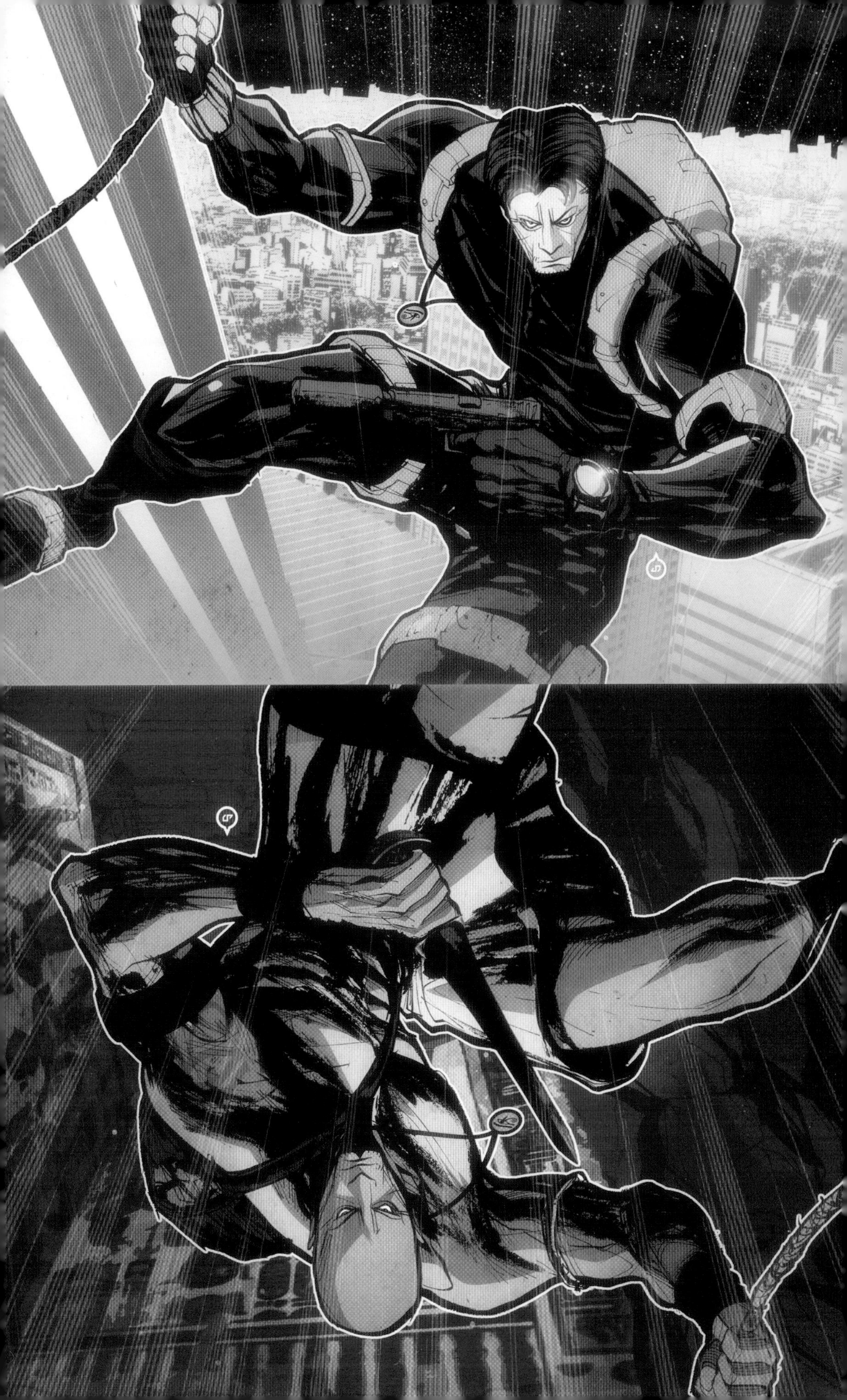

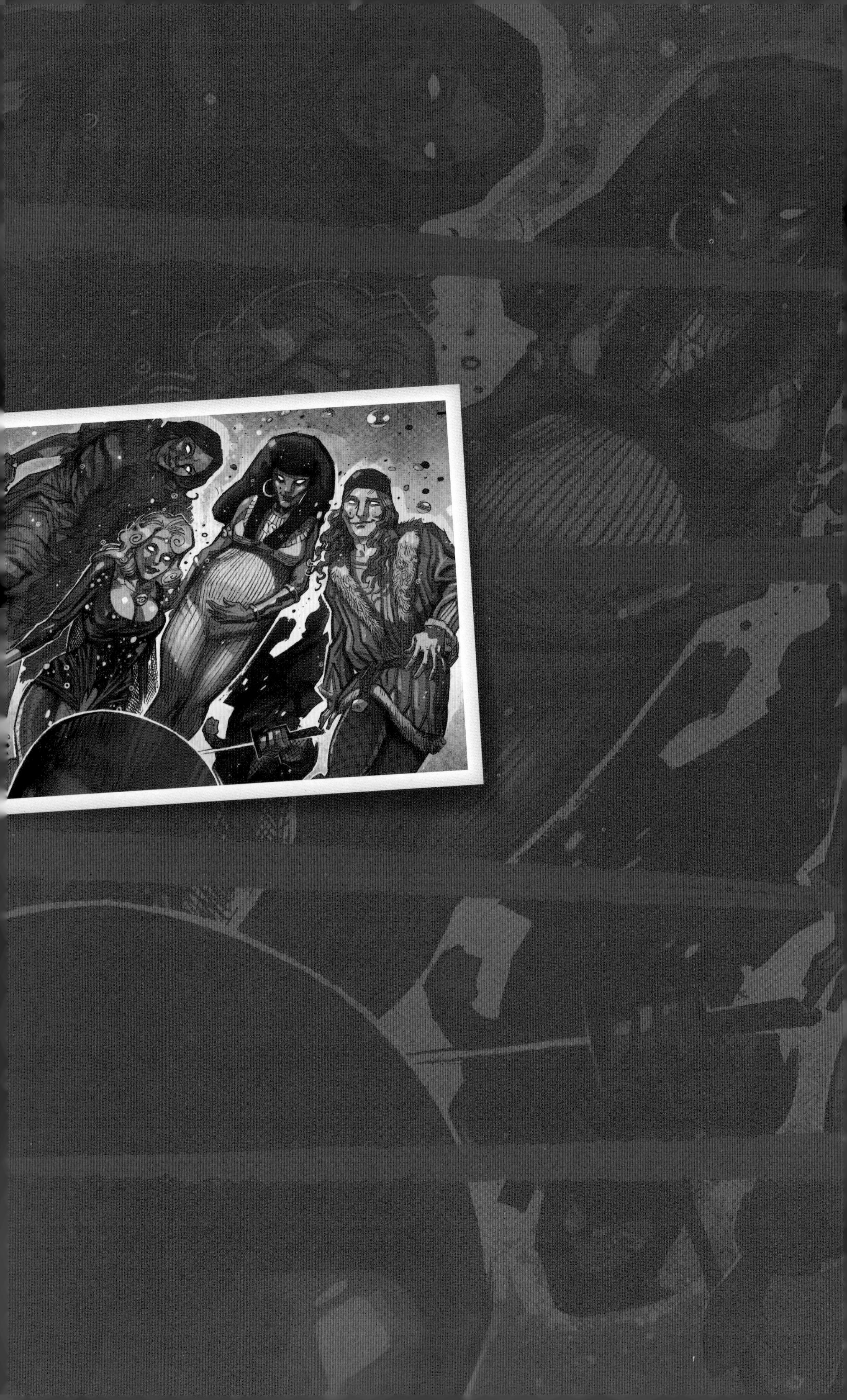

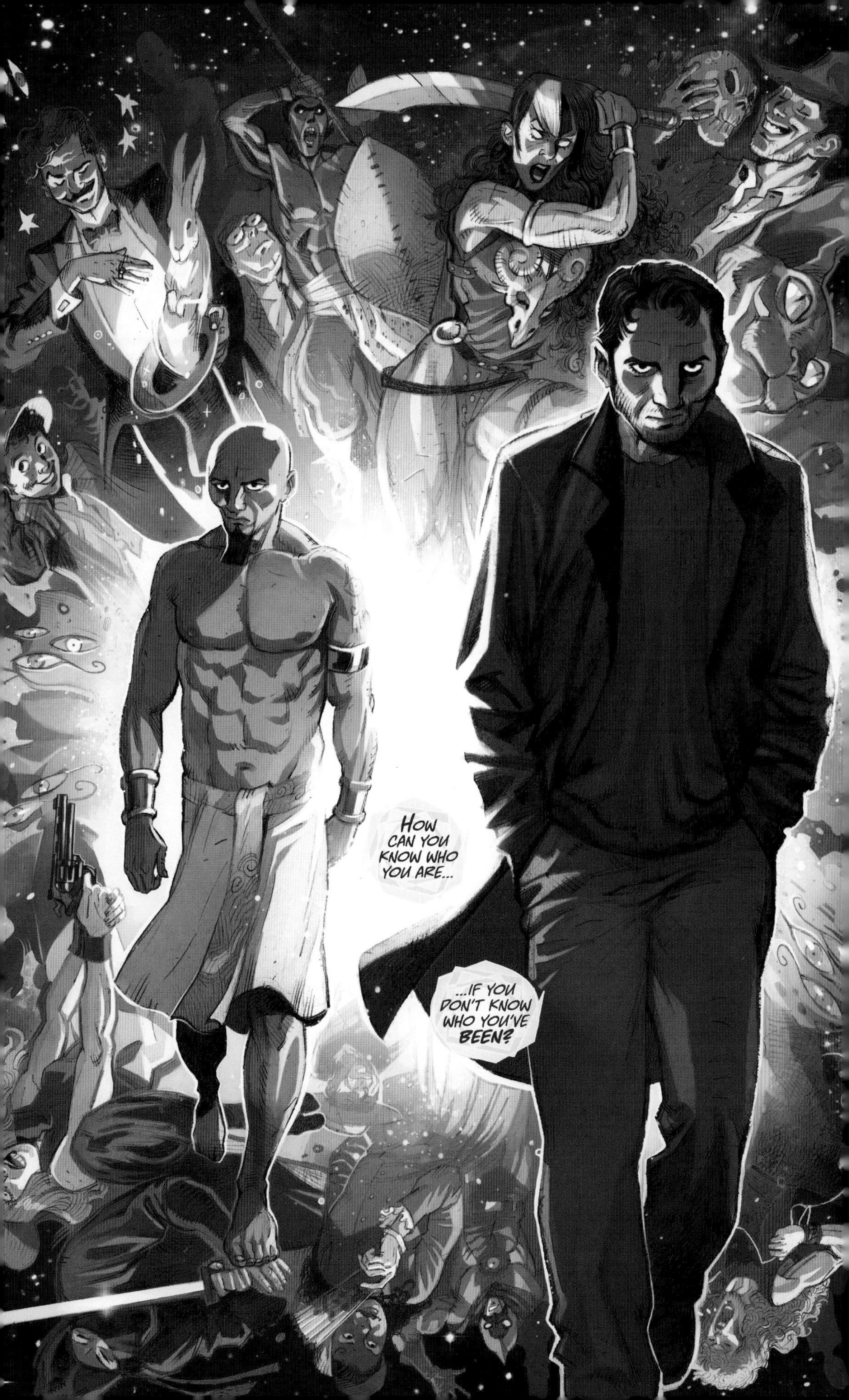
HOW CAN YOU KNOW WHO YOU ARE...
...IF YOU DON'T KNOW WHO YOU'VE BEEN?

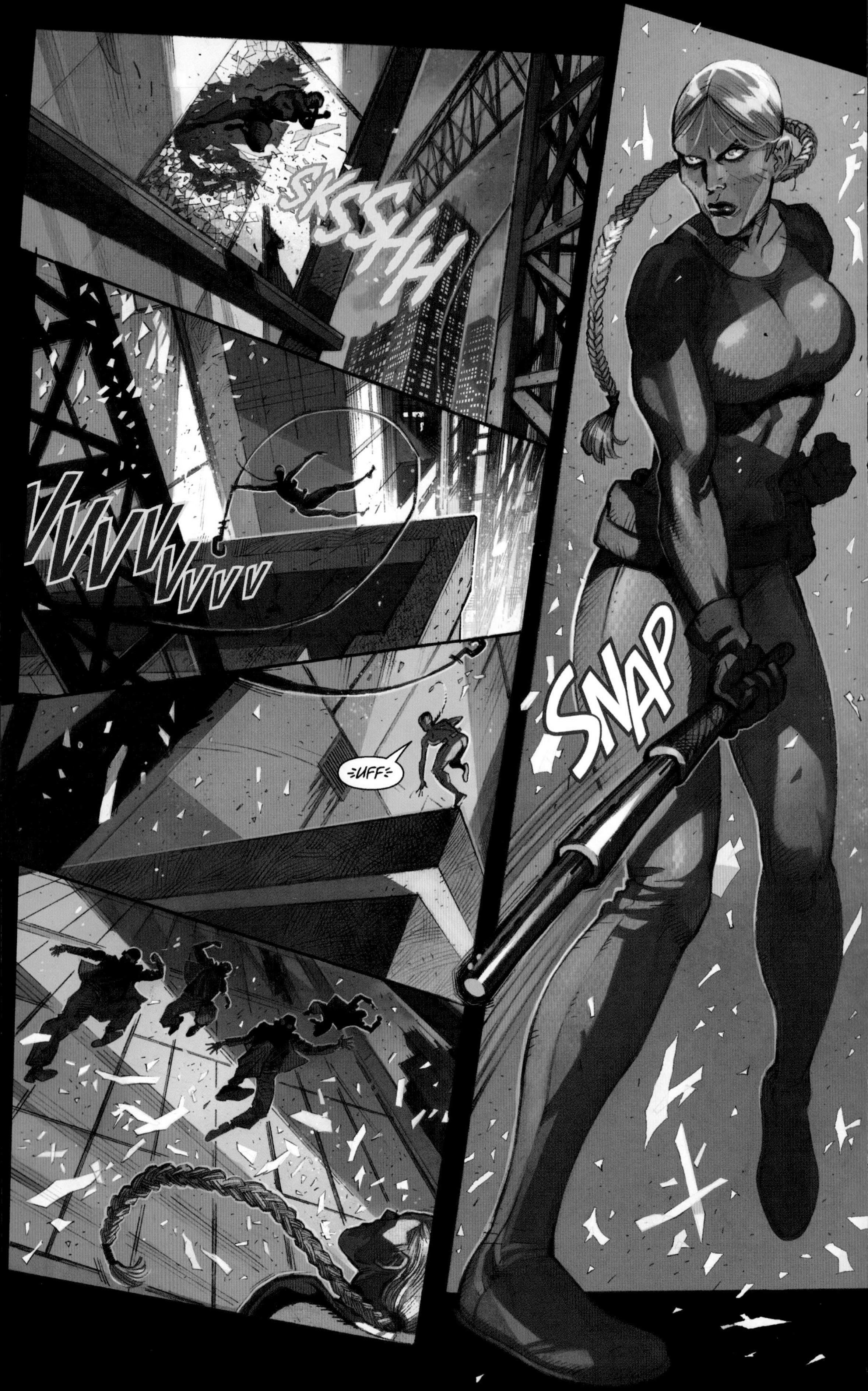
SKSSHH
VVVVVVVVVV
UFF
SNAP

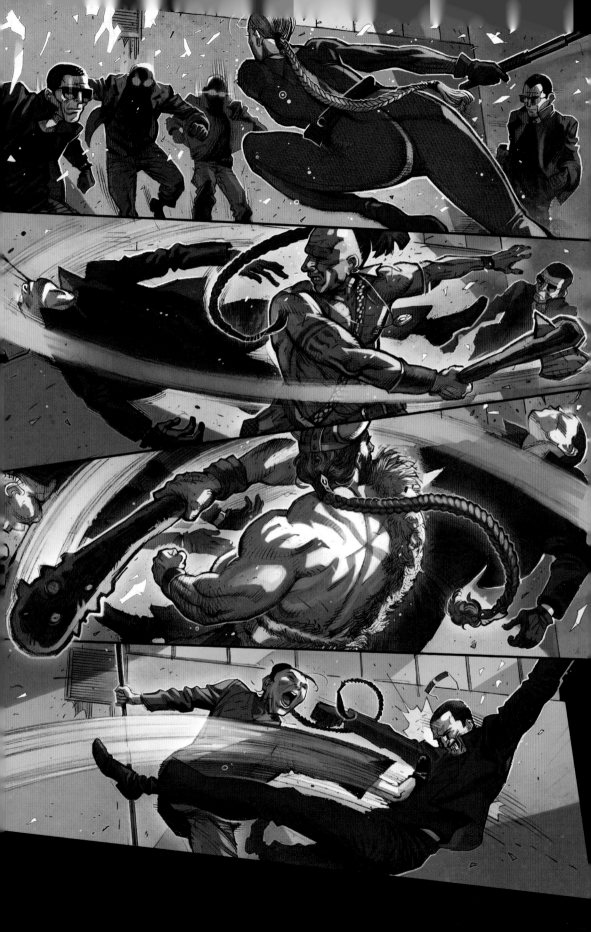

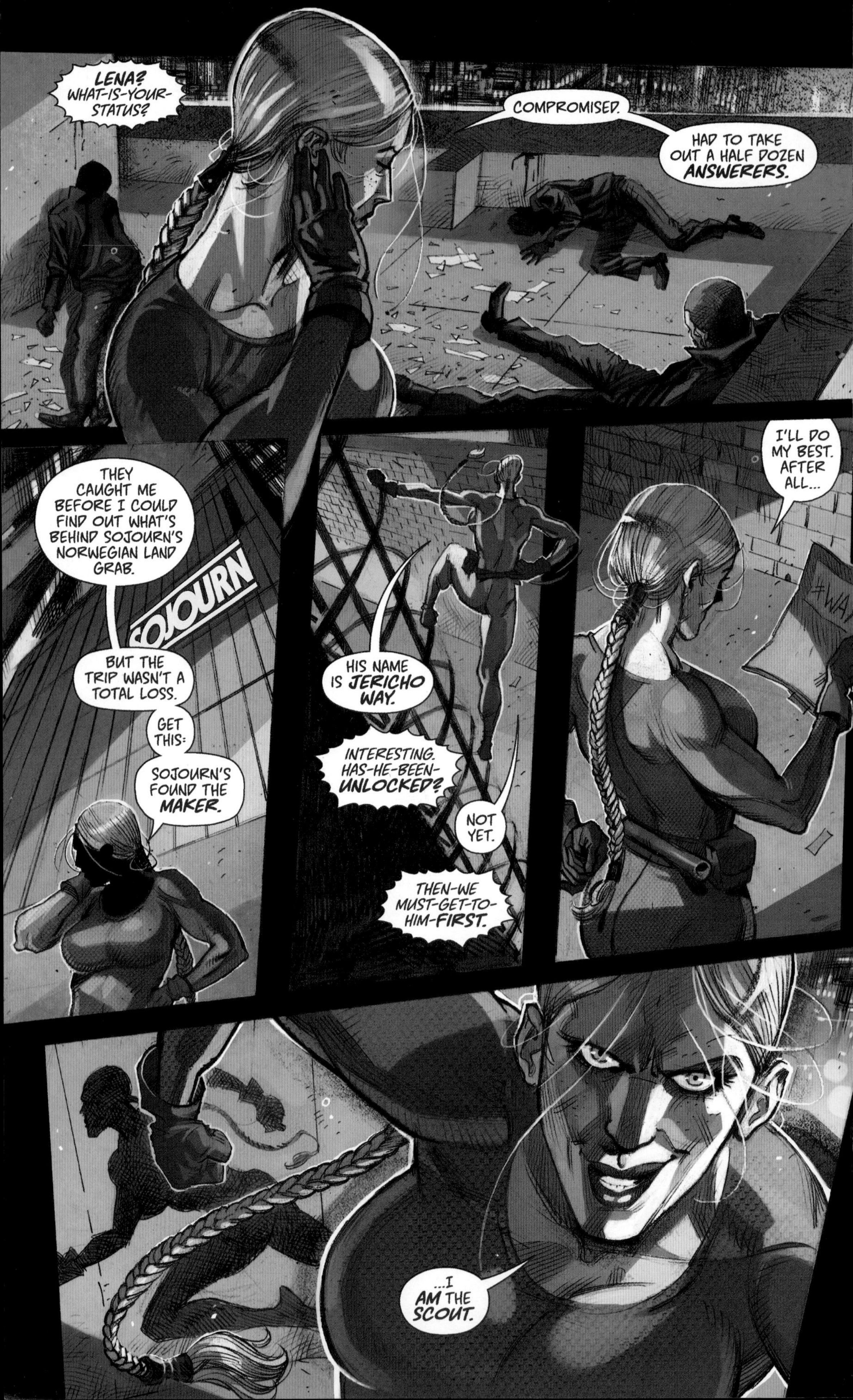
LENA? WHAT-IS-YOUR-STATUS?
COMPROMISED.
HAD TO TAKE OUT A HALF DOZEN **ANSWERERS.**
THEY CAUGHT ME BEFORE I COULD FIND OUT WHAT'S BEHIND SOJOURN'S NORWEGIAN LAND GRAB.
SOJOURN
BUT THE TRIP WASN'T A TOTAL LOSS.
GET THIS:
SOJOURN'S FOUND THE **MAKER.**
HIS NAME IS **JERICHO WAY.**
INTERESTING. HAS-HE-BEEN-**UNLOCKED?**
NOT YET.
THEN-WE MUST-GET-TO-HIM-**FIRST.**
I'LL DO MY BEST. AFTER ALL...
...I **AM** THE **SCOUT.**

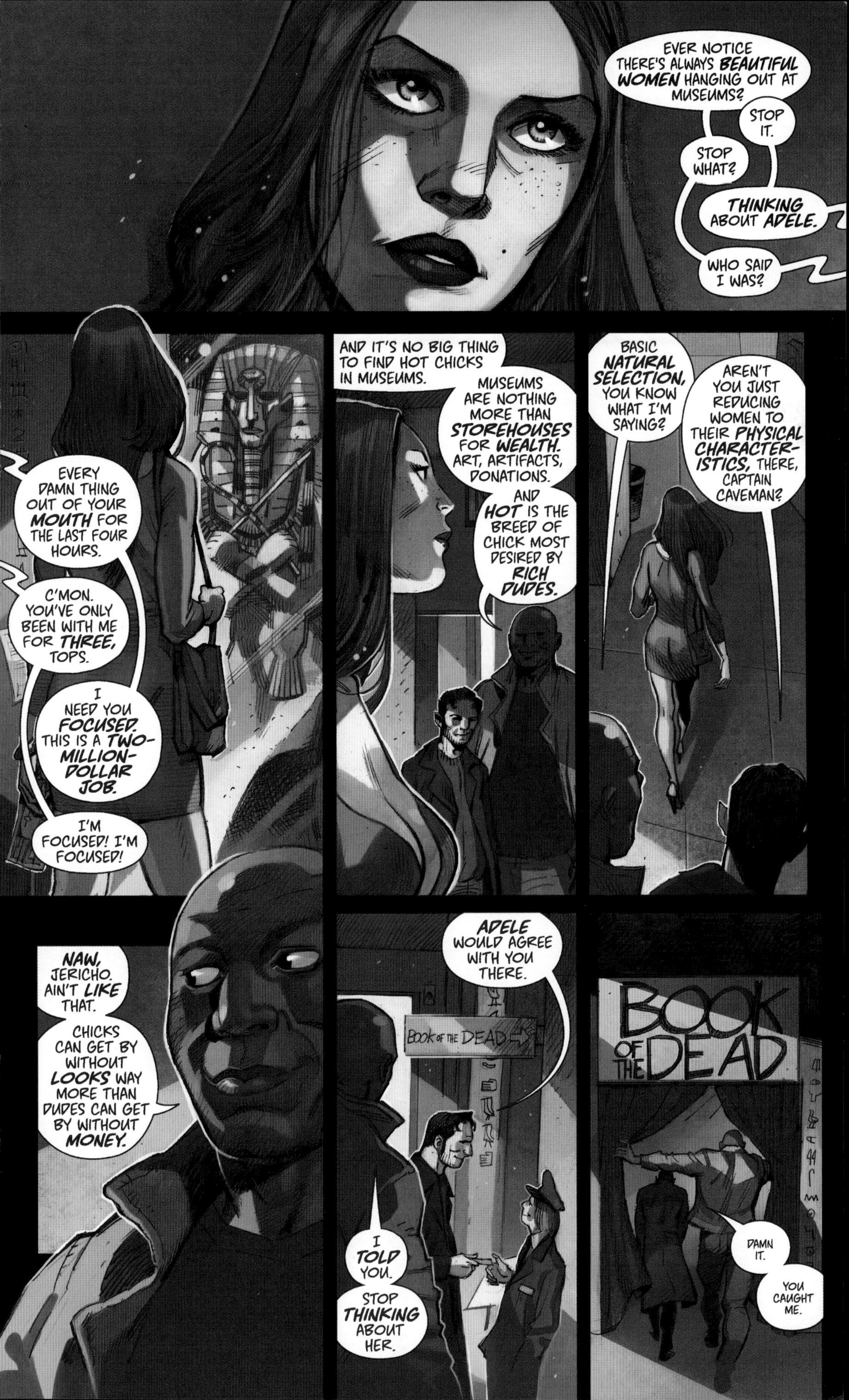
EVER NOTICE THERE'S ALWAYS BEAUTIFUL WOMEN HANGING OUT AT MUSEUMS?
STOP IT.
STOP WHAT?
THINKING ABOUT ADELE.
WHO SAID I WAS?
EVERY DAMN THING OUT OF YOUR MOUTH FOR THE LAST FOUR HOURS.
C'MON. YOU'VE ONLY BEEN WITH ME FOR THREE, TOPS.
I NEED YOU FOCUSED. THIS IS A TWO-MILLION-DOLLAR JOB.
I'M FOCUSED! I'M FOCUSED!
AND IT'S NO BIG THING TO FIND HOT CHICKS IN MUSEUMS.
MUSEUMS ARE NOTHING MORE THAN STOREHOUSES FOR WEALTH. ART, ARTIFACTS, DONATIONS.
AND HOT IS THE BREED OF CHICK MOST DESIRED BY RICH DUDES.
BASIC NATURAL SELECTION, YOU KNOW WHAT I'M SAYING?
AREN'T YOU JUST REDUCING WOMEN TO THEIR PHYSICAL CHARACTER-ISTICS, THERE, CAPTAIN CAVEMAN?
NAW, JERICHO. AIN'T LIKE THAT.
CHICKS CAN GET BY WITHOUT LOOKS WAY MORE THAN DUDES CAN GET BY WITHOUT MONEY.
ADELE WOULD AGREE WITH YOU THERE.
BOOK OF THE DEAD
I TOLD YOU.
STOP THINKING ABOUT HER.
BOOK OF THE DEAD
DAMN IT.
YOU CAUGHT ME.

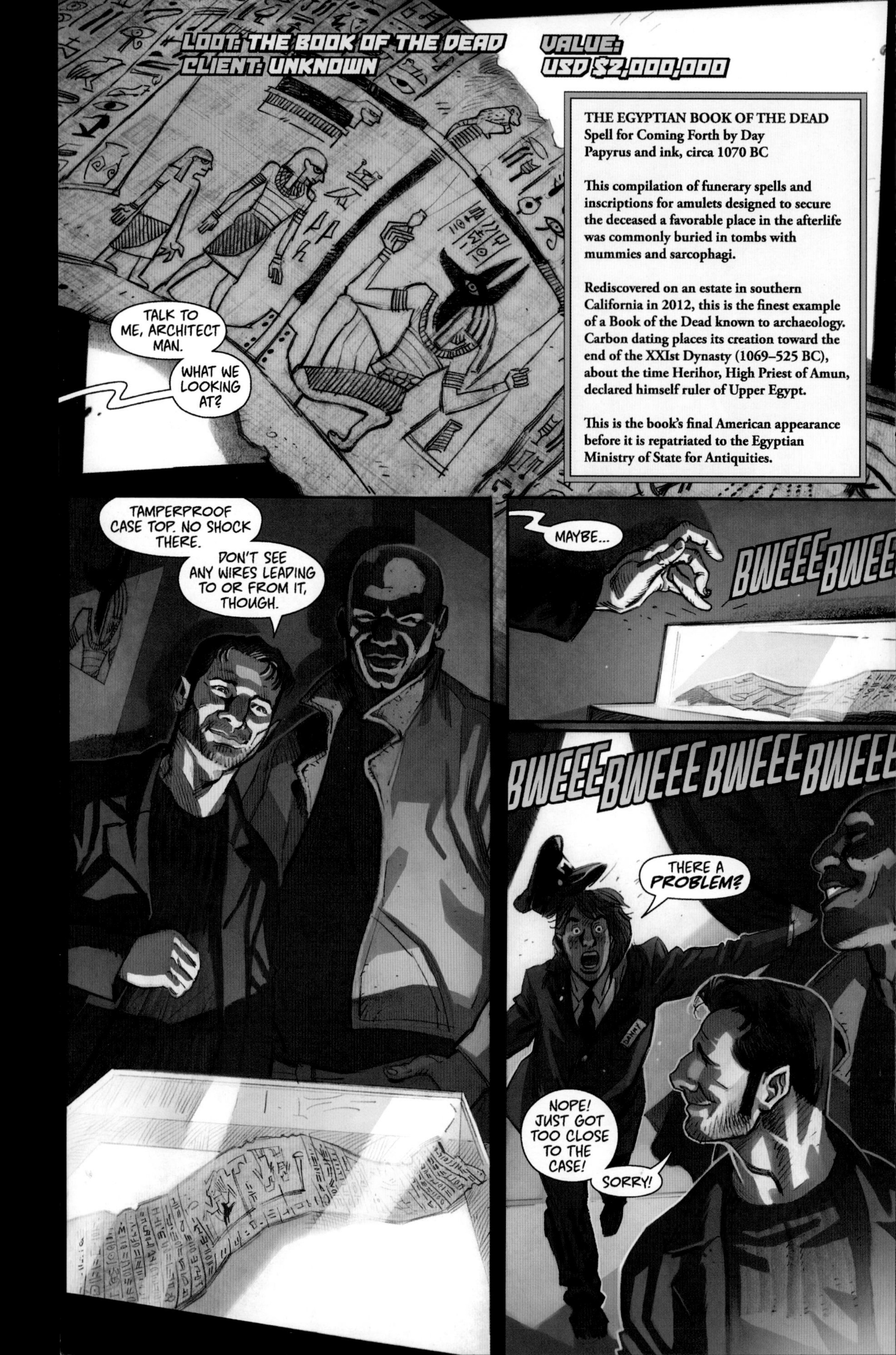
LOOT: THE BOOK OF THE DEAD
CLIENT: UNKNOWN
VALUE:
USD $2,000,000
THE EGYPTIAN BOOK OF THE DEAD
Spell for Coming Forth by Day
Papyrus and ink, circa 1070 BC
This compilation of funerary spells and inscriptions for amulets designed to secure the deceased a favorable place in the afterlife was commonly buried in tombs with mummies and sarcophagi.
Rediscovered on an estate in southern California in 2012, this is the finest example of a Book of the Dead known to archaeology. Carbon dating places its creation toward the end of the XXIst Dynasty (1069–525 BC), about the time Herihor, High Priest of Amun, declared himself ruler of Upper Egypt.
This is the book's final American appearance before it is repatriated to the Egyptian Ministry of State for Antiquities.
TALK TO ME, ARCHITECT MAN.
WHAT WE LOOKING AT?
TAMPERPROOF CASE TOP. NO SHOCK THERE.
DON'T SEE ANY WIRES LEADING TO OR FROM IT, THOUGH.
MAYBE...
BWEEE BWEE
BWEEE BWEEE BWEEE BWEEE
THERE A PROBLEM?
DANNY
NOPE! JUST GOT TOO CLOSE TO THE CASE!
SORRY!

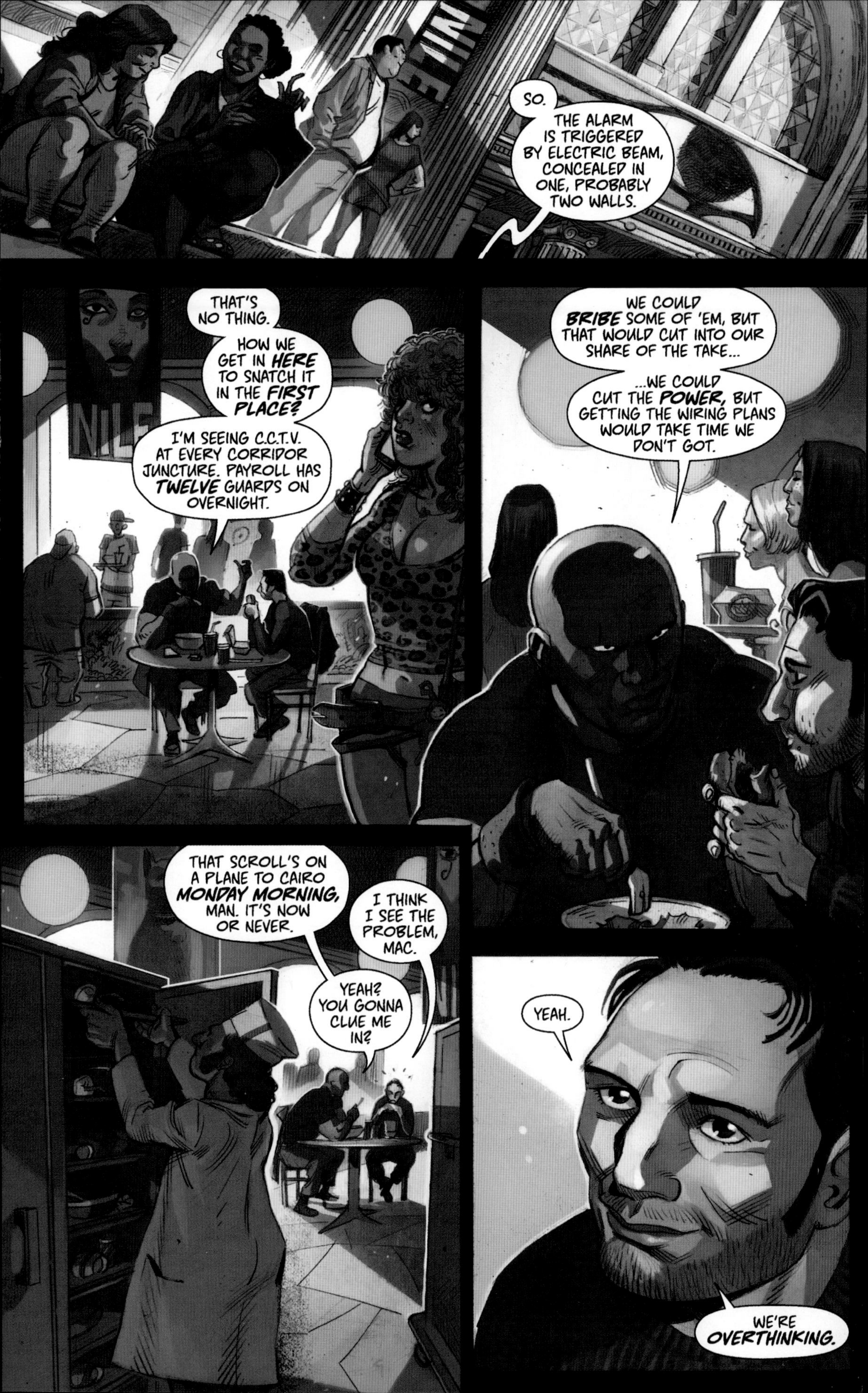
SO.
THE ALARM IS TRIGGERED BY ELECTRIC BEAM, CONCEALED IN ONE, PROBABLY TWO WALLS.
THAT'S NO THING.
HOW WE GET IN HERE TO SNATCH IT IN THE FIRST PLACE?
I'M SEEING C.C.T.V. AT EVERY CORRIDOR JUNCTURE. PAYROLL HAS TWELVE GUARDS ON OVERNIGHT.
WE COULD BRIBE SOME OF 'EM, BUT THAT WOULD CUT INTO OUR SHARE OF THE TAKE...
...WE COULD CUT THE POWER, BUT GETTING THE WIRING PLANS WOULD TAKE TIME WE DON'T GOT.
THAT SCROLL'S ON A PLANE TO CAIRO MONDAY MORNING, MAN. IT'S NOW OR NEVER.
I THINK I SEE THE PROBLEM, MAC.
YEAH? YOU GONNA CLUE ME IN?
YEAH.
WE'RE OVERTHINKING.

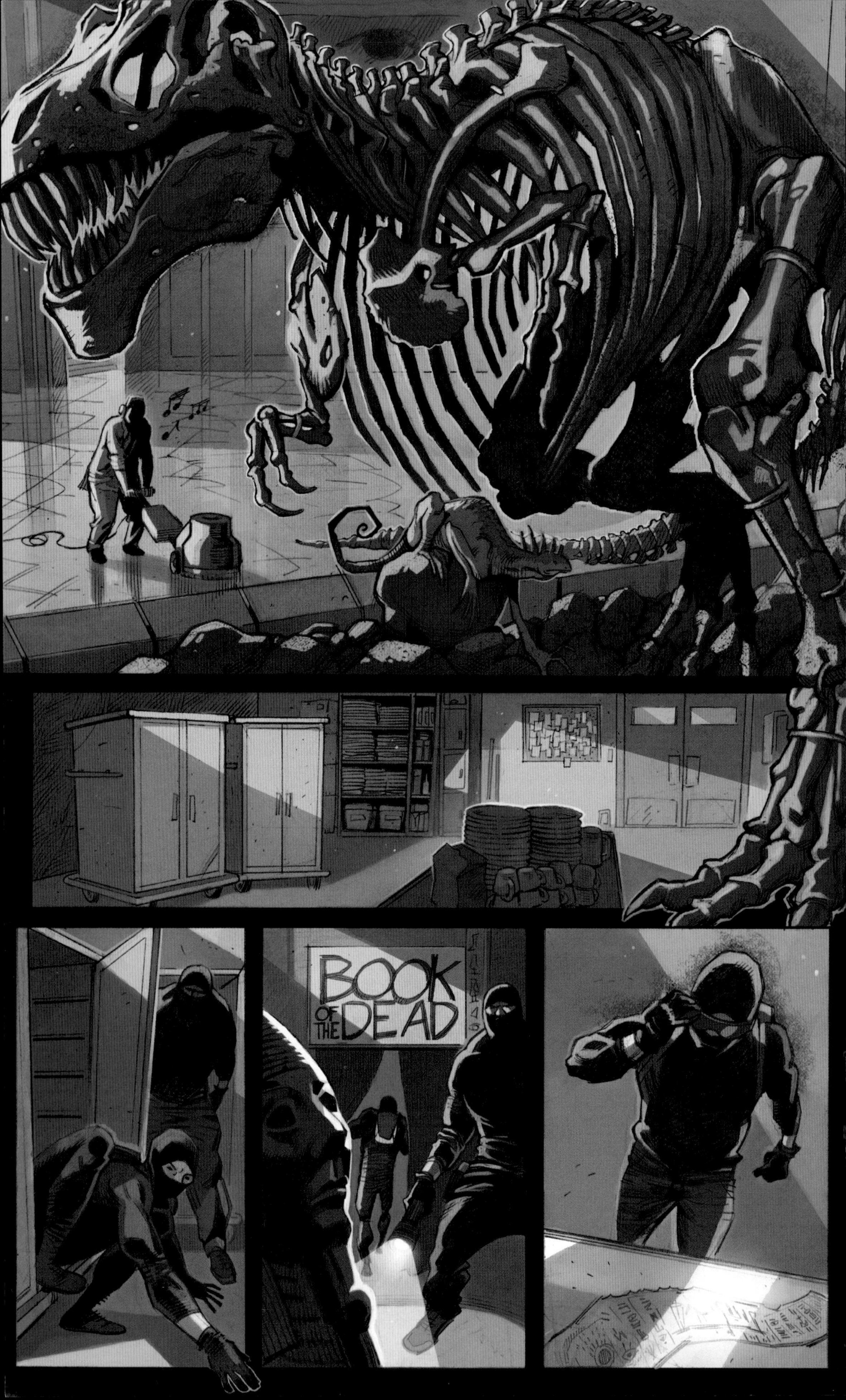
BOOK OF THE DEAD

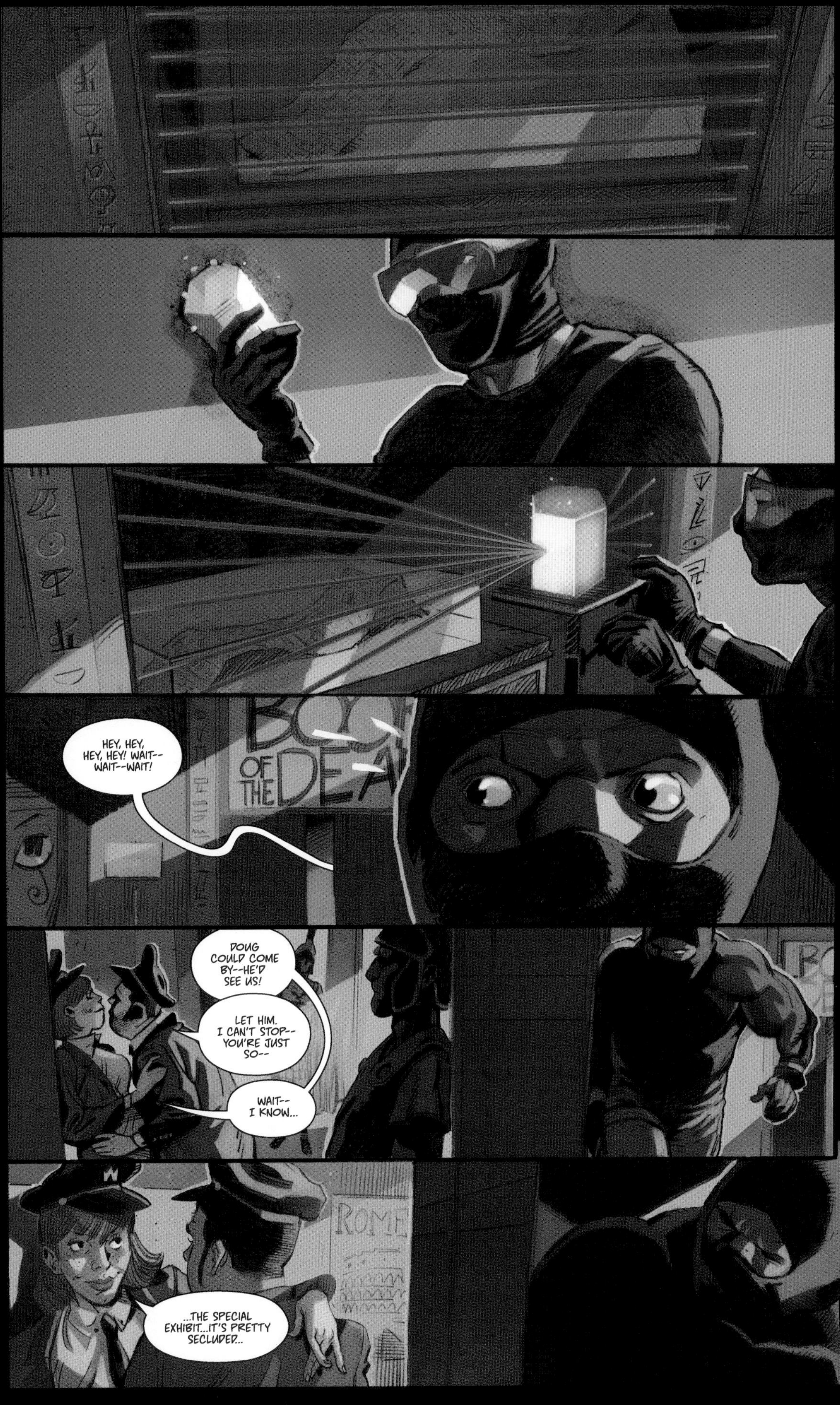

BOOK OF THE DEA
HEY, HEY, HEY, HEY! WAIT-- WAIT--WAIT!
DOUG COULD COME BY--HE'D SEE US!
LET HIM. I CAN'T STOP-- YOU'RE JUST SO--
WAIT-- I KNOW...
ROME
...THE SPECIAL EXHIBIT...IT'S PRETTY SECLUDED...

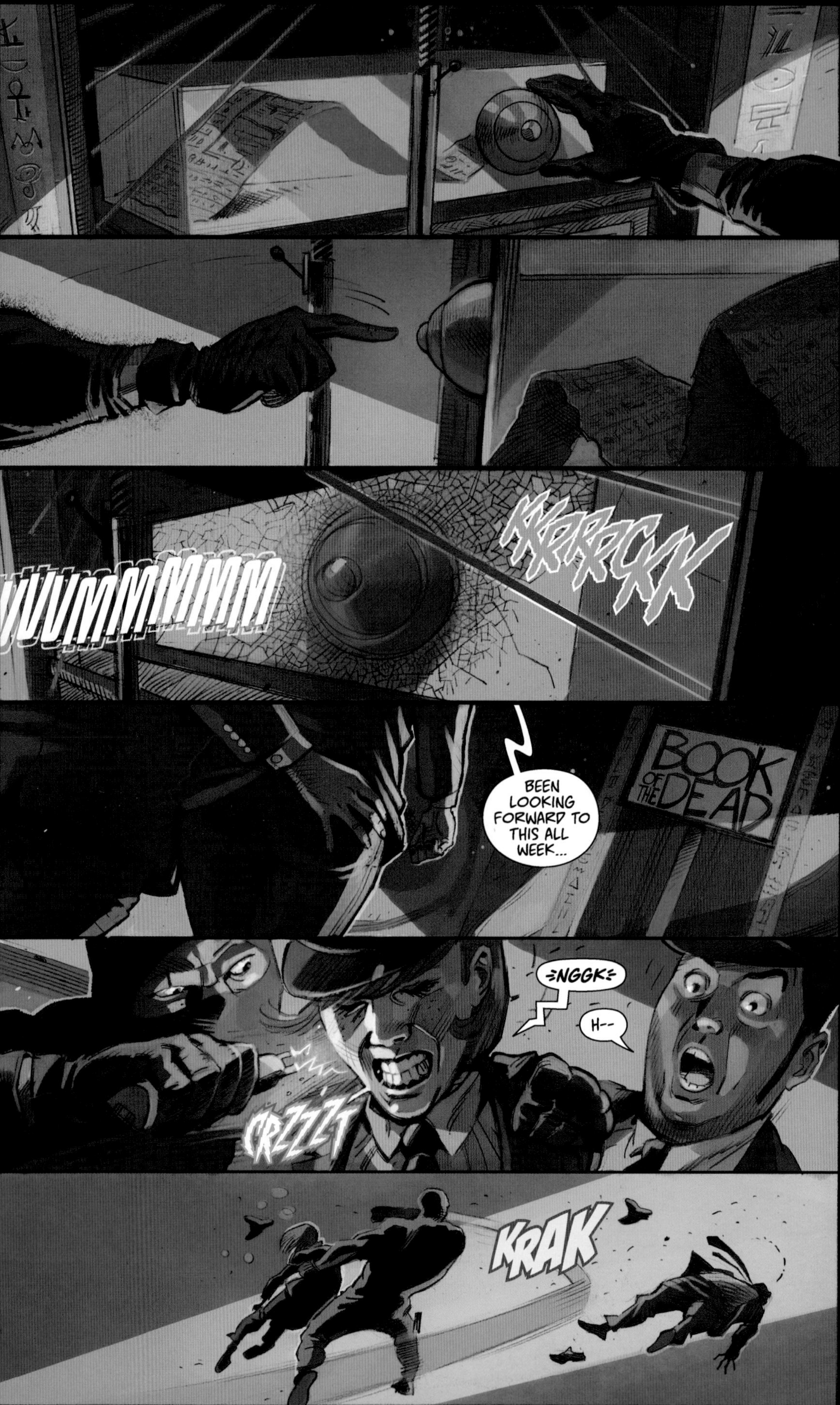

VVVUMMMMMMM
KKRRRCKK
BOOK OF THE DEAD
BEEN LOOKING FORWARD TO THIS ALL WEEK...
NGGK
H--
CRZZZT
KRAK

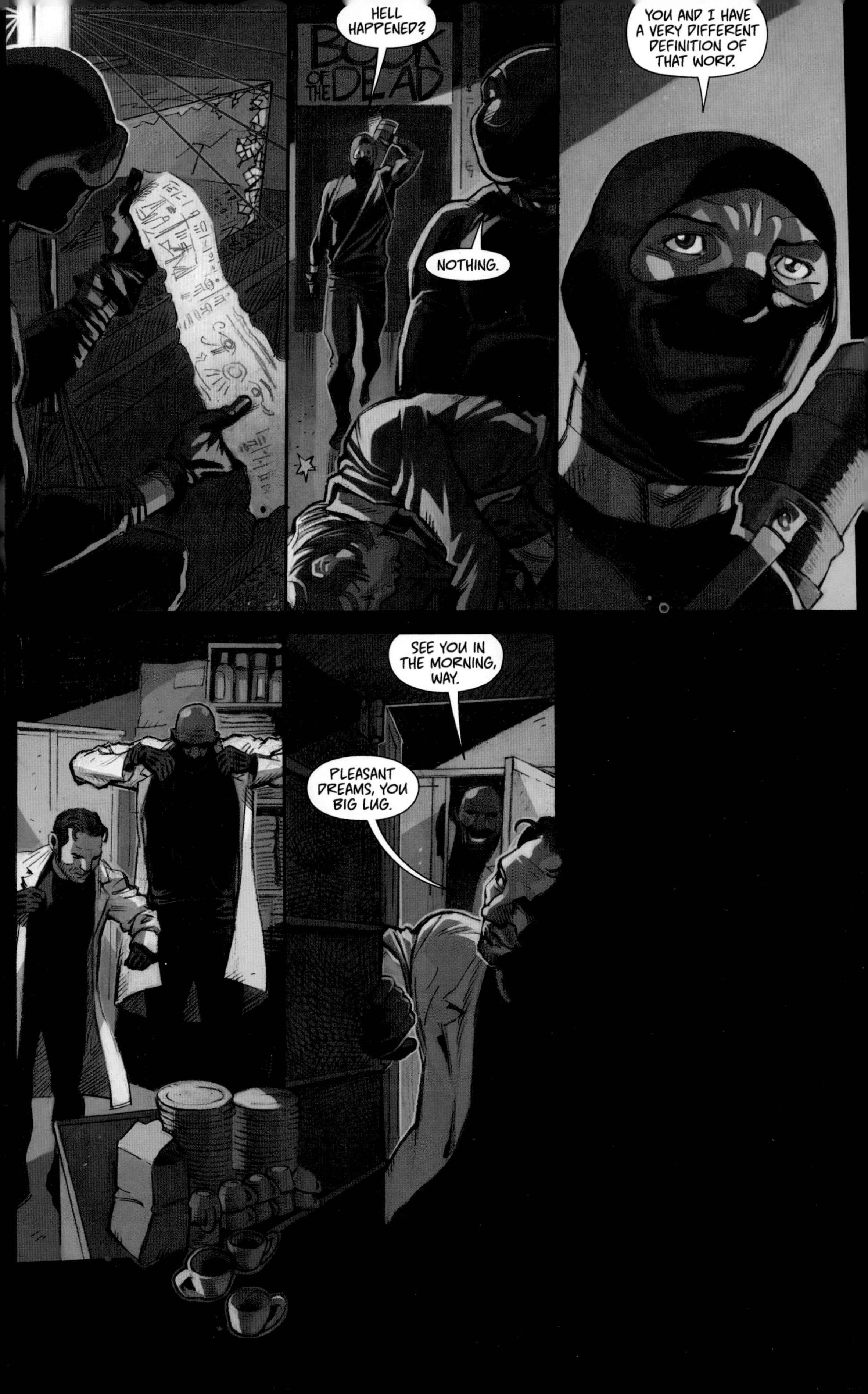
BOOK OF THE DEAD
HELL HAPPENED?
NOTHING.
YOU AND I HAVE A VERY DIFFERENT DEFINITION OF THAT WORD.
SEE YOU IN THE MORNING, WAY.
PLEASANT DREAMS, YOU BIG LUG.

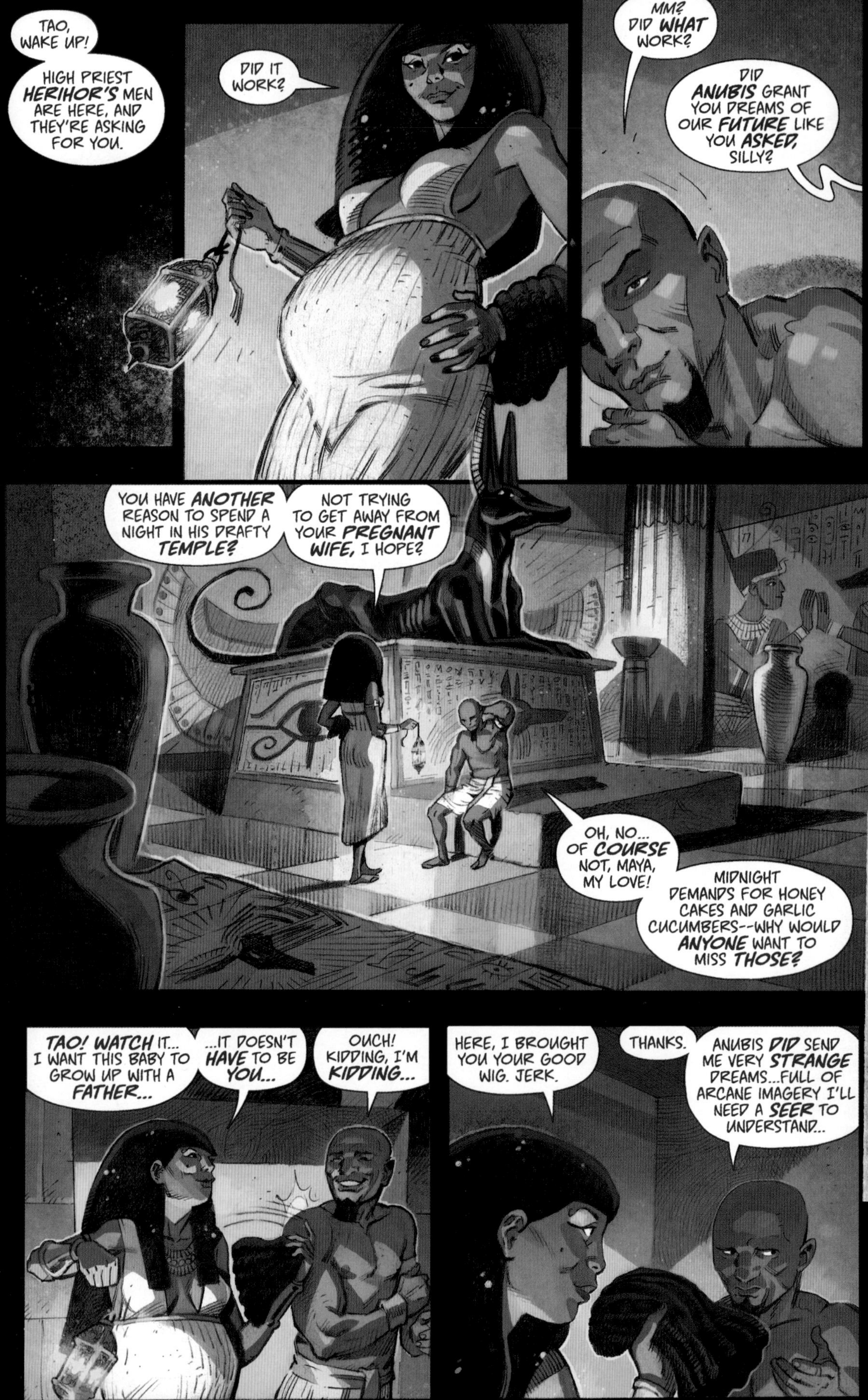
TAO, WAKE UP!
HIGH PRIEST HERIHOR'S MEN ARE HERE, AND THEY'RE ASKING FOR YOU.
DID IT WORK?
MM? DID WHAT WORK?
DID ANUBIS GRANT YOU DREAMS OF OUR FUTURE LIKE YOU ASKED, SILLY?
YOU HAVE ANOTHER REASON TO SPEND A NIGHT IN HIS DRAFTY TEMPLE?
NOT TRYING TO GET AWAY FROM YOUR PREGNANT WIFE, I HOPE?
OH, NO... OF COURSE NOT, MAYA, MY LOVE!
MIDNIGHT DEMANDS FOR HONEY CAKES AND GARLIC CUCUMBERS--WHY WOULD ANYONE WANT TO MISS THOSE?
TAO! WATCH IT... I WANT THIS BABY TO GROW UP WITH A FATHER...
...IT DOESN'T HAVE TO BE YOU...
OUCH! KIDDING, I'M KIDDING...
HERE, I BROUGHT YOU YOUR GOOD WIG. JERK.
THANKS.
ANUBIS DID SEND ME VERY STRANGE DREAMS...FULL OF ARCANE IMAGERY I'LL NEED A SEER TO UNDERSTAND...

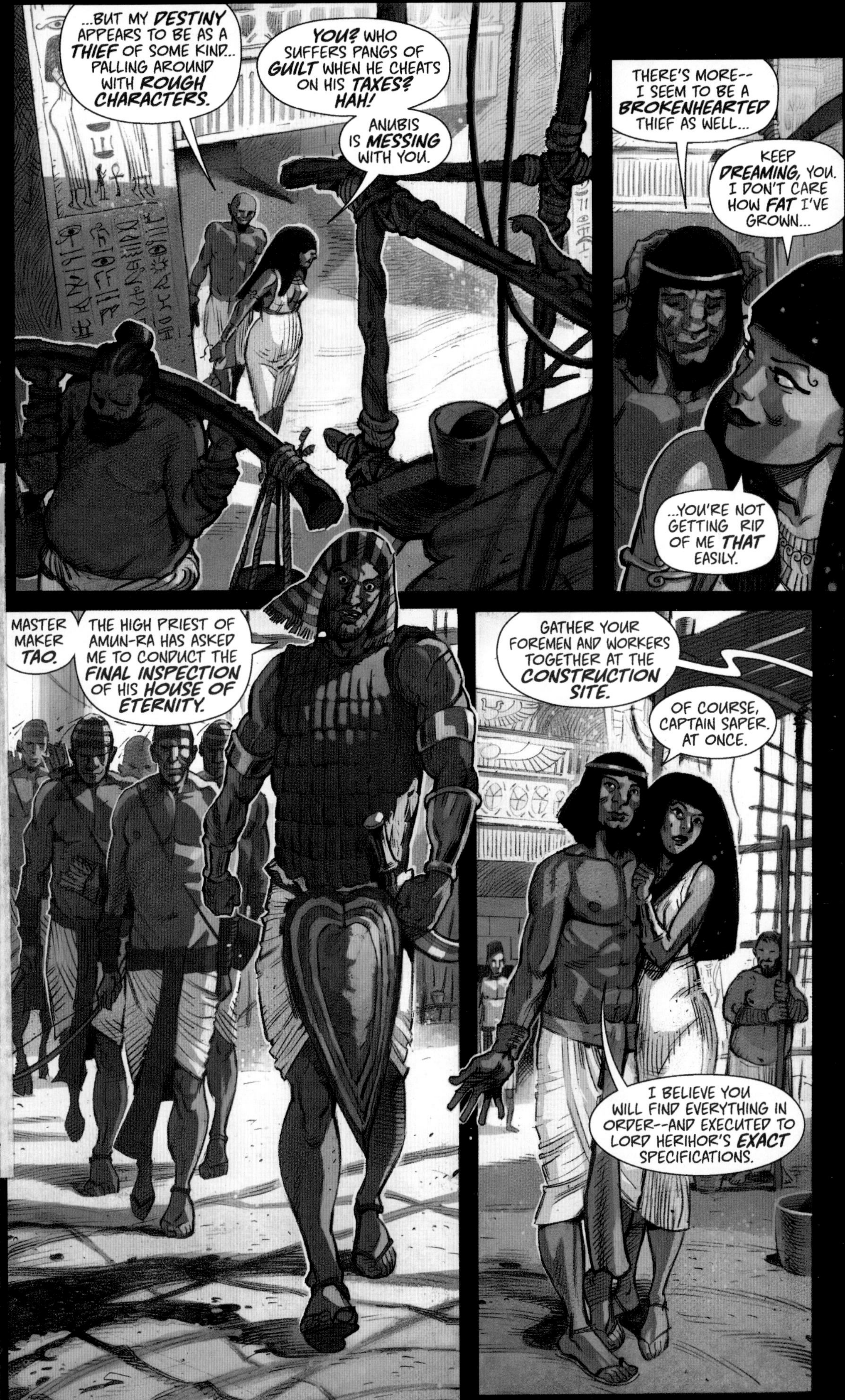
...BUT MY DESTINY APPEARS TO BE AS A THIEF OF SOME KIND... PALLING AROUND WITH ROUGH CHARACTERS.
YOU? WHO SUFFERS PANGS OF GUILT WHEN HE CHEATS ON HIS TAXES? HAH!
ANUBIS IS MESSING WITH YOU.
THERE'S MORE-- I SEEM TO BE A BROKENHEARTED THIEF AS WELL...
KEEP DREAMING, YOU. I DON'T CARE HOW FAT I'VE GROWN...
...YOU'RE NOT GETTING RID OF ME THAT EASILY.
MASTER MAKER TAO.
THE HIGH PRIEST OF AMUN-RA HAS ASKED ME TO CONDUCT THE FINAL INSPECTION OF HIS HOUSE OF ETERNITY.
GATHER YOUR FOREMEN AND WORKERS TOGETHER AT THE CONSTRUCTION SITE.
OF COURSE, CAPTAIN SAPER. AT ONCE.
I BELIEVE YOU WILL FIND EVERYTHING IN ORDER--AND EXECUTED TO LORD HERIHOR'S EXACT SPECIFICATIONS.

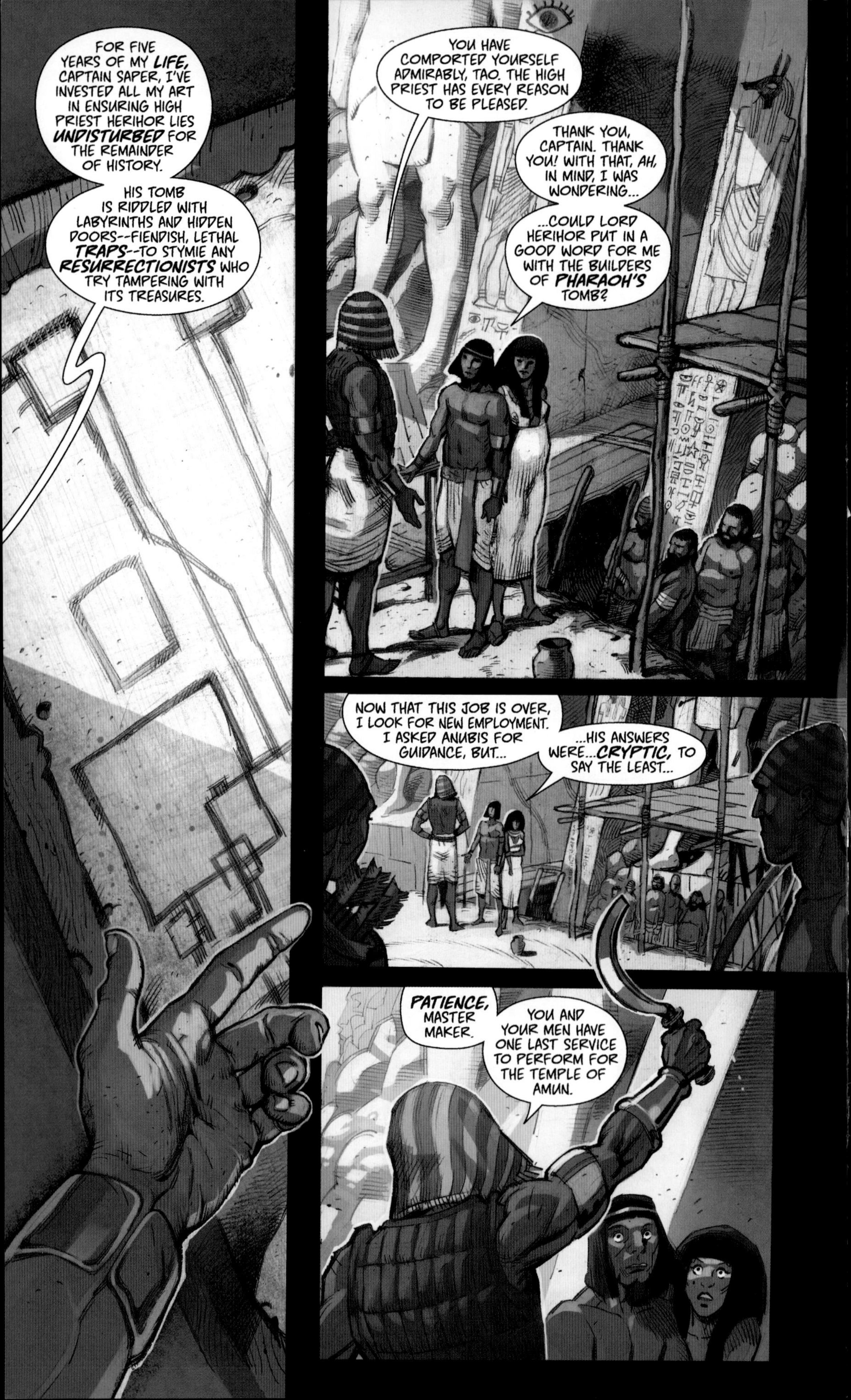
FOR FIVE YEARS OF MY LIFE, CAPTAIN SAPER, I'VE INVESTED ALL MY ART IN ENSURING HIGH PRIEST HERIHOR LIES UNDISTURBED FOR THE REMAINDER OF HISTORY.
HIS TOMB IS RIDDLED WITH LABYRINTHS AND HIDDEN DOORS--FIENDISH, LETHAL TRAPS--TO STYMIE ANY RESURRECTIONISTS WHO TRY TAMPERING WITH ITS TREASURES.
YOU HAVE COMPORTED YOURSELF ADMIRABLY, TAO. THE HIGH PRIEST HAS EVERY REASON TO BE PLEASED.
THANK YOU, CAPTAIN. THANK YOU! WITH THAT, AH, IN MIND, I WAS WONDERING...
...COULD LORD HERIHOR PUT IN A GOOD WORD FOR ME WITH THE BUILDERS OF PHARAOH'S TOMB?
NOW THAT THIS JOB IS OVER, I LOOK FOR NEW EMPLOYMENT. I ASKED ANUBIS FOR GUIDANCE, BUT...
...HIS ANSWERS WERE...CRYPTIC, TO SAY THE LEAST...
PATIENCE, MASTER MAKER.
YOU AND YOUR MEN HAVE ONE LAST SERVICE TO PERFORM FOR THE TEMPLE OF AMUN.

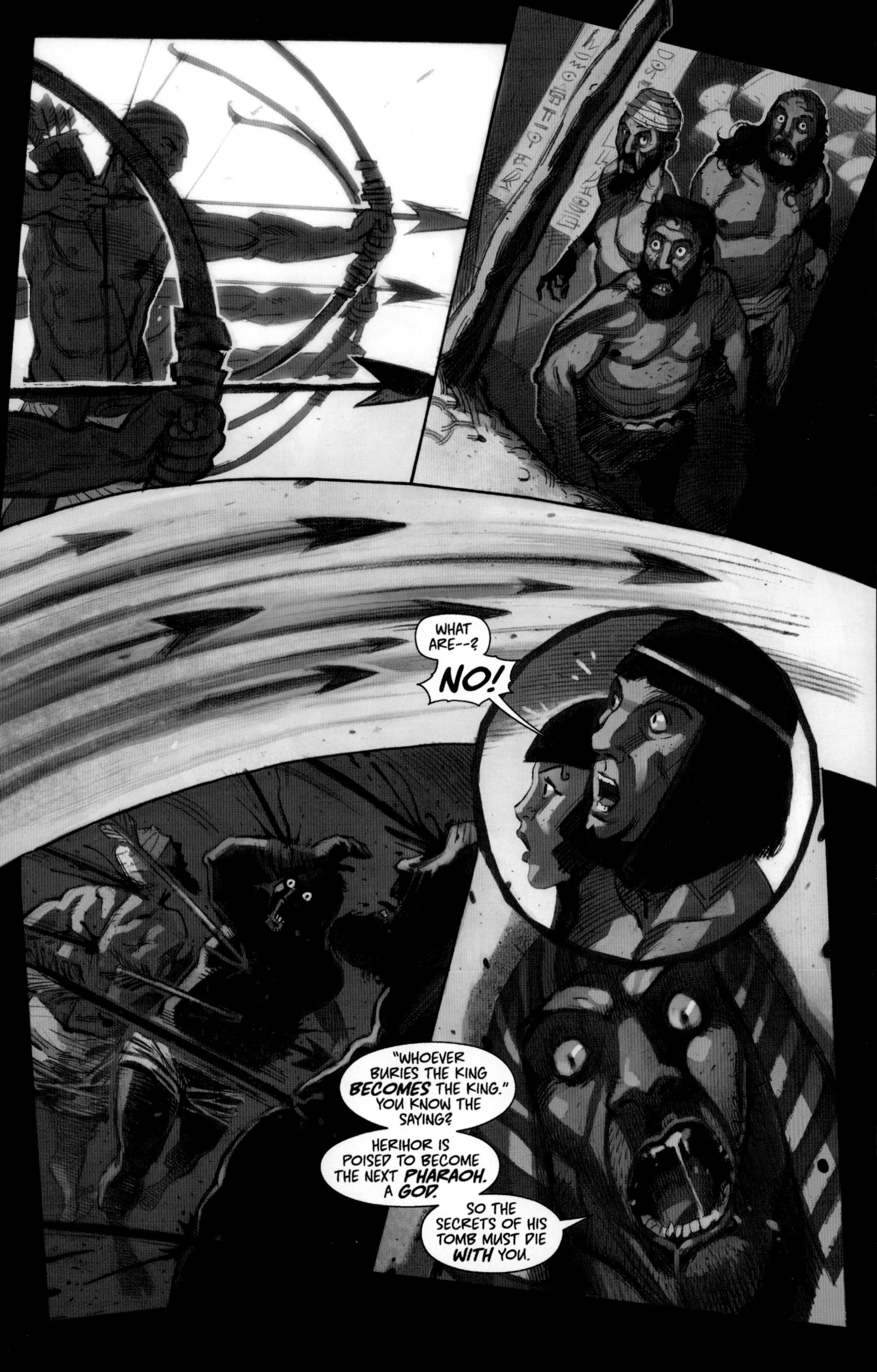
WHAT ARE--?
NO!
"WHOEVER BURIES THE KING BECOMES THE KING." YOU KNOW THE SAYING?
HERIHOR IS POISED TO BECOME THE NEXT PHARAOH. A GOD.
SO THE SECRETS OF HIS TOMB MUST DIE WITH YOU.

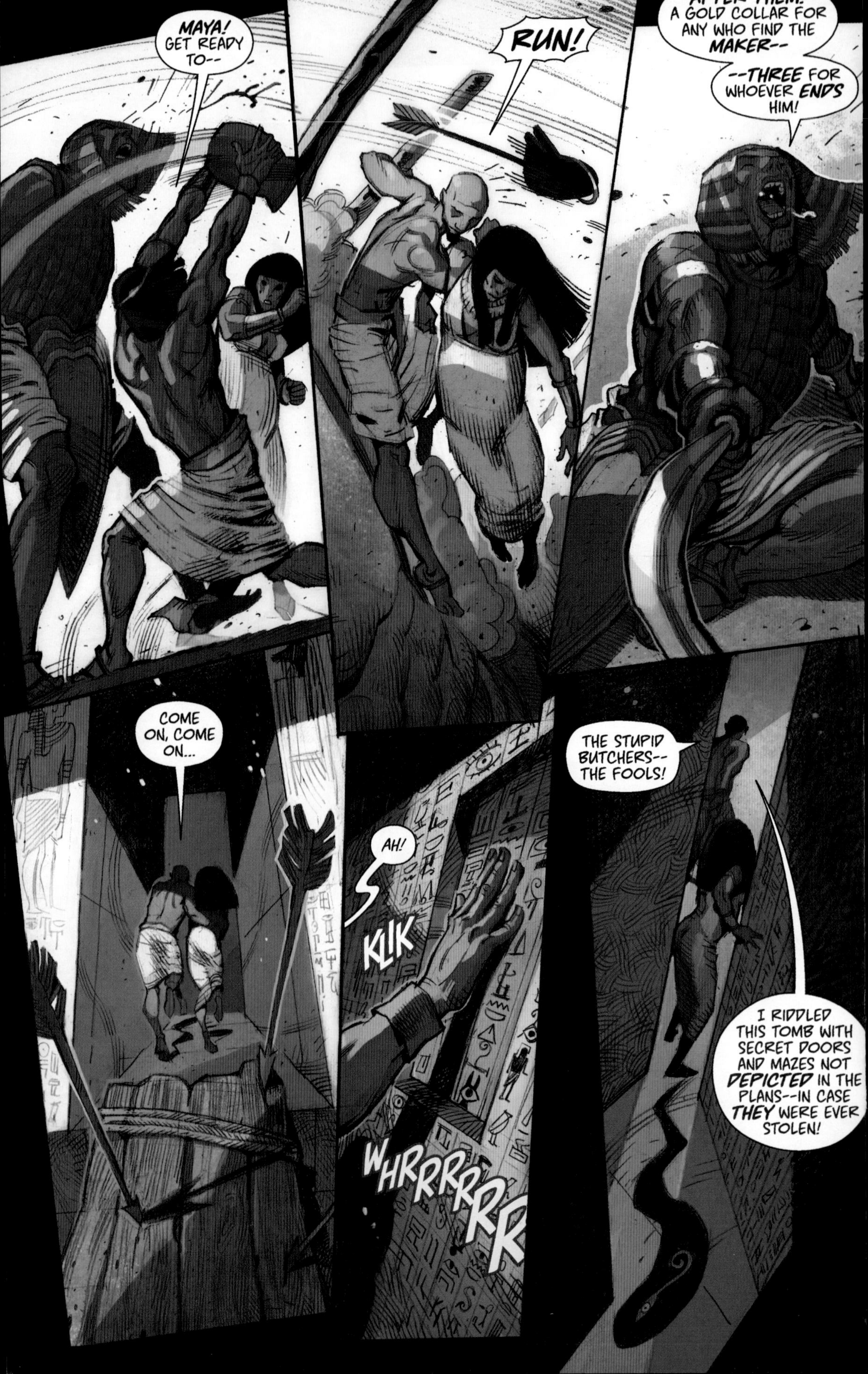
MAYA! GET READY TO--
RUN!
AFTER THEM! A GOLD COLLAR FOR ANY WHO FIND THE MAKER--
--THREE FOR WHOEVER ENDS HIM!
COME ON, COME ON...
AH!
KLIK
WHRRRRRR
THE STUPID BUTCHERS-- THE FOOLS!
I RIDDLED THIS TOMB WITH SECRET DOORS AND MAZES NOT DEPICTED IN THE PLANS--IN CASE THEY WERE EVER STOLEN!

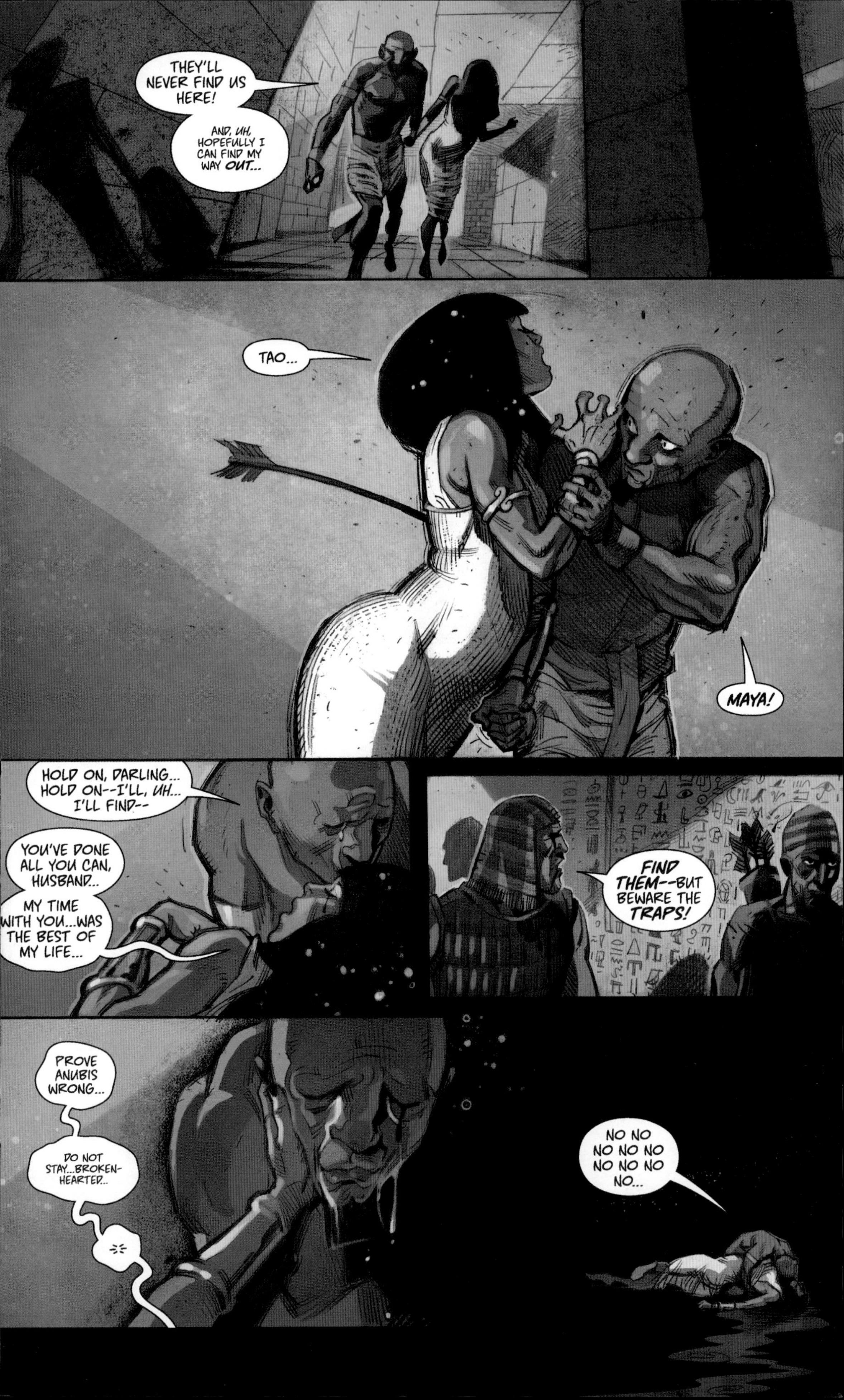
THEY'LL NEVER FIND US HERE!
AND, UH, HOPEFULLY I CAN FIND MY WAY OUT...
TAO...
MAYA!
HOLD ON, DARLING... HOLD ON--I'LL, UH... I'LL FIND--
YOU'VE DONE ALL YOU CAN, HUSBAND...
MY TIME WITH YOU...WAS THE BEST OF MY LIFE...
FIND THEM--BUT BEWARE THE TRAPS!
PROVE ANUBIS WRONG...
DO NOT STAY...BROKEN-HEARTED...
NO NO NO NO NO NO NO NO NO...

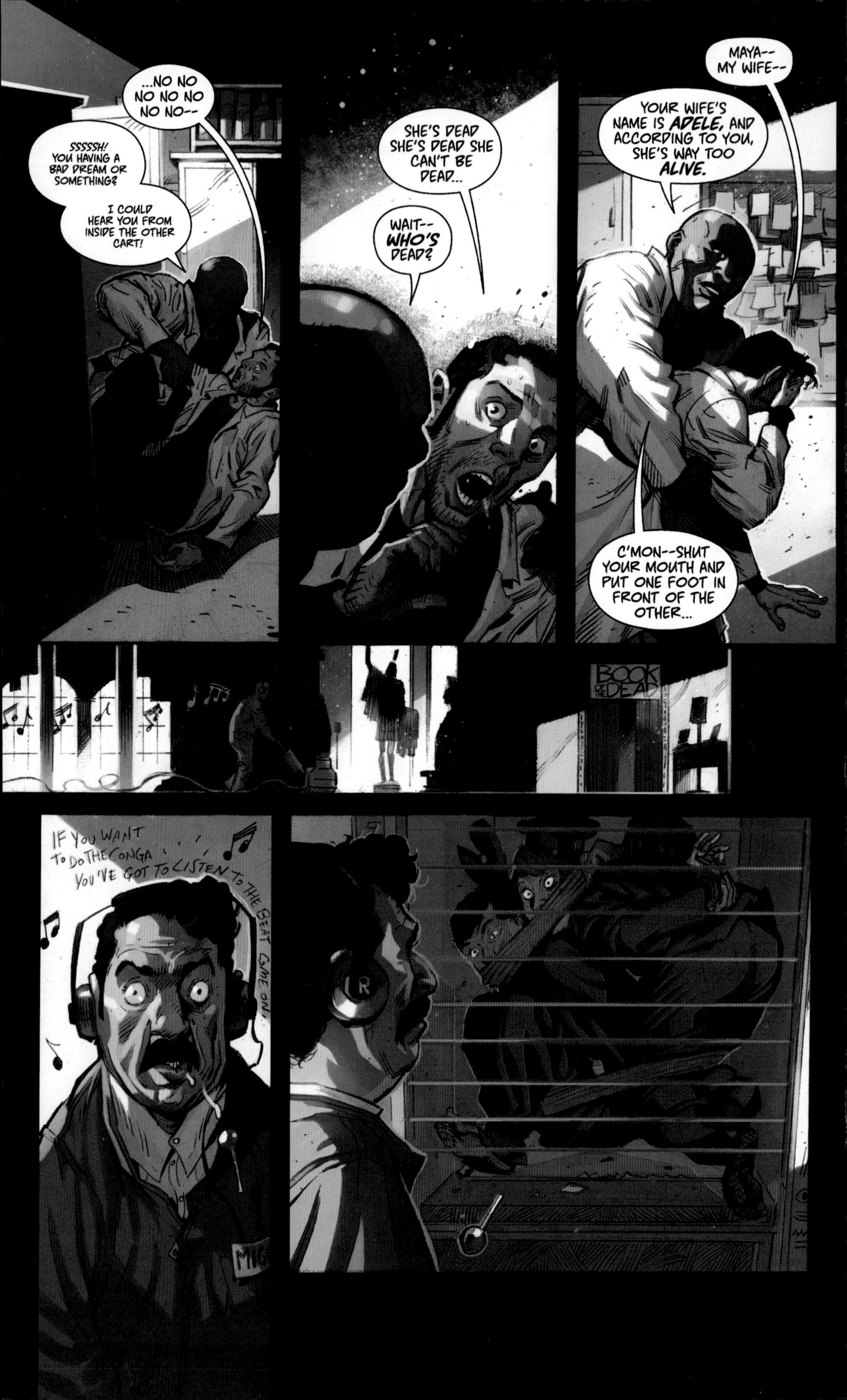

...NO NO NO NO NO NO NO--
SSSSSH! YOU HAVING A BAD DREAM OR SOMETHING?
I COULD HEAR YOU FROM INSIDE THE OTHER CART!
SHE'S DEAD SHE'S DEAD SHE CAN'T BE DEAD...
WAIT-- WHO'S DEAD?
MAYA-- MY WIFE--
YOUR WIFE'S NAME IS ADELE, AND ACCORDING TO YOU, SHE'S WAY TOO ALIVE.
C'MON--SHUT YOUR MOUTH AND PUT ONE FOOT IN FRONT OF THE OTHER...
BOOK OF THE DEAD
IF YOU WANT TO DO THE CONGA YOU'VE GOT TO LISTEN TO THE BEAT COME ON.

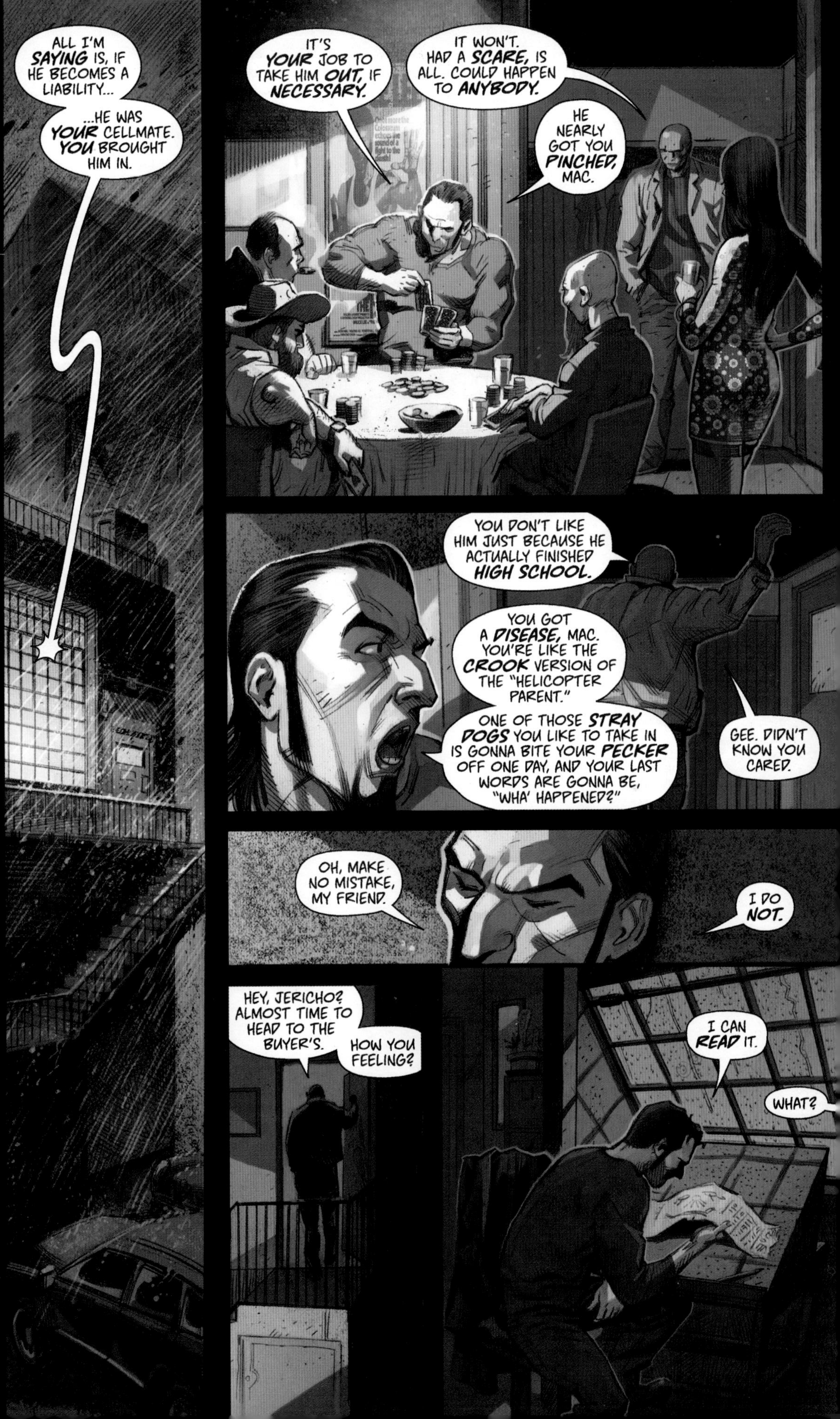
ALL I'M SAYING IS, IF HE BECOMES A LIABILITY...
IT'S YOUR JOB TO TAKE HIM OUT, IF NECESSARY.
IT WON'T. HAD A SCARE, IS ALL. COULD HAPPEN TO ANYBODY.
HE NEARLY GOT YOU PINCHED, MAC.
...HE WAS YOUR CELLMATE. YOU BROUGHT HIM IN.
YOU DON'T LIKE HIM JUST BECAUSE HE ACTUALLY FINISHED HIGH SCHOOL.
YOU GOT A DISEASE, MAC. YOU'RE LIKE THE CROOK VERSION OF THE "HELICOPTER PARENT."
ONE OF THOSE STRAY DOGS YOU LIKE TO TAKE IN IS GONNA BITE YOUR PECKER OFF ONE DAY, AND YOUR LAST WORDS ARE GONNA BE, "WHA' HAPPENED?"
GEE. DIDN'T KNOW YOU CARED.
OH, MAKE NO MISTAKE, MY FRIEND.
I DO NOT.
HEY, JERICHO? ALMOST TIME TO HEAD TO THE BUYER'S.
HOW YOU FEELING?
I CAN READ IT.
WHAT?

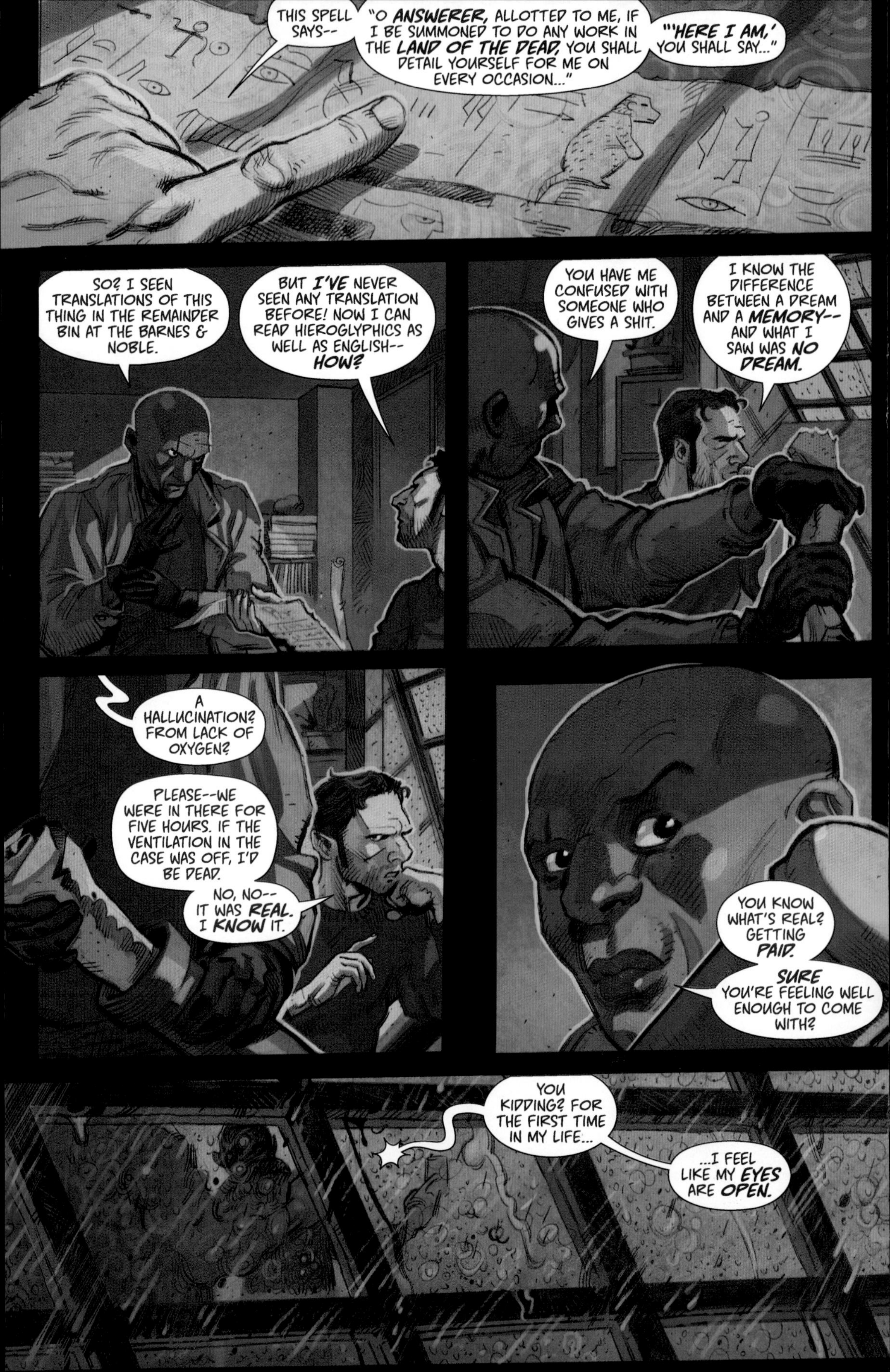

THIS SPELL SAYS--
"O ANSWERER, ALLOTTED TO ME, IF I BE SUMMONED TO DO ANY WORK IN THE LAND OF THE DEAD, YOU SHALL DETAIL YOURSELF FOR ME ON EVERY OCCASION..."
"'HERE I AM,' YOU SHALL SAY..."
SO? I SEEN TRANSLATIONS OF THIS THING IN THE REMAINDER BIN AT THE BARNES & NOBLE.
BUT I'VE NEVER SEEN ANY TRANSLATION BEFORE! NOW I CAN READ HIEROGLYPHICS AS WELL AS ENGLISH-- HOW?
YOU HAVE ME CONFUSED WITH SOMEONE WHO GIVES A SHIT.
I KNOW THE DIFFERENCE BETWEEN A DREAM AND A MEMORY-- AND WHAT I SAW WAS NO DREAM.
A HALLUCINATION? FROM LACK OF OXYGEN?
PLEASE--WE WERE IN THERE FOR FIVE HOURS. IF THE VENTILATION IN THE CASE WAS OFF, I'D BE DEAD.
NO, NO-- IT WAS REAL. I KNOW IT.
YOU KNOW WHAT'S REAL? GETTING PAID.
SURE YOU'RE FEELING WELL ENOUGH TO COME WITH?
YOU KIDDING? FOR THE FIRST TIME IN MY LIFE...
...I FEEL LIKE MY EYES ARE OPEN.

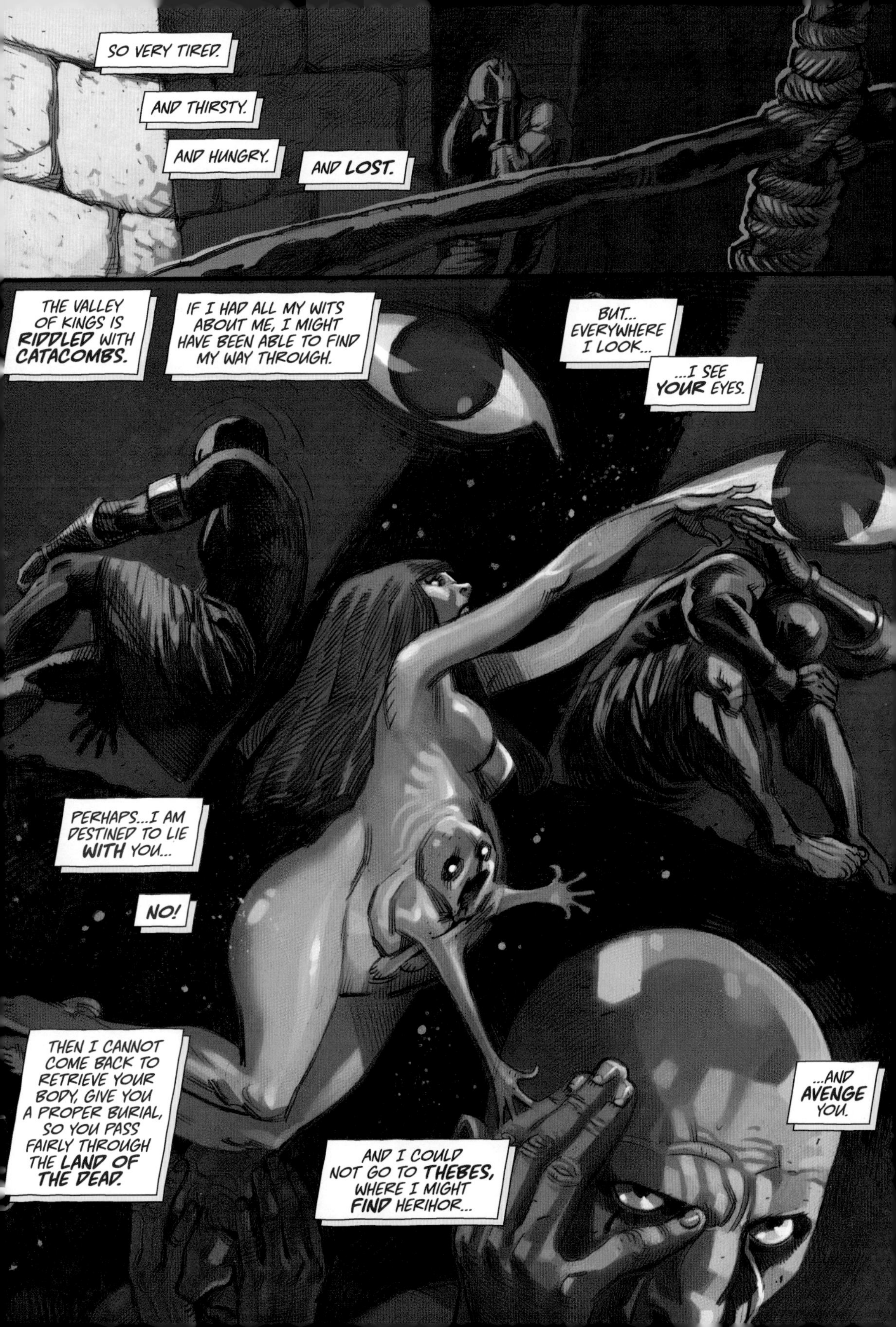
SO VERY TIRED.
AND THIRSTY.
AND HUNGRY.
AND LOST.
THE VALLEY OF KINGS IS RIDDLED WITH CATACOMBS.
IF I HAD ALL MY WITS ABOUT ME, I MIGHT HAVE BEEN ABLE TO FIND MY WAY THROUGH.
BUT... EVERYWHERE I LOOK...
...I SEE YOUR EYES.
PERHAPS...I AM DESTINED TO LIE WITH YOU...
NO!
THEN I CANNOT COME BACK TO RETRIEVE YOUR BODY, GIVE YOU A PROPER BURIAL, SO YOU PASS FAIRLY THROUGH THE LAND OF THE DEAD.
AND I COULD NOT GO TO THEBES, WHERE I MIGHT FIND HERIHOR...
...AND AVENGE YOU.

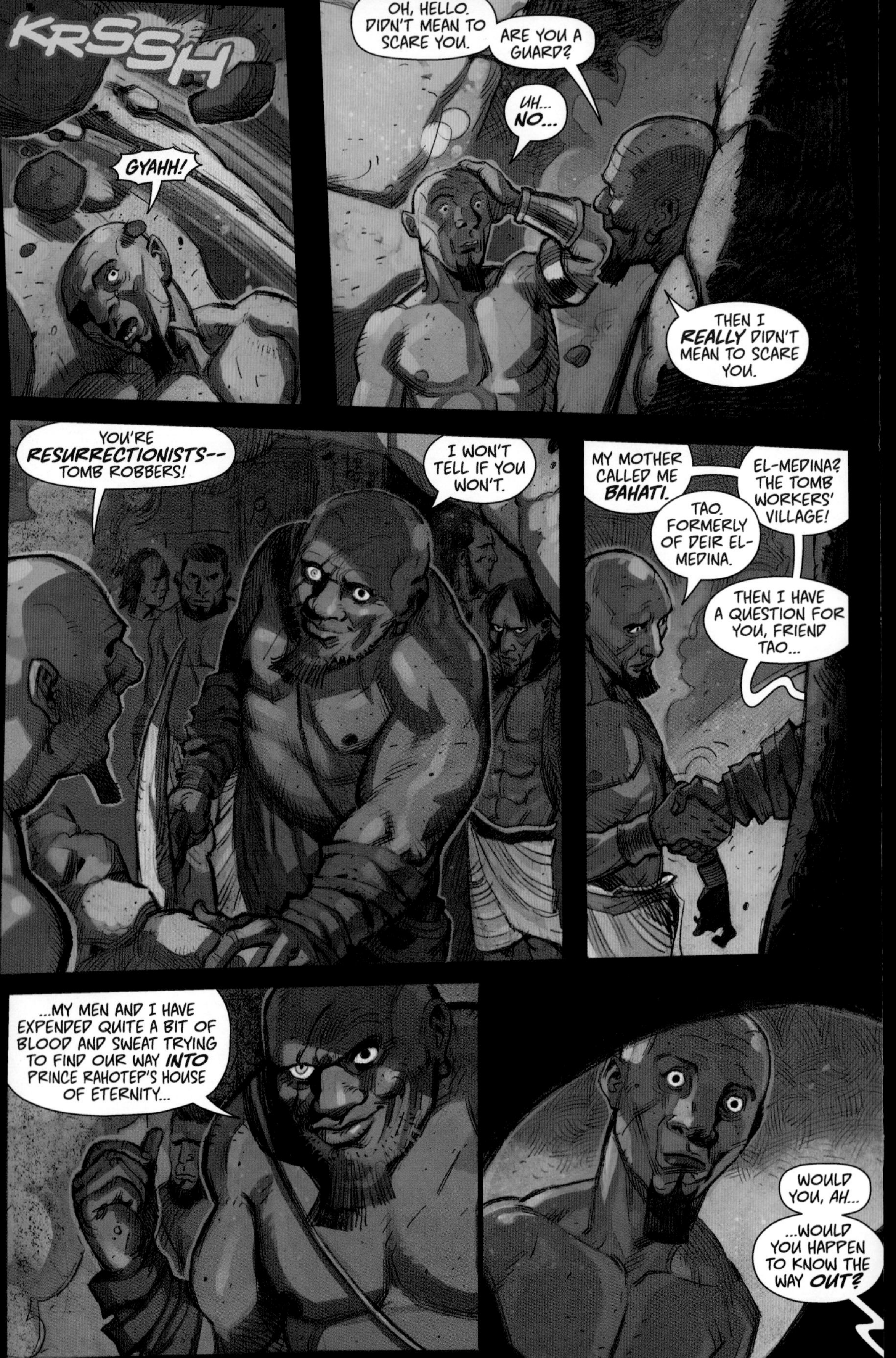
KRSSH
GYAHH!
OH, HELLO. DIDN'T MEAN TO SCARE YOU.
ARE YOU A GUARD?
UH... NO...
THEN I REALLY DIDN'T MEAN TO SCARE YOU.
YOU'RE RESURRECTIONISTS-- TOMB ROBBERS!
I WON'T TELL IF YOU WON'T.
MY MOTHER CALLED ME BAHATI.
TAO. FORMERLY OF DEIR EL-MEDINA.
EL-MEDINA? THE TOMB WORKERS' VILLAGE!
THEN I HAVE A QUESTION FOR YOU, FRIEND TAO...
...MY MEN AND I HAVE EXPENDED QUITE A BIT OF BLOOD AND SWEAT TRYING TO FIND OUR WAY INTO PRINCE RAHOTEP'S HOUSE OF ETERNITY...
WOULD YOU, AH...
...WOULD YOU HAPPEN TO KNOW THE WAY OUT?

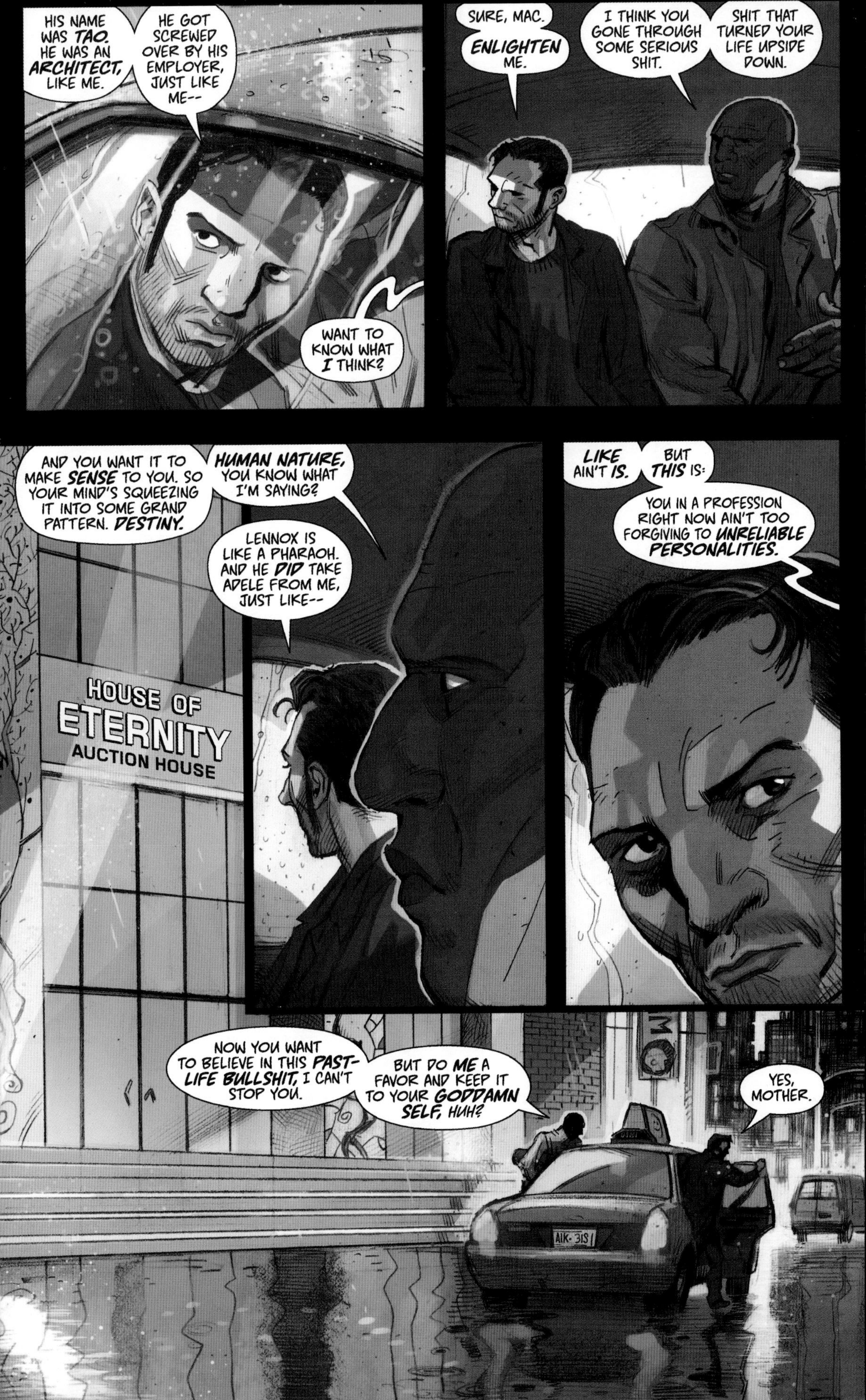
HIS NAME WAS TAO. HE WAS AN ARCHITECT, LIKE ME.
HE GOT SCREWED OVER BY HIS EMPLOYER, JUST LIKE ME--
WANT TO KNOW WHAT I THINK?
SURE, MAC. ENLIGHTEN ME.
I THINK YOU GONE THROUGH SOME SERIOUS SHIT.
SHIT THAT TURNED YOUR LIFE UPSIDE DOWN.
AND YOU WANT IT TO MAKE SENSE TO YOU. SO YOUR MIND'S SQUEEZING IT INTO SOME GRAND PATTERN. DESTINY.
HUMAN NATURE, YOU KNOW WHAT I'M SAYING?
LENNOX IS LIKE A PHARAOH. AND HE DID TAKE ADELE FROM ME, JUST LIKE--
HOUSE OF ETERNITY
AUCTION HOUSE
LIKE AIN'T IS.
BUT THIS IS:
YOU IN A PROFESSION RIGHT NOW AIN'T TOO FORGIVING TO UNRELIABLE PERSONALITIES.
NOW YOU WANT TO BELIEVE IN THIS PAST-LIFE BULLSHIT, I CAN'T STOP YOU.
BUT DO ME A FAVOR AND KEEP IT TO YOUR GODDAMN SELF, HUH?
YES, MOTHER.
AIK-315

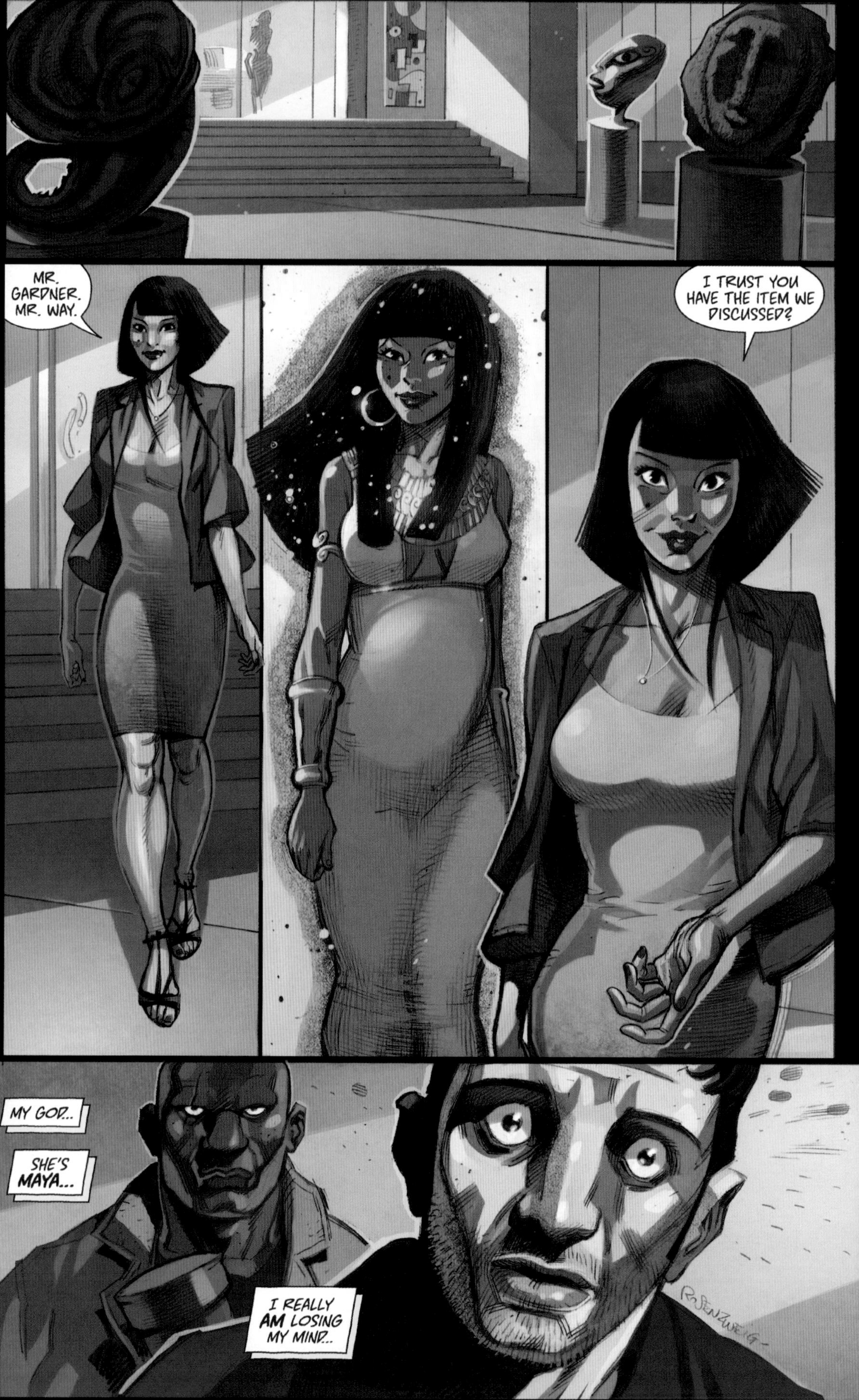
MR. GARDNER. MR. WAY.
I TRUST YOU HAVE THE ITEM WE DISCUSSED?
MY GOD...
SHE'S MAYA...
I REALLY AM LOSING MY MIND...

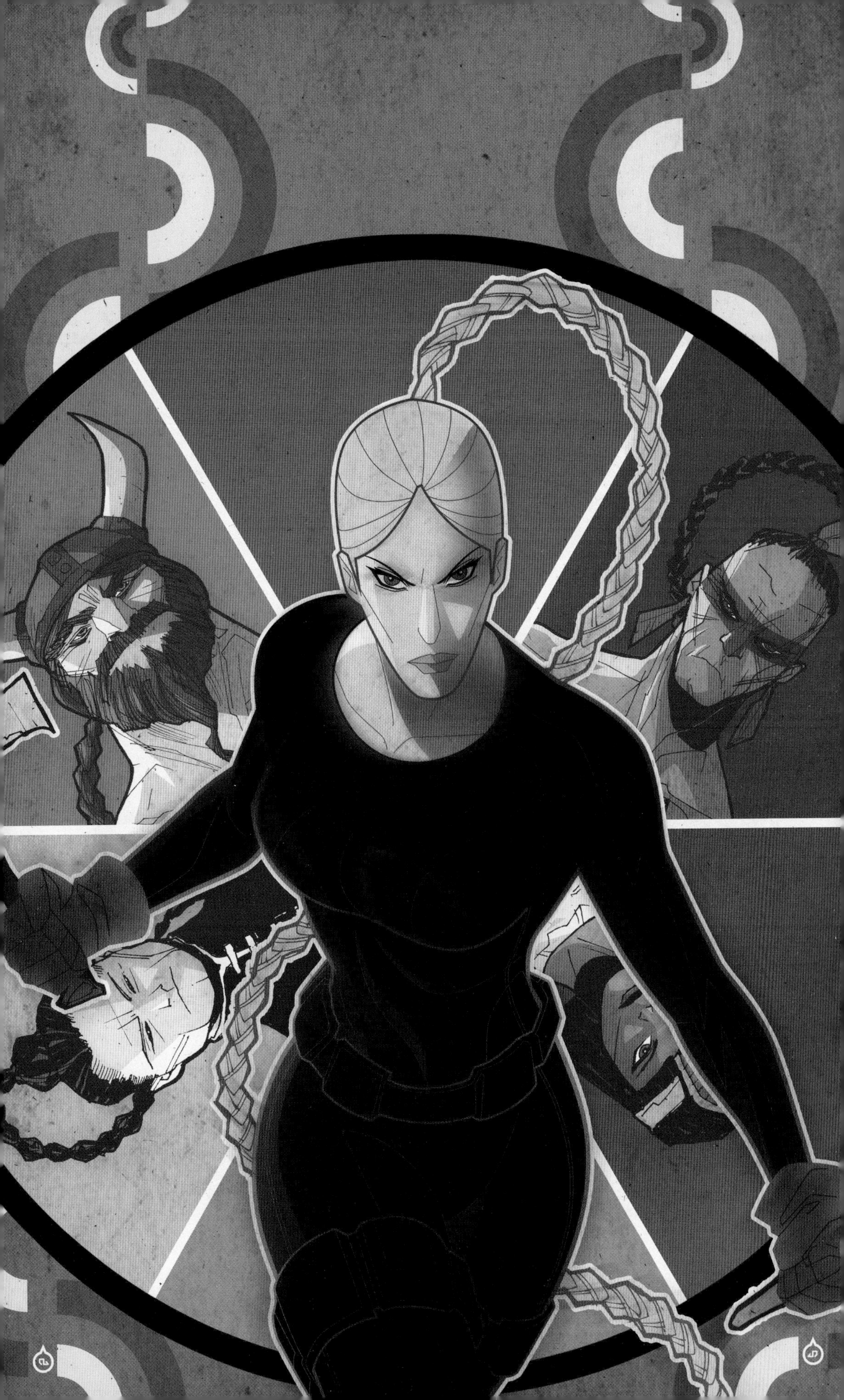

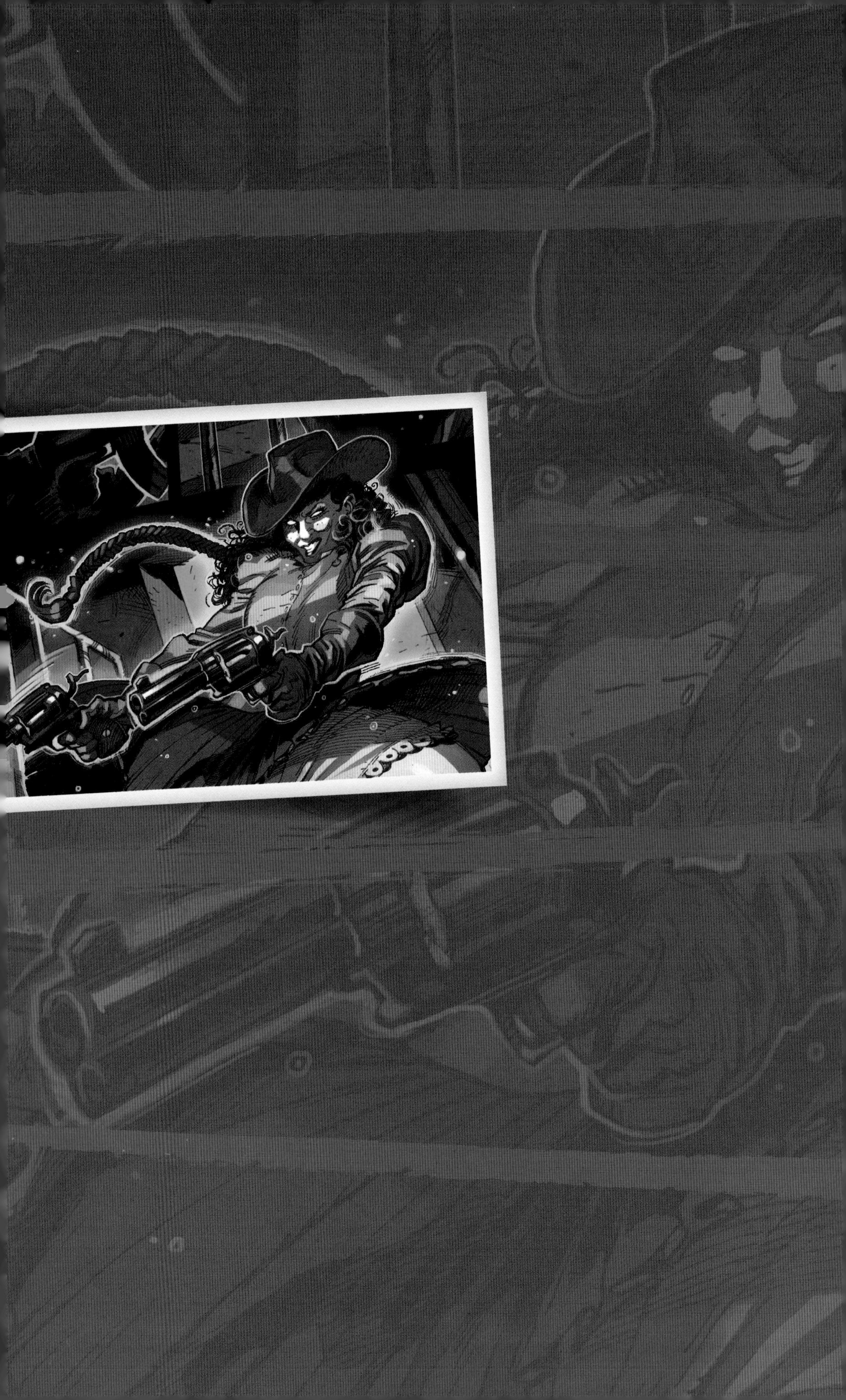

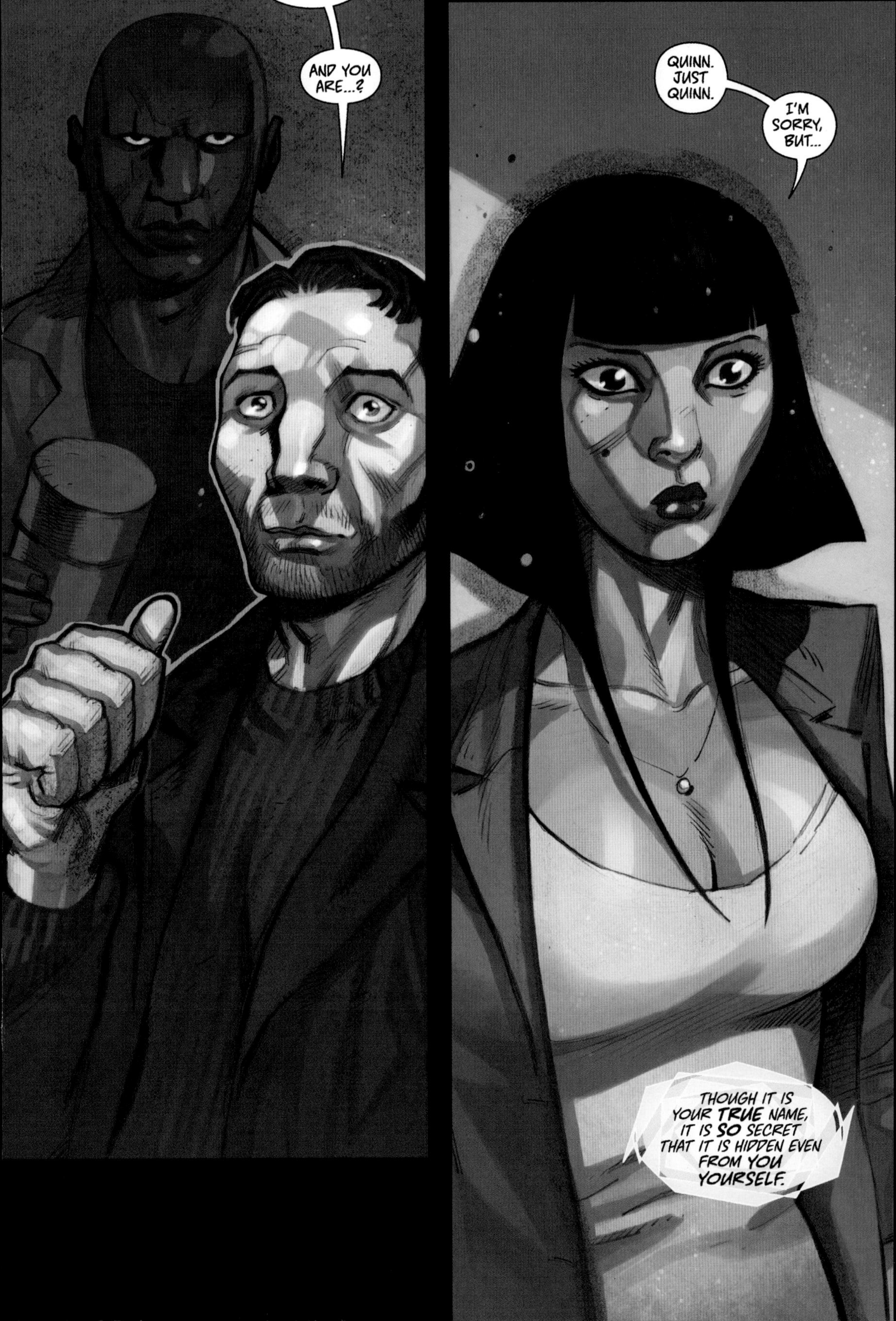
AND YOU ARE...?
QUINN. JUST QUINN.
I'M SORRY, BUT...
THOUGH IT IS YOUR TRUE NAME, IT IS SO SECRET THAT IT IS HIDDEN EVEN FROM YOU YOURSELF.

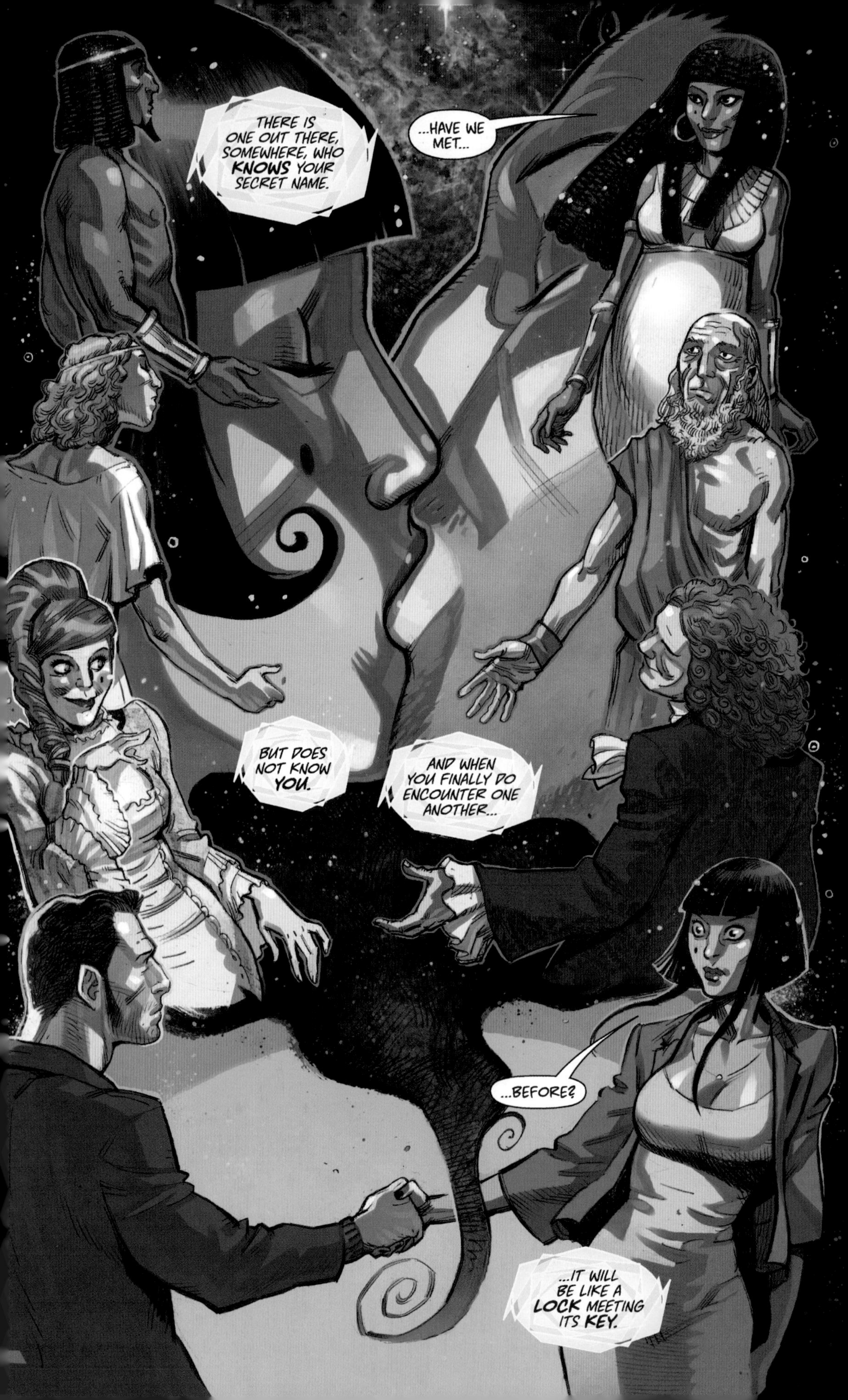
THERE IS ONE OUT THERE, SOMEWHERE, WHO KNOWS YOUR SECRET NAME.
...HAVE WE MET...
BUT DOES NOT KNOW YOU.
AND WHEN YOU FINALLY DO ENCOUNTER ONE ANOTHER...
...BEFORE?
...IT WILL BE LIKE A LOCK MEETING ITS KEY.

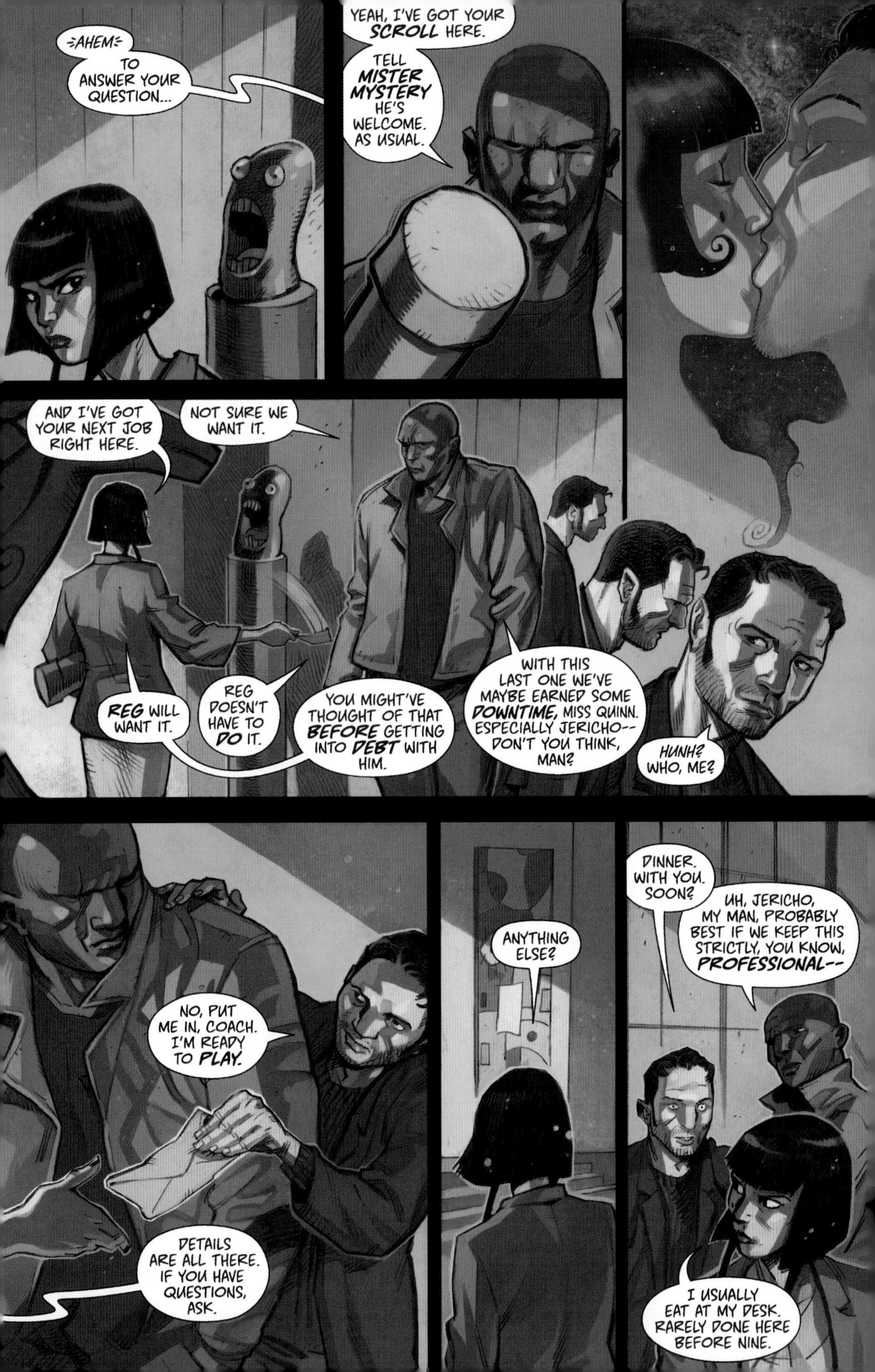

AHEM
TO ANSWER YOUR QUESTION...
YEAH, I'VE GOT YOUR SCROLL HERE.
TELL MISTER MYSTERY HE'S WELCOME. AS USUAL.
AND I'VE GOT YOUR NEXT JOB RIGHT HERE.
NOT SURE WE WANT IT.
REG WILL WANT IT.
REG DOESN'T HAVE TO DO IT.
YOU MIGHT'VE THOUGHT OF THAT BEFORE GETTING INTO DEBT WITH HIM.
WITH THIS LAST ONE WE'VE MAYBE EARNED SOME DOWNTIME, MISS QUINN. ESPECIALLY JERICHO-- DON'T YOU THINK, MAN?
HUNH? WHO, ME?
NO, PUT ME IN, COACH. I'M READY TO PLAY.
DETAILS ARE ALL THERE. IF YOU HAVE QUESTIONS, ASK.
ANYTHING ELSE?
DINNER. WITH YOU. SOON?
UH, JERICHO, MY MAN, PROBABLY BEST IF WE KEEP THIS STRICTLY, YOU KNOW, PROFESSIONAL--
I USUALLY EAT AT MY DESK. RARELY DONE HERE BEFORE NINE.

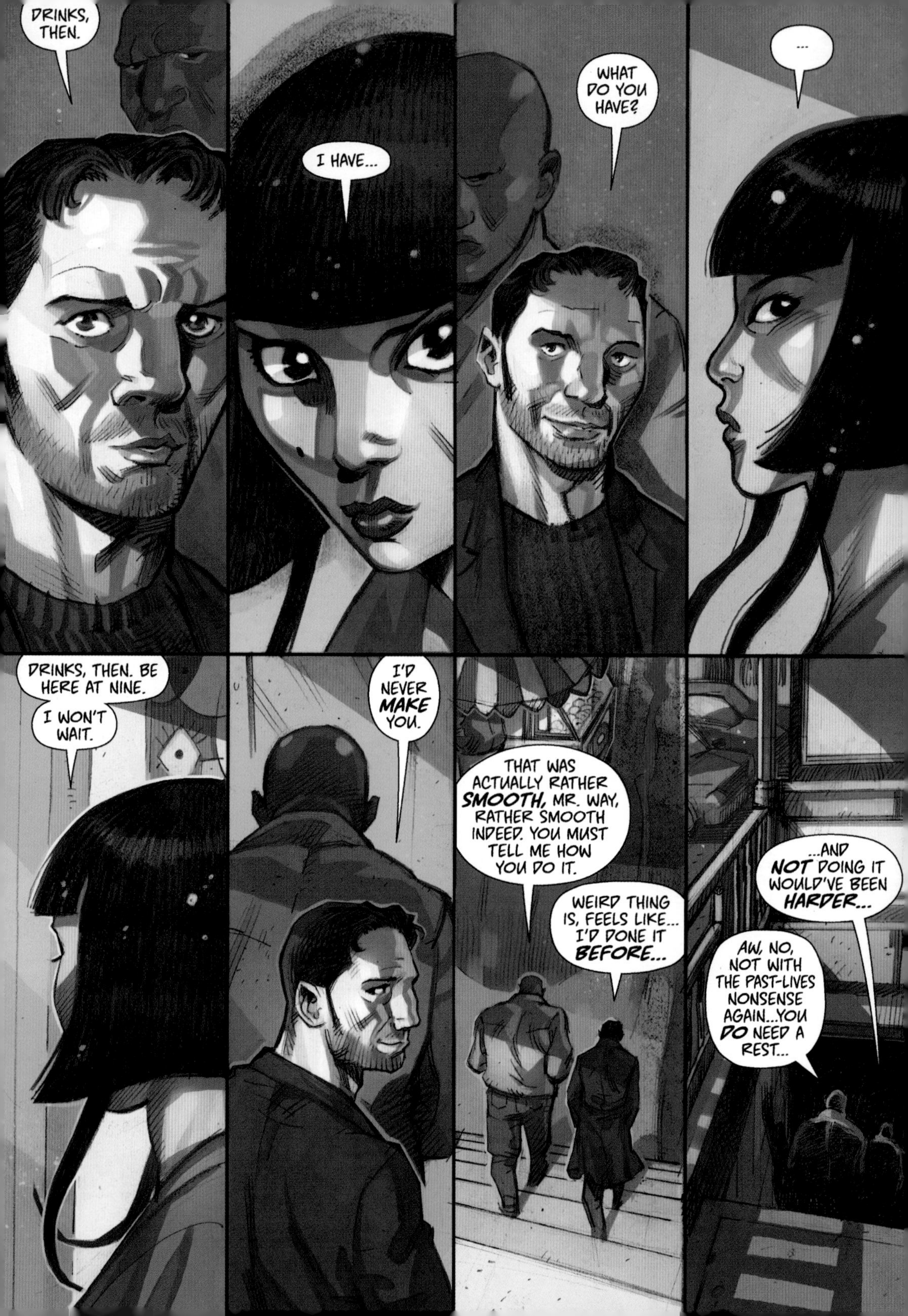
DRINKS, THEN.
I HAVE...
WHAT DO YOU HAVE?
...
DRINKS, THEN. BE HERE AT NINE.
I WON'T WAIT.
I'D NEVER MAKE YOU.
THAT WAS ACTUALLY RATHER SMOOTH, MR. WAY, RATHER SMOOTH INDEED. YOU MUST TELL ME HOW YOU DO IT.
WEIRD THING IS, FEELS LIKE... I'D DONE IT BEFORE...
...AND NOT DOING IT WOULD'VE BEEN HARDER...
AW, NO, NOT WITH THE PAST-LIVES NONSENSE AGAIN...YOU DO NEED A REST...

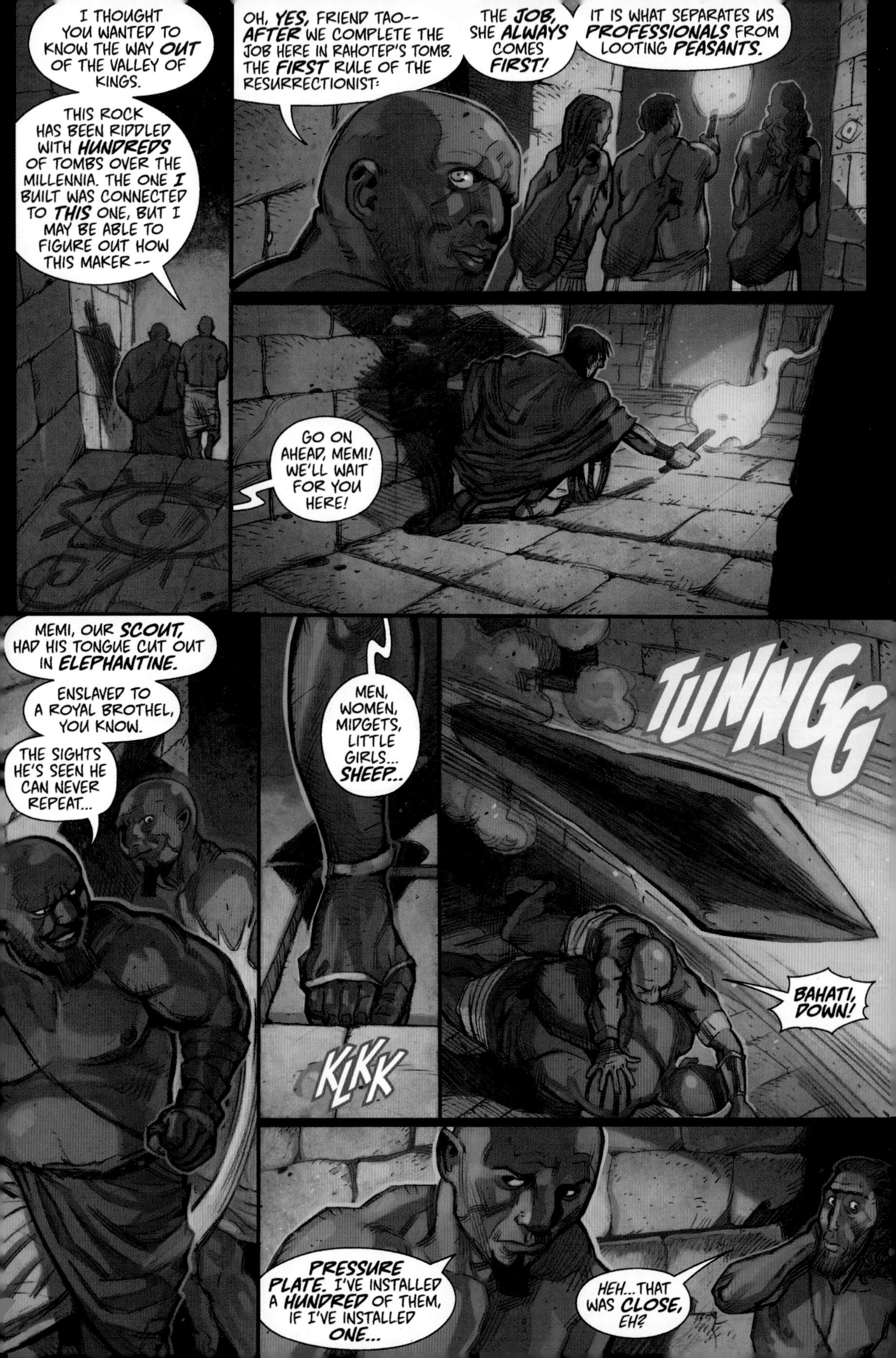
I THOUGHT YOU WANTED TO KNOW THE WAY *OUT* OF THE VALLEY OF KINGS.
THIS ROCK HAS BEEN RIDDLED WITH *HUNDREDS* OF TOMBS OVER THE MILLENNIA. THE ONE *I* BUILT WAS CONNECTED TO *THIS* ONE, BUT I MAY BE ABLE TO FIGURE OUT HOW THIS MAKER --
OH, *YES,* FRIEND TAO-- *AFTER* WE COMPLETE THE JOB HERE IN RAHOTEP'S TOMB. THE *FIRST* RULE OF THE RESURRECTIONIST:
THE *JOB,* SHE *ALWAYS* COMES *FIRST!*
IT IS WHAT SEPARATES US *PROFESSIONALS* FROM LOOTING *PEASANTS.*
GO ON AHEAD, MEMI! WE'LL WAIT FOR YOU HERE!
MEMI, OUR *SCOUT,* HAD HIS TONGUE CUT OUT IN *ELEPHANTINE.*
ENSLAVED TO A ROYAL BROTHEL, YOU KNOW.
THE SIGHTS HE'S SEEN HE CAN NEVER REPEAT...
MEN, WOMEN, MIDGETS, LITTLE GIRLS... *SHEEP...*
KLIKK
TUNNGG
BAHATI, DOWN!
PRESSURE PLATE. I'VE INSTALLED A *HUNDRED* OF THEM, IF I'VE INSTALLED *ONE...*
HEH...THAT WAS *CLOSE,* EH?

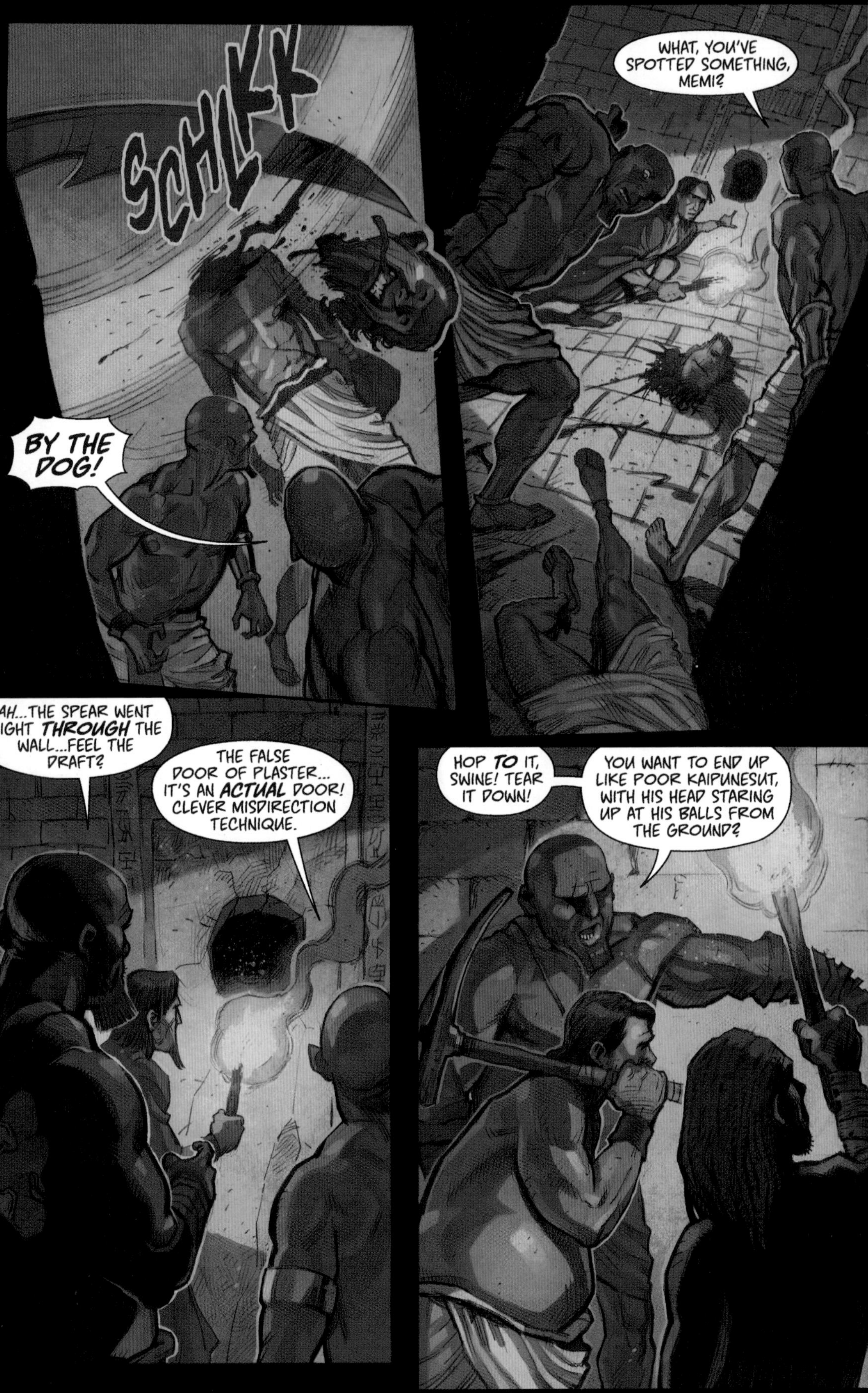
SCHKK
BY THE DOG!
WHAT, YOU'VE SPOTTED SOMETHING, MEMI?
AH...THE SPEAR WENT RIGHT THROUGH THE WALL...FEEL THE DRAFT?
THE FALSE DOOR OF PLASTER... IT'S AN ACTUAL DOOR! CLEVER MISDIRECTION TECHNIQUE.
HOP TO IT, SWINE! TEAR IT DOWN!
YOU WANT TO END UP LIKE POOR KAIPUNESUT, WITH HIS HEAD STARING UP AT HIS BALLS FROM THE GROUND?

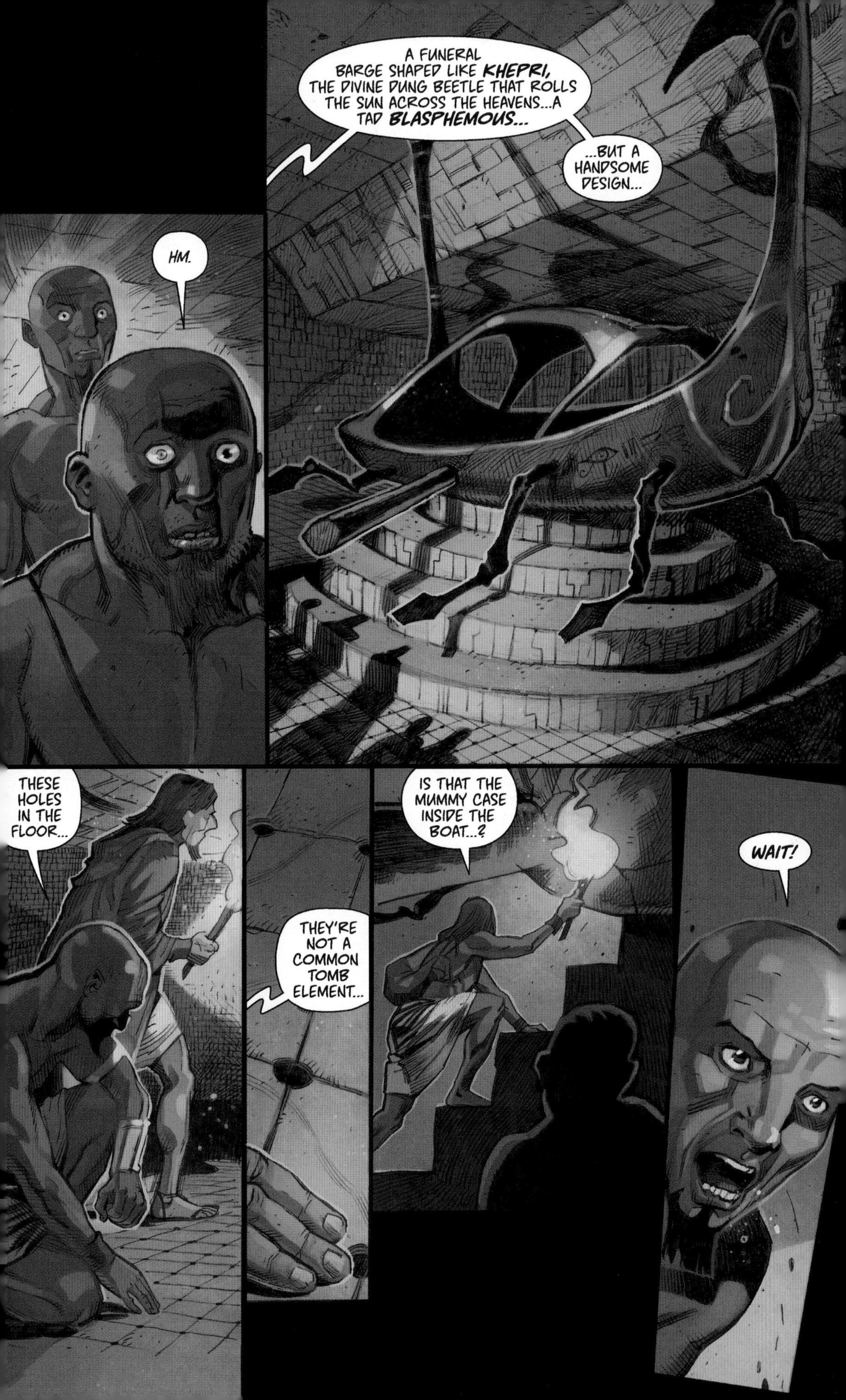
A FUNERAL BARGE SHAPED LIKE KHEPRI, THE DIVINE DUNG BEETLE THAT ROLLS THE SUN ACROSS THE HEAVENS...A TAD BLASPHEMOUS...
...BUT A HANDSOME DESIGN...
HM.
THESE HOLES IN THE FLOOR...
THEY'RE NOT A COMMON TOMB ELEMENT...
IS THAT THE MUMMY CASE INSIDE THE BOAT...?
WAIT!

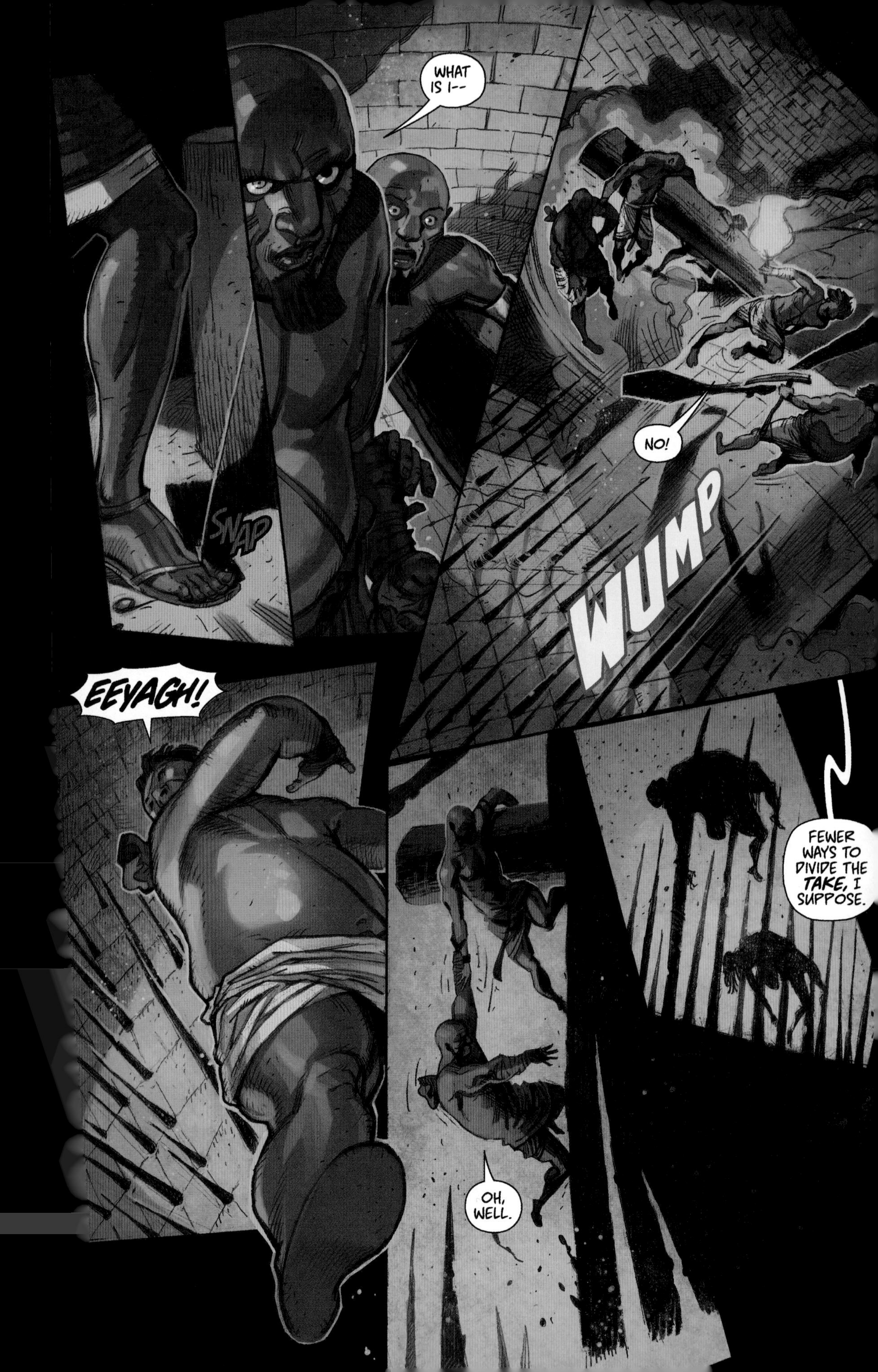
WHAT IS I--
SNAP
NO!
WUMP
EEYAGH!
FEWER WAYS TO DIVIDE THE TAKE, I SUPPOSE.
OH, WELL.

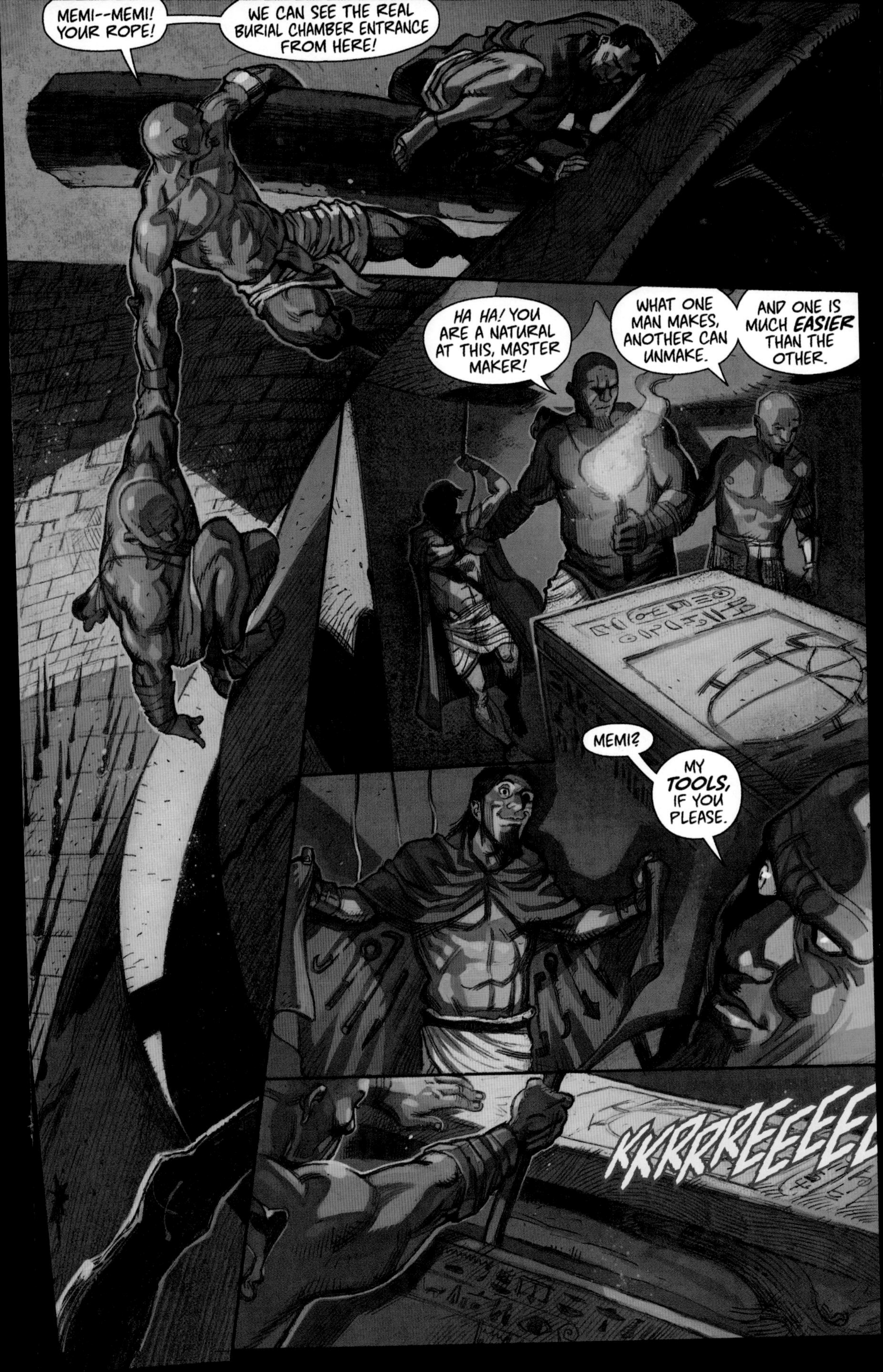
MEMI--MEMI! YOUR ROPE!
WE CAN SEE THE REAL BURIAL CHAMBER ENTRANCE FROM HERE!
HA HA! YOU ARE A NATURAL AT THIS, MASTER MAKER!
WHAT ONE MAN MAKES, ANOTHER CAN UNMAKE.
AND ONE IS MUCH EASIER THAN THE OTHER.
MEMI?
MY TOOLS, IF YOU PLEASE.
KKRRREEEEE

LOOT: SARCOPHAGUS OF PRINCE RAHOTEP
CLIENT: TEMPLE OF SOBEK

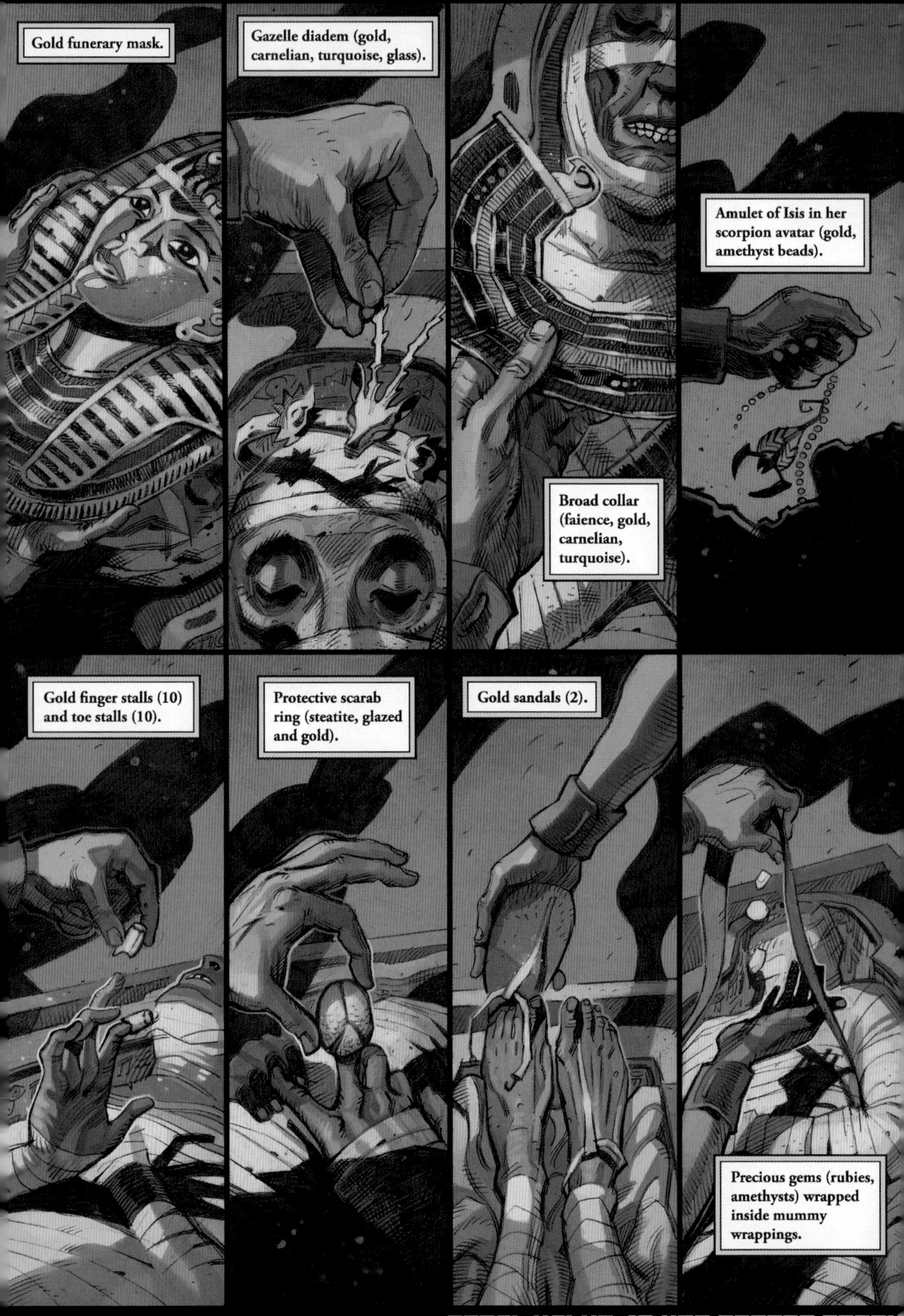

Gold funerary mask.
Gazelle diadem (gold, carnelian, turquoise, glass).
Broad collar (faience, gold, carnelian, turquoise).
Amulet of Isis in her scorpion avatar (gold, amethyst beads).
Gold finger stalls (10) and toe stalls (10).
Protective scarab ring (steatite, glazed and gold).
Gold sandals (2).
Precious gems (rubies, amethysts) wrapped inside mummy wrappings.

TOTAL VALUE: 16,490 COPPER DEBEN

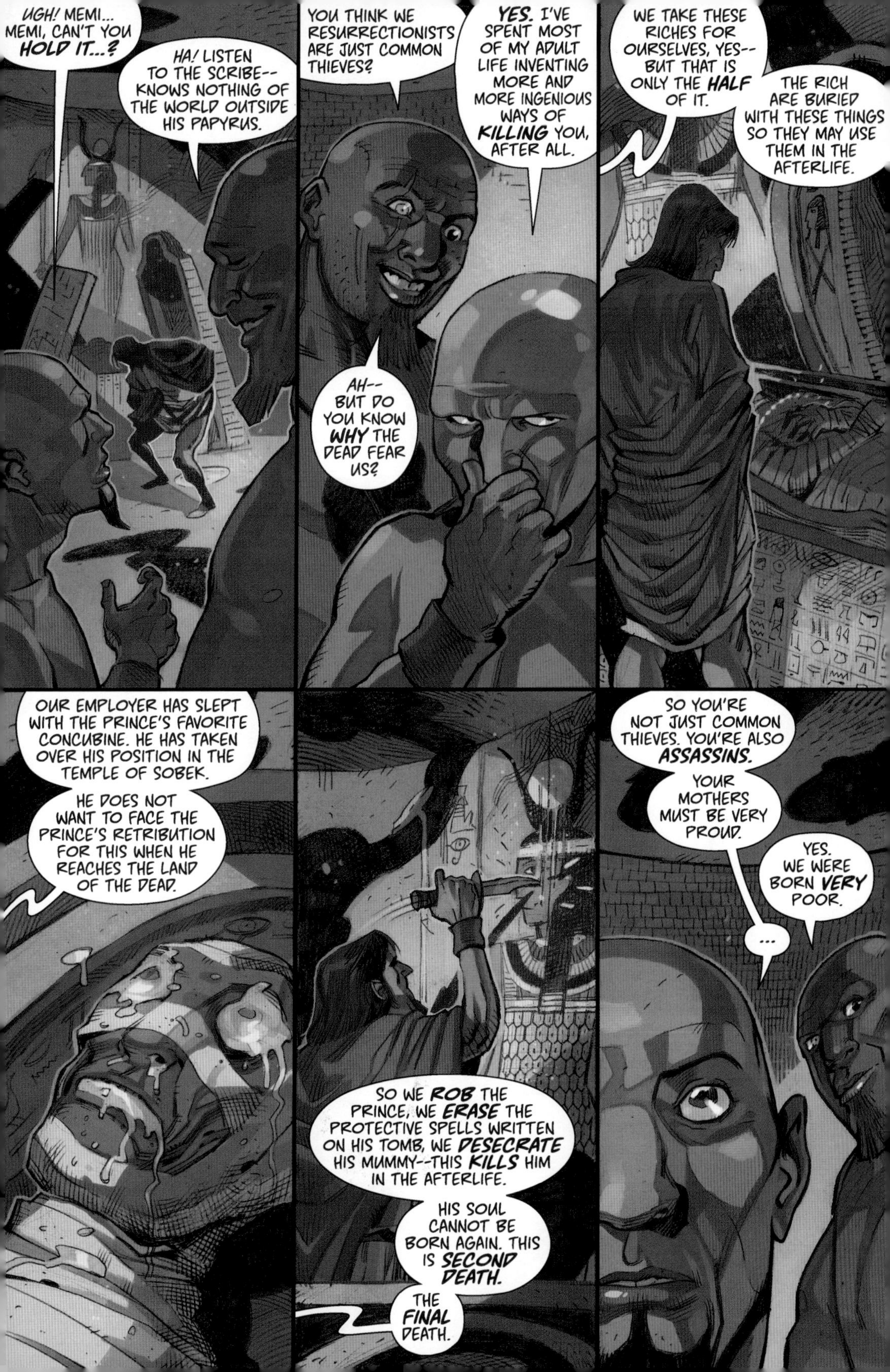
UGH! MEMI... MEMI, CAN'T YOU HOLD IT...?
HA! LISTEN TO THE SCRIBE-- KNOWS NOTHING OF THE WORLD OUTSIDE HIS PAPYRUS.
YOU THINK WE RESURRECTIONISTS ARE JUST COMMON THIEVES?
YES. I'VE SPENT MOST OF MY ADULT LIFE INVENTING MORE AND MORE INGENIOUS WAYS OF KILLING YOU, AFTER ALL.
AH-- BUT DO YOU KNOW WHY THE DEAD FEAR US?
WE TAKE THESE RICHES FOR OURSELVES, YES-- BUT THAT IS ONLY THE HALF OF IT.
THE RICH ARE BURIED WITH THESE THINGS SO THEY MAY USE THEM IN THE AFTERLIFE.
OUR EMPLOYER HAS SLEPT WITH THE PRINCE'S FAVORITE CONCUBINE. HE HAS TAKEN OVER HIS POSITION IN THE TEMPLE OF SOBEK.
HE DOES NOT WANT TO FACE THE PRINCE'S RETRIBUTION FOR THIS WHEN HE REACHES THE LAND OF THE DEAD.
SO WE ROB THE PRINCE, WE ERASE THE PROTECTIVE SPELLS WRITTEN ON HIS TOMB, WE DESECRATE HIS MUMMY--THIS KILLS HIM IN THE AFTERLIFE.
HIS SOUL CANNOT BE BORN AGAIN. THIS IS SECOND DEATH.
THE FINAL DEATH.
SO YOU'RE NOT JUST COMMON THIEVES. YOU'RE ALSO ASSASSINS.
YOUR MOTHERS MUST BE VERY PROUD.
YES. WE WERE BORN VERY POOR.
...

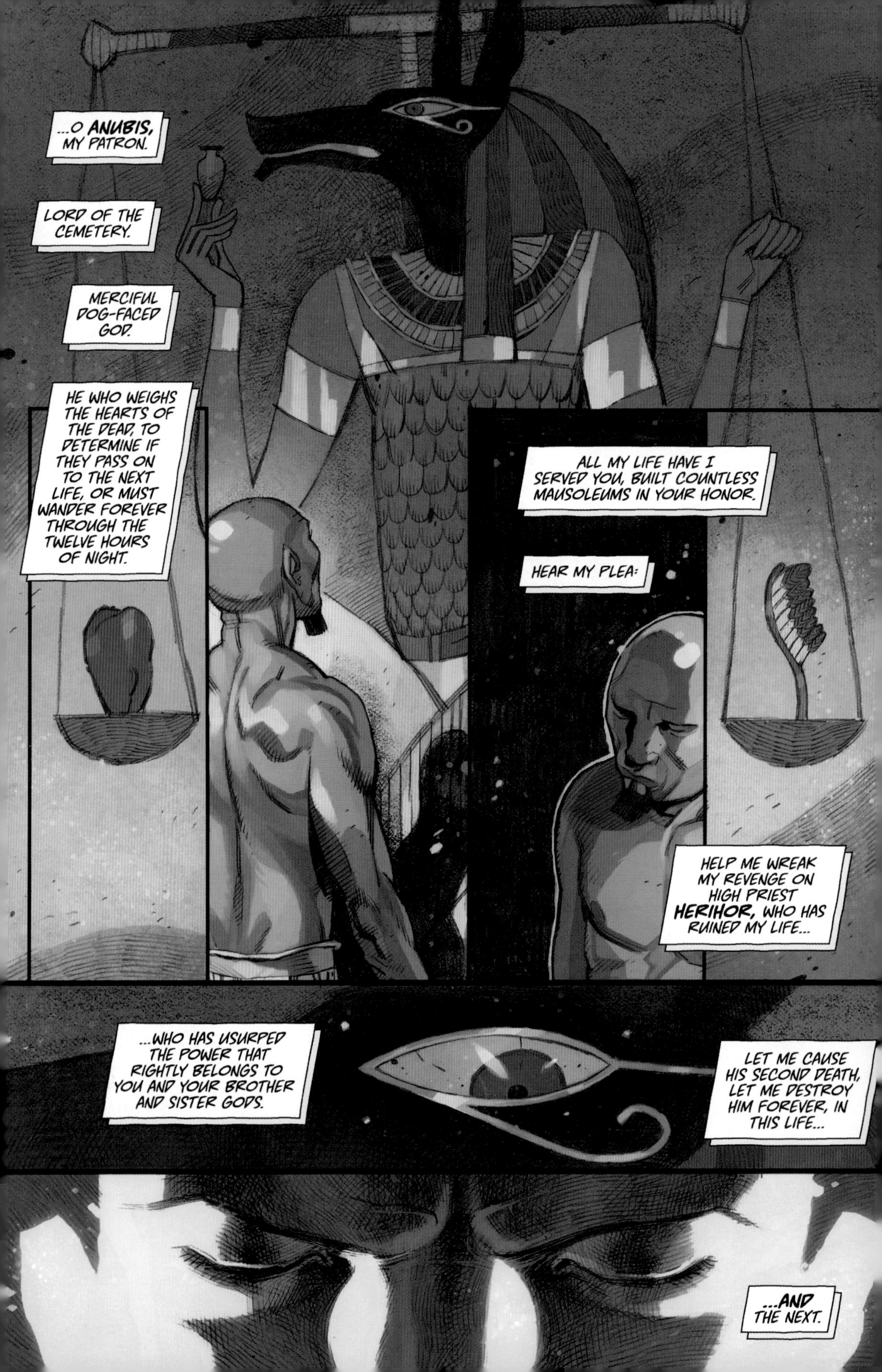

...O ANUBIS, MY PATRON.
LORD OF THE CEMETERY.
MERCIFUL DOG-FACED GOD.
HE WHO WEIGHS THE HEARTS OF THE DEAD, TO DETERMINE IF THEY PASS ON TO THE NEXT LIFE, OR MUST WANDER FOREVER THROUGH THE TWELVE HOURS OF NIGHT.
ALL MY LIFE HAVE I SERVED YOU, BUILT COUNTLESS MAUSOLEUMS IN YOUR HONOR.
HEAR MY PLEA:
HELP ME WREAK MY REVENGE ON HIGH PRIEST HERIHOR, WHO HAS RUINED MY LIFE...
...WHO HAS USURPED THE POWER THAT RIGHTLY BELONGS TO YOU AND YOUR BROTHER AND SISTER GODS.
LET ME CAUSE HIS SECOND DEATH, LET ME DESTROY HIM FOREVER, IN THIS LIFE...
...AND THE NEXT.

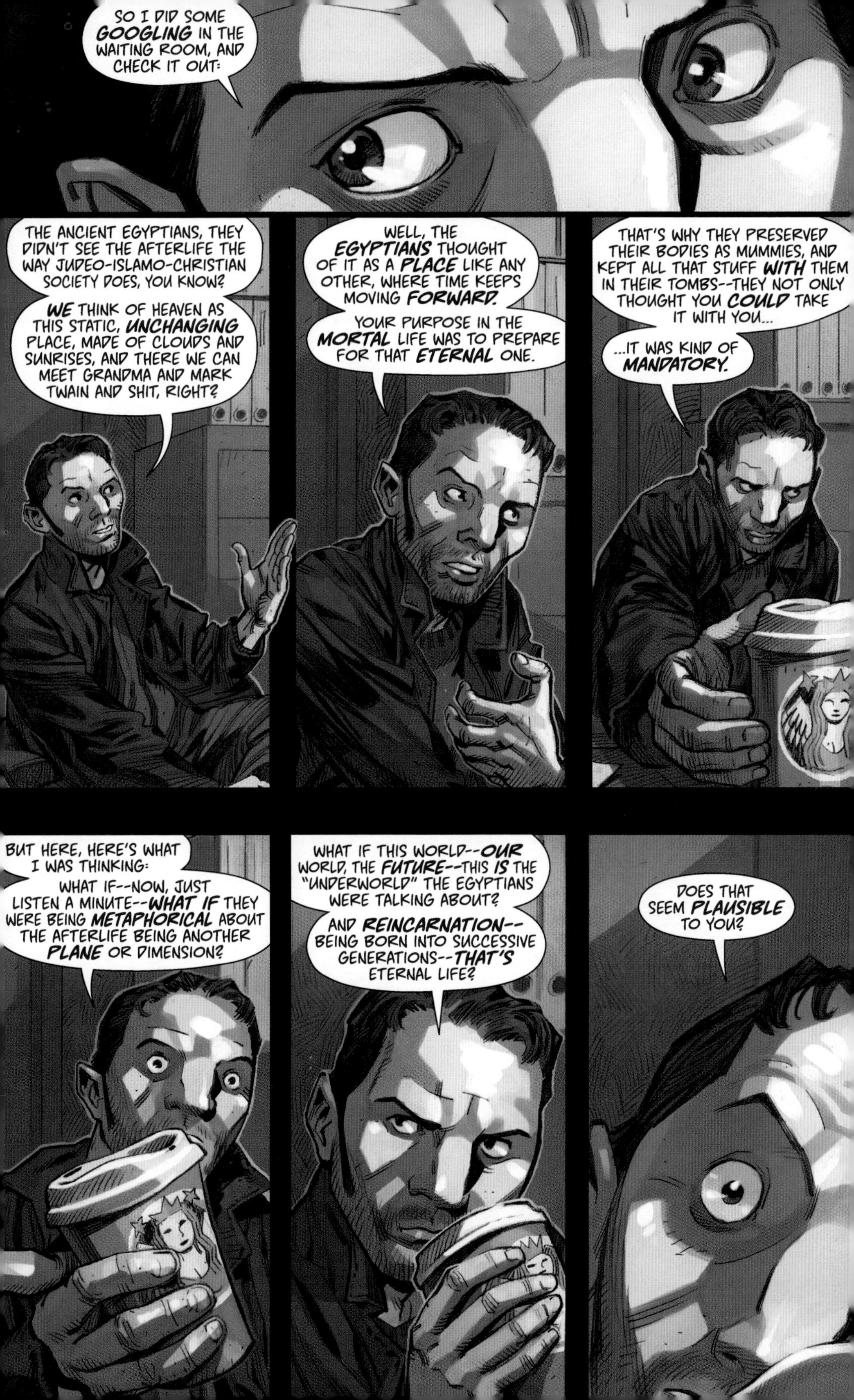
SO I DID SOME GOOGLING IN THE WAITING ROOM, AND CHECK IT OUT:
THE ANCIENT EGYPTIANS, THEY DIDN'T SEE THE AFTERLIFE THE WAY JUDEO-ISLAMO-CHRISTIAN SOCIETY DOES, YOU KNOW?
WE THINK OF HEAVEN AS THIS STATIC, UNCHANGING PLACE, MADE OF CLOUDS AND SUNRISES, AND THERE WE CAN MEET GRANDMA AND MARK TWAIN AND SHIT, RIGHT?
WELL, THE EGYPTIANS THOUGHT OF IT AS A PLACE LIKE ANY OTHER, WHERE TIME KEEPS MOVING FORWARD.
YOUR PURPOSE IN THE MORTAL LIFE WAS TO PREPARE FOR THAT ETERNAL ONE.
THAT'S WHY THEY PRESERVED THEIR BODIES AS MUMMIES, AND KEPT ALL THAT STUFF WITH THEM IN THEIR TOMBS--THEY NOT ONLY THOUGHT YOU COULD TAKE IT WITH YOU...
...IT WAS KIND OF MANDATORY.
BUT HERE, HERE'S WHAT I WAS THINKING:
WHAT IF--NOW, JUST LISTEN A MINUTE--WHAT IF THEY WERE BEING METAPHORICAL ABOUT THE AFTERLIFE BEING ANOTHER PLANE OR DIMENSION?
WHAT IF THIS WORLD--OUR WORLD, THE FUTURE--THIS IS THE "UNDERWORLD" THE EGYPTIANS WERE TALKING ABOUT?
AND REINCARNATION--BEING BORN INTO SUCCESSIVE GENERATIONS--THAT'S ETERNAL LIFE?
DOES THAT SEEM PLAUSIBLE TO YOU?

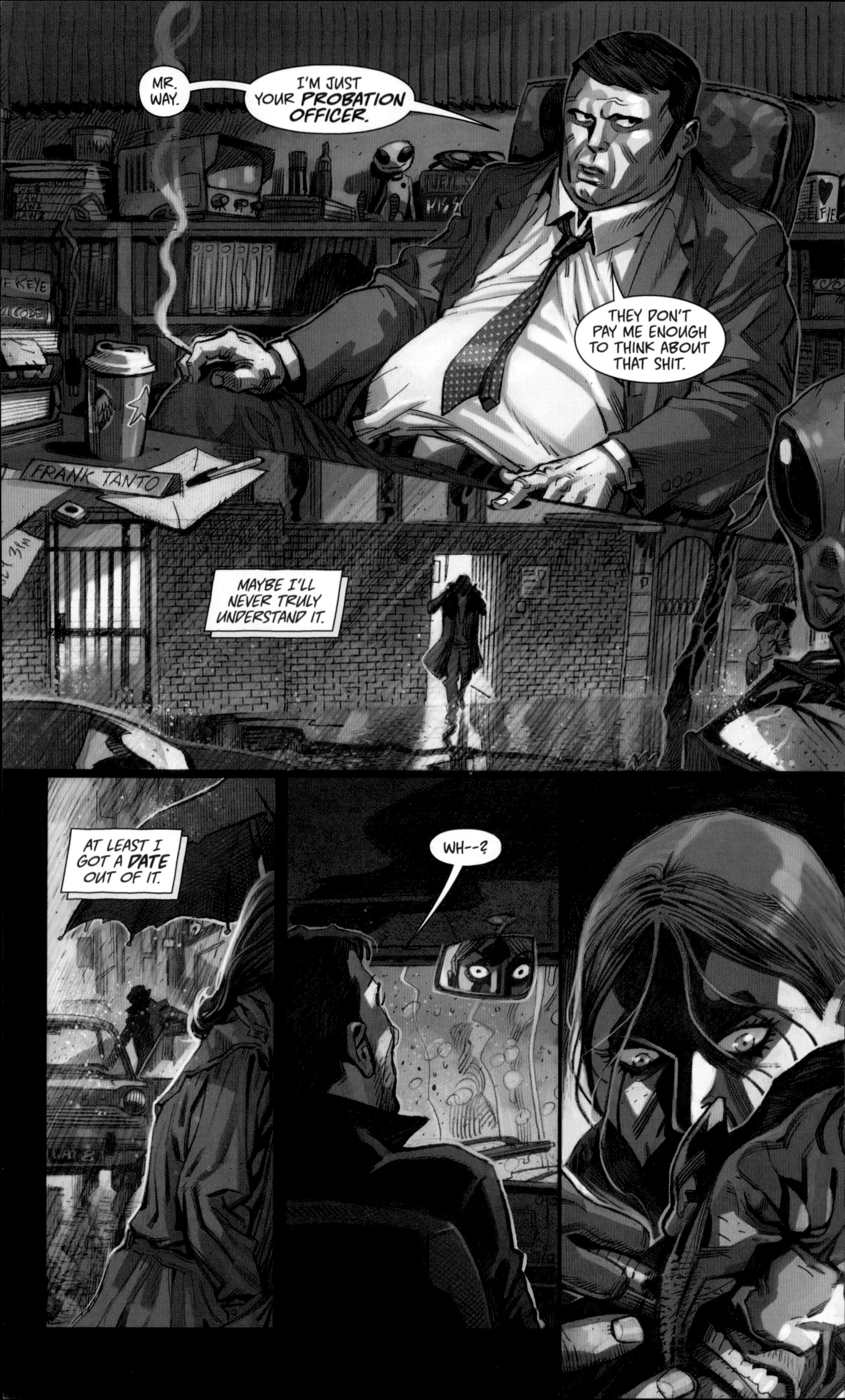

MR. WAY.
I'M JUST YOUR PROBATION OFFICER.
THEY DON'T PAY ME ENOUGH TO THINK ABOUT THAT SHIT.
FRANK TANTO
MAYBE I'LL NEVER TRULY UNDERSTAND IT.
AT LEAST I GOT A DATE OUT OF IT.
WH--?

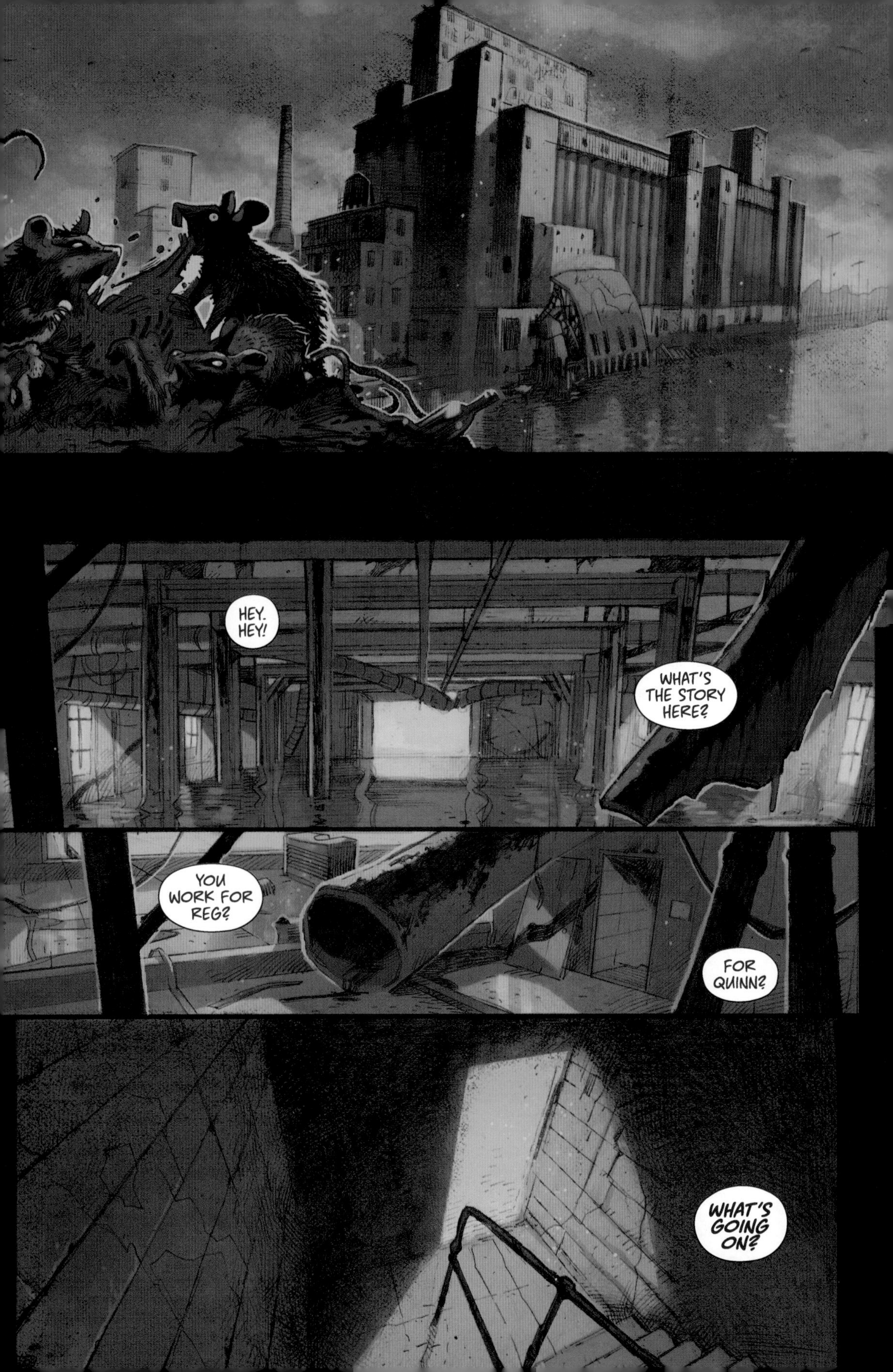
HEY. HEY!
WHAT'S THE STORY HERE?
YOU WORK FOR REG?
FOR QUINN?
WHAT'S GOING ON?

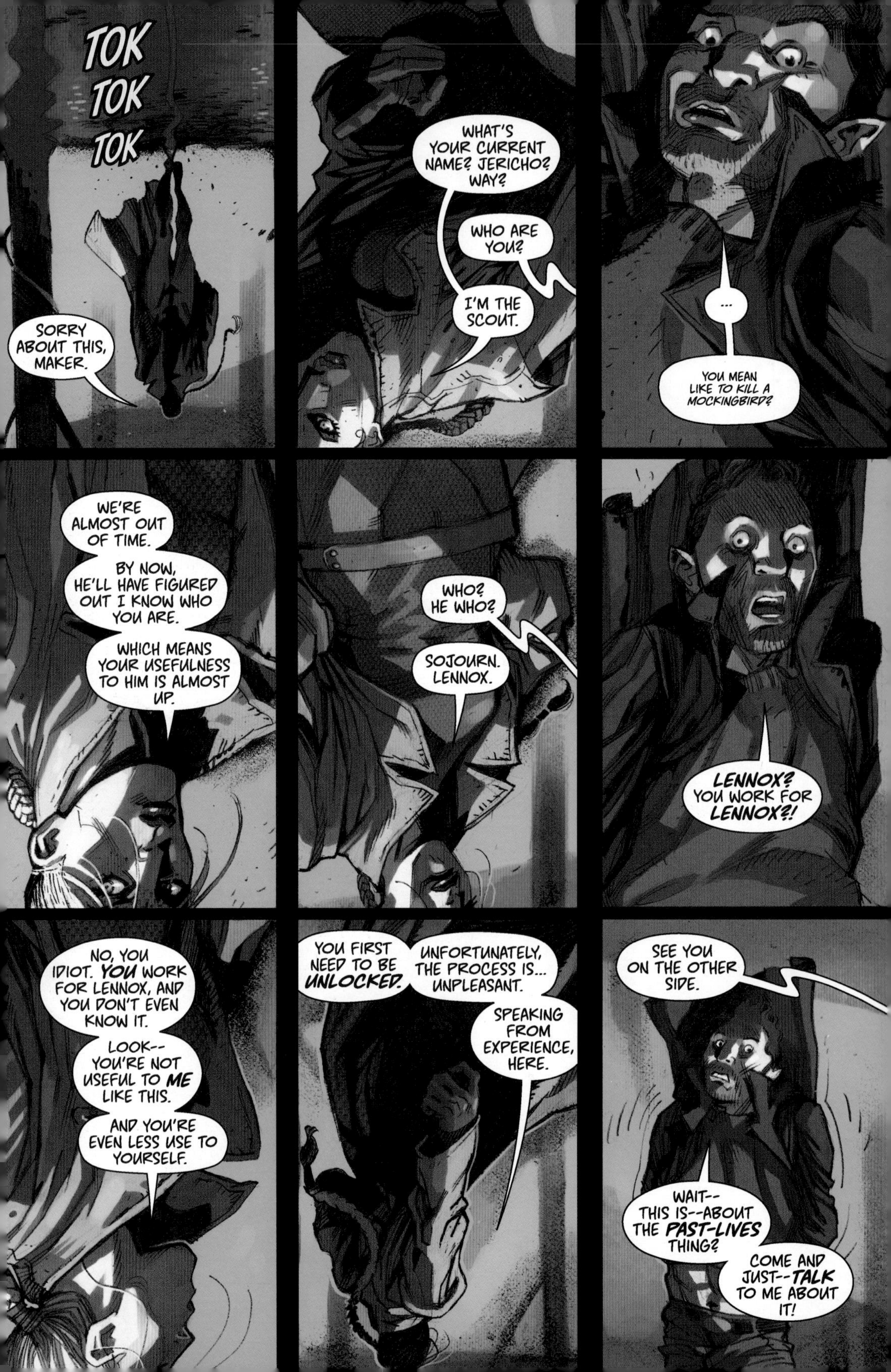
TOK
TOK
TOK
SORRY ABOUT THIS, MAKER.
WHAT'S YOUR CURRENT NAME? JERICHO? WAY?
WHO ARE YOU?
I'M THE SCOUT.
...
YOU MEAN LIKE TO KILL A MOCKINGBIRD?
WE'RE ALMOST OUT OF TIME.
BY NOW, HE'LL HAVE FIGURED OUT I KNOW WHO YOU ARE.
WHICH MEANS YOUR USEFULNESS TO HIM IS ALMOST UP.
WHO? HE WHO?
SOJOURN. LENNOX.
LENNOX? YOU WORK FOR LENNOX?!
NO, YOU IDIOT. YOU WORK FOR LENNOX, AND YOU DON'T EVEN KNOW IT.
LOOK-- YOU'RE NOT USEFUL TO ME LIKE THIS.
AND YOU'RE EVEN LESS USE TO YOURSELF.
YOU FIRST NEED TO BE UNLOCKED.
UNFORTUNATELY, THE PROCESS IS... UNPLEASANT.
SPEAKING FROM EXPERIENCE, HERE.
SEE YOU ON THE OTHER SIDE.
WAIT-- THIS IS--ABOUT THE PAST-LIVES THING?
COME AND JUST--TALK TO ME ABOUT IT!

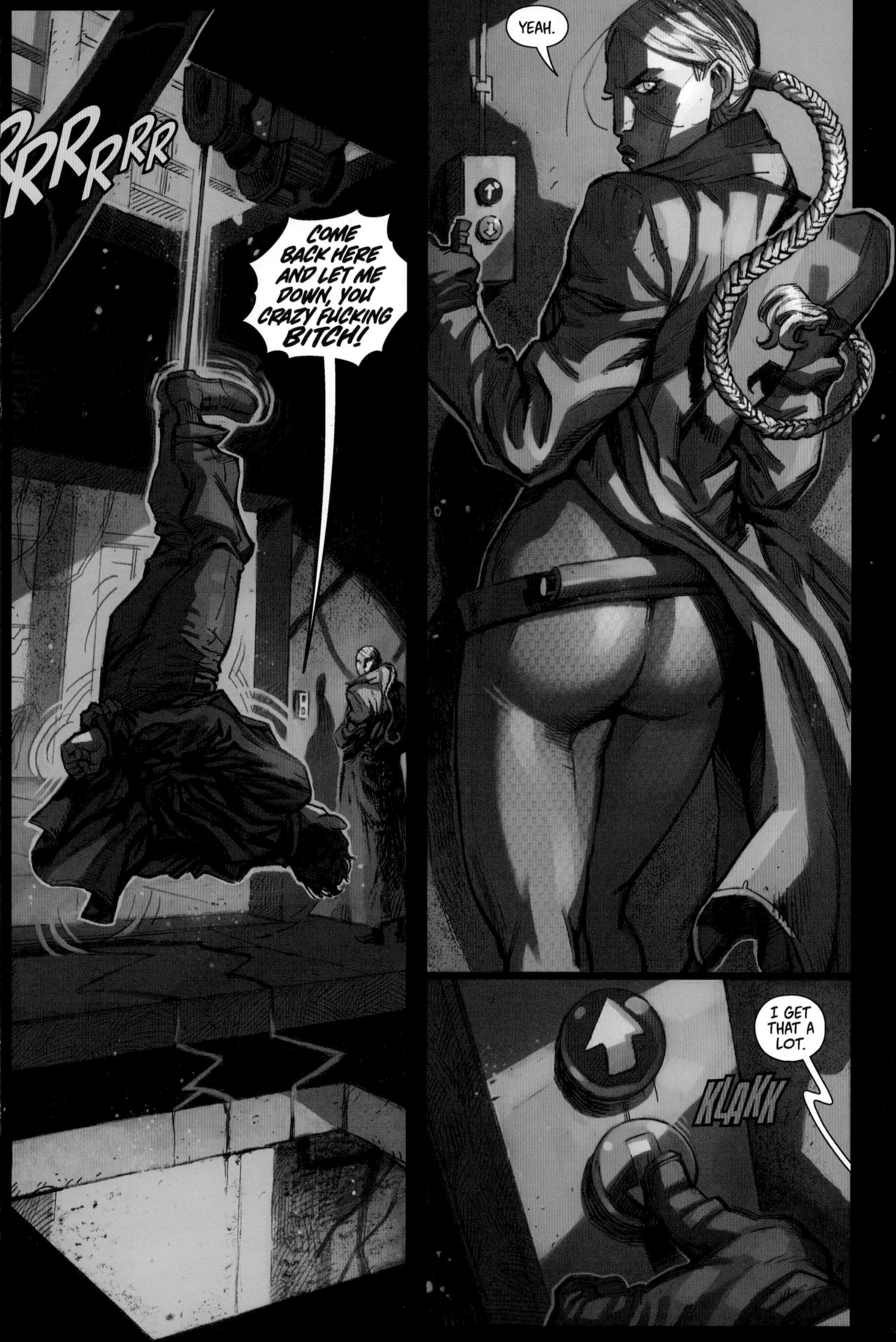
RRRRRR
COME BACK HERE AND LET ME DOWN, YOU CRAZY FUCKING BITCH!
YEAH.
KLAKK
I GET THAT A LOT.

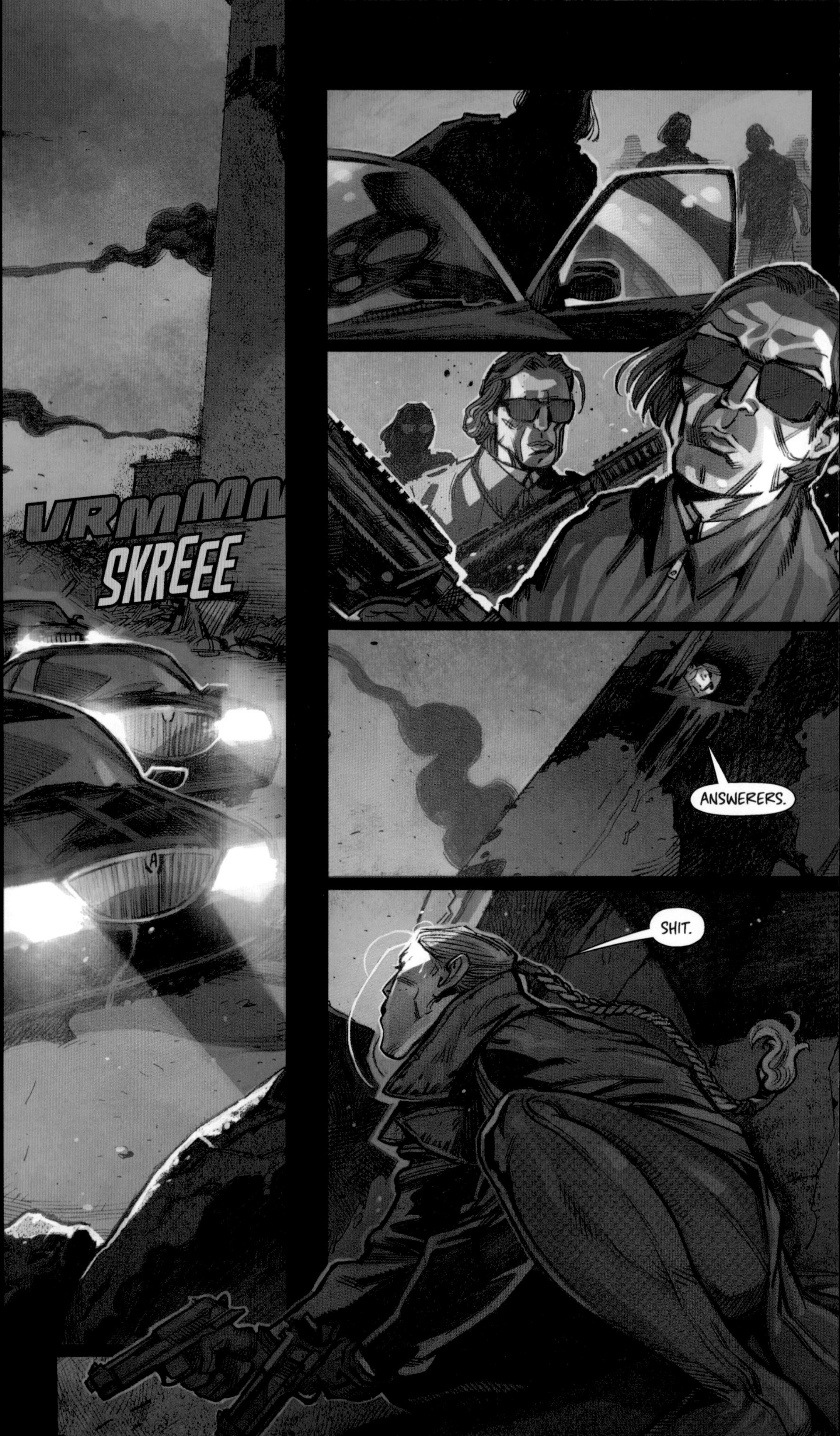
VRMMM
SKREEE
ANSWERERS.
SHIT.

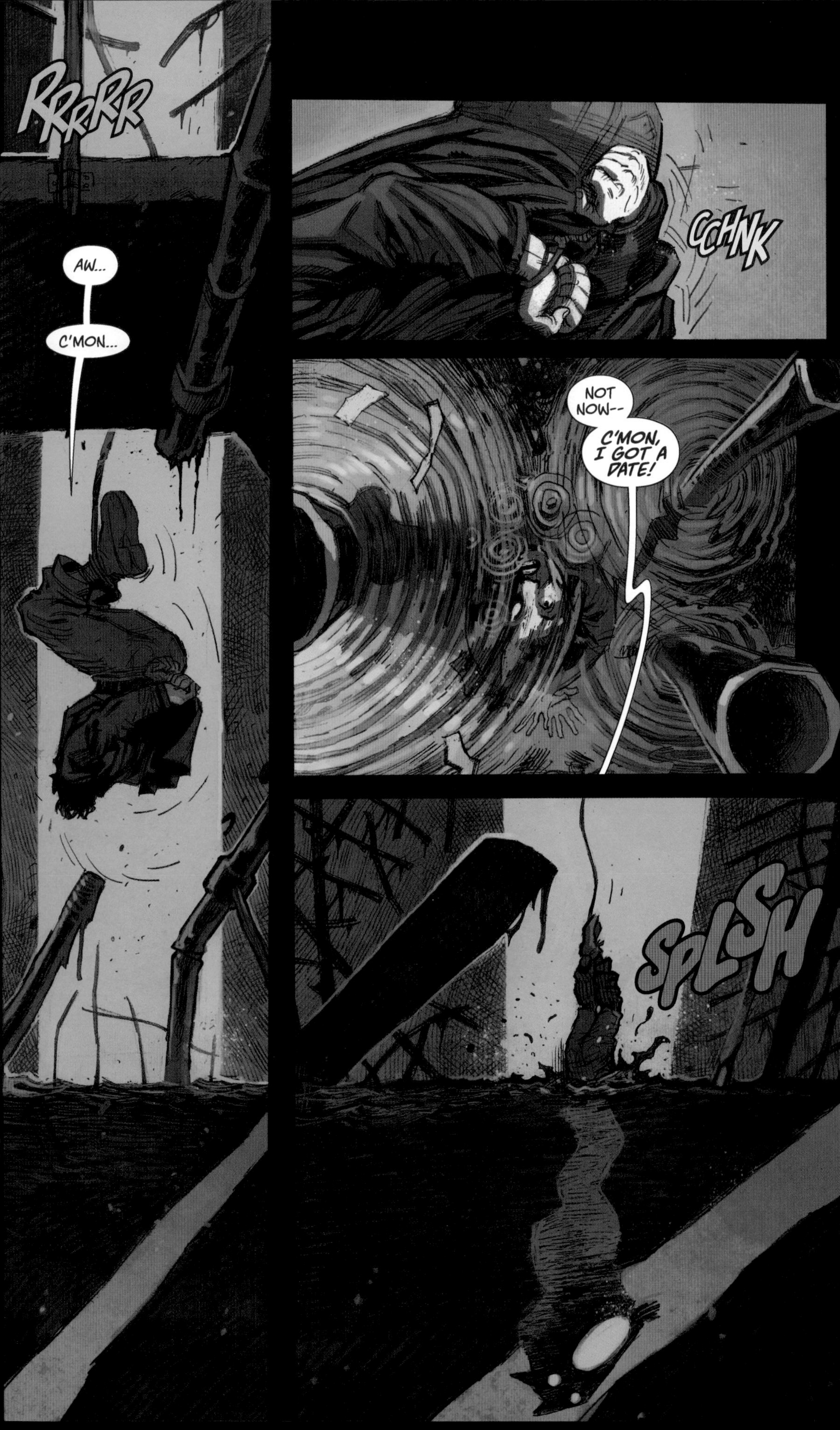
RRRRR
AW...
C'MON...
CCHNK
NOT NOW--
C'MON, I GOT A DATE!
SPLSH

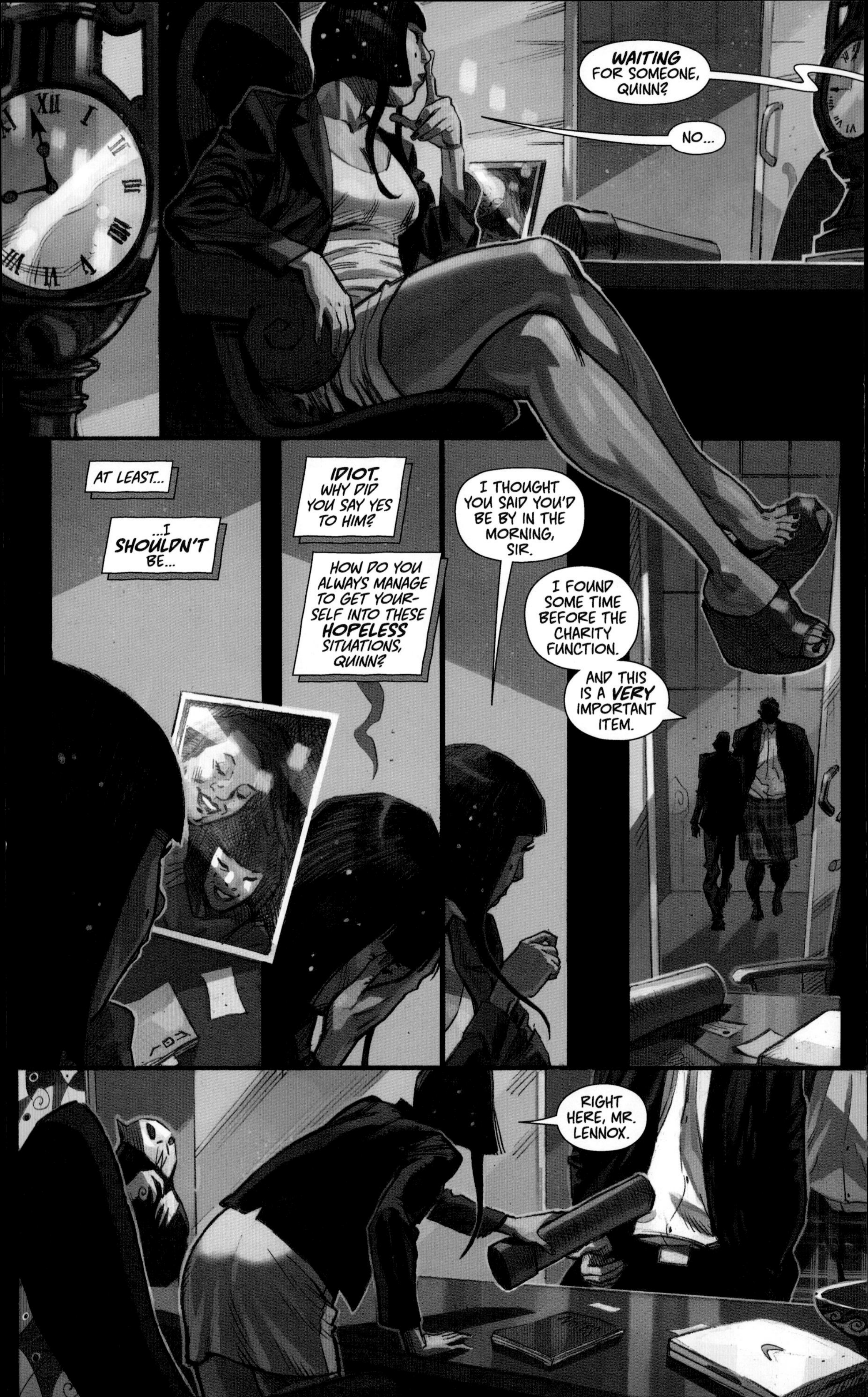
WAITING FOR SOMEONE, QUINN?
NO...
AT LEAST...
...I SHOULDN'T BE...
IDIOT. WHY DID YOU SAY YES TO HIM?
HOW DO YOU ALWAYS MANAGE TO GET YOURSELF INTO THESE HOPELESS SITUATIONS, QUINN?
I THOUGHT YOU SAID YOU'D BE BY IN THE MORNING, SIR.
I FOUND SOME TIME BEFORE THE CHARITY FUNCTION.
AND THIS IS A VERY IMPORTANT ITEM.
RIGHT HERE, MR. LENNOX.

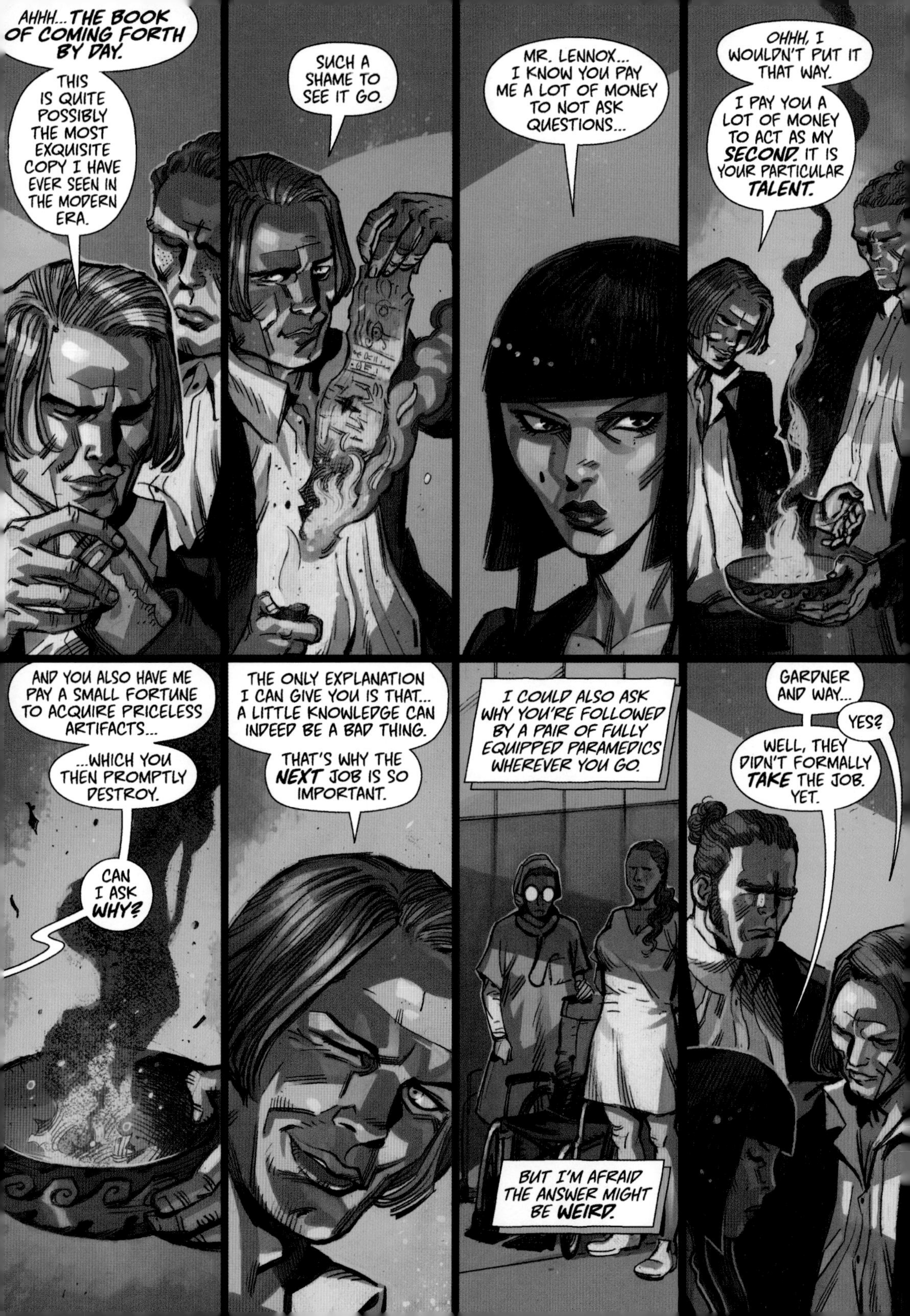

AHHH... THE BOOK OF COMING FORTH BY DAY.
THIS IS QUITE POSSIBLY THE MOST EXQUISITE COPY I HAVE EVER SEEN IN THE MODERN ERA.
SUCH A SHAME TO SEE IT GO.
MR. LENNOX... I KNOW YOU PAY ME A LOT OF MONEY TO NOT ASK QUESTIONS...
OHHH, I WOULDN'T PUT IT THAT WAY.
I PAY YOU A LOT OF MONEY TO ACT AS MY SECOND. IT IS YOUR PARTICULAR TALENT.
AND YOU ALSO HAVE ME PAY A SMALL FORTUNE TO ACQUIRE PRICELESS ARTIFACTS...
...WHICH YOU THEN PROMPTLY DESTROY.
CAN I ASK WHY?
THE ONLY EXPLANATION I CAN GIVE YOU IS THAT... A LITTLE KNOWLEDGE CAN INDEED BE A BAD THING.
THAT'S WHY THE NEXT JOB IS SO IMPORTANT.
I COULD ALSO ASK WHY YOU'RE FOLLOWED BY A PAIR OF FULLY EQUIPPED PARAMEDICS WHEREVER YOU GO.
BUT I'M AFRAID THE ANSWER MIGHT BE WEIRD.
GARDNER AND WAY...
YES?
WELL, THEY DIDN'T FORMALLY TAKE THE JOB. YET.

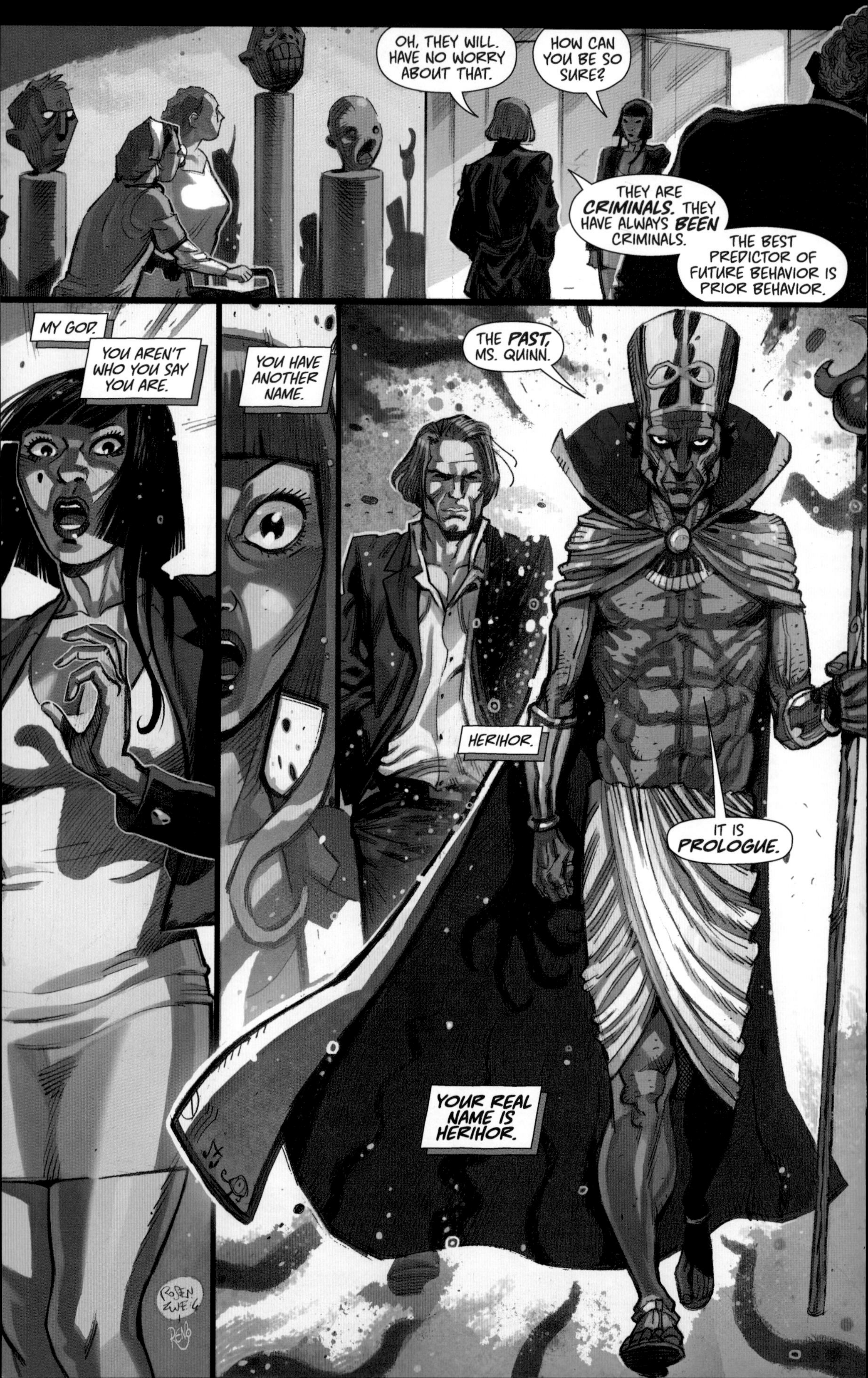

OH, THEY WILL. HAVE NO WORRY ABOUT THAT.
HOW CAN YOU BE SO SURE?
THEY ARE CRIMINALS. THEY HAVE ALWAYS BEEN CRIMINALS.
THE BEST PREDICTOR OF FUTURE BEHAVIOR IS PRIOR BEHAVIOR.
MY GOD.
YOU AREN'T WHO YOU SAY YOU ARE.
YOU HAVE ANOTHER NAME.
THE PAST, MS. QUINN.
HERIHOR.
IT IS PROLOGUE.
YOUR REAL NAME IS HERIHOR.

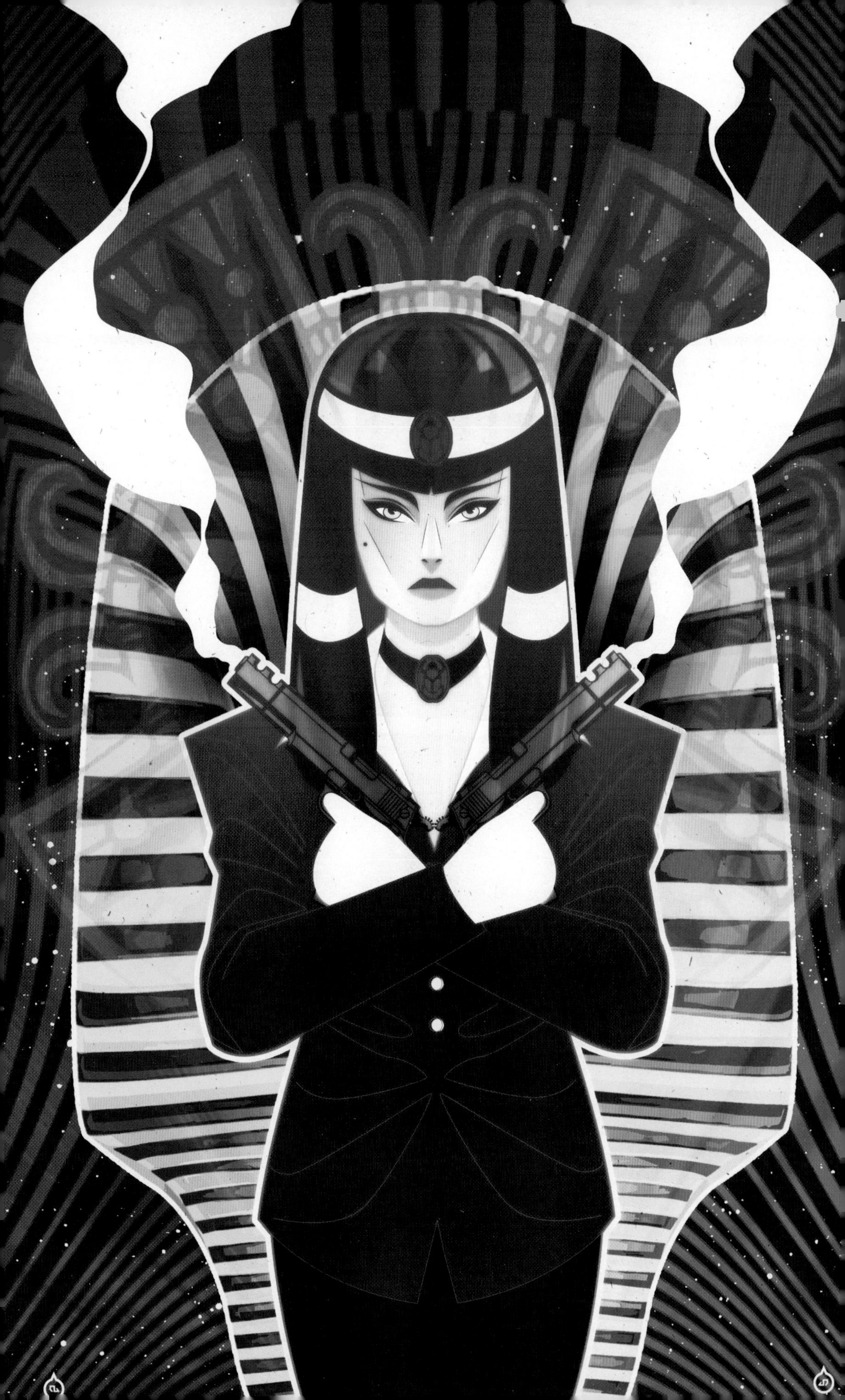

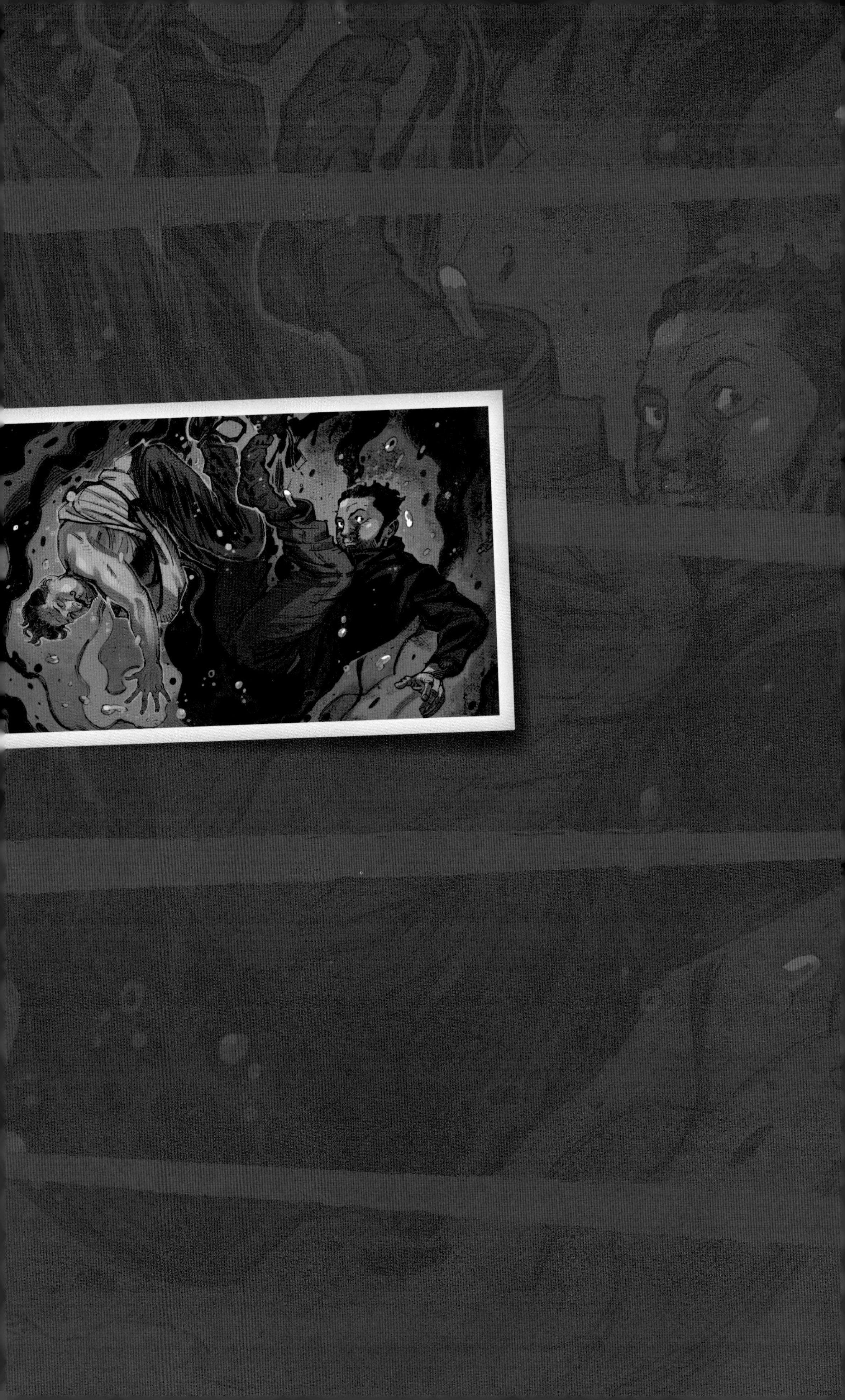

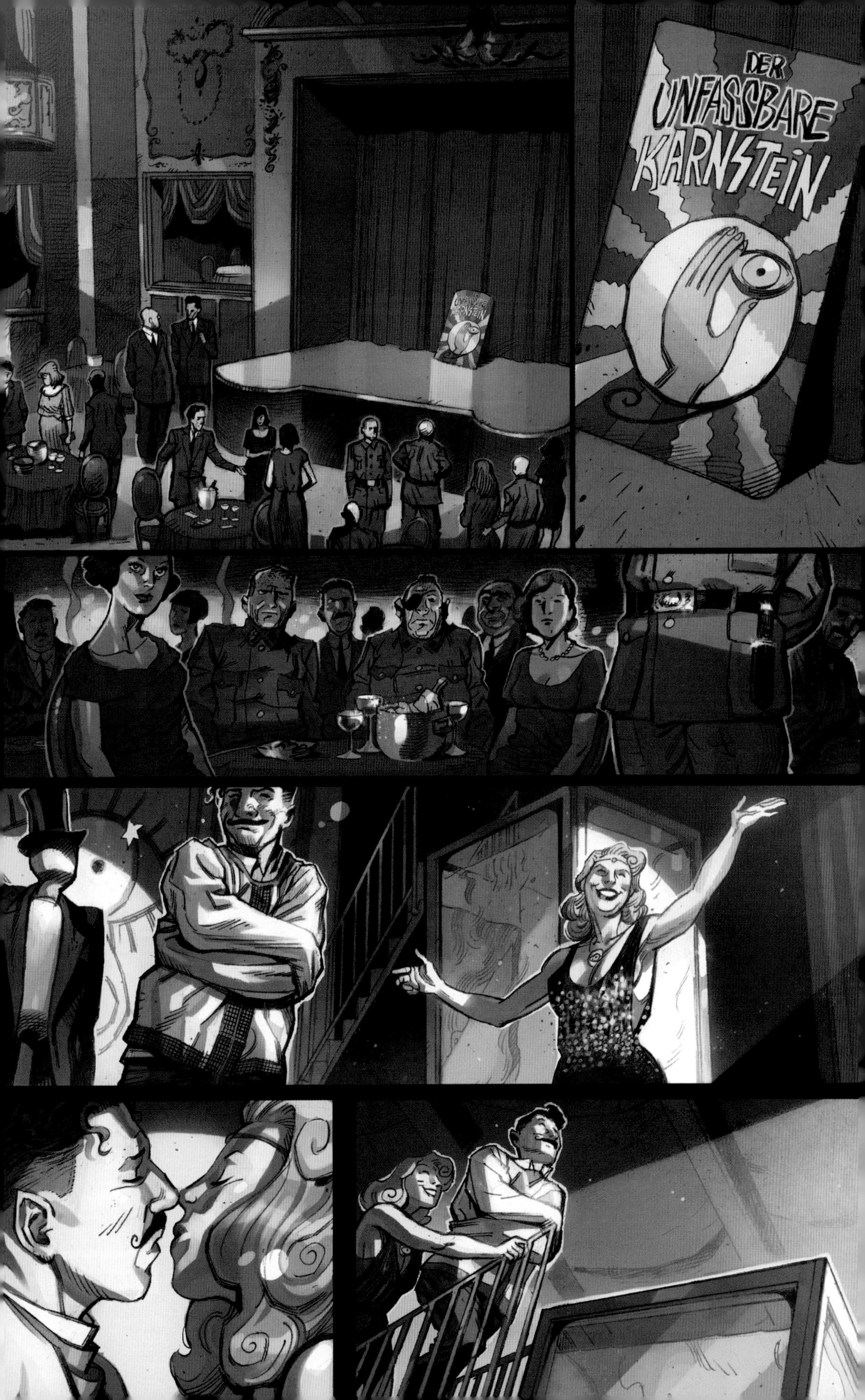
DER
UNFASSBARE
KARNSTEIN

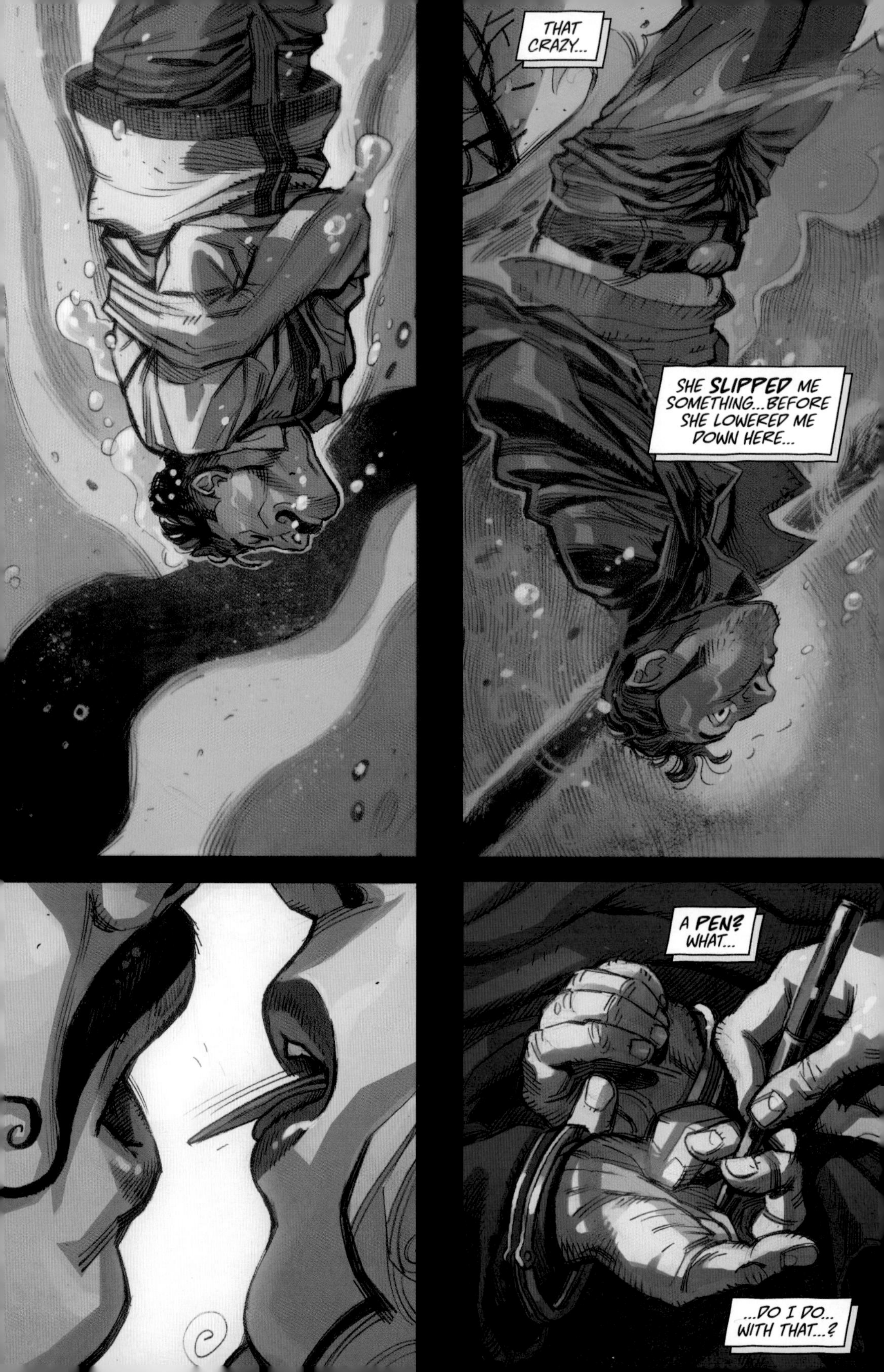
THAT CRAZY...
SHE SLIPPED ME SOMETHING...BEFORE SHE LOWERED ME DOWN HERE...
A PEN? WHAT...
...DO I DO... WITH THAT...?

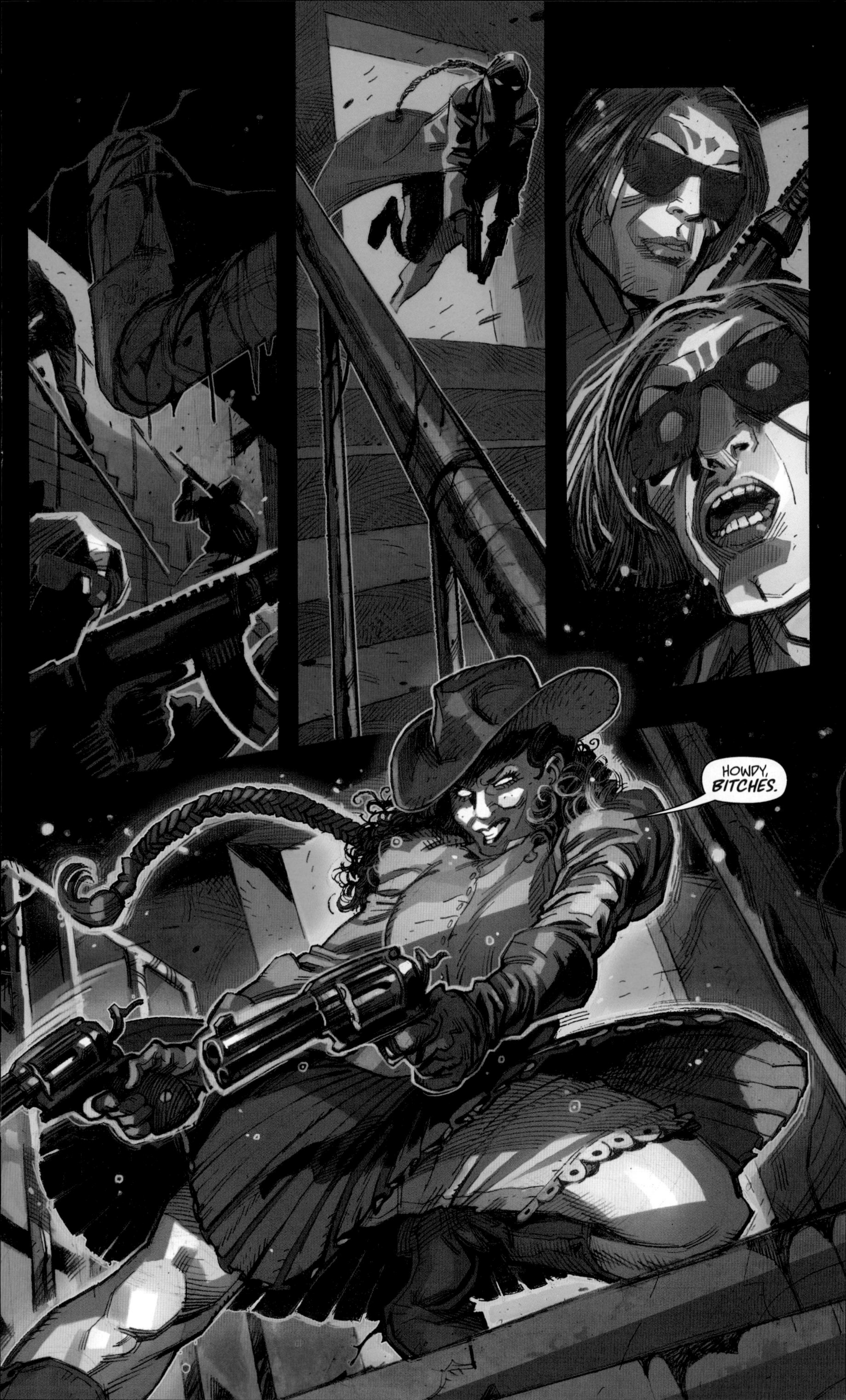
HOWDY,
BITCHES.

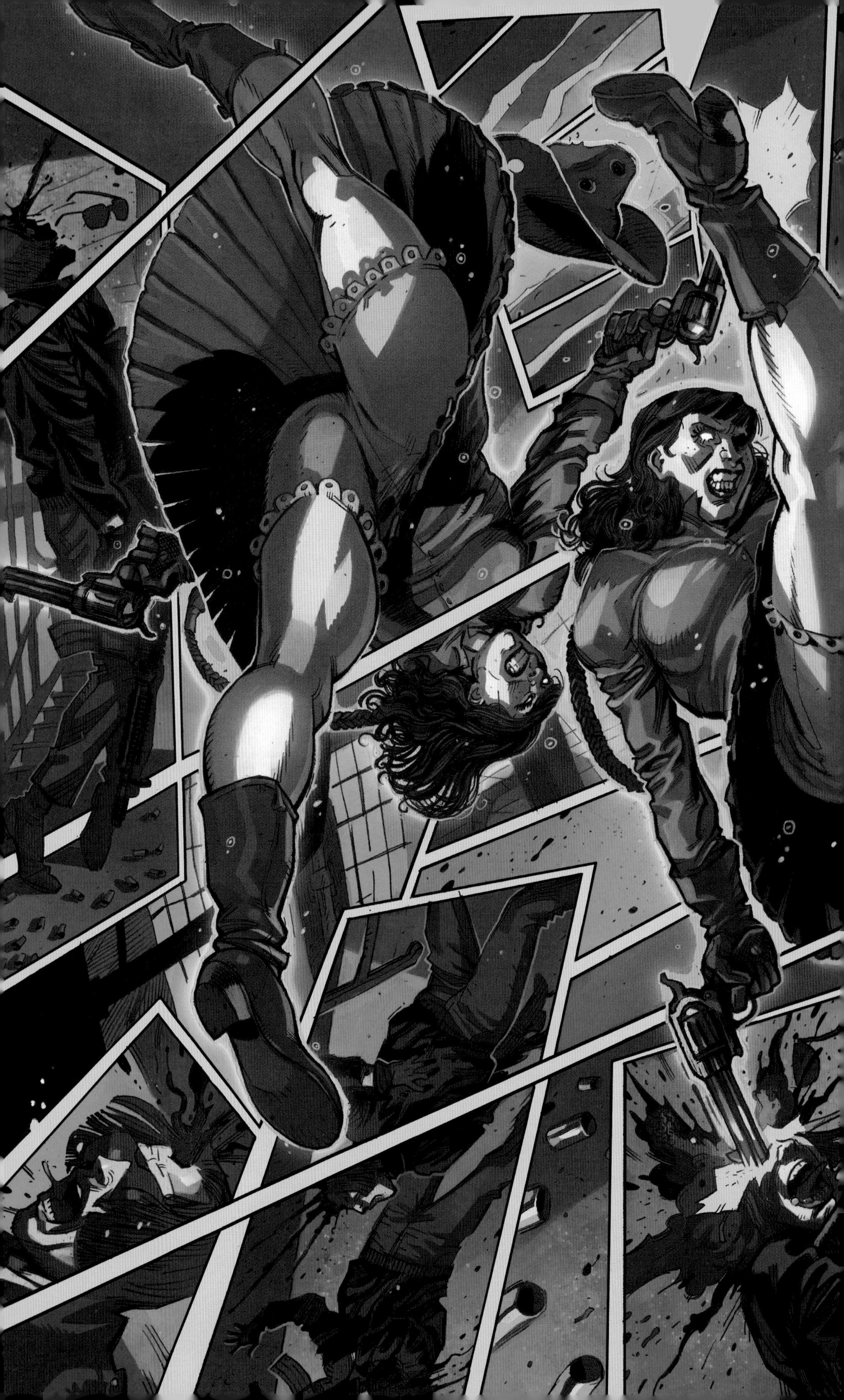

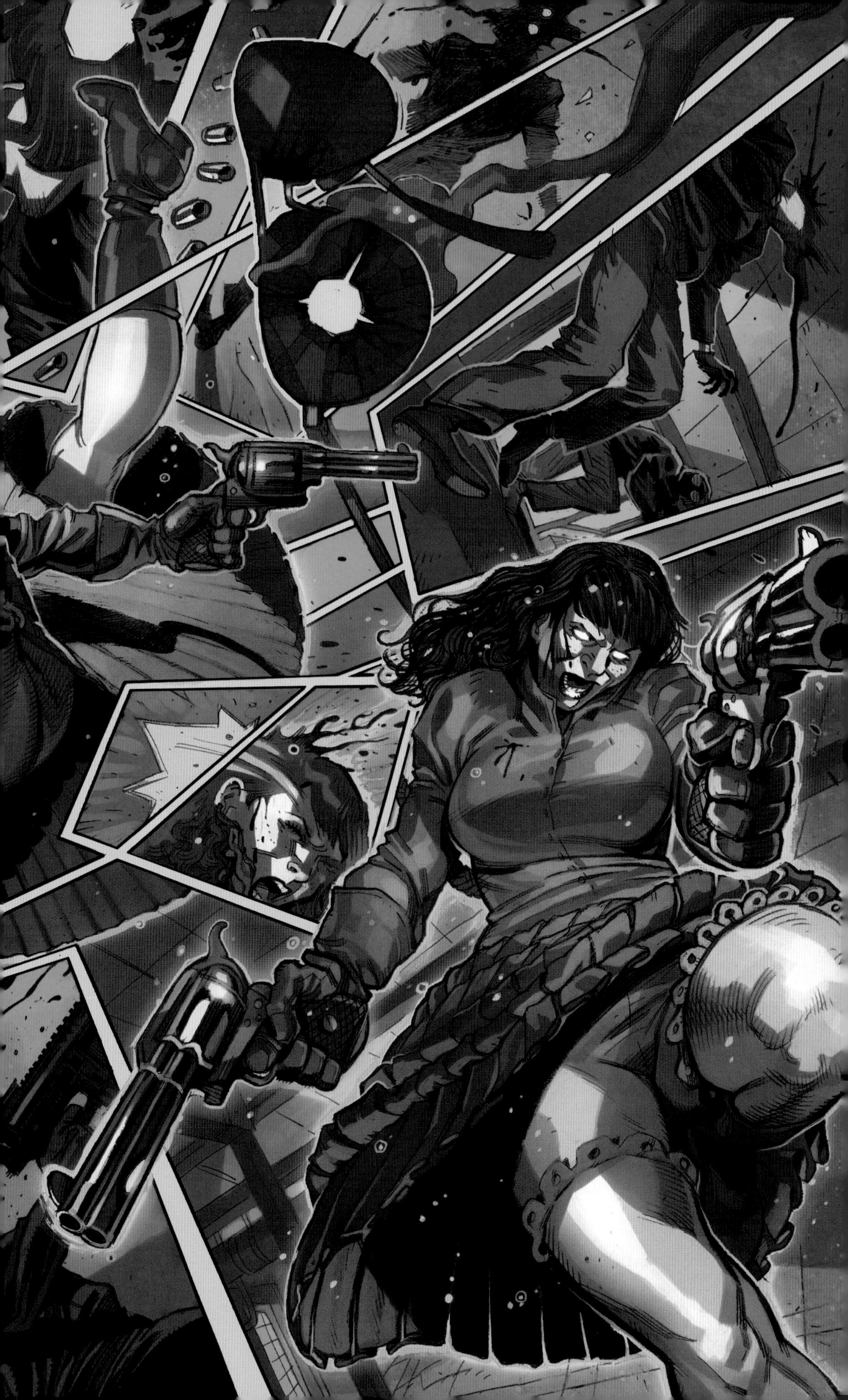

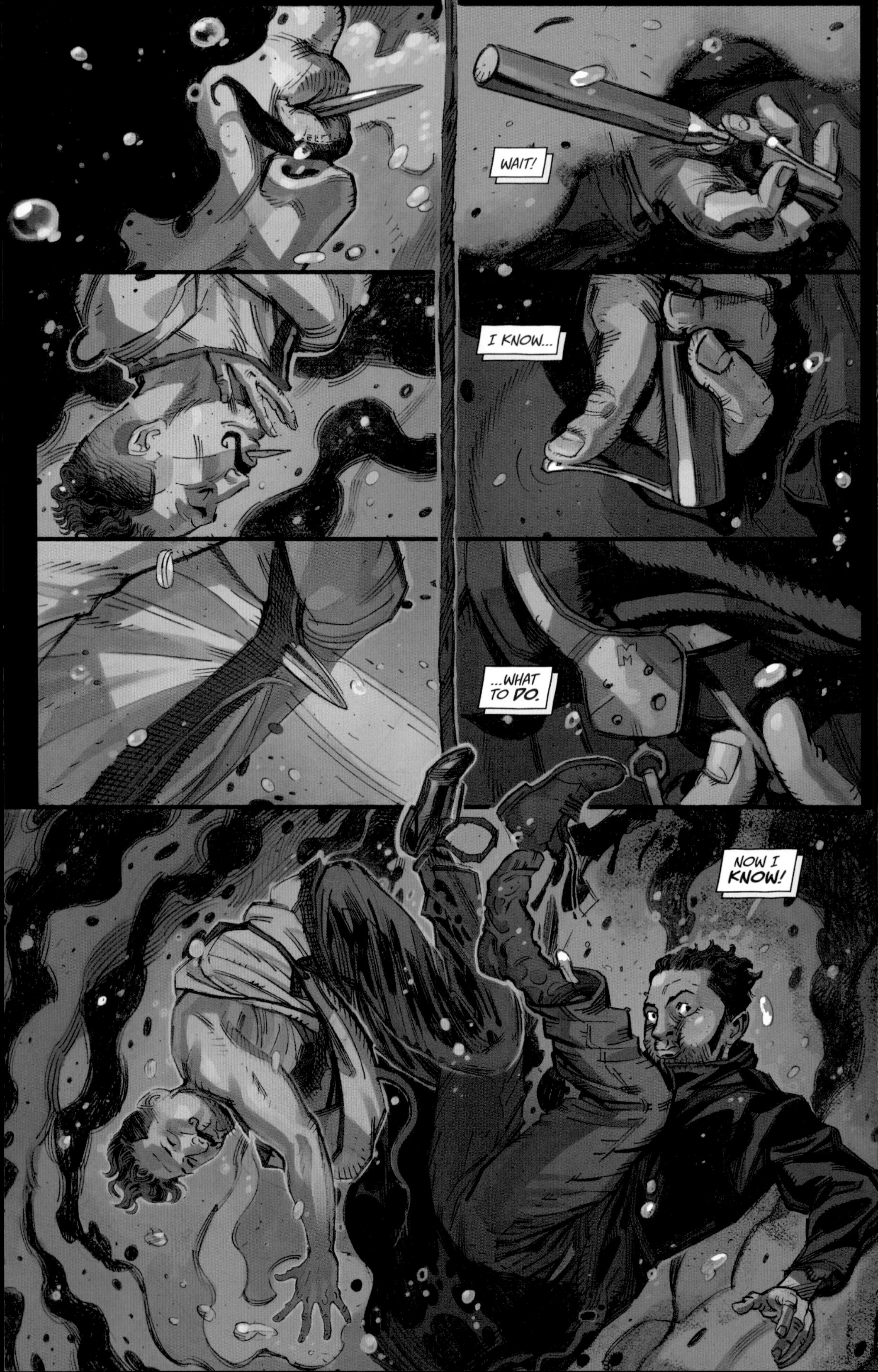
WAIT!
I KNOW...
...WHAT TO DO.
NOW I KNOW!

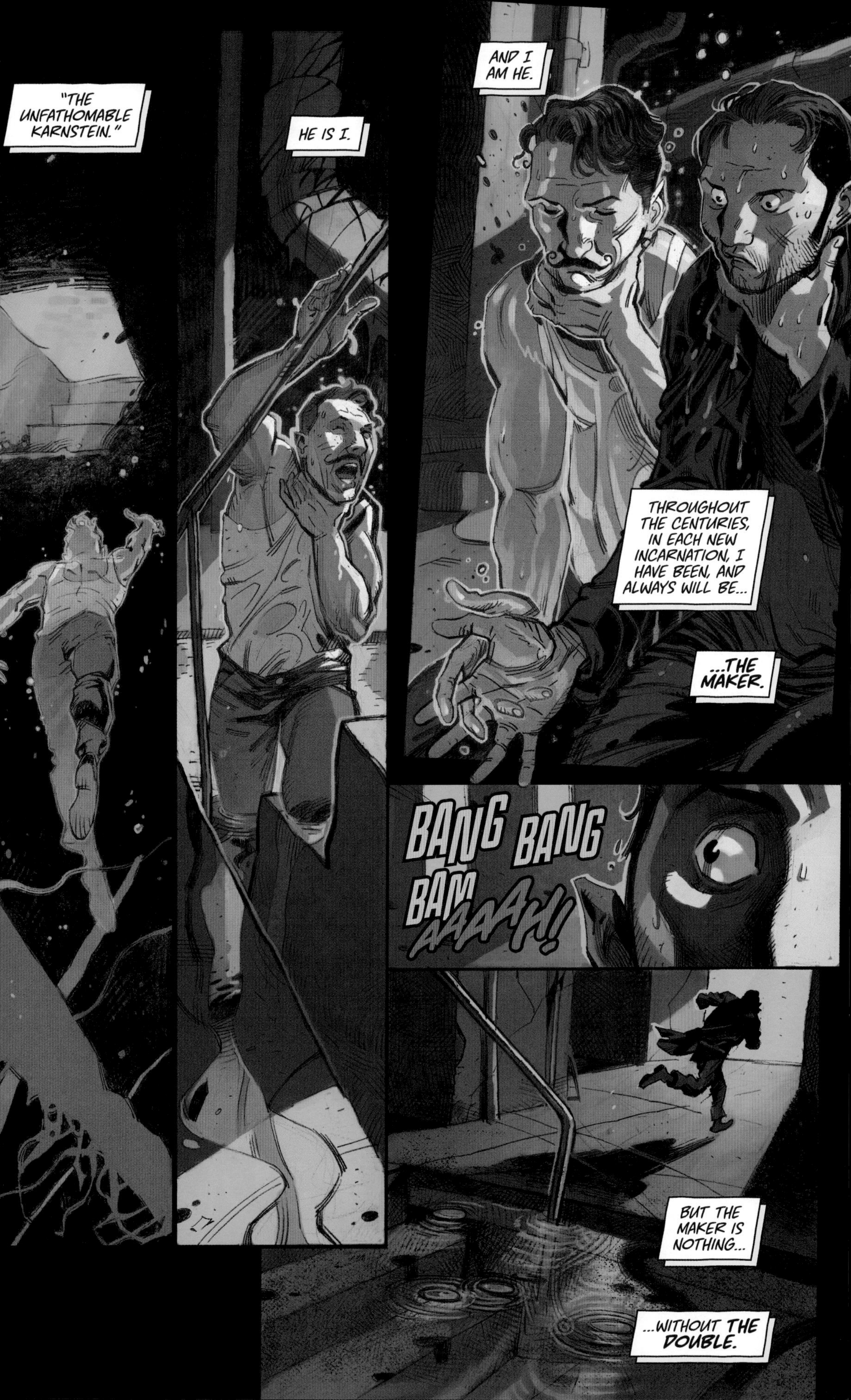
"THE UNFATHOMABLE KARNSTEIN."
HE IS I.
AND I AM HE.
THROUGHOUT THE CENTURIES, IN EACH NEW INCARNATION, I HAVE BEEN, AND ALWAYS WILL BE...
...THE MAKER.
BANG BANG
BAM
AAAAH!
BUT THE MAKER IS NOTHING...
...WITHOUT THE DOUBLE.

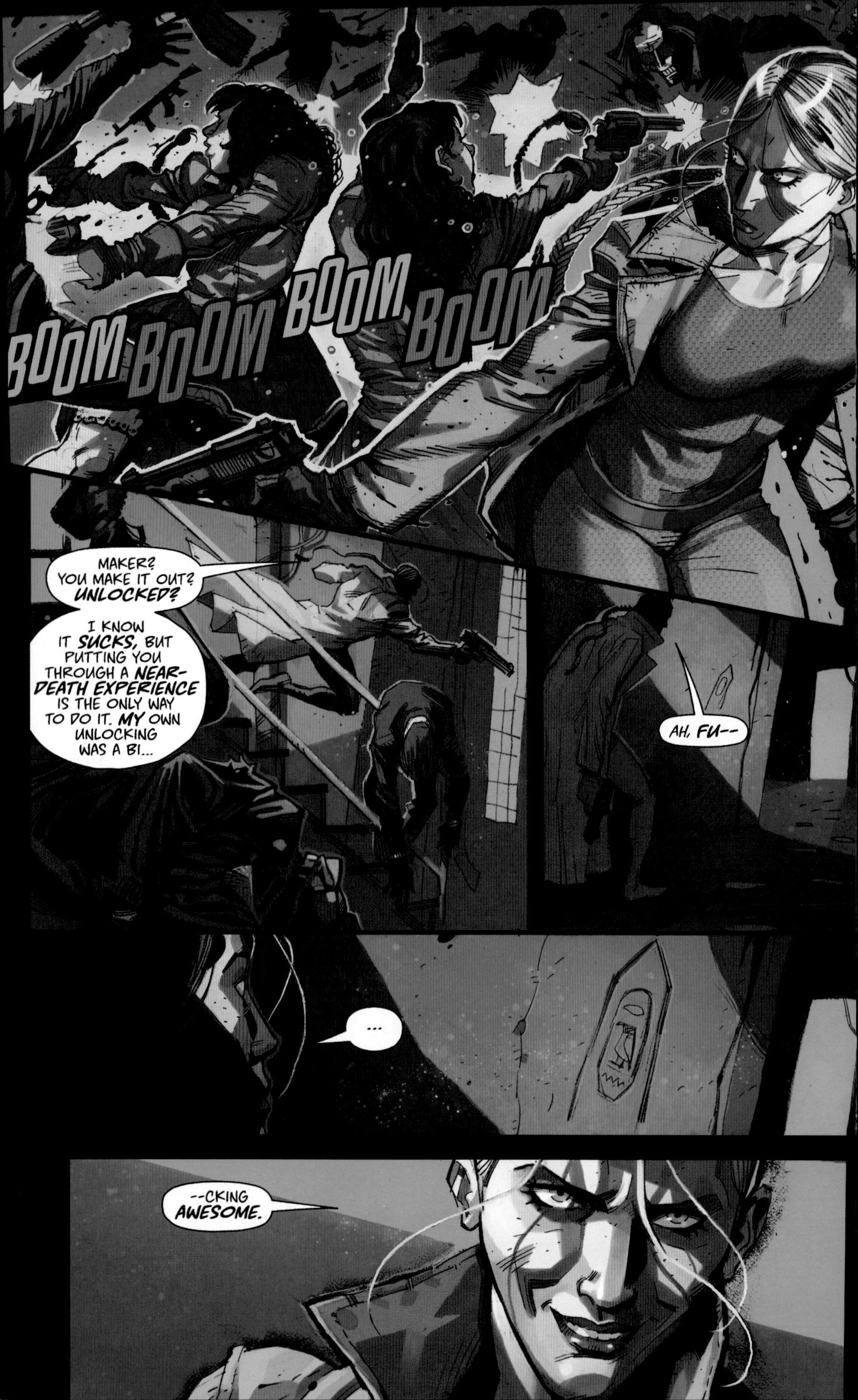
BOOM BOOM BOOM BOOM
MAKER? YOU MAKE IT OUT? UNLOCKED?
I KNOW IT SUCKS, BUT PUTTING YOU THROUGH A NEAR-DEATH EXPERIENCE IS THE ONLY WAY TO DO IT. MY OWN UNLOCKING WAS A BI...
AH, FU--
...
--CKING AWESOME.

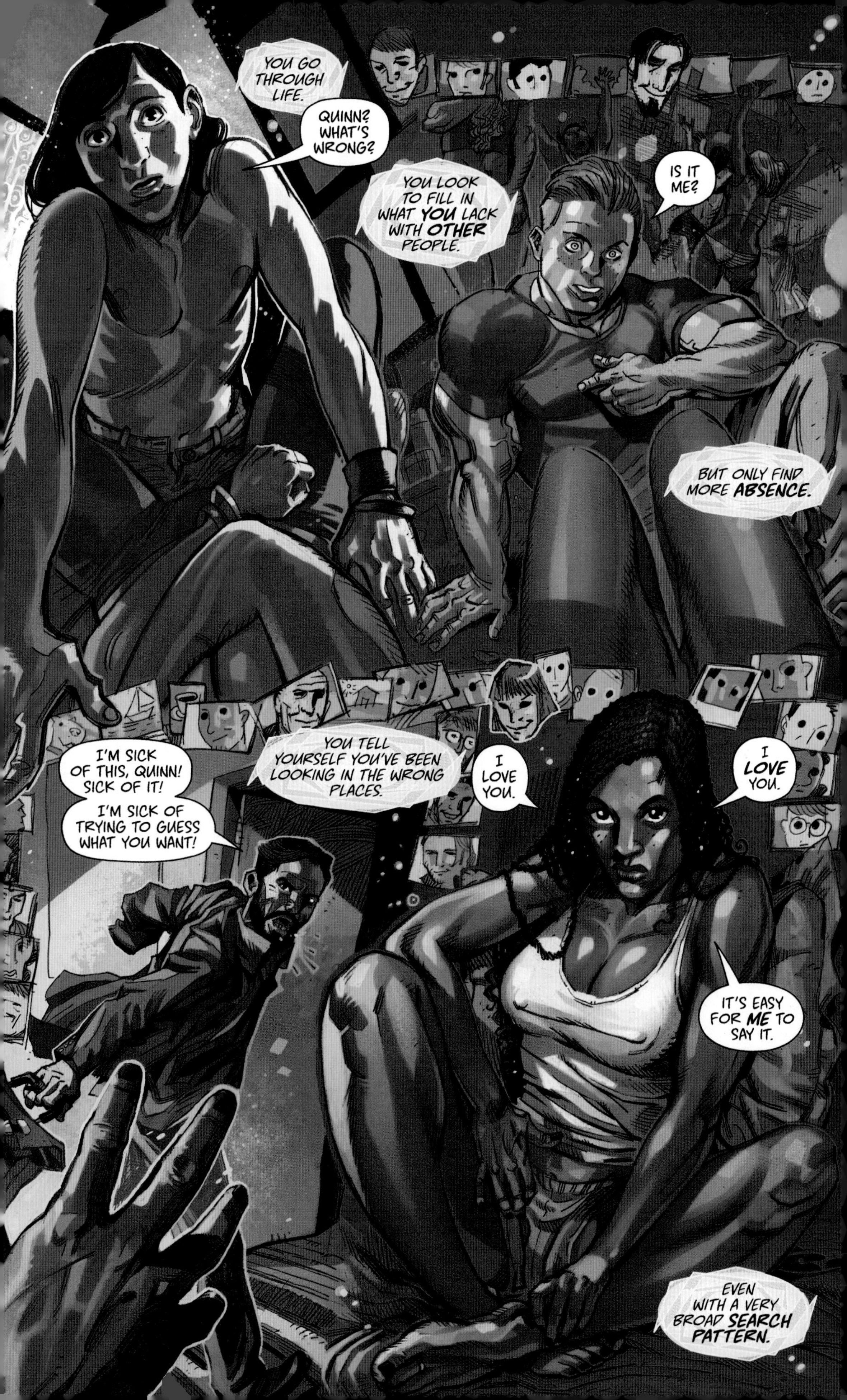
YOU GO THROUGH LIFE.
QUINN? WHAT'S WRONG?
YOU LOOK TO FILL IN WHAT **YOU** LACK WITH **OTHER** PEOPLE.
IS IT ME?
BUT ONLY FIND MORE **ABSENCE.**
I'M SICK OF THIS, QUINN! SICK OF IT!
I'M SICK OF TRYING TO GUESS WHAT YOU WANT!
YOU TELL YOURSELF YOU'VE BEEN LOOKING IN THE WRONG PLACES.
I LOVE YOU.
I **LOVE** YOU.
IT'S EASY FOR **ME** TO SAY IT.
EVEN WITH A VERY BROAD **SEARCH PATTERN.**

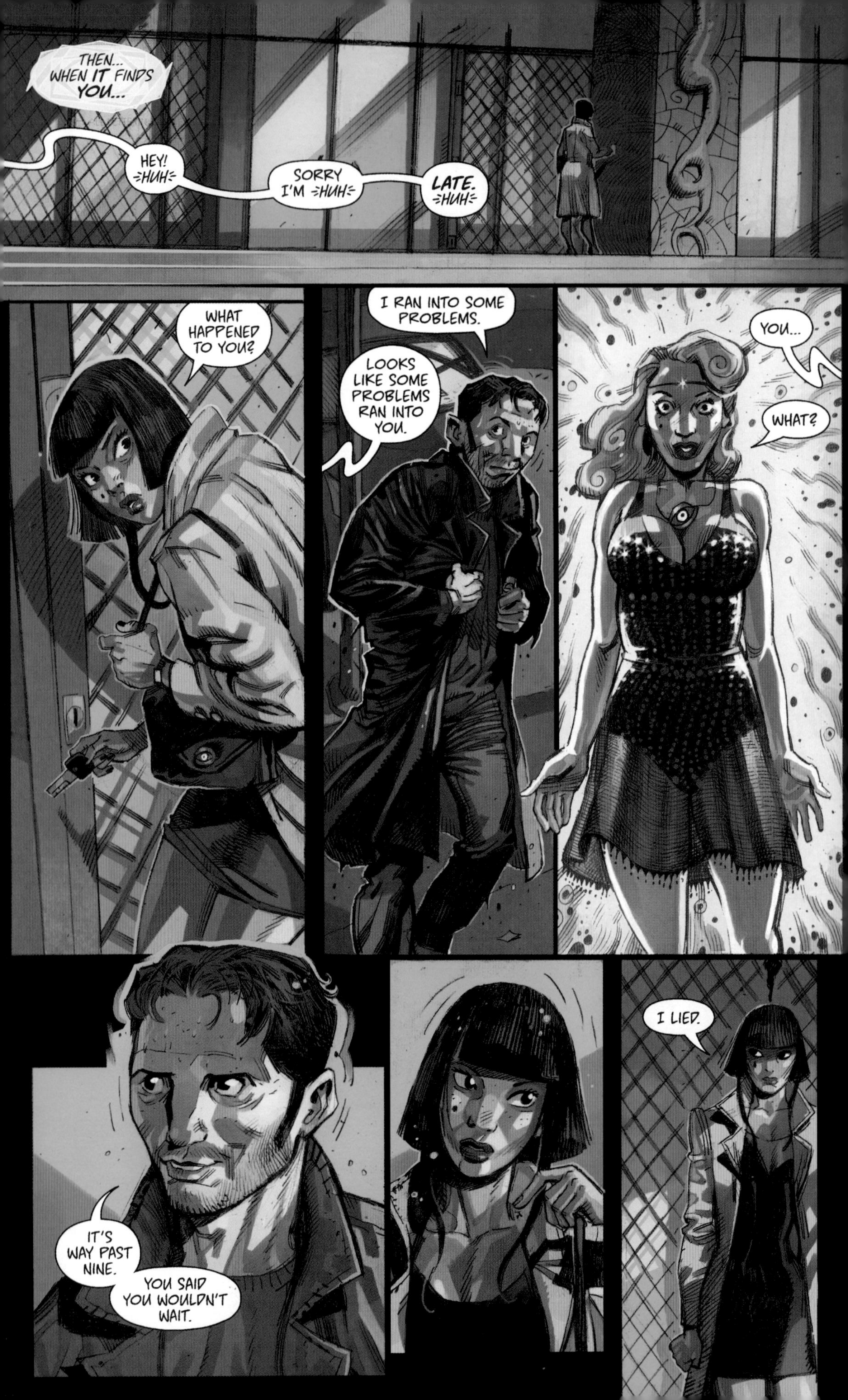
THEN... WHEN IT FINDS YOU...
HEY! ≈HUH≈
SORRY I'M ≈HUH≈
LATE. ≈HUH≈
WHAT HAPPENED TO YOU?
I RAN INTO SOME PROBLEMS.
LOOKS LIKE SOME PROBLEMS RAN INTO YOU.
YOU...
WHAT?
IT'S WAY PAST NINE.
YOU SAID YOU WOULDN'T WAIT.
I LIED.

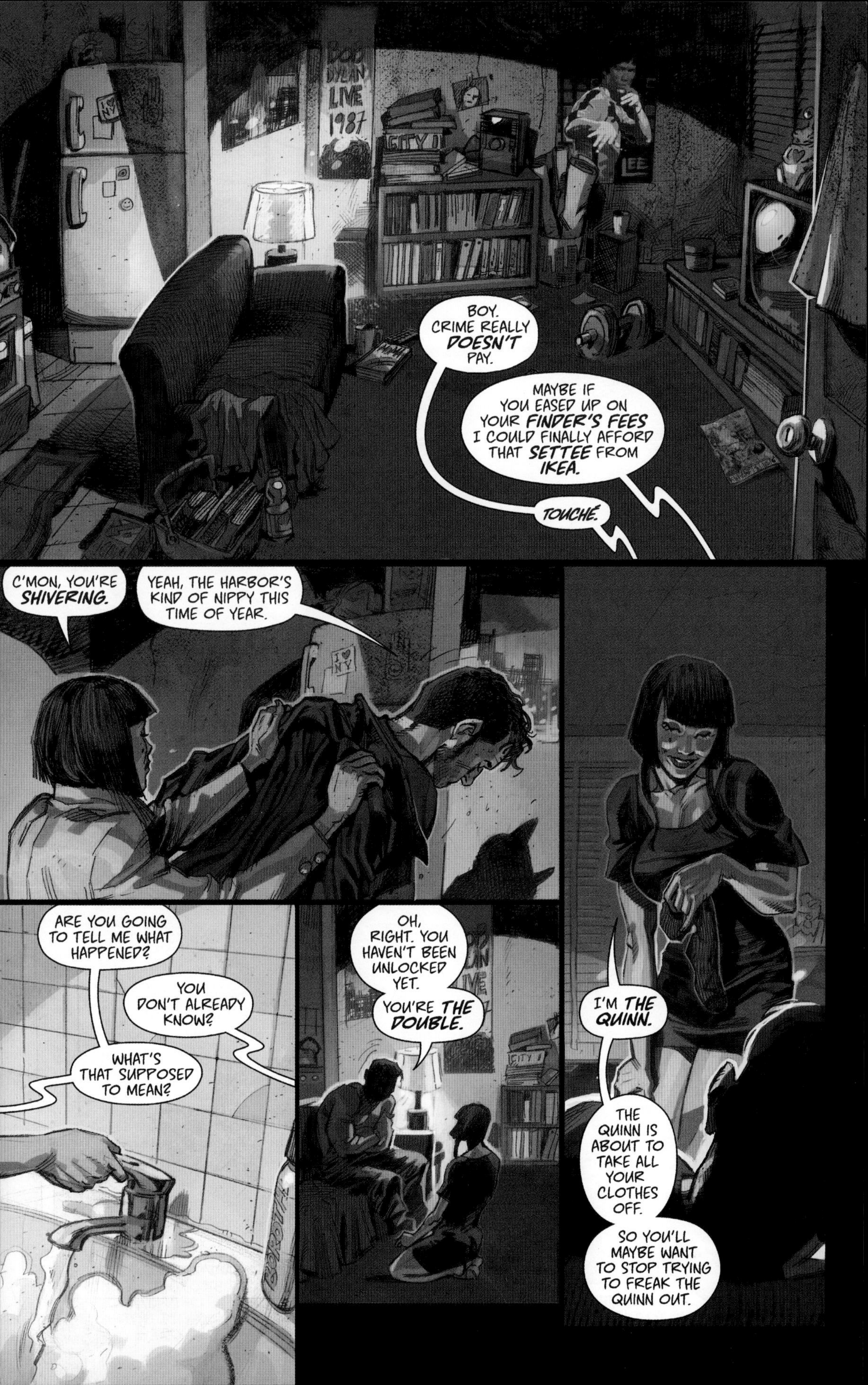
BOY. CRIME REALLY DOESN'T PAY.
MAYBE IF YOU EASED UP ON YOUR FINDER'S FEES I COULD FINALLY AFFORD THAT SETTEE FROM IKEA.
TOUCHÉ.
C'MON, YOU'RE SHIVERING.
YEAH, THE HARBOR'S KIND OF NIPPY THIS TIME OF YEAR.
ARE YOU GOING TO TELL ME WHAT HAPPENED?
YOU DON'T ALREADY KNOW?
WHAT'S THAT SUPPOSED TO MEAN?
OH, RIGHT. YOU HAVEN'T BEEN UNLOCKED YET.
YOU'RE THE DOUBLE.
I'M THE QUINN.
THE QUINN IS ABOUT TO TAKE ALL YOUR CLOTHES OFF.
SO YOU'LL MAYBE WANT TO STOP TRYING TO FREAK THE QUINN OUT.

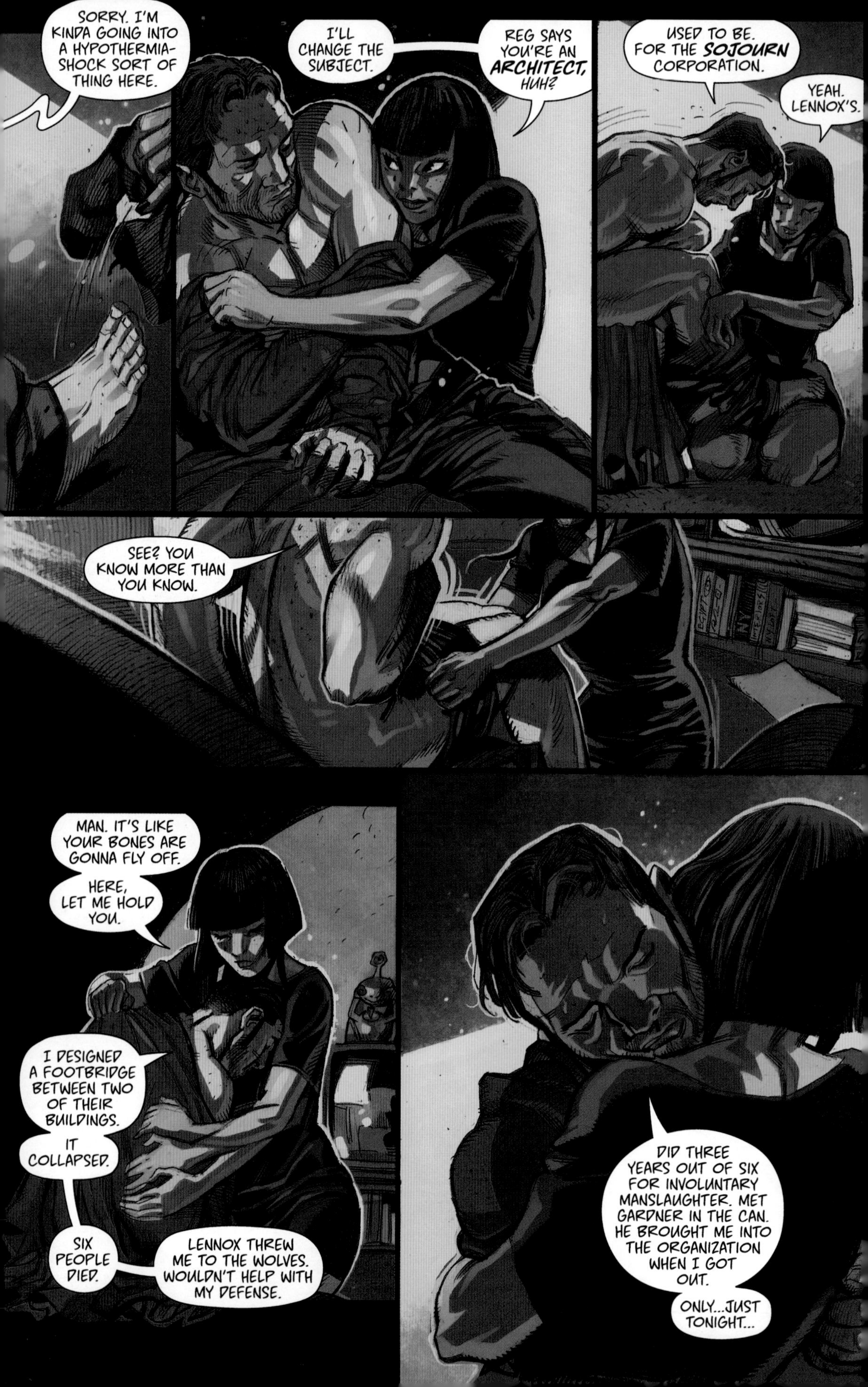
SORRY. I'M KINDA GOING INTO A HYPOTHERMIA-SHOCK SORT OF THING HERE.
I'LL CHANGE THE SUBJECT.
REG SAYS YOU'RE AN **ARCHITECT,** HUH?
USED TO BE. FOR THE **SOJOURN** CORPORATION.
YEAH. LENNOX'S.
SEE? YOU KNOW MORE THAN YOU KNOW.
MAN. IT'S LIKE YOUR BONES ARE GONNA FLY OFF.
HERE, LET ME HOLD YOU.
I DESIGNED A FOOTBRIDGE BETWEEN TWO OF THEIR BUILDINGS.
IT COLLAPSED.
SIX PEOPLE DIED.
LENNOX THREW ME TO THE WOLVES. WOULDN'T HELP WITH MY DEFENSE.
DID THREE YEARS OUT OF SIX FOR INVOLUNTARY MANSLAUGHTER. MET GARDNER IN THE CAN. HE BROUGHT ME INTO THE ORGANIZATION WHEN I GOT OUT.
ONLY...JUST TONIGHT...

...I LEARNED THERE'S A LITTLE MORE *TO* IT THAN I THOUGHT.

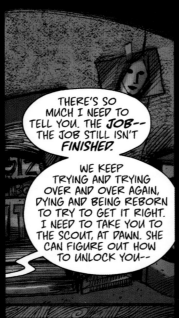

THERE'S SO MUCH I NEED TO TELL YOU. THE *JOB*-- THE JOB STILL ISN'T *FINISHED.*

WE KEEP TRYING AND TRYING OVER AND OVER AGAIN, DYING AND BEING REBORN TO TRY TO GET IT RIGHT. I NEED TO TAKE YOU TO THE SCOUT, AT DAWN. SHE CAN FIGURE OUT HOW TO UNLOCK YOU--

THEN, WHEN WHAT YOU'RE LOOKING FOR FINDS *YOU*...

--THOUGH I GOTTA WARN YOU, IT'S NOT VERY *PLEASANT*--

...IT'S LIKE AN *ANCHOR* AROUND YOUR *NECK.*

MAYA? WHAT'S WRON--

MY *NAME* IS *QUINN!*

QUINN--I KNOW--I'M SORRY--I JUST--

NO...*I'M* SORRY... I...

QUINN!

PULLING YOU DOWN, DOWN, DOWN.

INTO *DARKNESS.*

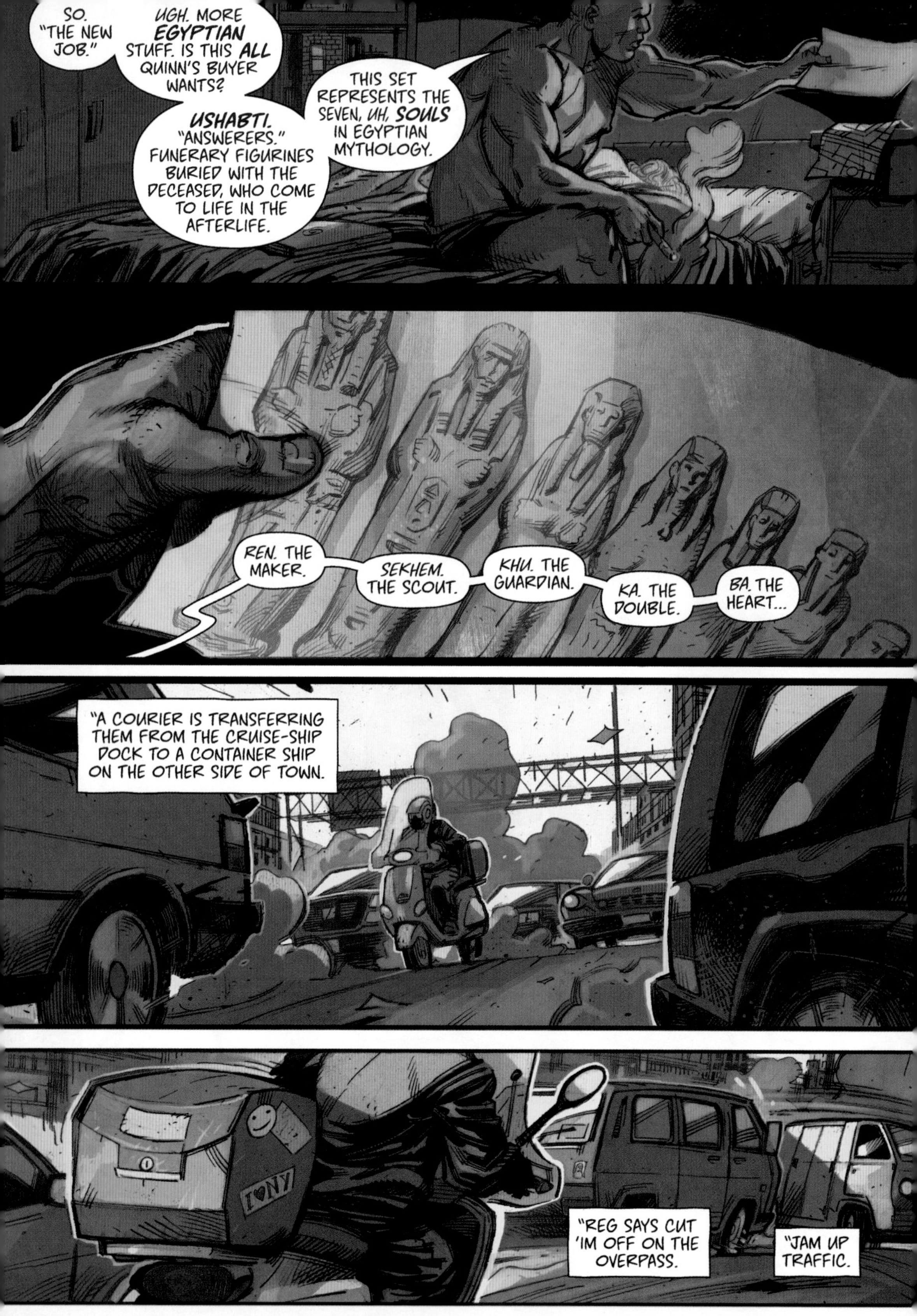
SO. "THE NEW JOB."
UGH. MORE EGYPTIAN STUFF. IS THIS ALL QUINN'S BUYER WANTS?
USHABTI. "ANSWERERS." FUNERARY FIGURINES BURIED WITH THE DECEASED, WHO COME TO LIFE IN THE AFTERLIFE.
THIS SET REPRESENTS THE SEVEN, UH, SOULS IN EGYPTIAN MYTHOLOGY.
REN. THE MAKER.
SEKHEM. THE SCOUT.
KHU. THE GUARDIAN.
KA. THE DOUBLE.
BA. THE HEART...
"A COURIER IS TRANSFERRING THEM FROM THE CRUISE-SHIP DOCK TO A CONTAINER SHIP ON THE OTHER SIDE OF TOWN.
I ♥ NY
"REG SAYS CUT 'IM OFF ON THE OVERPASS.
"JAM UP TRAFFIC.

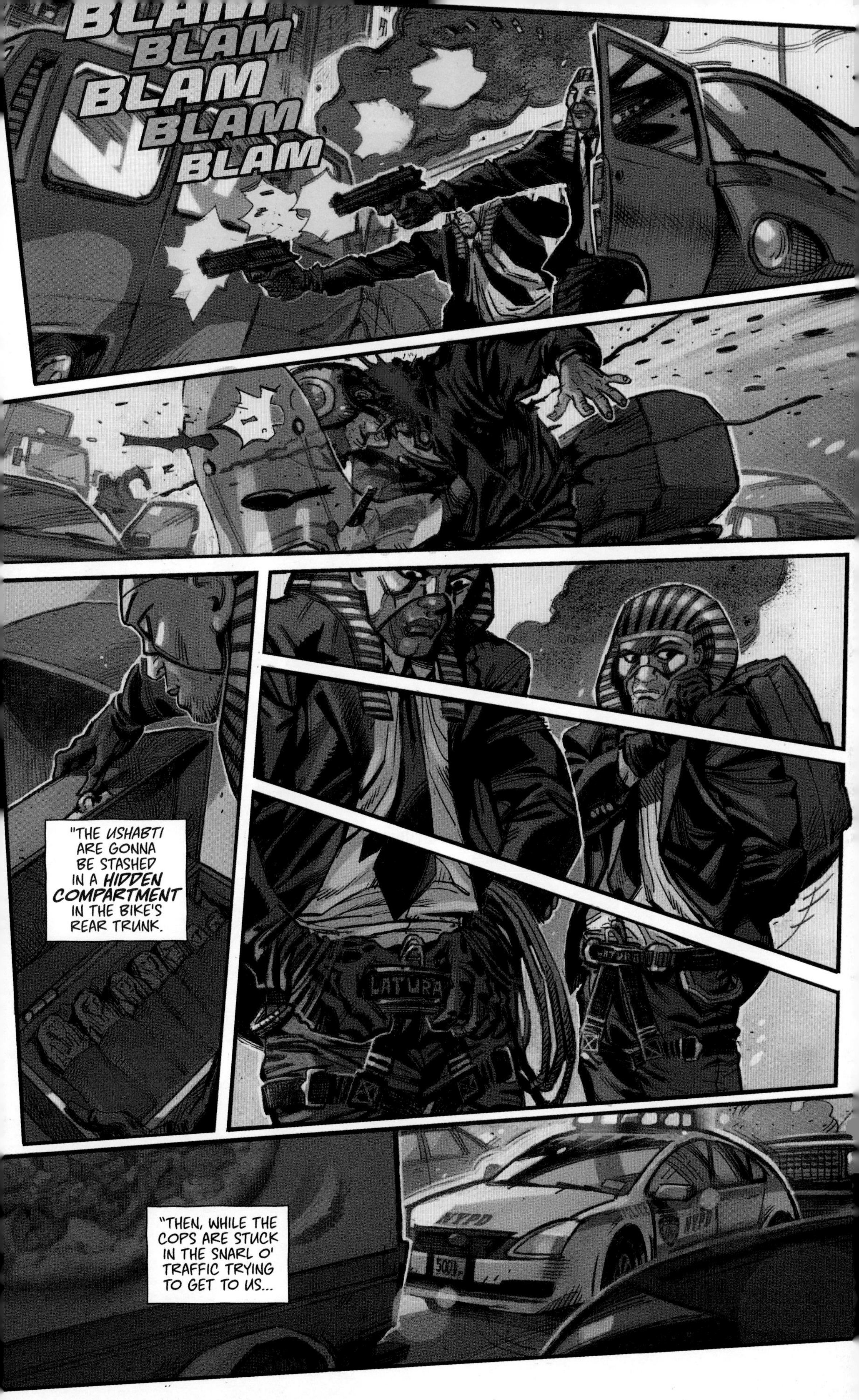
BLAM
BLAM
BLAM
BLAM
BLAM
"THE USHABTI ARE GONNA BE STASHED IN A HIDDEN COMPARTMENT IN THE BIKE'S REAR TRUNK.
LATURA
"THEN, WHILE THE COPS ARE STUCK IN THE SNARL O' TRAFFIC TRYING TO GET TO US...
NYPD
NYPD
5001

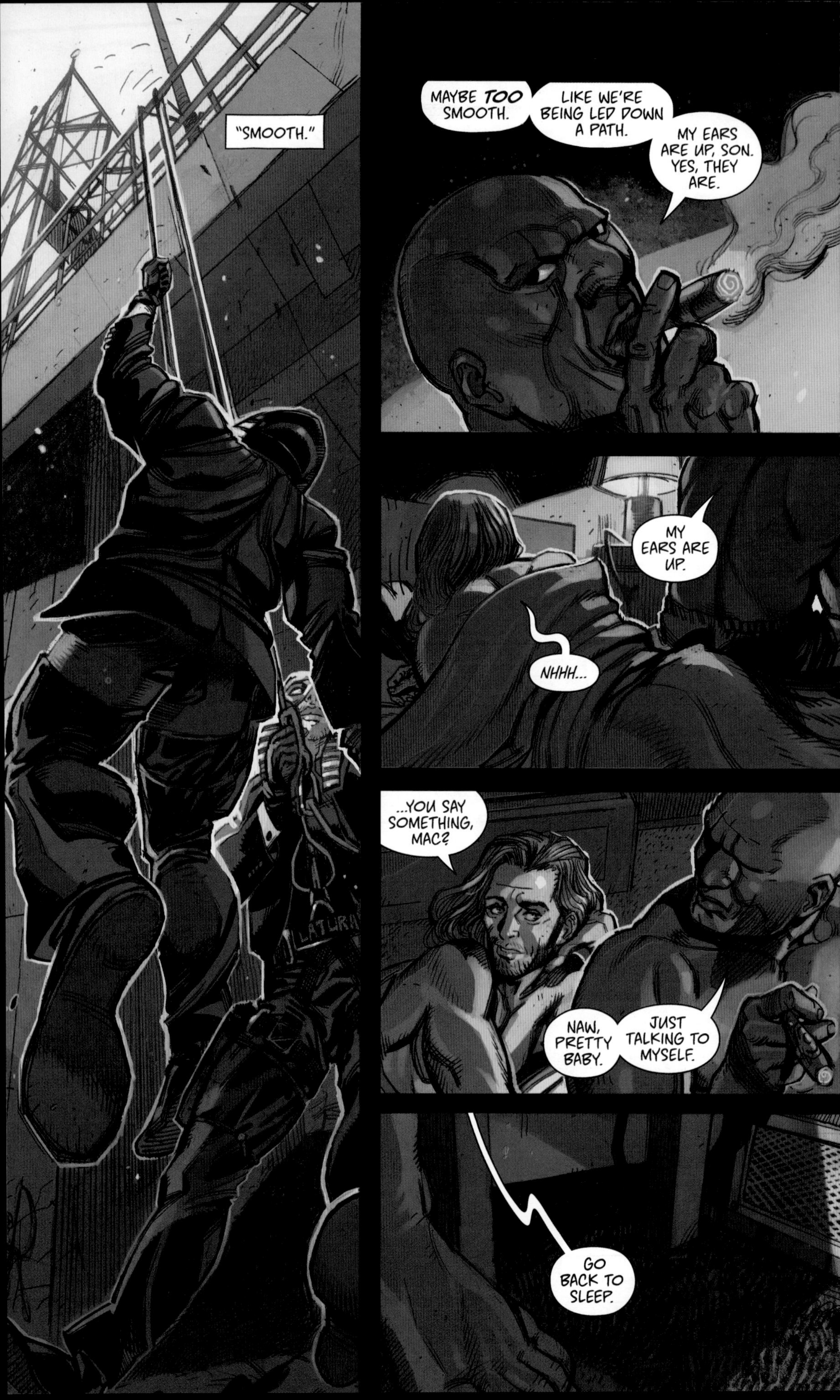
"SMOOTH."
MAYBE TOO SMOOTH.
LIKE WE'RE BEING LED DOWN A PATH.
MY EARS ARE UP, SON. YES, THEY ARE.
MY EARS ARE UP.
NHHH...
...YOU SAY SOMETHING, MAC?
NAW, PRETTY BABY.
JUST TALKING TO MYSELF.
GO BACK TO SLEEP.
LATURA

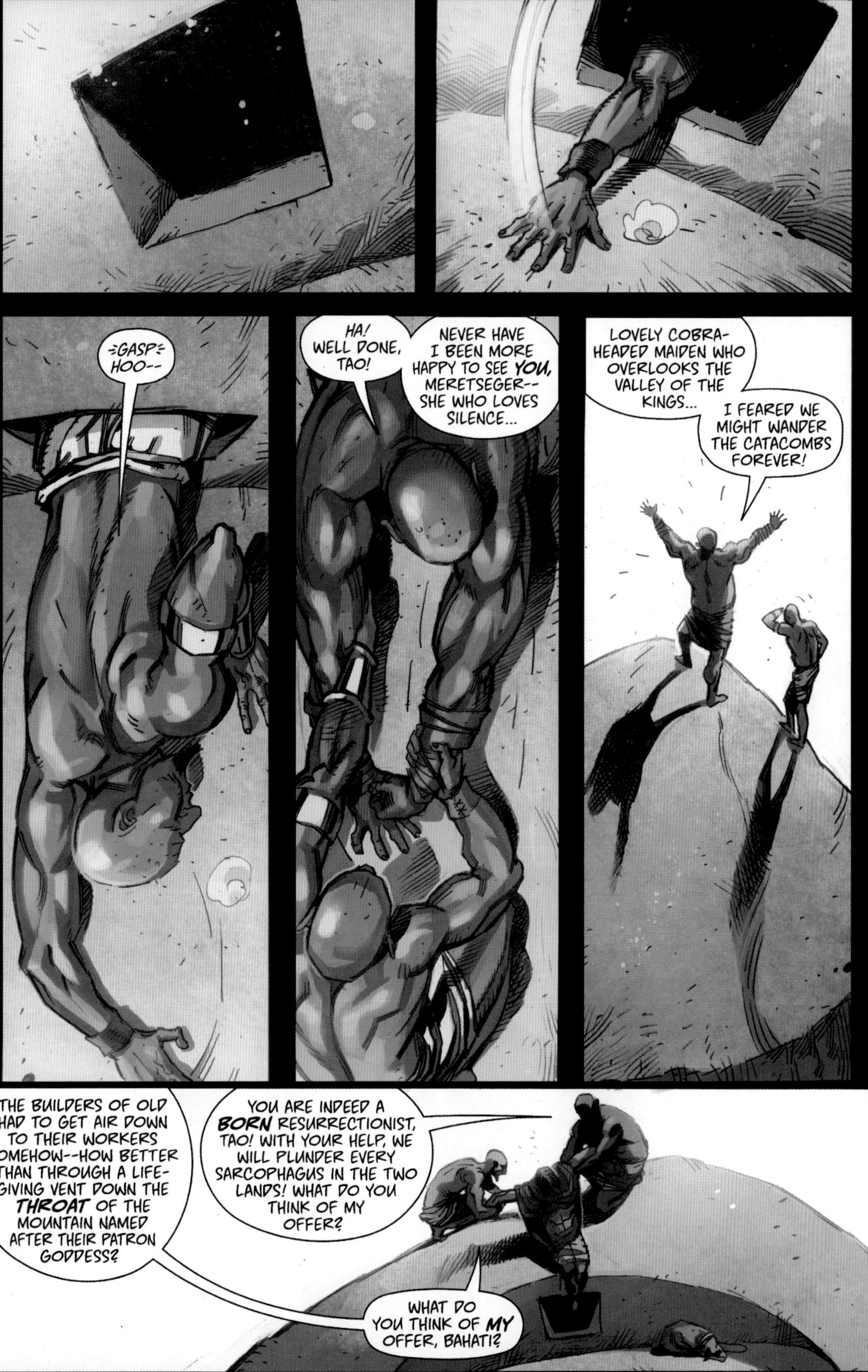

GASP HOO--
HA! WELL DONE, TAO!
NEVER HAVE I BEEN MORE HAPPY TO SEE YOU, MERETSEGER-- SHE WHO LOVES SILENCE...
LOVELY COBRA-HEADED MAIDEN WHO OVERLOOKS THE VALLEY OF THE KINGS...
I FEARED WE MIGHT WANDER THE CATACOMBS FOREVER!
THE BUILDERS OF OLD HAD TO GET AIR DOWN TO THEIR WORKERS SOMEHOW--HOW BETTER THAN THROUGH A LIFE-GIVING VENT DOWN THE THROAT OF THE MOUNTAIN NAMED AFTER THEIR PATRON GODDESS?
YOU ARE INDEED A BORN RESURRECTIONIST, TAO! WITH YOUR HELP, WE WILL PLUNDER EVERY SARCOPHAGUS IN THE TWO LANDS! WHAT DO YOU THINK OF MY OFFER?
WHAT DO YOU THINK OF MY OFFER, BAHATI?

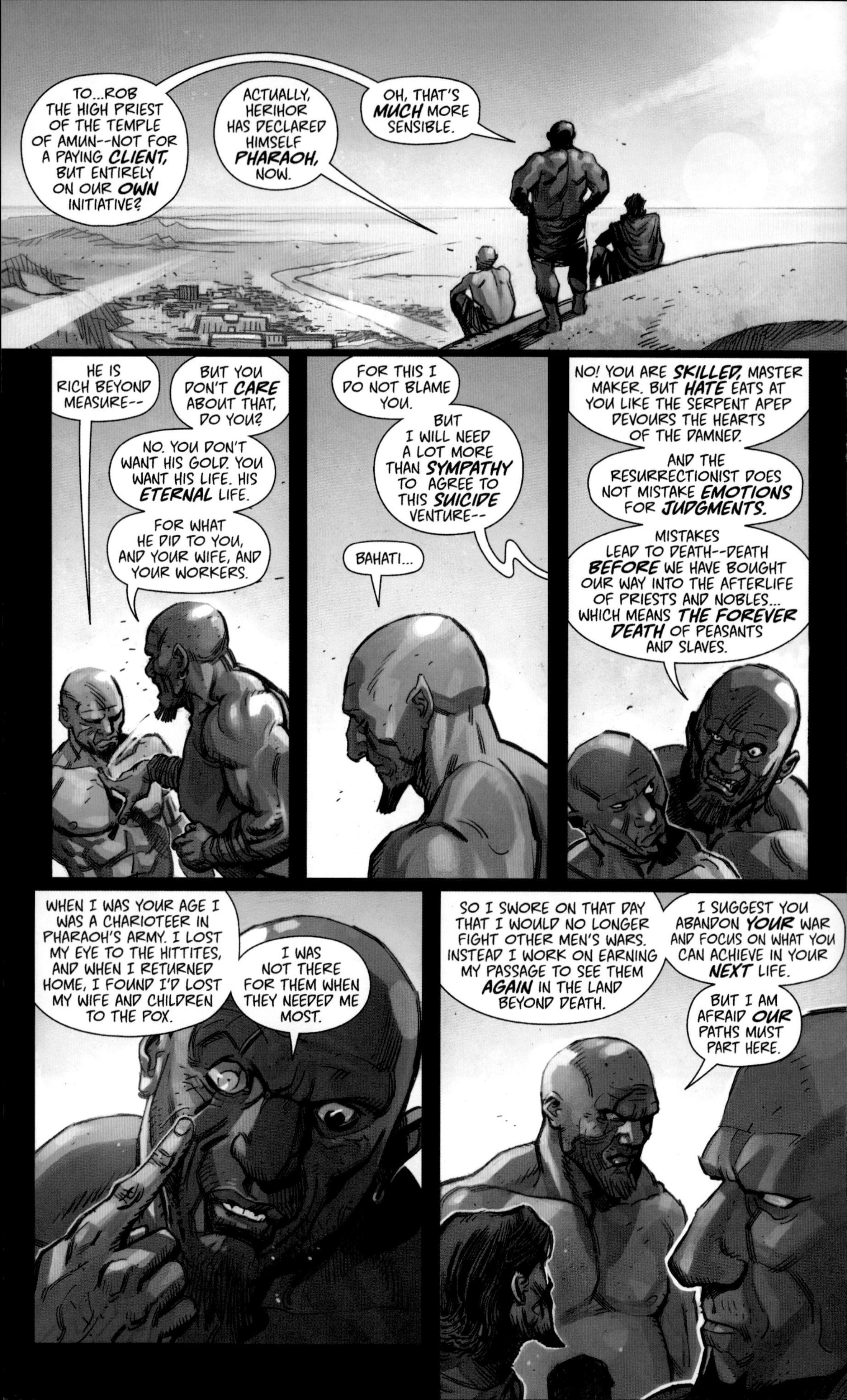
TO...ROB THE HIGH PRIEST OF THE TEMPLE OF AMUN--NOT FOR A PAYING CLIENT, BUT ENTIRELY ON OUR OWN INITIATIVE?
ACTUALLY, HERIHOR HAS DECLARED HIMSELF PHARAOH, NOW.
OH, THAT'S MUCH MORE SENSIBLE.
HE IS RICH BEYOND MEASURE--
BUT YOU DON'T CARE ABOUT THAT, DO YOU?
NO. YOU DON'T WANT HIS GOLD. YOU WANT HIS LIFE. HIS ETERNAL LIFE.
FOR WHAT HE DID TO YOU, AND YOUR WIFE, AND YOUR WORKERS.
FOR THIS I DO NOT BLAME YOU.
BUT I WILL NEED A LOT MORE THAN SYMPATHY TO AGREE TO THIS SUICIDE VENTURE--
BAHATI...
NO! YOU ARE SKILLED, MASTER MAKER. BUT HATE EATS AT YOU LIKE THE SERPENT APEP DEVOURS THE HEARTS OF THE DAMNED.
AND THE RESURRECTIONIST DOES NOT MISTAKE EMOTIONS FOR JUDGMENTS.
MISTAKES LEAD TO DEATH--DEATH BEFORE WE HAVE BOUGHT OUR WAY INTO THE AFTERLIFE OF PRIESTS AND NOBLES... WHICH MEANS THE FOREVER DEATH OF PEASANTS AND SLAVES.
WHEN I WAS YOUR AGE I WAS A CHARIOTEER IN PHARAOH'S ARMY. I LOST MY EYE TO THE HITTITES, AND WHEN I RETURNED HOME, I FOUND I'D LOST MY WIFE AND CHILDREN TO THE POX.
I WAS NOT THERE FOR THEM WHEN THEY NEEDED ME MOST.
SO I SWORE ON THAT DAY THAT I WOULD NO LONGER FIGHT OTHER MEN'S WARS. INSTEAD I WORK ON EARNING MY PASSAGE TO SEE THEM AGAIN IN THE LAND BEYOND DEATH.
I SUGGEST YOU ABANDON YOUR WAR AND FOCUS ON WHAT YOU CAN ACHIEVE IN YOUR NEXT LIFE.
BUT I AM AFRAID OUR PATHS MUST PART HERE.

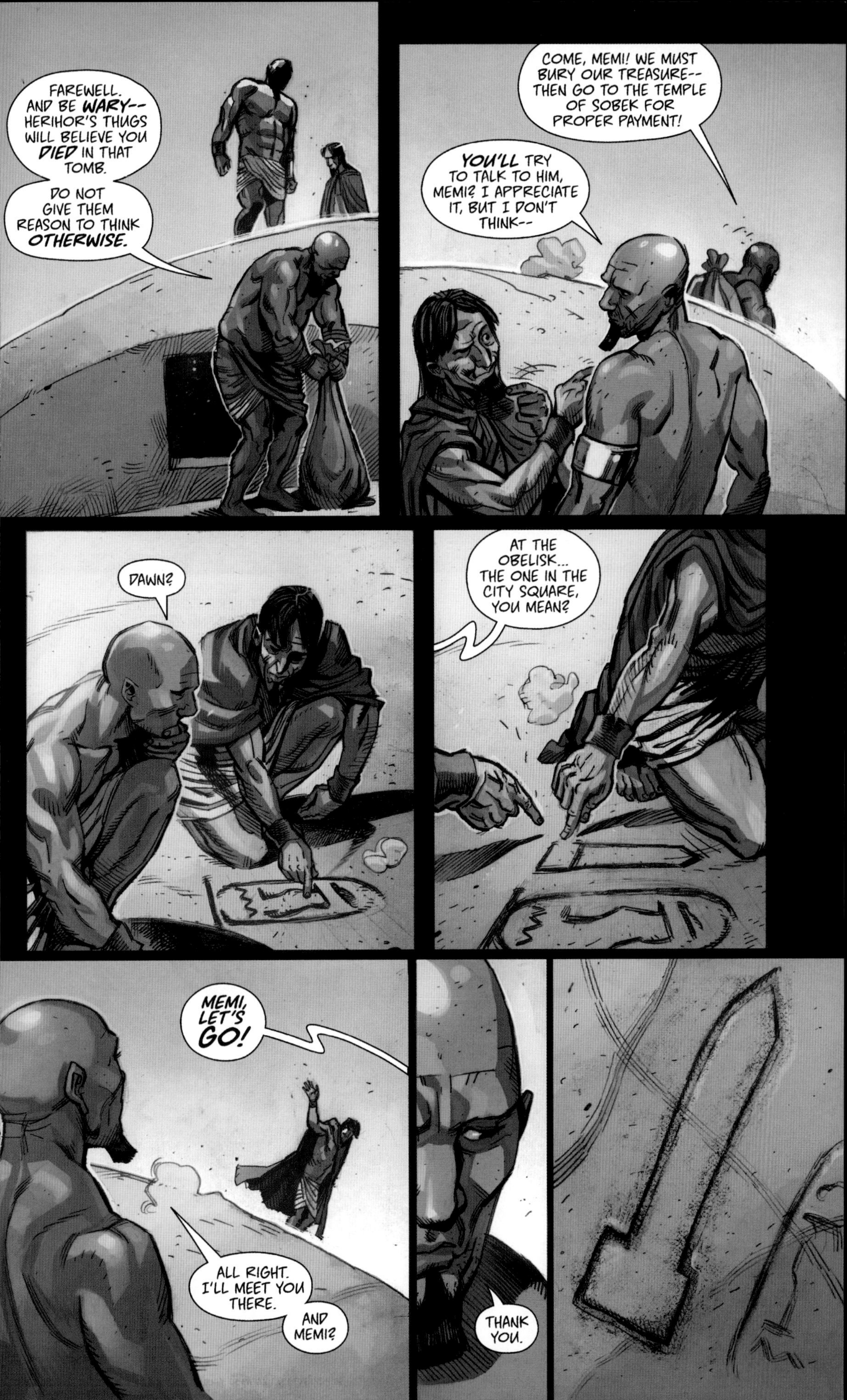
FAREWELL. AND BE WARY-- HERIHOR'S THUGS WILL BELIEVE YOU DIED IN THAT TOMB.
DO NOT GIVE THEM REASON TO THINK OTHERWISE.
COME, MEMI! WE MUST BURY OUR TREASURE-- THEN GO TO THE TEMPLE OF SOBEK FOR PROPER PAYMENT!
YOU'LL TRY TO TALK TO HIM, MEMI? I APPRECIATE IT, BUT I DON'T THINK--
DAWN?
AT THE OBELISK... THE ONE IN THE CITY SQUARE, YOU MEAN?
MEMI, LET'S GO!
ALL RIGHT. I'LL MEET YOU THERE.
AND MEMI?
THANK YOU.

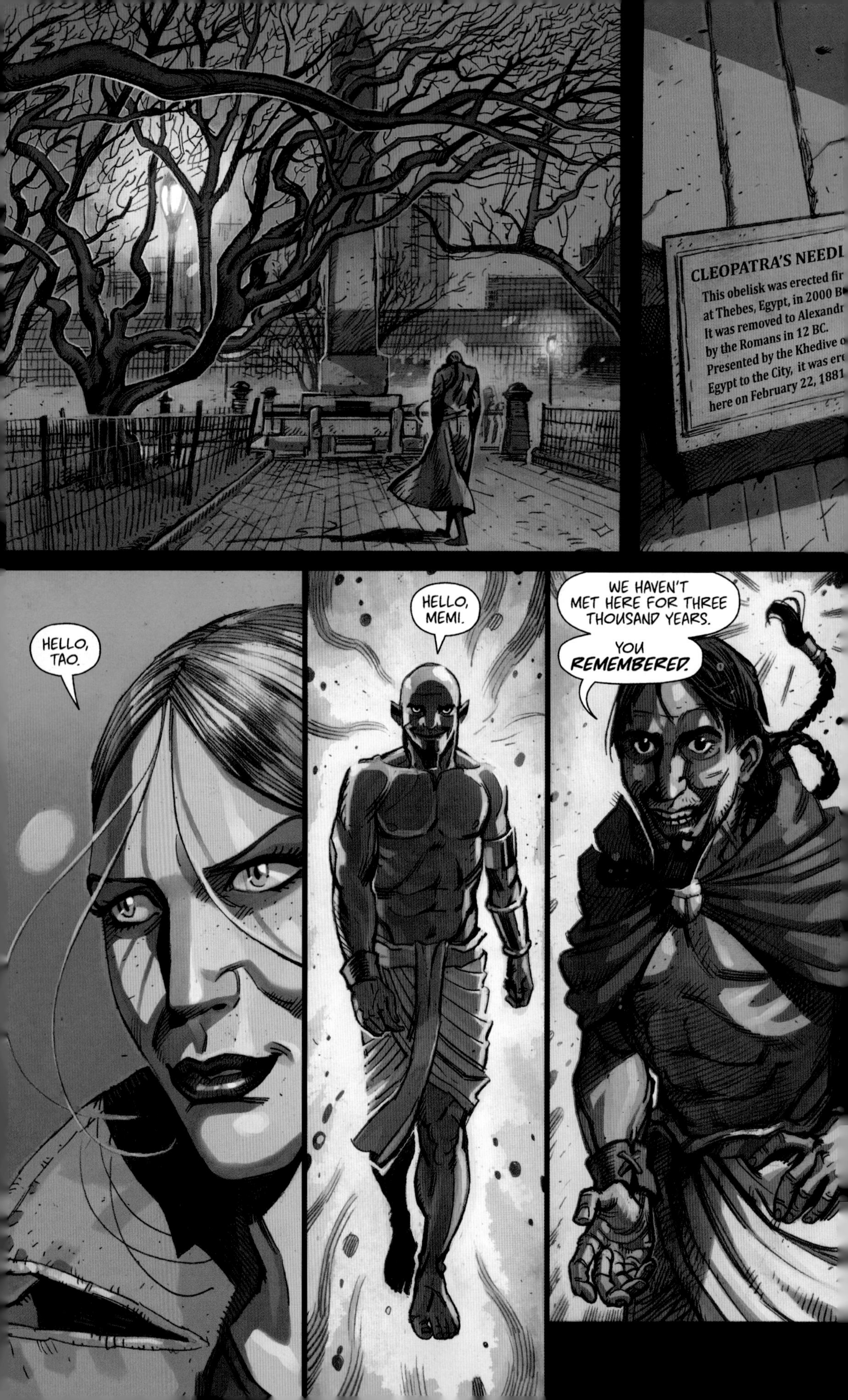
CLEOPATRA'S NEEDL
This obelisk was erected fir
at Thebes, Egypt, in 2000 B
It was removed to Alexandr
by the Romans in 12 BC.
Presented by the Khedive o
Egypt to the City, it was ere
here on February 22, 1881
HELLO, TAO.
HELLO, MEMI.
WE HAVEN'T MET HERE FOR THREE THOUSAND YEARS.
YOU *REMEMBERED.*

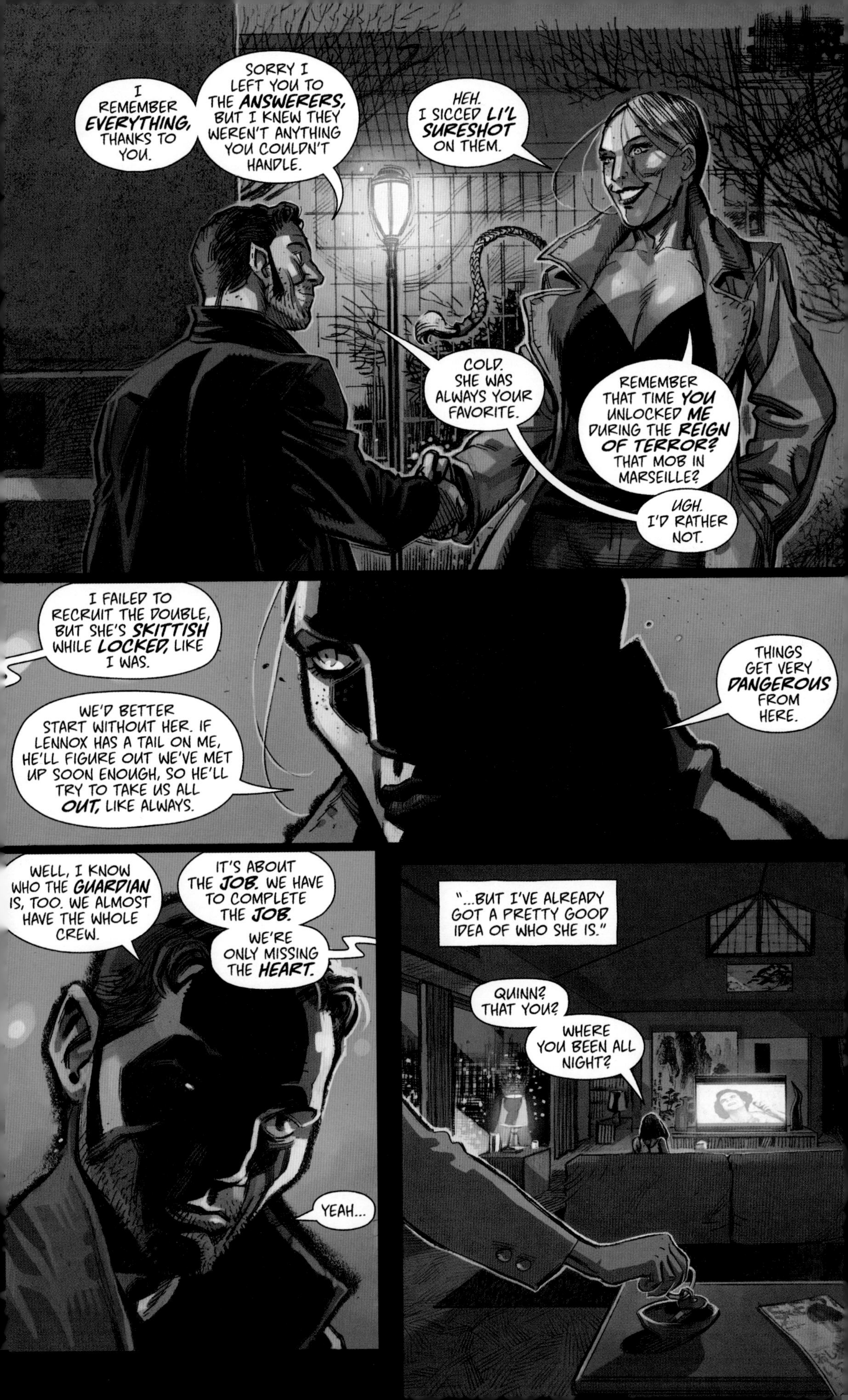

I REMEMBER EVERYTHING, THANKS TO YOU.
SORRY I LEFT YOU TO THE ANSWERERS, BUT I KNEW THEY WEREN'T ANYTHING YOU COULDN'T HANDLE.
HEH. I SICCED LI'L SURESHOT ON THEM.
COLD. SHE WAS ALWAYS YOUR FAVORITE.
REMEMBER THAT TIME YOU UNLOCKED ME DURING THE REIGN OF TERROR? THAT MOB IN MARSEILLE?
UGH. I'D RATHER NOT.
I FAILED TO RECRUIT THE DOUBLE, BUT SHE'S SKITTISH WHILE LOCKED, LIKE I WAS.
WE'D BETTER START WITHOUT HER. IF LENNOX HAS A TAIL ON ME, HE'LL FIGURE OUT WE'VE MET UP SOON ENOUGH, SO HE'LL TRY TO TAKE US ALL OUT, LIKE ALWAYS.
THINGS GET VERY DANGEROUS FROM HERE.
WELL, I KNOW WHO THE GUARDIAN IS, TOO. WE ALMOST HAVE THE WHOLE CREW.
IT'S ABOUT THE JOB. WE HAVE TO COMPLETE THE JOB.
WE'RE ONLY MISSING THE HEART.
YEAH...
"...BUT I'VE ALREADY GOT A PRETTY GOOD IDEA OF WHO SHE IS."
QUINN? THAT YOU?
WHERE YOU BEEN ALL NIGHT?

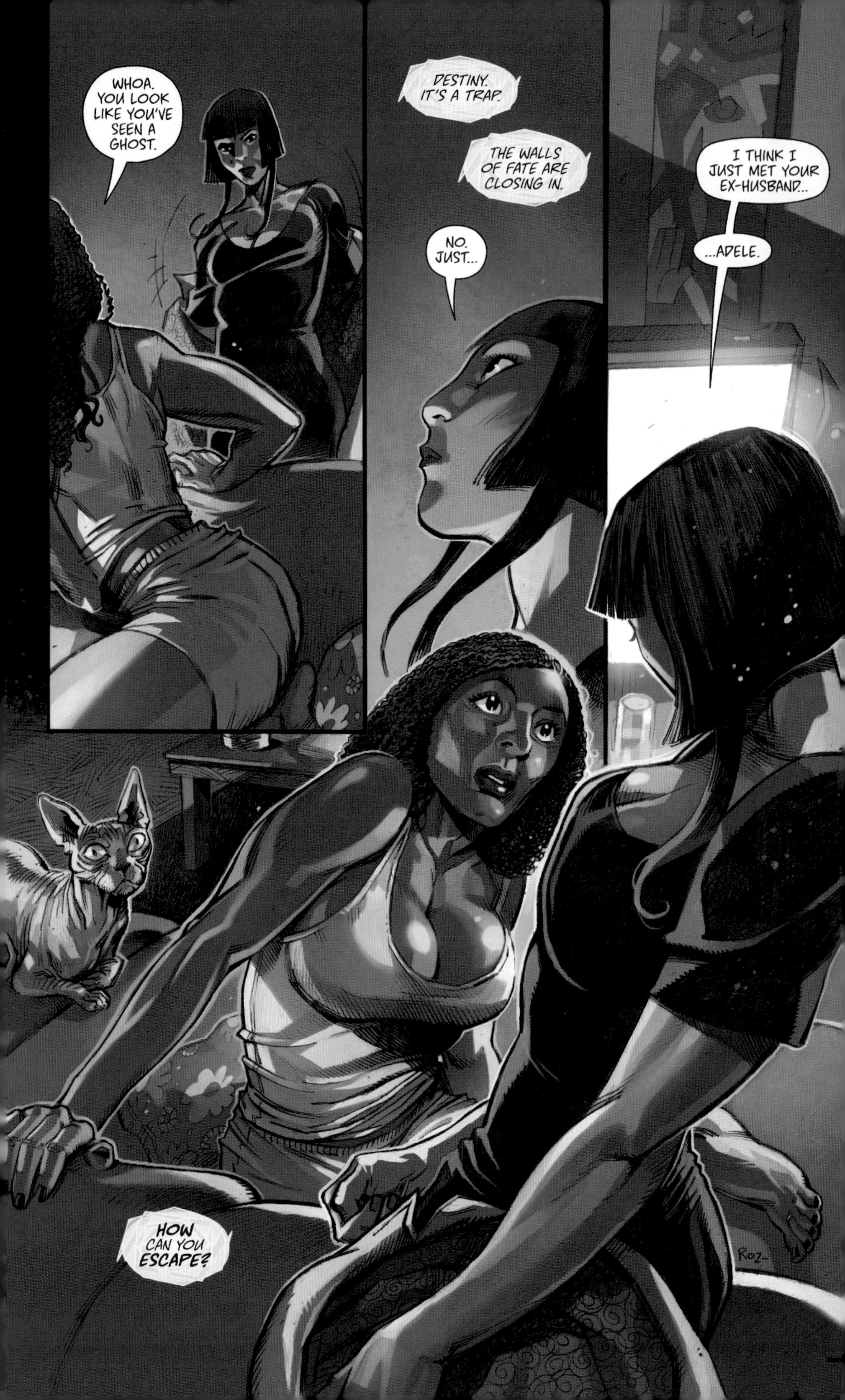
WHOA. YOU LOOK LIKE YOU'VE SEEN A GHOST.
DESTINY. IT'S A TRAP.
THE WALLS OF FATE ARE CLOSING IN.
NO. JUST...
I THINK I JUST MET YOUR EX-HUSBAND...
...ADELE.
HOW CAN YOU ESCAPE?
ROZ

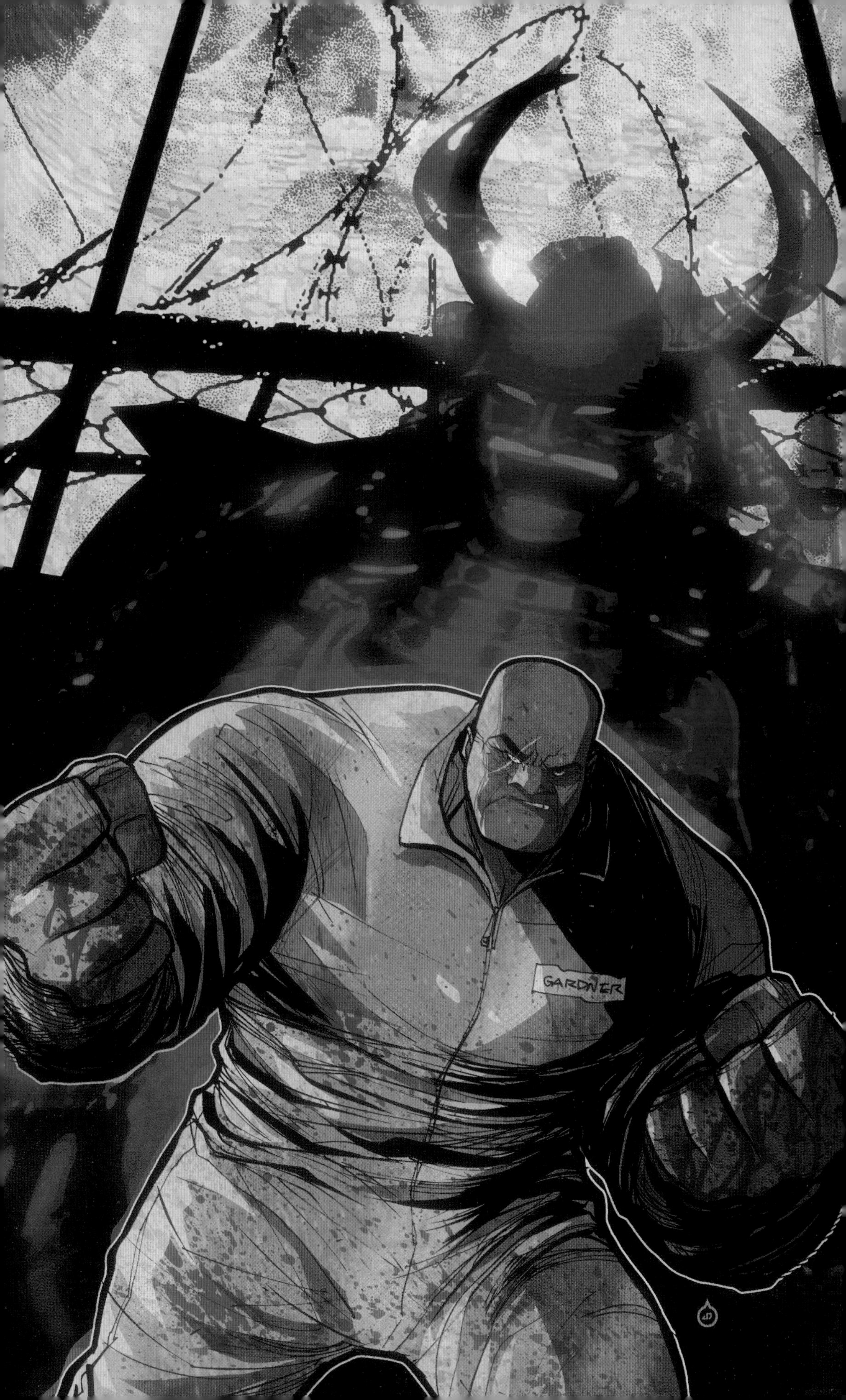
GARDNER

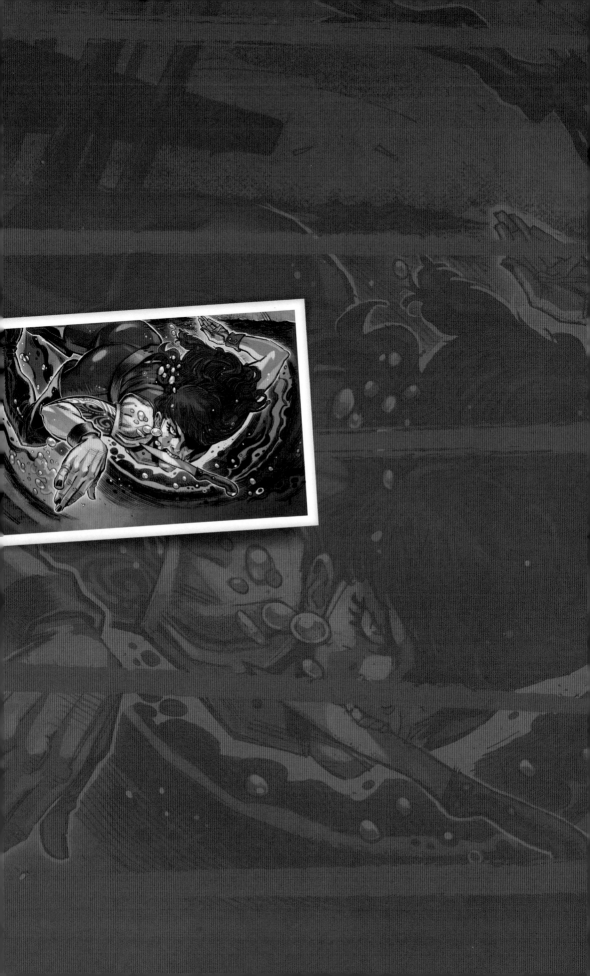

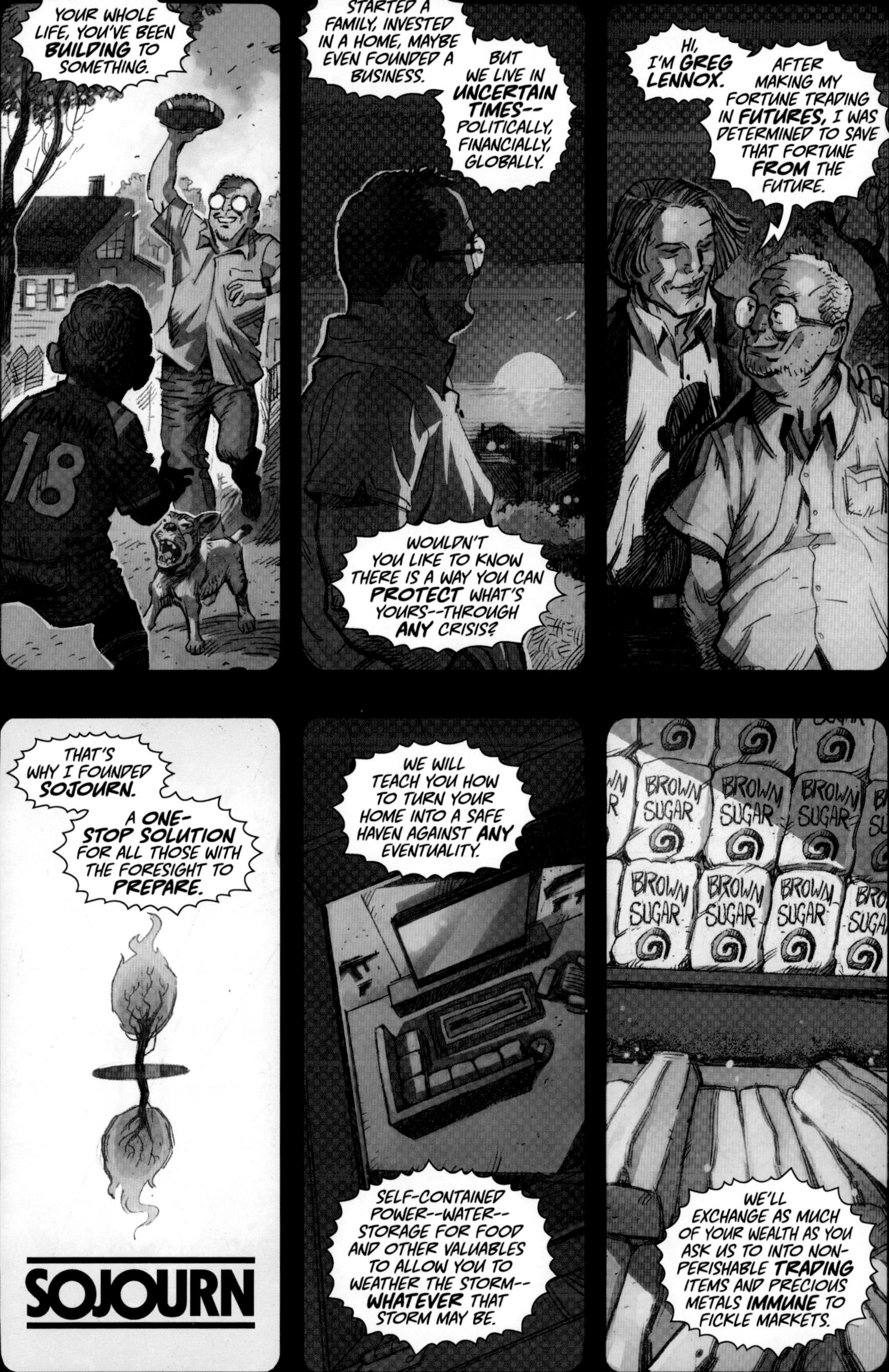

YOUR WHOLE LIFE, YOU'VE BEEN BUILDING TO SOMETHING.
MANNING
18
STARTED A FAMILY, INVESTED IN A HOME, MAYBE EVEN FOUNDED A BUSINESS.
BUT WE LIVE IN UNCERTAIN TIMES--POLITICALLY, FINANCIALLY, GLOBALLY.
WOULDN'T YOU LIKE TO KNOW THERE IS A WAY YOU CAN PROTECT WHAT'S YOURS--THROUGH ANY CRISIS?
HI, I'M GREG LENNOX.
AFTER MAKING MY FORTUNE TRADING IN FUTURES, I WAS DETERMINED TO SAVE THAT FORTUNE FROM THE FUTURE.
THAT'S WHY I FOUNDED SOJOURN.
A ONE-STOP SOLUTION FOR ALL THOSE WITH THE FORESIGHT TO PREPARE.
SOJOURN
WE WILL TEACH YOU HOW TO TURN YOUR HOME INTO A SAFE HAVEN AGAINST ANY EVENTUALITY.
SELF-CONTAINED POWER--WATER--STORAGE FOR FOOD AND OTHER VALUABLES TO ALLOW YOU TO WEATHER THE STORM--WHATEVER THAT STORM MAY BE.
BROWN SUGAR
WE'LL EXCHANGE AS MUCH OF YOUR WEALTH AS YOU ASK US TO INTO NON-PERISHABLE TRADING ITEMS AND PRECIOUS METALS IMMUNE TO FICKLE MARKETS.

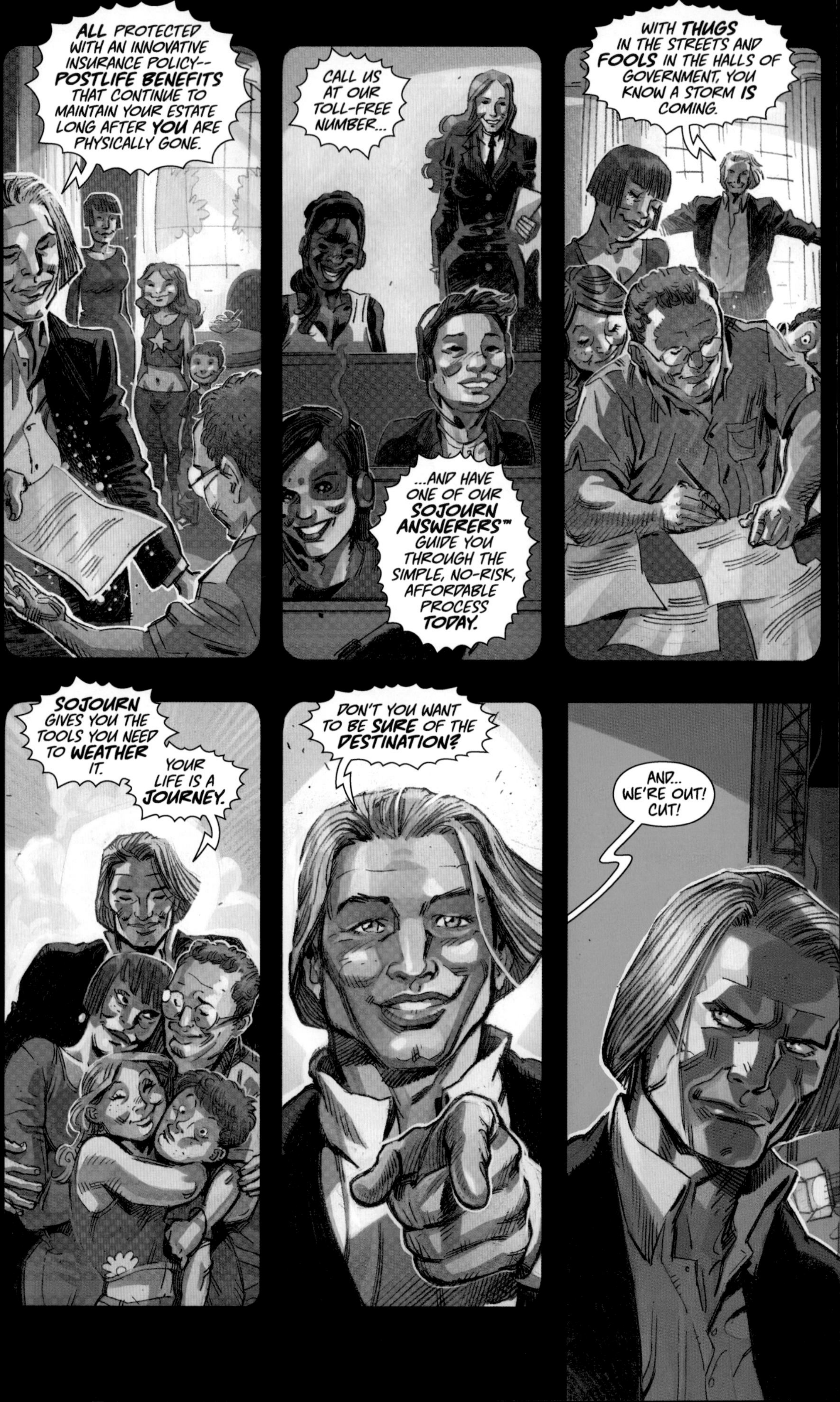
ALL PROTECTED WITH AN INNOVATIVE INSURANCE POLICY-- POSTLIFE BENEFITS THAT CONTINUE TO MAINTAIN YOUR ESTATE LONG AFTER YOU ARE PHYSICALLY GONE.
CALL US AT OUR TOLL-FREE NUMBER...
...AND HAVE ONE OF OUR SOJOURN ANSWERERS™ GUIDE YOU THROUGH THE SIMPLE, NO-RISK, AFFORDABLE PROCESS TODAY.
WITH THUGS IN THE STREETS AND FOOLS IN THE HALLS OF GOVERNMENT, YOU KNOW A STORM IS COMING.
SOJOURN GIVES YOU THE TOOLS YOU NEED TO WEATHER IT.
YOUR LIFE IS A JOURNEY.
DON'T YOU WANT TO BE SURE OF THE DESTINATION?
AND... WE'RE OUT! CUT!

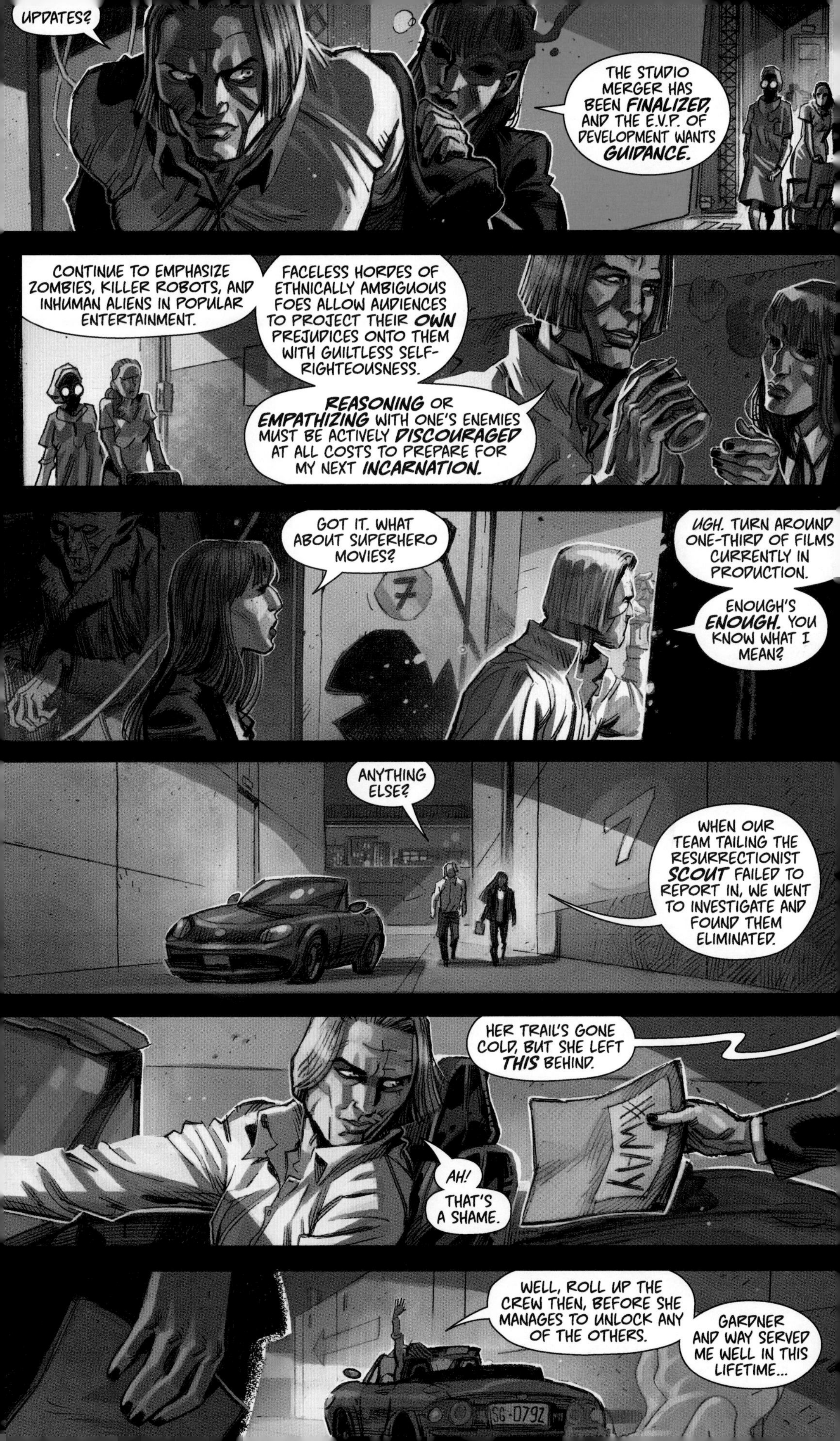
UPDATES?
THE STUDIO MERGER HAS BEEN FINALIZED, AND THE E.V.P. OF DEVELOPMENT WANTS GUIDANCE.
CONTINUE TO EMPHASIZE ZOMBIES, KILLER ROBOTS, AND INHUMAN ALIENS IN POPULAR ENTERTAINMENT.
FACELESS HORDES OF ETHNICALLY AMBIGUOUS FOES ALLOW AUDIENCES TO PROJECT THEIR OWN PREJUDICES ONTO THEM WITH GUILTLESS SELF-RIGHTEOUSNESS.
REASONING OR EMPATHIZING WITH ONE'S ENEMIES MUST BE ACTIVELY DISCOURAGED AT ALL COSTS TO PREPARE FOR MY NEXT INCARNATION.
GOT IT. WHAT ABOUT SUPERHERO MOVIES?
UGH. TURN AROUND ONE-THIRD OF FILMS CURRENTLY IN PRODUCTION.
ENOUGH'S ENOUGH. YOU KNOW WHAT I MEAN?
7
ANYTHING ELSE?
WHEN OUR TEAM TAILING THE RESURRECTIONIST SCOUT FAILED TO REPORT IN, WE WENT TO INVESTIGATE AND FOUND THEM ELIMINATED.
HER TRAIL'S GONE COLD, BUT SHE LEFT THIS BEHIND.
AH!
THAT'S A SHAME.
WELL, ROLL UP THE CREW THEN, BEFORE SHE MANAGES TO UNLOCK ANY OF THE OTHERS.
GARDNER AND WAY SERVED ME WELL IN THIS LIFETIME...
SG-079Z

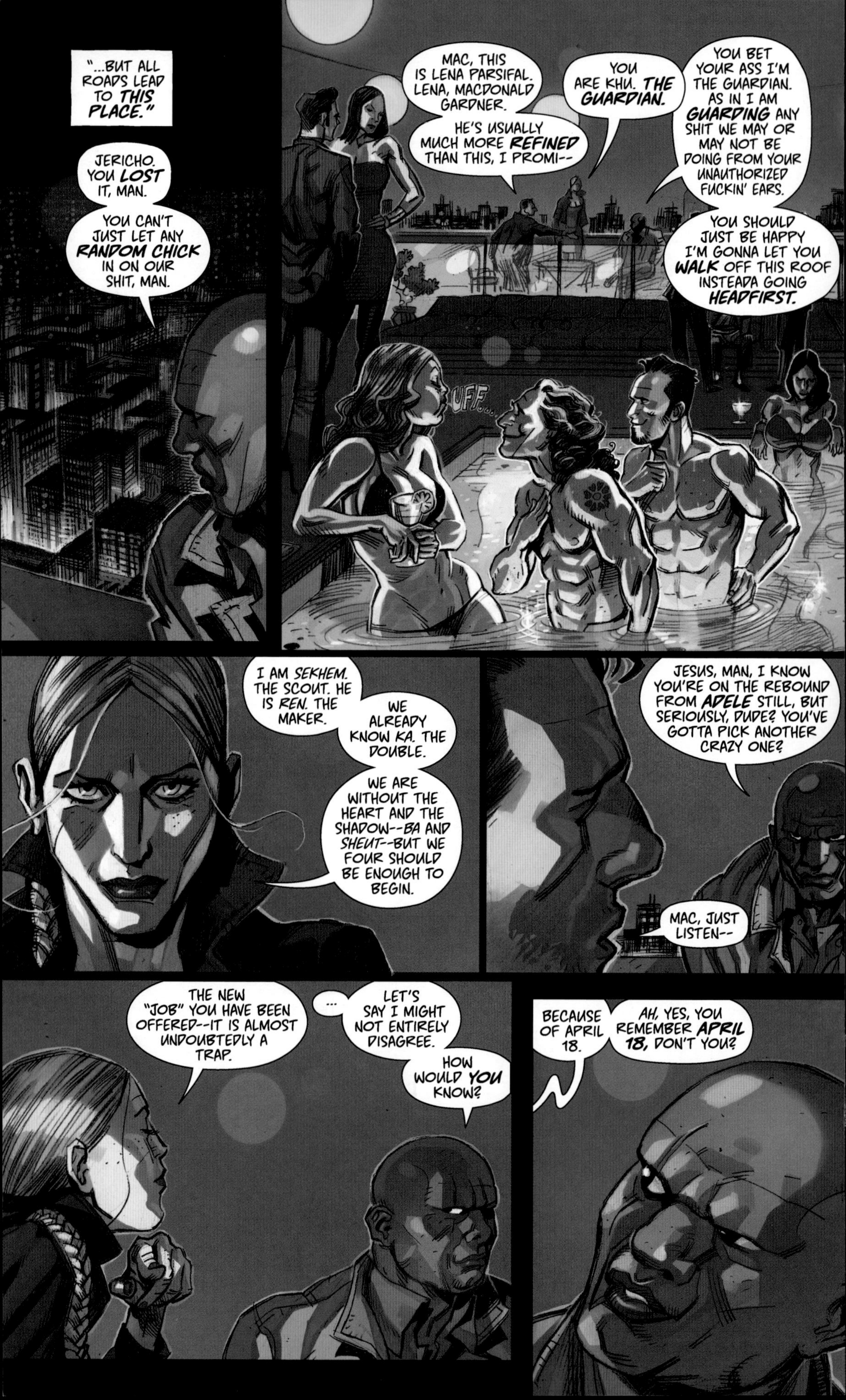
"...BUT ALL ROADS LEAD TO THIS PLACE."
MAC, THIS IS LENA PARSIFAL. LENA, MACDONALD GARDNER.
HE'S USUALLY MUCH MORE REFINED THAN THIS, I PROMI--
YOU ARE KHU. THE GUARDIAN.
YOU BET YOUR ASS I'M THE GUARDIAN. AS IN I AM GUARDING ANY SHIT WE MAY OR MAY NOT BE DOING FROM YOUR UNAUTHORIZED FUCKIN' EARS.
YOU SHOULD JUST BE HAPPY I'M GONNA LET YOU WALK OFF THIS ROOF INSTEADA GOING HEADFIRST.
UFF...
JERICHO. YOU LOST IT, MAN.
YOU CAN'T JUST LET ANY RANDOM CHICK IN ON OUR SHIT, MAN.
I AM SEKHEM. THE SCOUT. HE IS REN. THE MAKER.
WE ALREADY KNOW KA. THE DOUBLE.
WE ARE WITHOUT THE HEART AND THE SHADOW--BA AND SHEUT--BUT WE FOUR SHOULD BE ENOUGH TO BEGIN.
JESUS, MAN, I KNOW YOU'RE ON THE REBOUND FROM ADELE STILL, BUT SERIOUSLY, DUDE? YOU'VE GOTTA PICK ANOTHER CRAZY ONE?
MAC, JUST LISTEN--
THE NEW "JOB" YOU HAVE BEEN OFFERED--IT IS ALMOST UNDOUBTEDLY A TRAP.
...
LET'S SAY I MIGHT NOT ENTIRELY DISAGREE.
HOW WOULD YOU KNOW?
BECAUSE OF APRIL 18.
AH, YES, YOU REMEMBER APRIL 18, DON'T YOU?

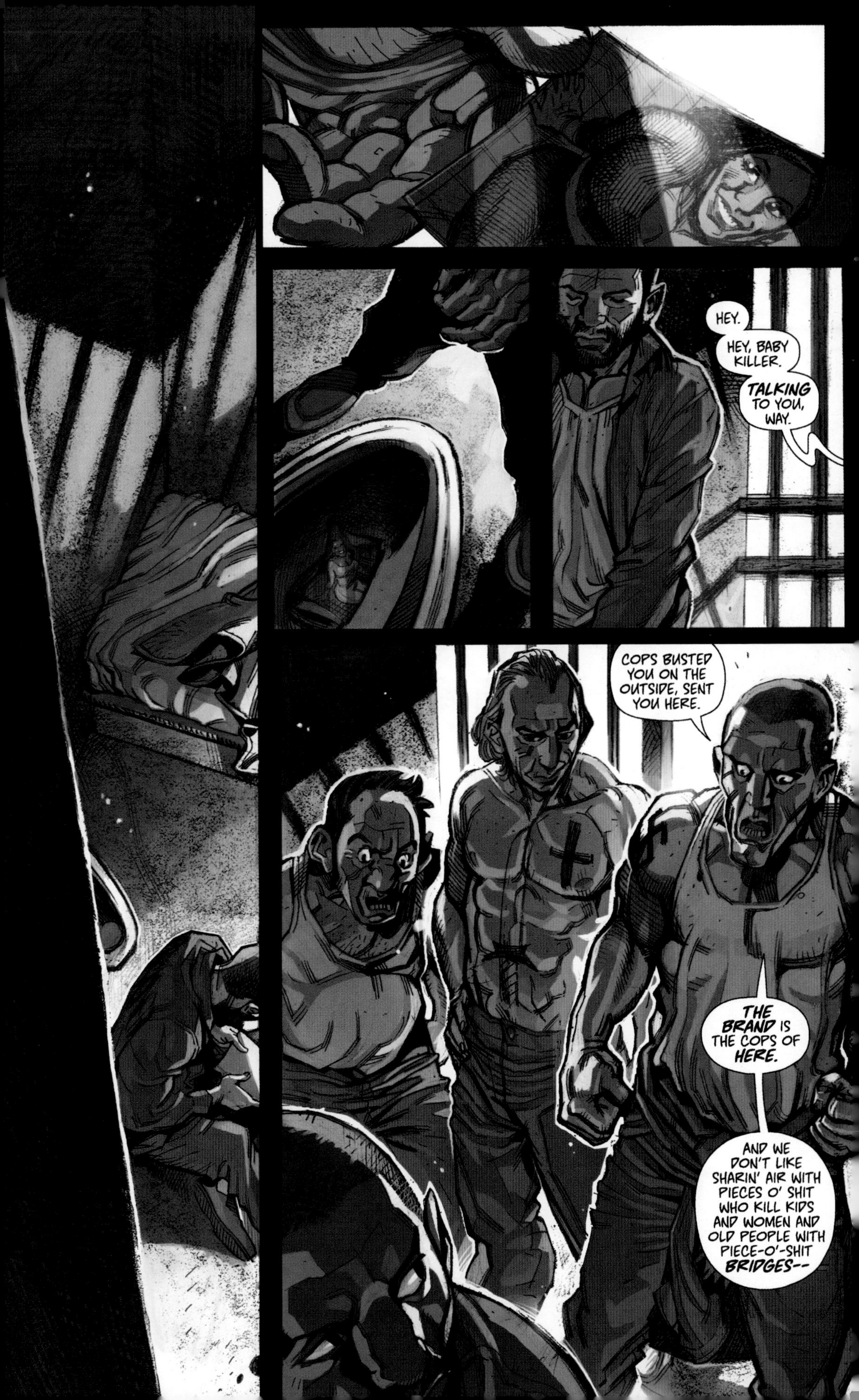
HEY.
HEY, BABY KILLER.
TALKING TO YOU, WAY.
COPS BUSTED YOU ON THE OUTSIDE, SENT YOU HERE.
THE BRAND IS THE COPS OF HERE.
AND WE DON'T LIKE SHARIN' AIR WITH PIECES O' SHIT WHO KILL KIDS AND WOMEN AND OLD PEOPLE WITH PIECE-O'-SHIT BRIDGES--

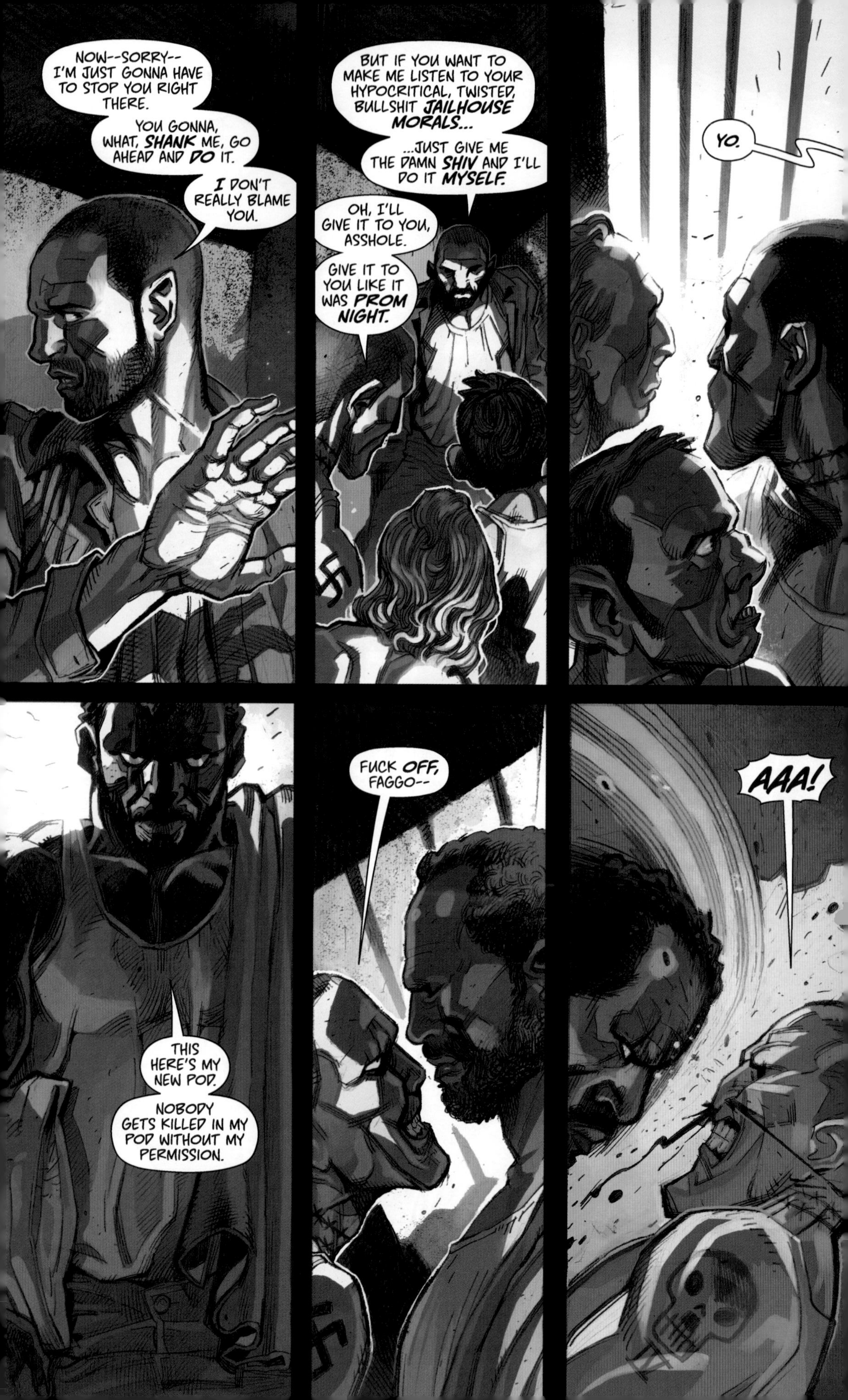
NOW--SORRY-- I'M JUST GONNA HAVE TO STOP YOU RIGHT THERE.
YOU GONNA, WHAT, SHANK ME, GO AHEAD AND DO IT.
I DON'T REALLY BLAME YOU.
BUT IF YOU WANT TO MAKE ME LISTEN TO YOUR HYPOCRITICAL, TWISTED, BULLSHIT JAILHOUSE MORALS...
...JUST GIVE ME THE DAMN SHIV AND I'LL DO IT MYSELF.
OH, I'LL GIVE IT TO YOU, ASSHOLE.
GIVE IT TO YOU LIKE IT WAS PROM NIGHT.
YO.
THIS HERE'S MY NEW POD.
NOBODY GETS KILLED IN MY POD WITHOUT MY PERMISSION.
FUCK OFF, FAGGO--
AAA!

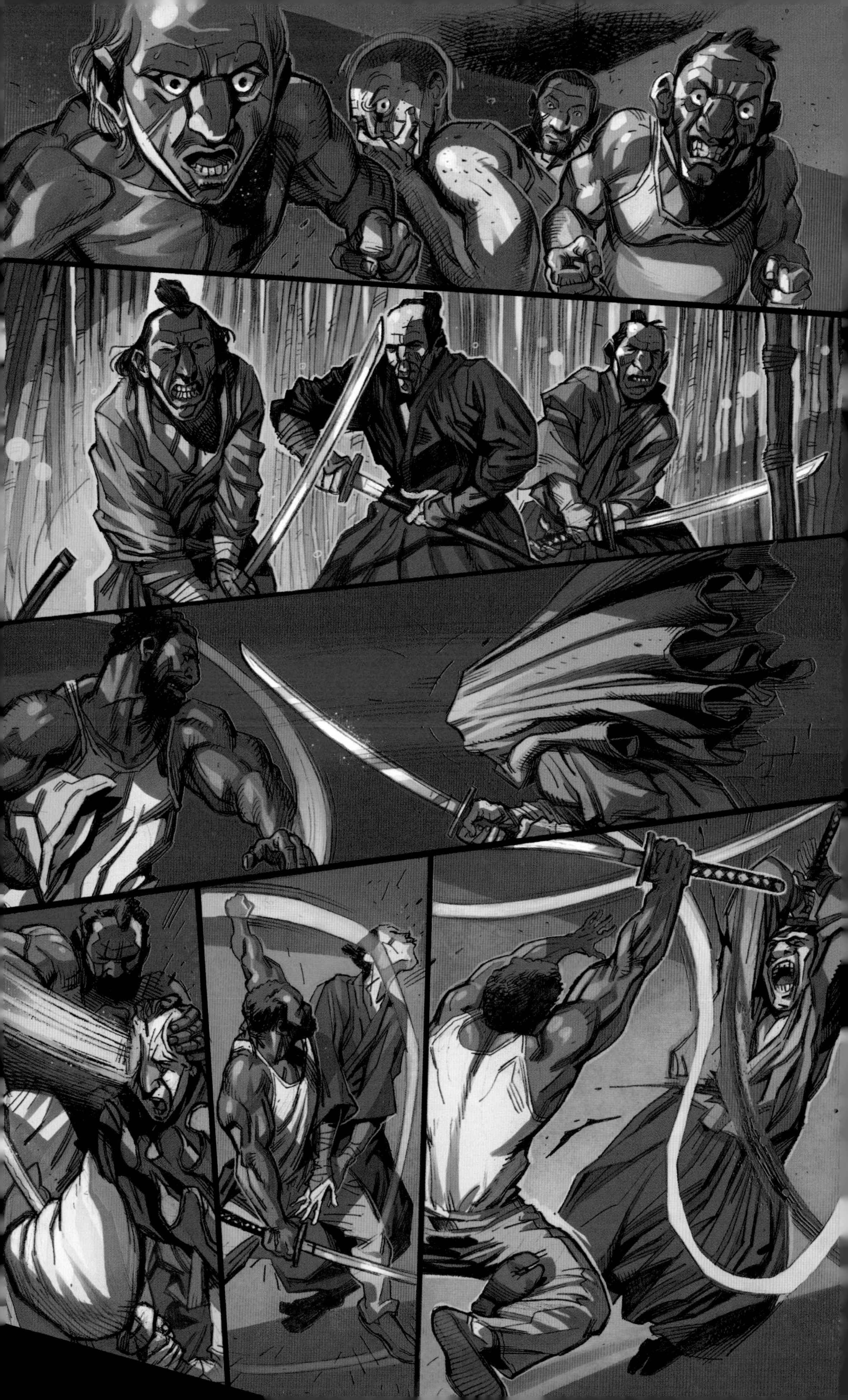

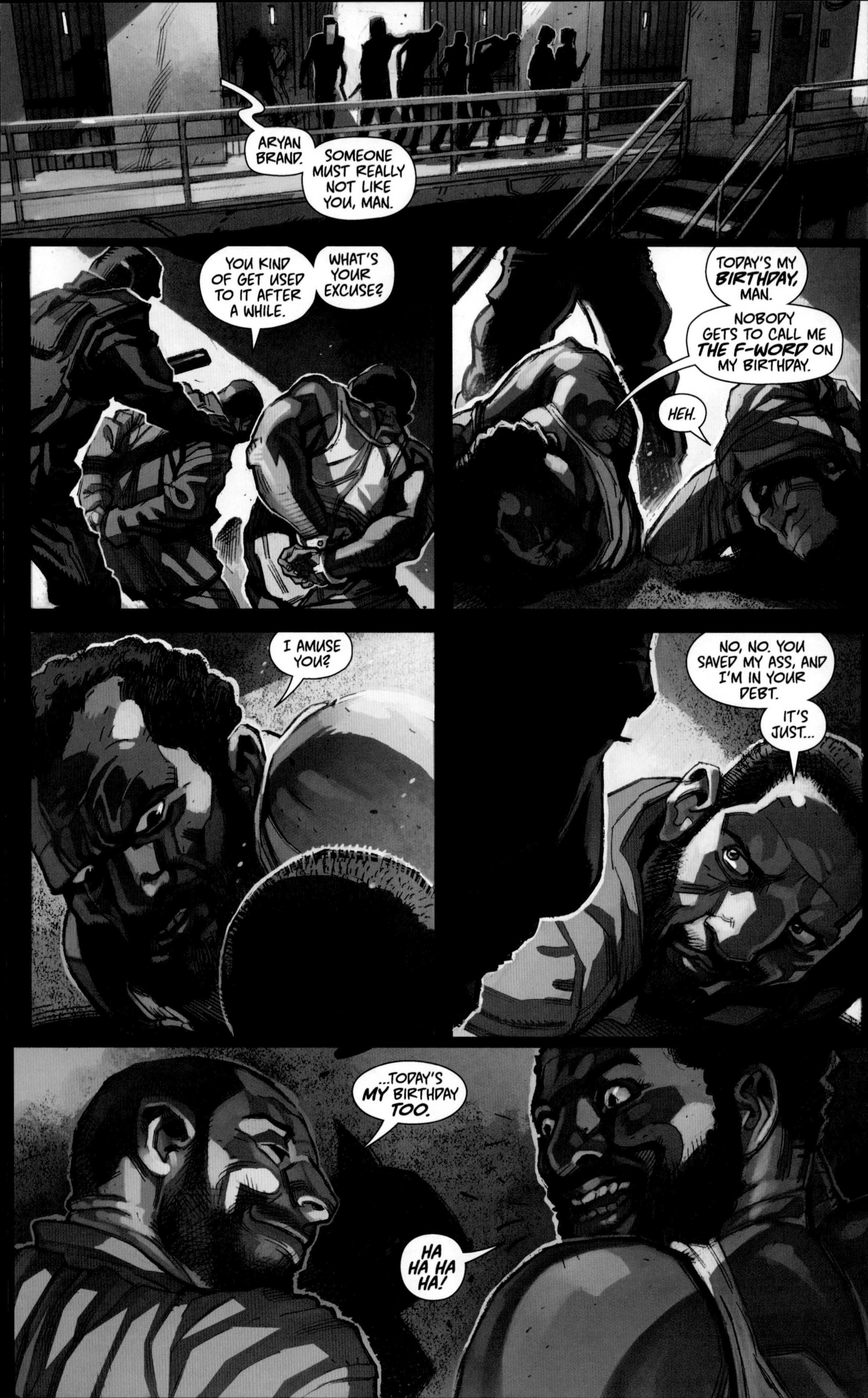
ARYAN BRAND.
SOMEONE MUST REALLY NOT LIKE YOU, MAN.
YOU KIND OF GET USED TO IT AFTER A WHILE.
WHAT'S YOUR EXCUSE?
TODAY'S MY BIRTHDAY, MAN.
NOBODY GETS TO CALL ME THE F-WORD ON MY BIRTHDAY.
HEH.
I AMUSE YOU?
NO, NO. YOU SAVED MY ASS, AND I'M IN YOUR DEBT.
IT'S JUST...
...TODAY'S MY BIRTHDAY TOO.
HA HA HA HA!

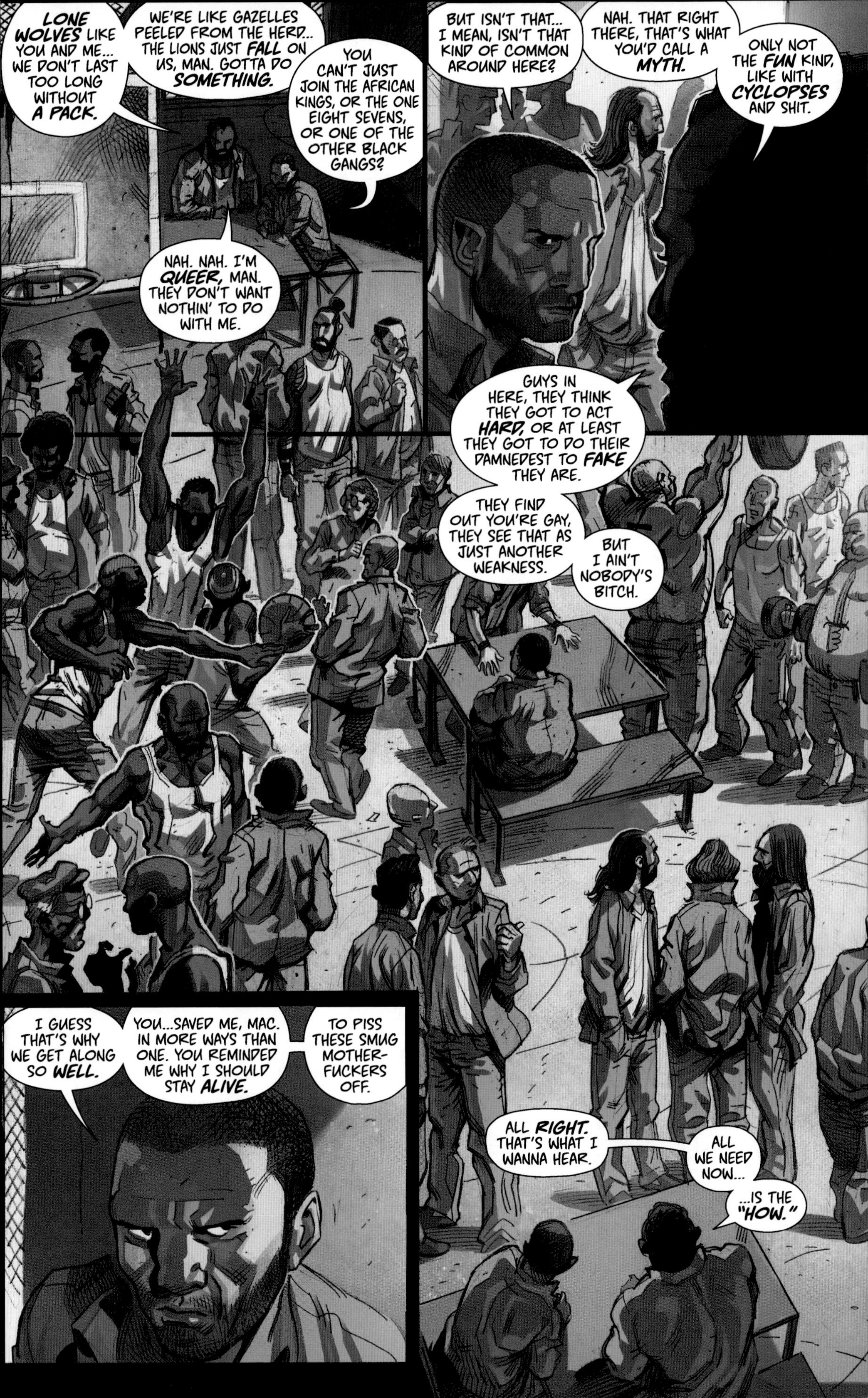
LONE WOLVES LIKE YOU AND ME... WE DON'T LAST TOO LONG WITHOUT A PACK.
WE'RE LIKE GAZELLES PEELED FROM THE HERD... THE LIONS JUST FALL ON US, MAN. GOTTA DO SOMETHING.
YOU CAN'T JUST JOIN THE AFRICAN KINGS, OR THE ONE EIGHT SEVENS, OR ONE OF THE OTHER BLACK GANGS?
NAH. NAH. I'M QUEER, MAN. THEY DON'T WANT NOTHIN' TO DO WITH ME.
BUT ISN'T THAT... I MEAN, ISN'T THAT KIND OF COMMON AROUND HERE?
NAH. THAT RIGHT THERE, THAT'S WHAT YOU'D CALL A MYTH.
ONLY NOT THE FUN KIND, LIKE WITH CYCLOPSES AND SHIT.
GUYS IN HERE, THEY THINK THEY GOT TO ACT HARD, OR AT LEAST THEY GOT TO DO THEIR DAMNEDEST TO FAKE THEY ARE.
THEY FIND OUT YOU'RE GAY, THEY SEE THAT AS JUST ANOTHER WEAKNESS.
BUT I AIN'T NOBODY'S BITCH.
I GUESS THAT'S WHY WE GET ALONG SO WELL.
YOU...SAVED ME, MAC. IN MORE WAYS THAN ONE. YOU REMINDED ME WHY I SHOULD STAY ALIVE.
TO PISS THESE SMUG MOTHER-FUCKERS OFF.
ALL RIGHT. THAT'S WHAT I WANNA HEAR.
ALL WE NEED NOW...
...IS THE "HOW."

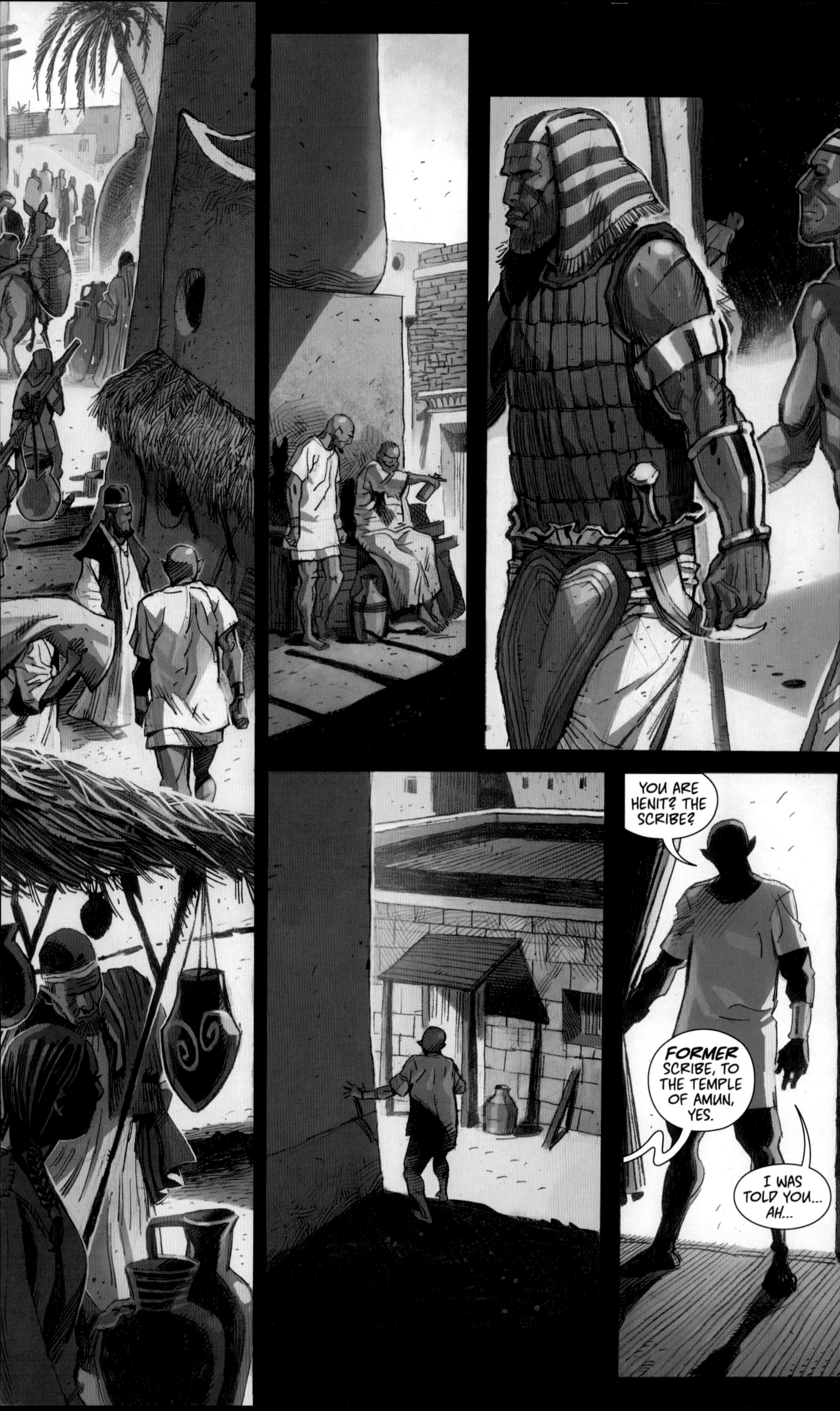
YOU ARE HENIT? THE SCRIBE?
FORMER SCRIBE, TO THE TEMPLE OF AMUN, YES.
I WAS TOLD YOU... AH...

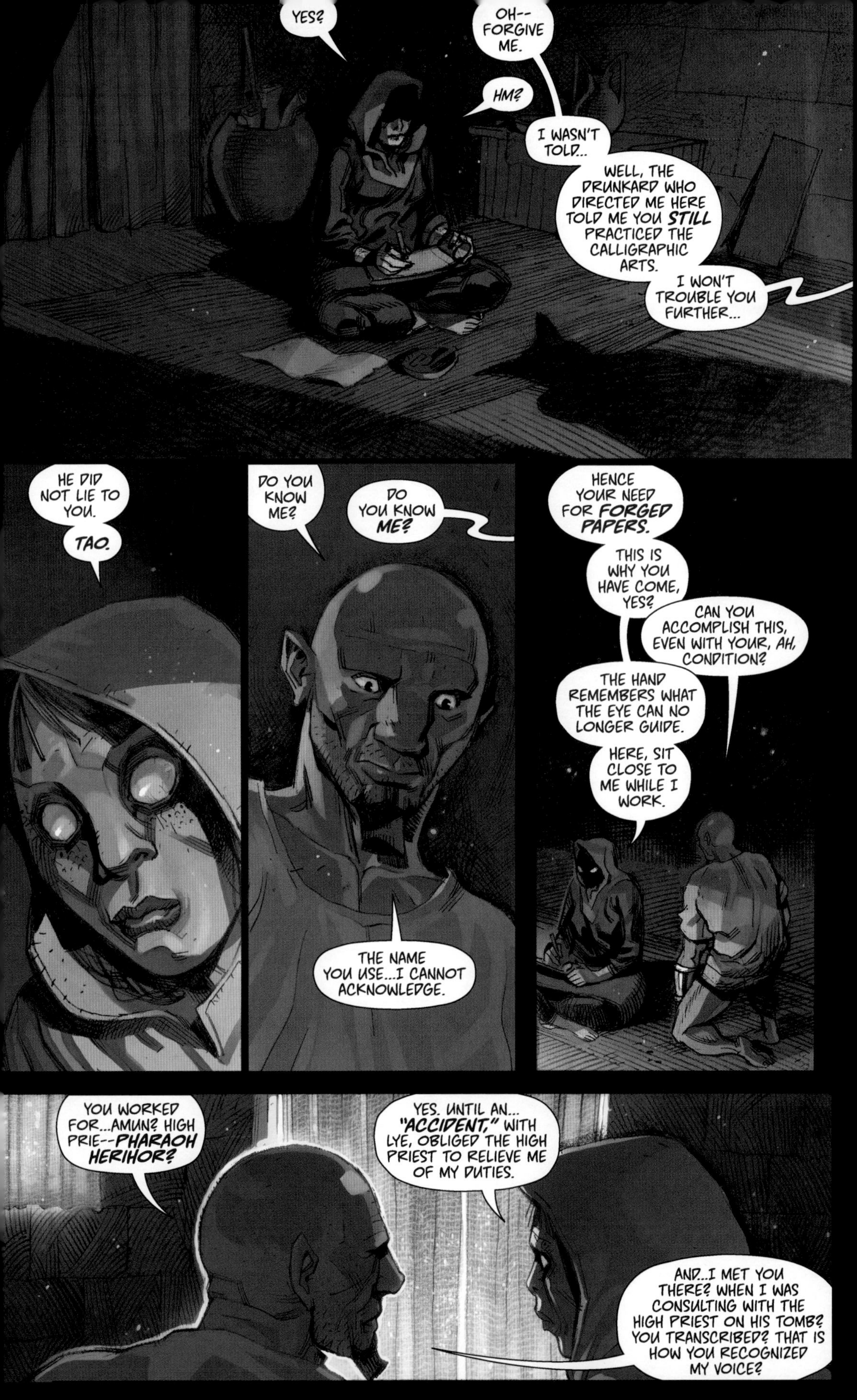
YES?
OH--FORGIVE ME.
HM?
I WASN'T TOLD...
WELL, THE DRUNKARD WHO DIRECTED ME HERE TOLD ME YOU STILL PRACTICED THE CALLIGRAPHIC ARTS.
I WON'T TROUBLE YOU FURTHER...
HE DID NOT LIE TO YOU.
TAO.
DO YOU KNOW ME?
DO YOU KNOW ME?
THE NAME YOU USE...I CANNOT ACKNOWLEDGE.
HENCE YOUR NEED FOR FORGED PAPERS.
THIS IS WHY YOU HAVE COME, YES?
CAN YOU ACCOMPLISH THIS, EVEN WITH YOUR, AH, CONDITION?
THE HAND REMEMBERS WHAT THE EYE CAN NO LONGER GUIDE.
HERE, SIT CLOSE TO ME WHILE I WORK.
YOU WORKED FOR...AMUN? HIGH PRIE--PHARAOH HERIHOR?
YES. UNTIL AN... "ACCIDENT," WITH LYE, OBLIGED THE HIGH PRIEST TO RELIEVE ME OF MY DUTIES.
AND...I MET YOU THERE? WHEN I WAS CONSULTING WITH THE HIGH PRIEST ON HIS TOMB? YOU TRANSCRIBED? THAT IS HOW YOU RECOGNIZED MY VOICE?

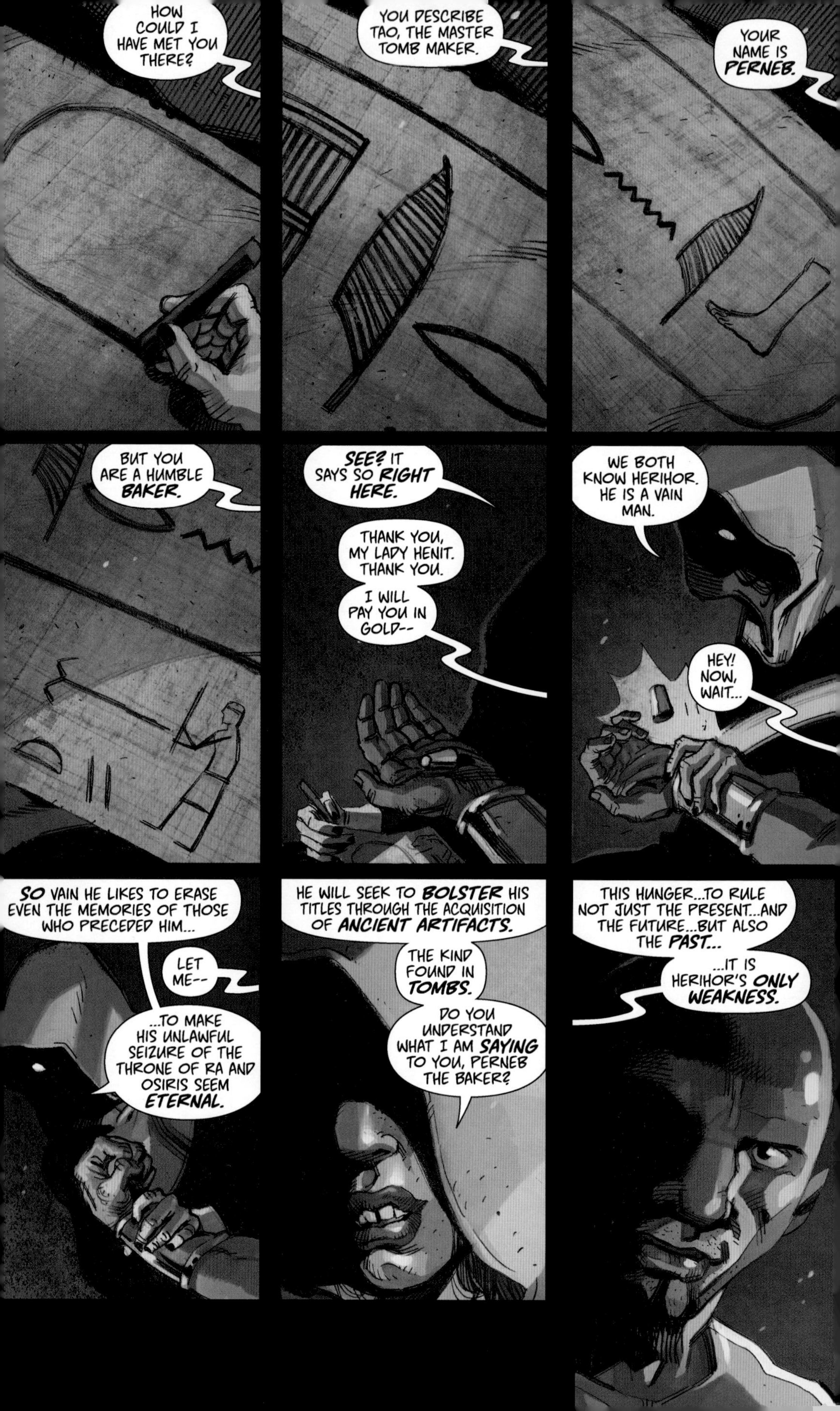
HOW COULD I HAVE MET YOU THERE?
YOU DESCRIBE TAO, THE MASTER TOMB MAKER.
YOUR NAME IS PERNEB.
BUT YOU ARE A HUMBLE BAKER.
SEE? IT SAYS SO RIGHT HERE.
THANK YOU, MY LADY HENIT. THANK YOU.
I WILL PAY YOU IN GOLD--
WE BOTH KNOW HERIHOR. HE IS A VAIN MAN.
HEY! NOW, WAIT...
SO VAIN HE LIKES TO ERASE EVEN THE MEMORIES OF THOSE WHO PRECEDED HIM...
LET ME--
...TO MAKE HIS UNLAWFUL SEIZURE OF THE THRONE OF RA AND OSIRIS SEEM ETERNAL.
HE WILL SEEK TO BOLSTER HIS TITLES THROUGH THE ACQUISITION OF ANCIENT ARTIFACTS.
THE KIND FOUND IN TOMBS.
DO YOU UNDERSTAND WHAT I AM SAYING TO YOU, PERNEB THE BAKER?
THIS HUNGER...TO RULE NOT JUST THE PRESENT...AND THE FUTURE...BUT ALSO THE PAST...
...IT IS HERIHOR'S ONLY WEAKNESS.

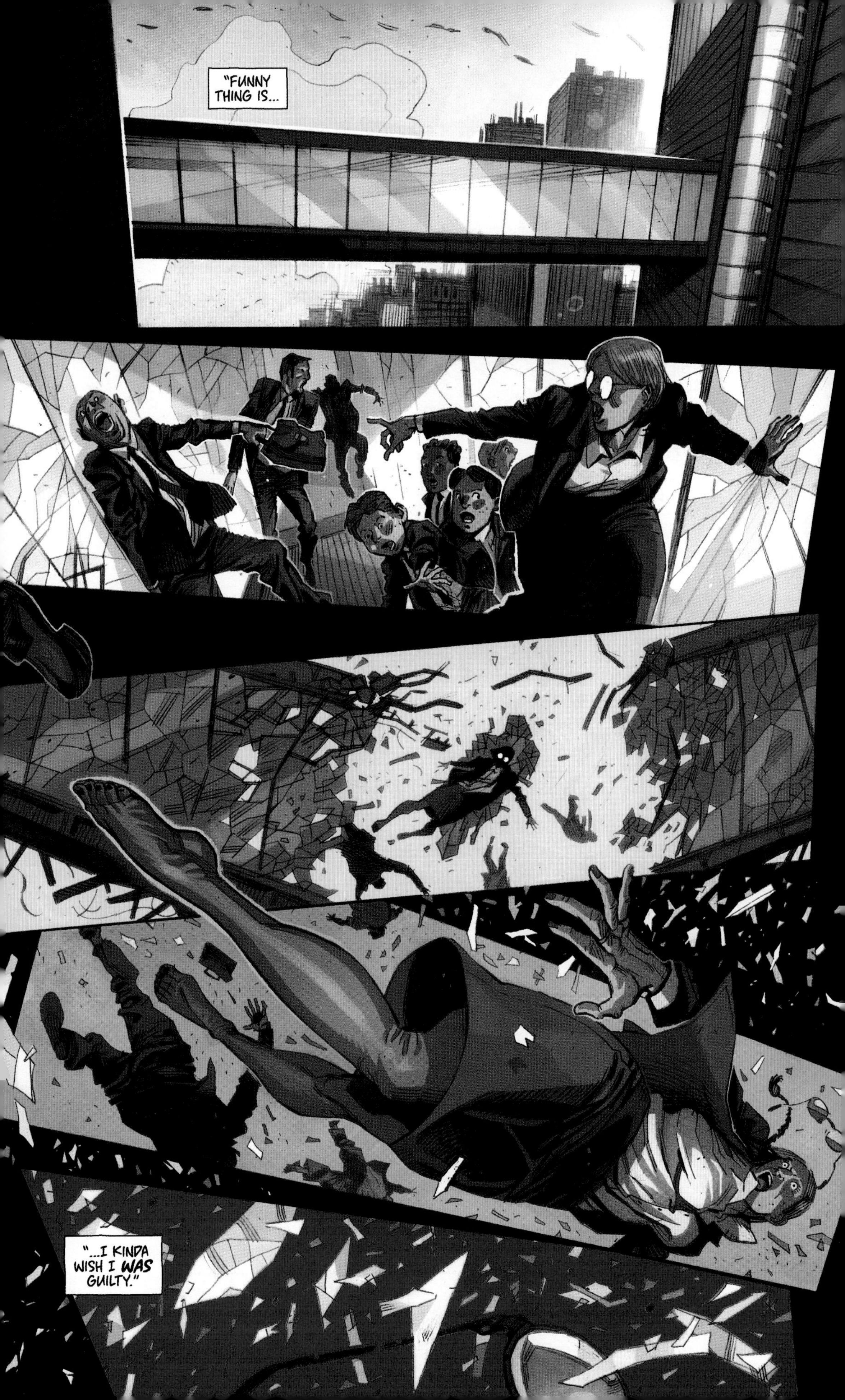
"FUNNY THING IS...
"...I KINDA WISH I WAS GUILTY."

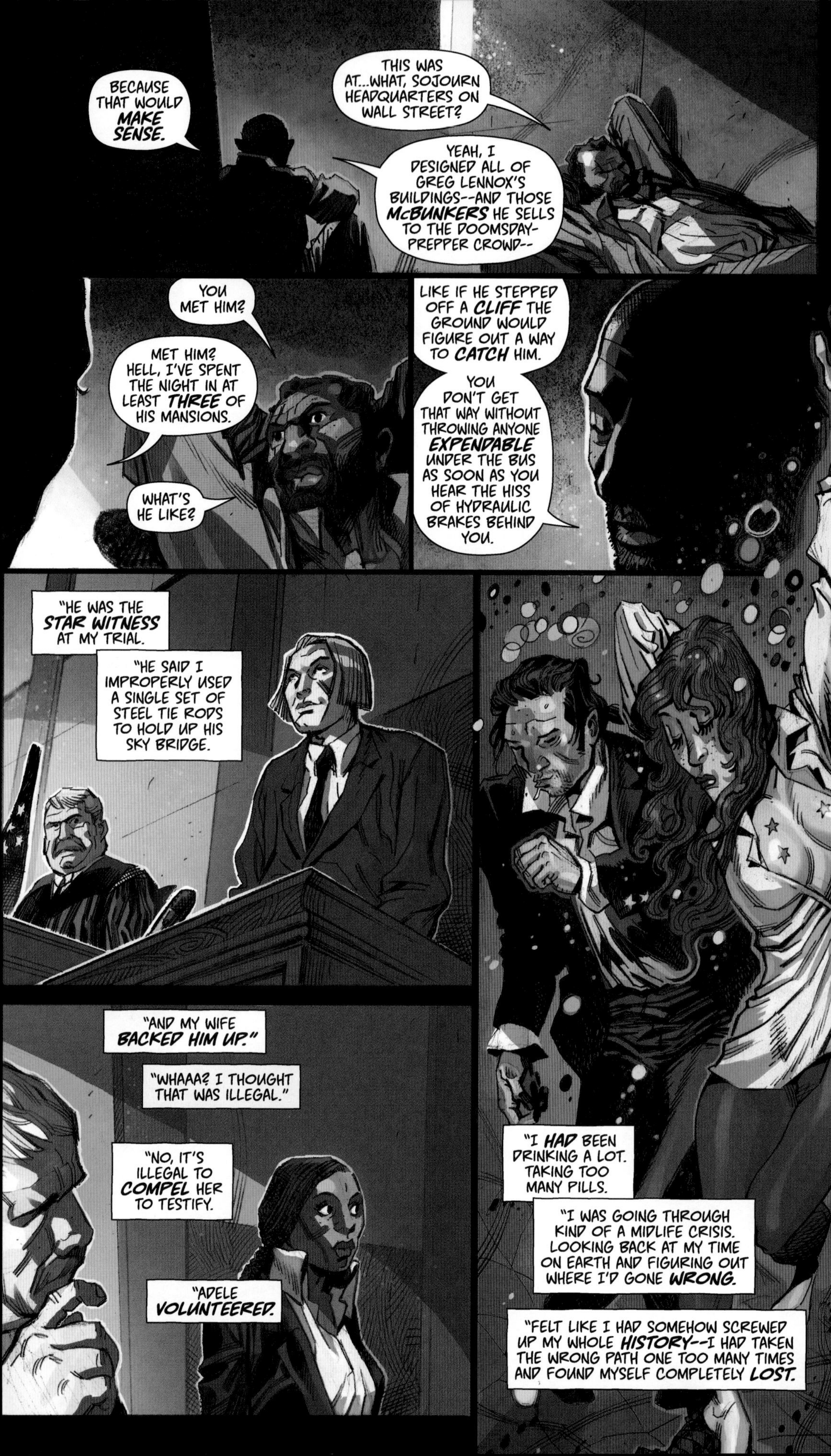
BECAUSE THAT WOULD MAKE SENSE.
THIS WAS AT...WHAT, SOJOURN HEADQUARTERS ON WALL STREET?
YEAH, I DESIGNED ALL OF GREG LENNOX'S BUILDINGS--AND THOSE McBUNKERS HE SELLS TO THE DOOMSDAY-PREPPER CROWD--
YOU MET HIM?
MET HIM? HELL, I'VE SPENT THE NIGHT IN AT LEAST THREE OF HIS MANSIONS.
WHAT'S HE LIKE?
LIKE IF HE STEPPED OFF A CLIFF THE GROUND WOULD FIGURE OUT A WAY TO CATCH HIM.
YOU DON'T GET THAT WAY WITHOUT THROWING ANYONE EXPENDABLE UNDER THE BUS AS SOON AS YOU HEAR THE HISS OF HYDRAULIC BRAKES BEHIND YOU.
"HE WAS THE STAR WITNESS AT MY TRIAL.
"HE SAID I IMPROPERLY USED A SINGLE SET OF STEEL TIE RODS TO HOLD UP HIS SKY BRIDGE.
"AND MY WIFE BACKED HIM UP."
"WHAAA? I THOUGHT THAT WAS ILLEGAL."
"NO, IT'S ILLEGAL TO COMPEL HER TO TESTIFY.
"ADELE VOLUNTEERED.
"I HAD BEEN DRINKING A LOT. TAKING TOO MANY PILLS.
"I WAS GOING THROUGH KIND OF A MIDLIFE CRISIS. LOOKING BACK AT MY TIME ON EARTH AND FIGURING OUT WHERE I'D GONE WRONG.
"FELT LIKE I HAD SOMEHOW SCREWED UP MY WHOLE HISTORY--I HAD TAKEN THE WRONG PATH ONE TOO MANY TIMES AND FOUND MYSELF COMPLETELY LOST.

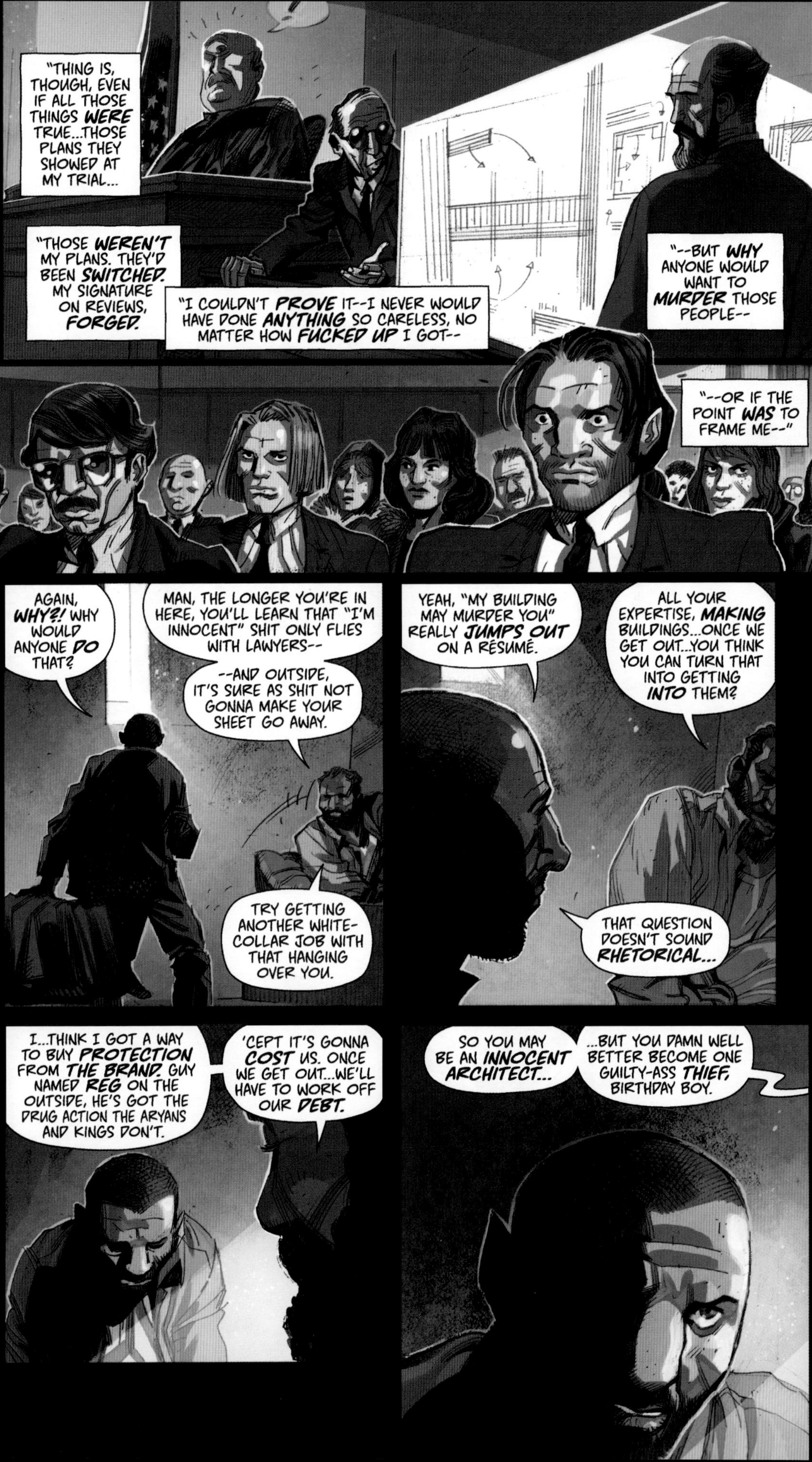
"THING IS, THOUGH, EVEN IF ALL THOSE THINGS WERE TRUE...THOSE PLANS THEY SHOWED AT MY TRIAL...
"THOSE WEREN'T MY PLANS. THEY'D BEEN SWITCHED. MY SIGNATURE ON REVIEWS, FORGED.
"I COULDN'T PROVE IT--I NEVER WOULD HAVE DONE ANYTHING SO CARELESS, NO MATTER HOW FUCKED UP I GOT--
"--BUT WHY ANYONE WOULD WANT TO MURDER THOSE PEOPLE--
"--OR IF THE POINT WAS TO FRAME ME--"
AGAIN, WHY?! WHY WOULD ANYONE DO THAT?
MAN, THE LONGER YOU'RE IN HERE, YOU'LL LEARN THAT "I'M INNOCENT" SHIT ONLY FLIES WITH LAWYERS--
--AND OUTSIDE, IT'S SURE AS SHIT NOT GONNA MAKE YOUR SHEET GO AWAY.
TRY GETTING ANOTHER WHITE-COLLAR JOB WITH THAT HANGING OVER YOU.
YEAH, "MY BUILDING MAY MURDER YOU" REALLY JUMPS OUT ON A RÉSUMÉ.
ALL YOUR EXPERTISE, MAKING BUILDINGS...ONCE WE GET OUT...YOU THINK YOU CAN TURN THAT INTO GETTING INTO THEM?
THAT QUESTION DOESN'T SOUND RHETORICAL...
I...THINK I GOT A WAY TO BUY PROTECTION FROM THE BRAND. GUY NAMED REG ON THE OUTSIDE, HE'S GOT THE DRUG ACTION THE ARYANS AND KINGS DON'T.
'CEPT IT'S GONNA COST US. ONCE WE GET OUT...WE'LL HAVE TO WORK OFF OUR DEBT.
SO YOU MAY BE AN INNOCENT ARCHITECT...
...BUT YOU DAMN WELL BETTER BECOME ONE GUILTY-ASS THIEF, BIRTHDAY BOY.

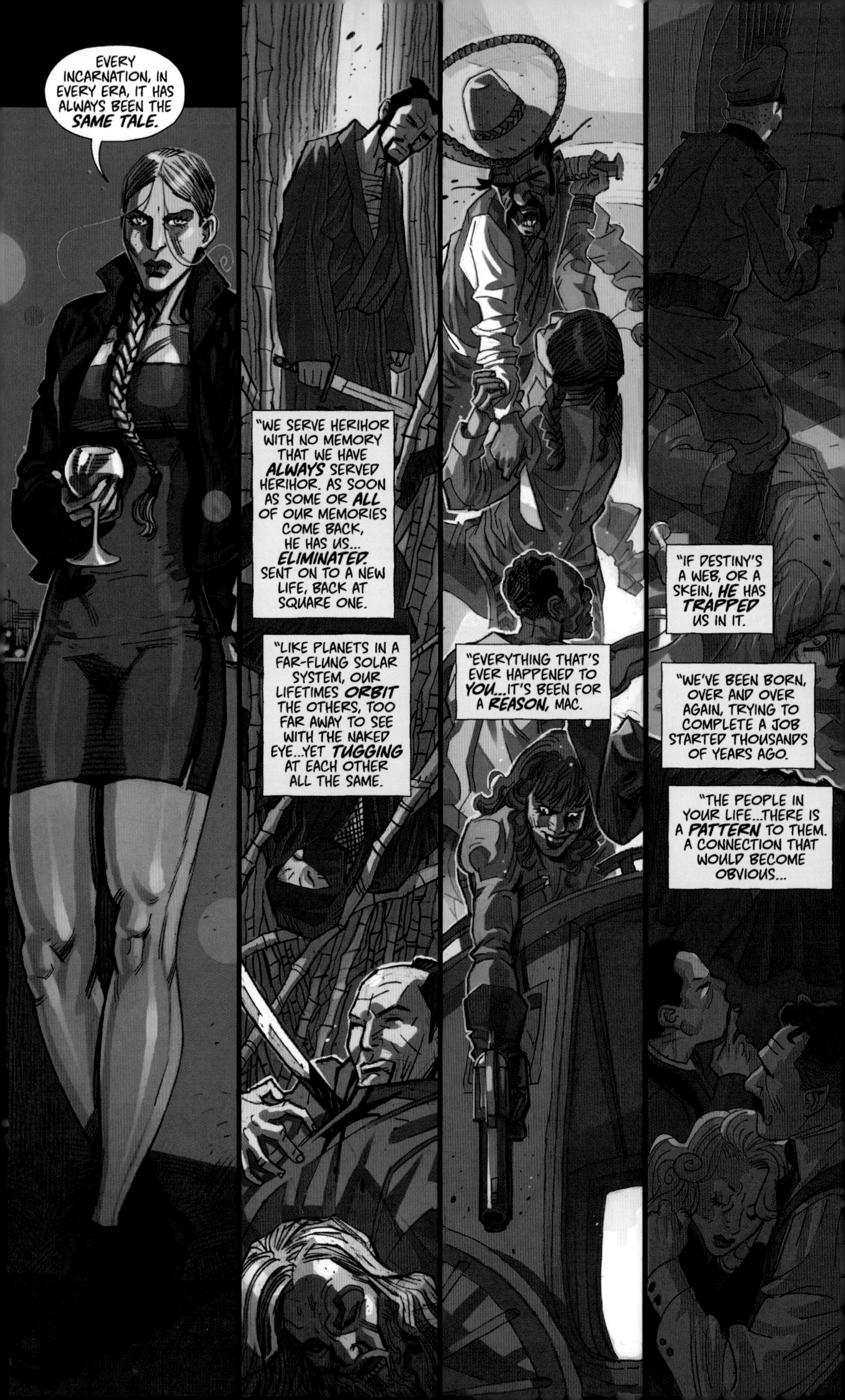
EVERY INCARNATION, IN EVERY ERA, IT HAS ALWAYS BEEN THE SAME TALE.
"WE SERVE HERIHOR WITH NO MEMORY THAT WE HAVE ALWAYS SERVED HERIHOR. AS SOON AS SOME OR ALL OF OUR MEMORIES COME BACK, HE HAS US... ELIMINATED. SENT ON TO A NEW LIFE, BACK AT SQUARE ONE.
"LIKE PLANETS IN A FAR-FLUNG SOLAR SYSTEM, OUR LIFETIMES ORBIT THE OTHERS, TOO FAR AWAY TO SEE WITH THE NAKED EYE...YET TUGGING AT EACH OTHER ALL THE SAME.
"EVERYTHING THAT'S EVER HAPPENED TO YOU...IT'S BEEN FOR A REASON, MAC.
"IF DESTINY'S A WEB, OR A SKEIN, HE HAS TRAPPED US IN IT.
"WE'VE BEEN BORN, OVER AND OVER AGAIN, TRYING TO COMPLETE A JOB STARTED THOUSANDS OF YEARS AGO.
"THE PEOPLE IN YOUR LIFE...THERE IS A PATTERN TO THEM. A CONNECTION THAT WOULD BECOME OBVIOUS...

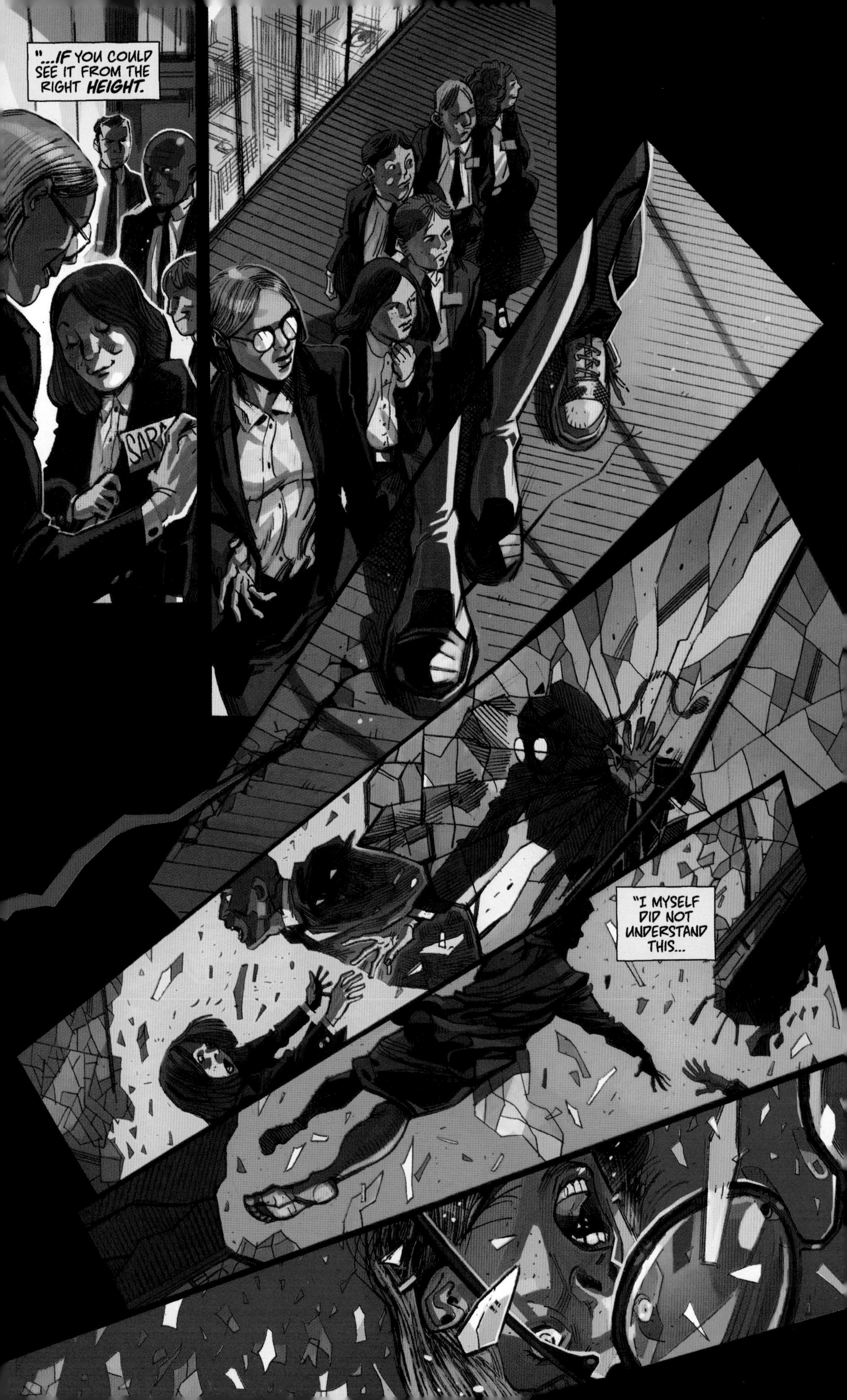
"...IF YOU COULD SEE IT FROM THE RIGHT HEIGHT.
SARA
"I MYSELF DID NOT UNDERSTAND THIS...

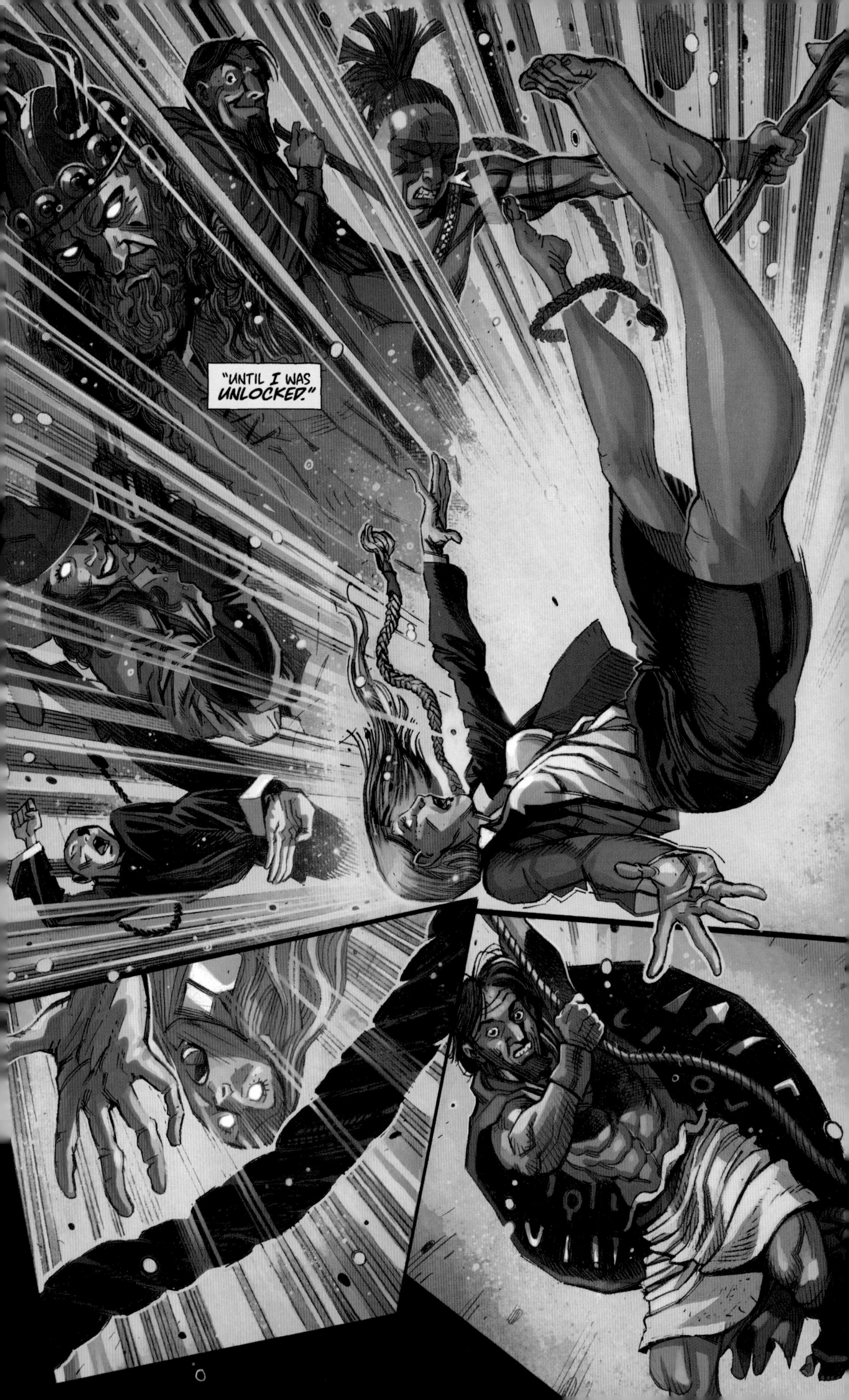
"UNTIL I WAS UNLOCKED."

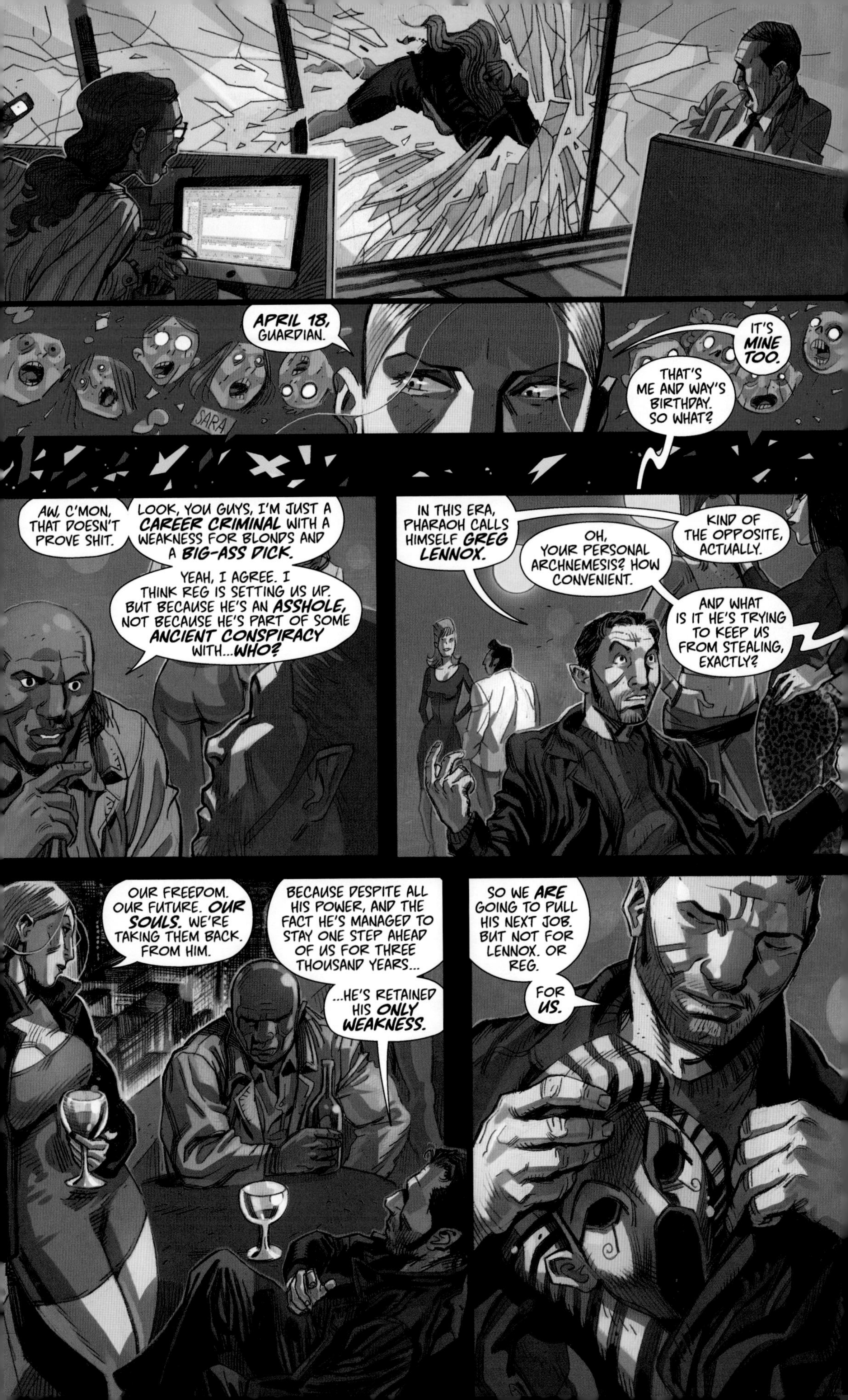
SARA
APRIL 18, GUARDIAN.
THAT'S ME AND WAY'S BIRTHDAY. SO WHAT?
IT'S MINE TOO.
AW, C'MON, THAT DOESN'T PROVE SHIT.
LOOK, YOU GUYS, I'M JUST A CAREER CRIMINAL WITH A WEAKNESS FOR BLONDS AND A BIG-ASS DICK.
YEAH, I AGREE. I THINK REG IS SETTING US UP. BUT BECAUSE HE'S AN ASSHOLE, NOT BECAUSE HE'S PART OF SOME ANCIENT CONSPIRACY WITH...WHO?
IN THIS ERA, PHARAOH CALLS HIMSELF GREG LENNOX.
OH, YOUR PERSONAL ARCHNEMESIS? HOW CONVENIENT.
KIND OF THE OPPOSITE, ACTUALLY.
AND WHAT IS IT HE'S TRYING TO KEEP US FROM STEALING, EXACTLY?
OUR FREEDOM. OUR FUTURE. OUR SOULS. WE'RE TAKING THEM BACK. FROM HIM.
BECAUSE DESPITE ALL HIS POWER, AND THE FACT HE'S MANAGED TO STAY ONE STEP AHEAD OF US FOR THREE THOUSAND YEARS...
...HE'S RETAINED HIS ONLY WEAKNESS.
SO WE ARE GOING TO PULL HIS NEXT JOB. BUT NOT FOR LENNOX. OR REG.
FOR US.

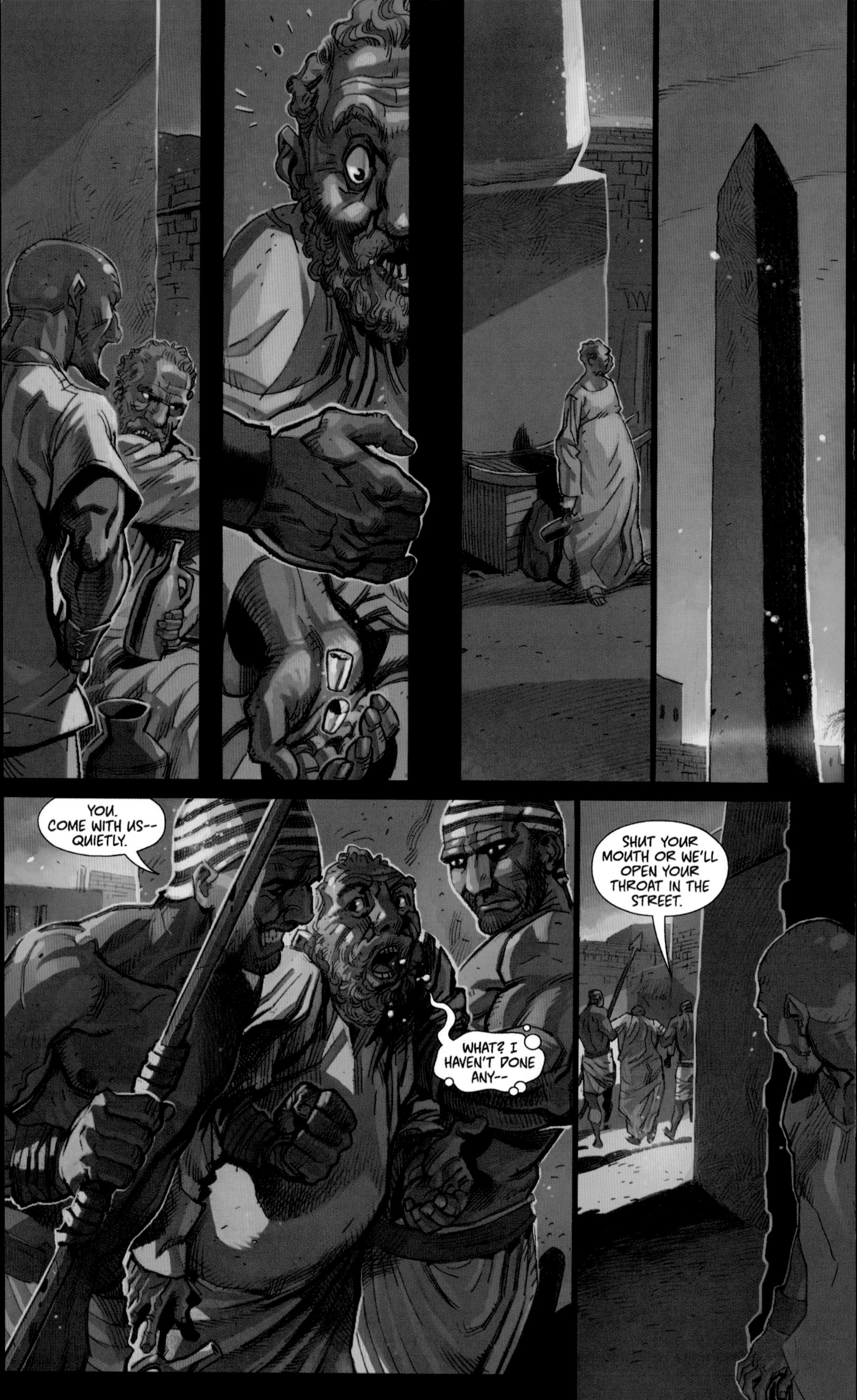
YOU. COME WITH US-- QUIETLY.
WHAT? I HAVEN'T DONE ANY--
SHUT YOUR MOUTH OR WE'LL OPEN YOUR THROAT IN THE STREET.

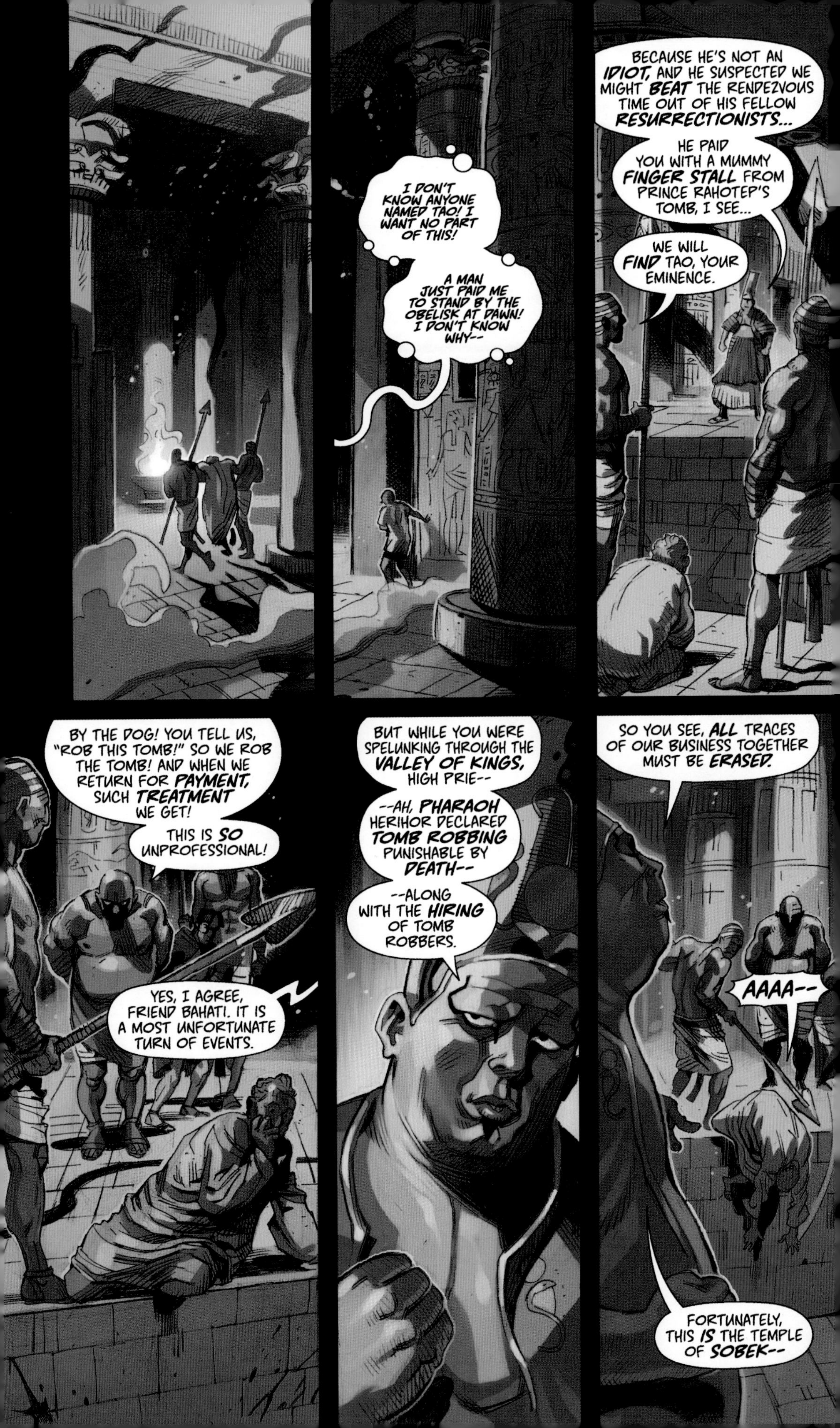

I DON'T KNOW ANYONE NAMED TAO! I WANT NO PART OF THIS!
A MAN JUST PAID ME TO STAND BY THE OBELISK AT DAWN! I DON'T KNOW WHY--
BECAUSE HE'S NOT AN IDIOT, AND HE SUSPECTED WE MIGHT BEAT THE RENDEZVOUS TIME OUT OF HIS FELLOW RESURRECTIONISTS...
HE PAID YOU WITH A MUMMY FINGER STALL FROM PRINCE RAHOTEP'S TOMB, I SEE...
WE WILL FIND TAO, YOUR EMINENCE.
BY THE DOG! YOU TELL US, "ROB THIS TOMB!" SO WE ROB THE TOMB! AND WHEN WE RETURN FOR PAYMENT, SUCH TREATMENT WE GET!
THIS IS SO UNPROFESSIONAL!
YES, I AGREE, FRIEND BAHATI. IT IS A MOST UNFORTUNATE TURN OF EVENTS.
BUT WHILE YOU WERE SPELUNKING THROUGH THE VALLEY OF KINGS, HIGH PRIE--
--AH, PHARAOH HERIHOR DECLARED TOMB ROBBING PUNISHABLE BY DEATH--
--ALONG WITH THE HIRING OF TOMB ROBBERS.
SO YOU SEE, ALL TRACES OF OUR BUSINESS TOGETHER MUST BE ERASED.
AAAA--
FORTUNATELY, THIS IS THE TEMPLE OF SOBEK--

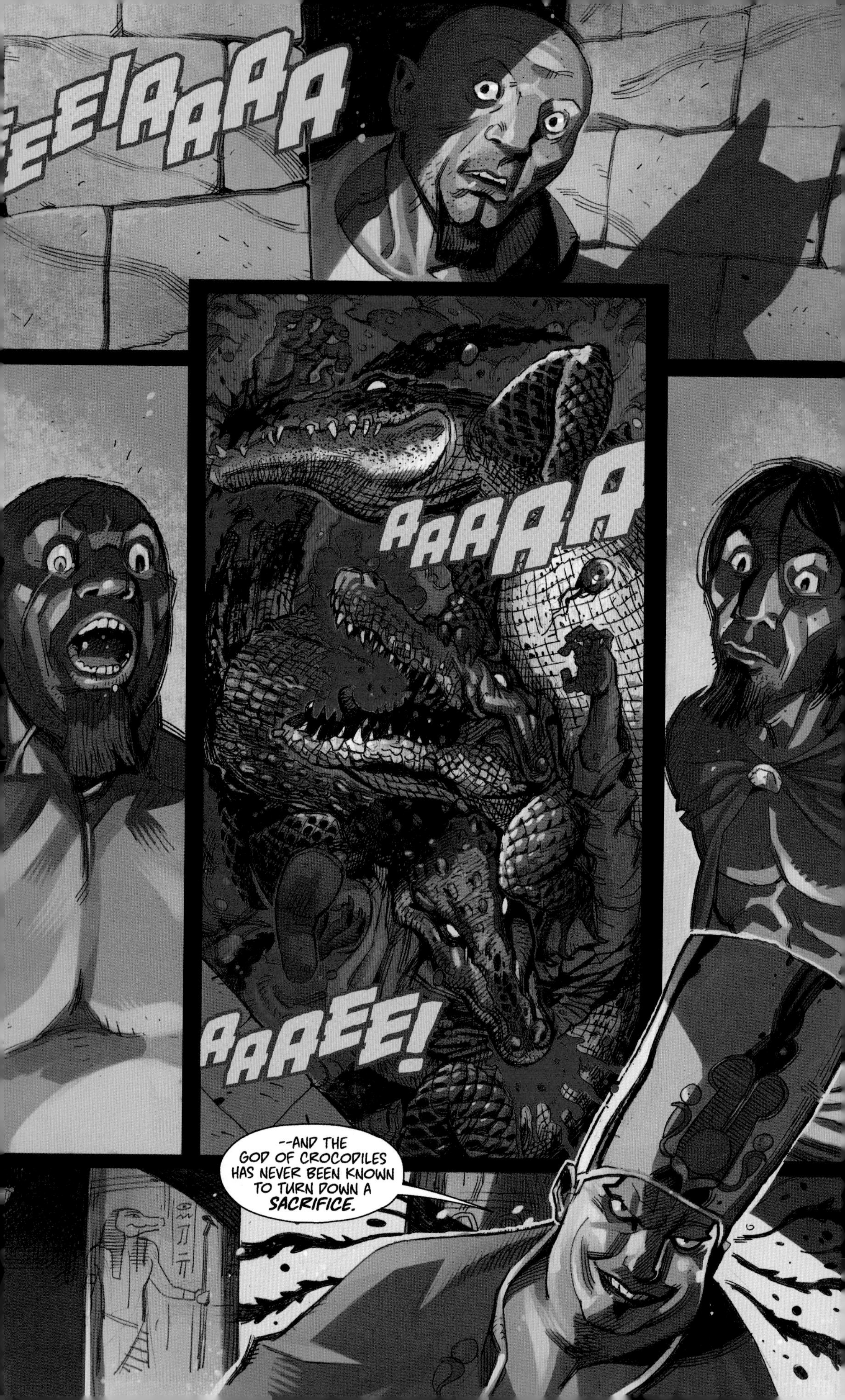
EEIAAAAA
AAAAAA
AAAEE!
--AND THE GOD OF CROCODILES HAS NEVER BEEN KNOWN TO TURN DOWN A SACRIFICE.

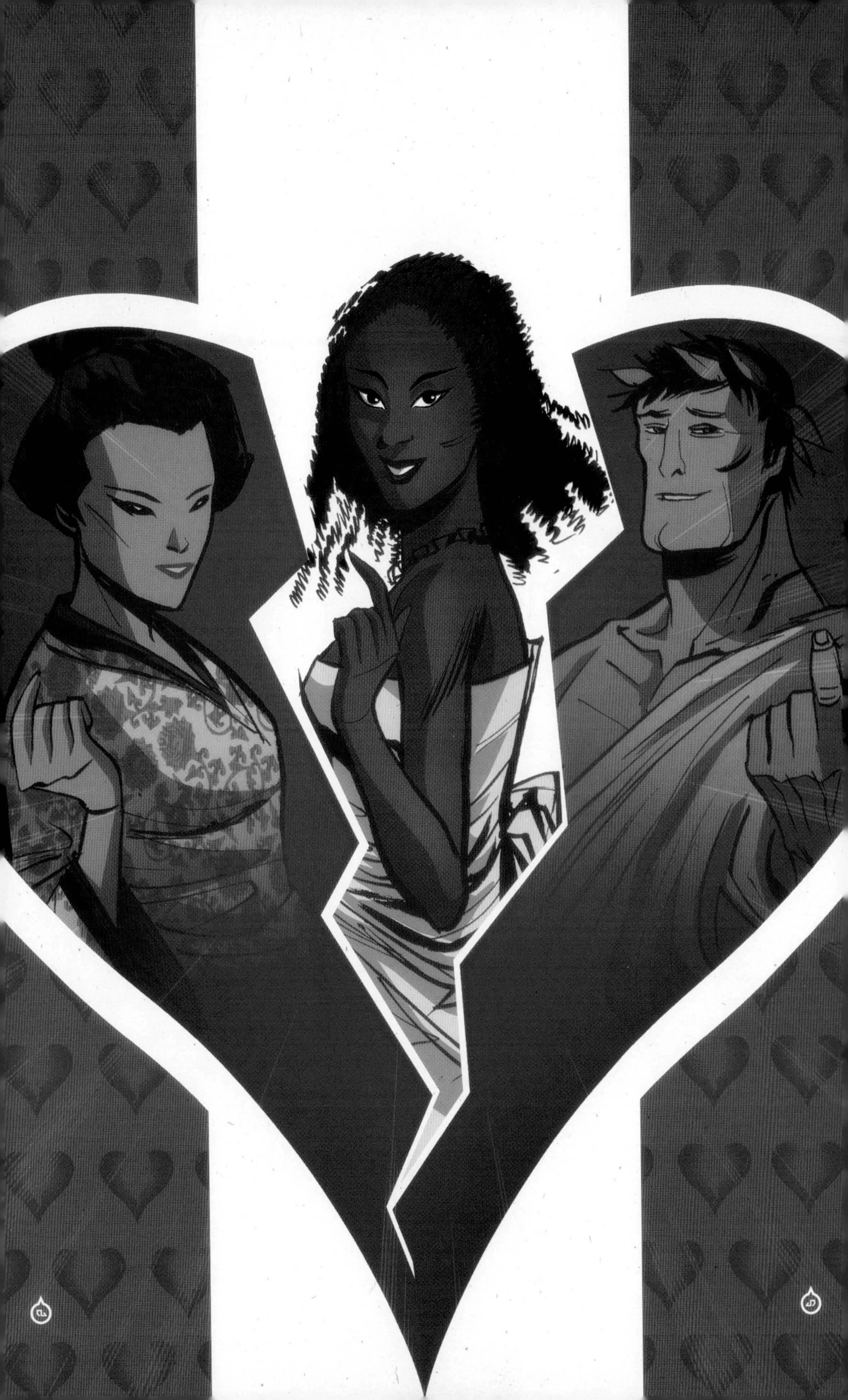

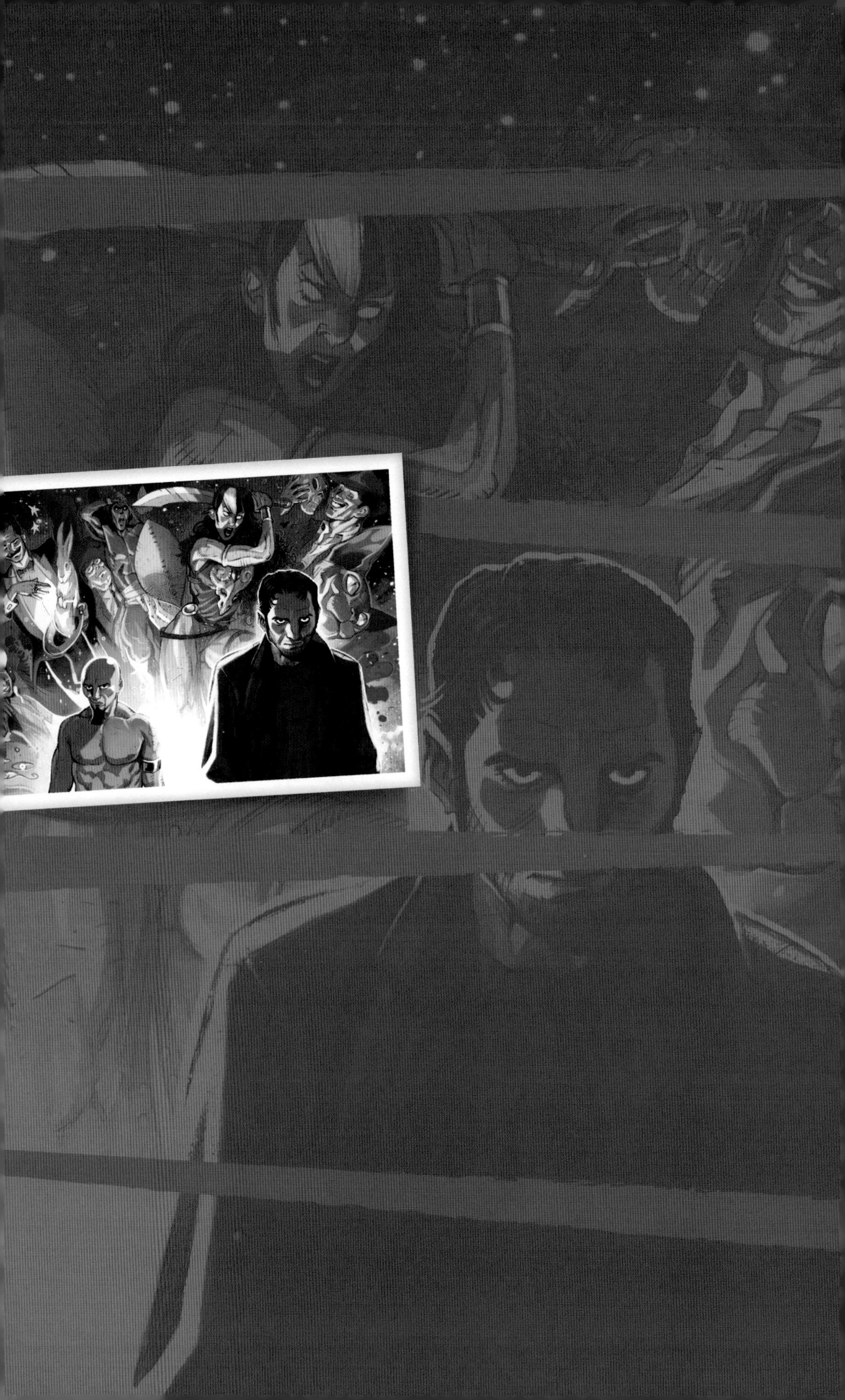

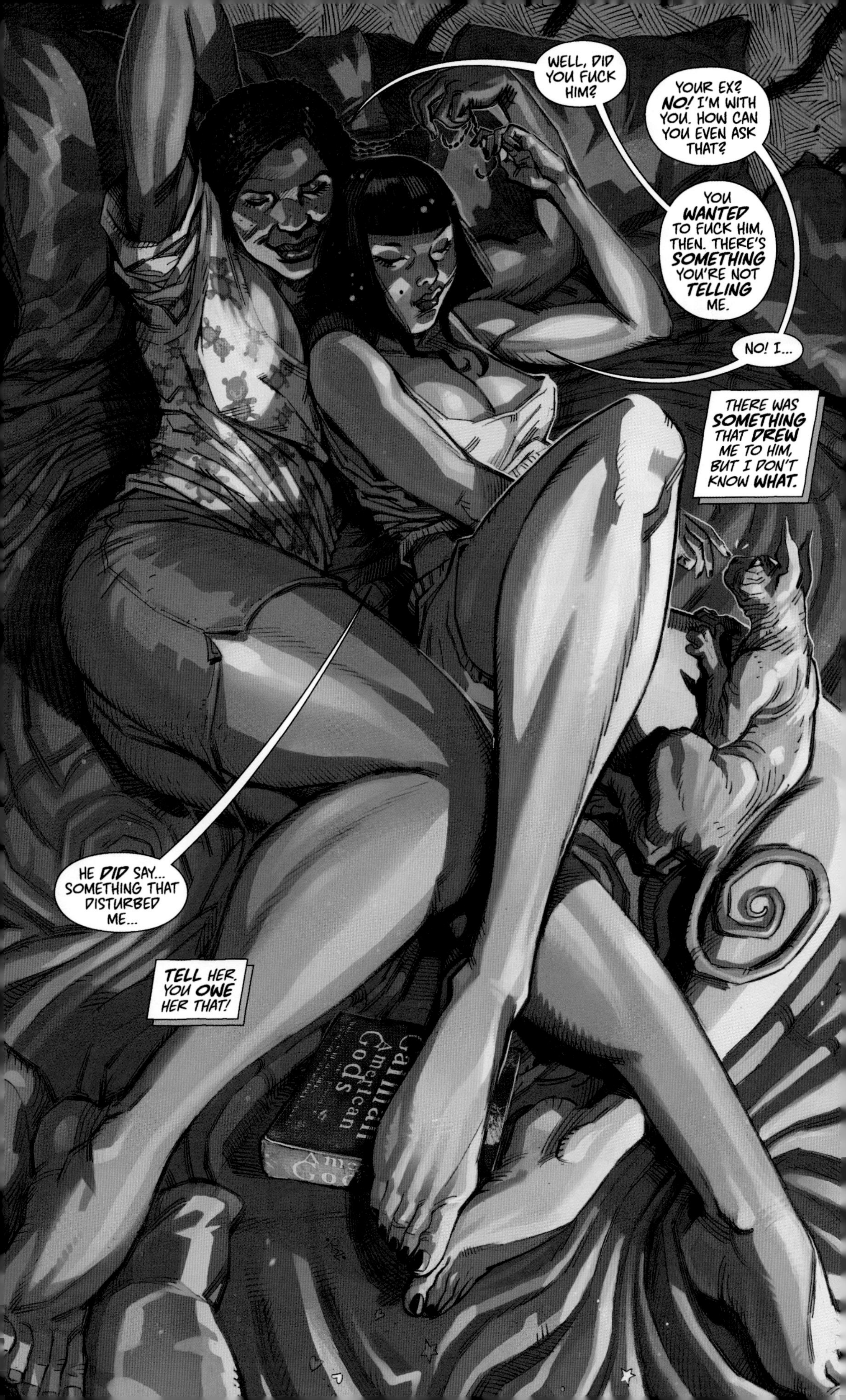
WELL, DID YOU FUCK HIM?
YOUR EX? NO! I'M WITH YOU. HOW CAN YOU EVEN ASK THAT?
YOU WANTED TO FUCK HIM, THEN. THERE'S SOMETHING YOU'RE NOT TELLING ME.
NO! I...
THERE WAS SOMETHING THAT DREW ME TO HIM, BUT I DON'T KNOW WHAT.
HE DID SAY... SOMETHING THAT DISTURBED ME...
TELL HER. YOU OWE HER THAT!
American Gods

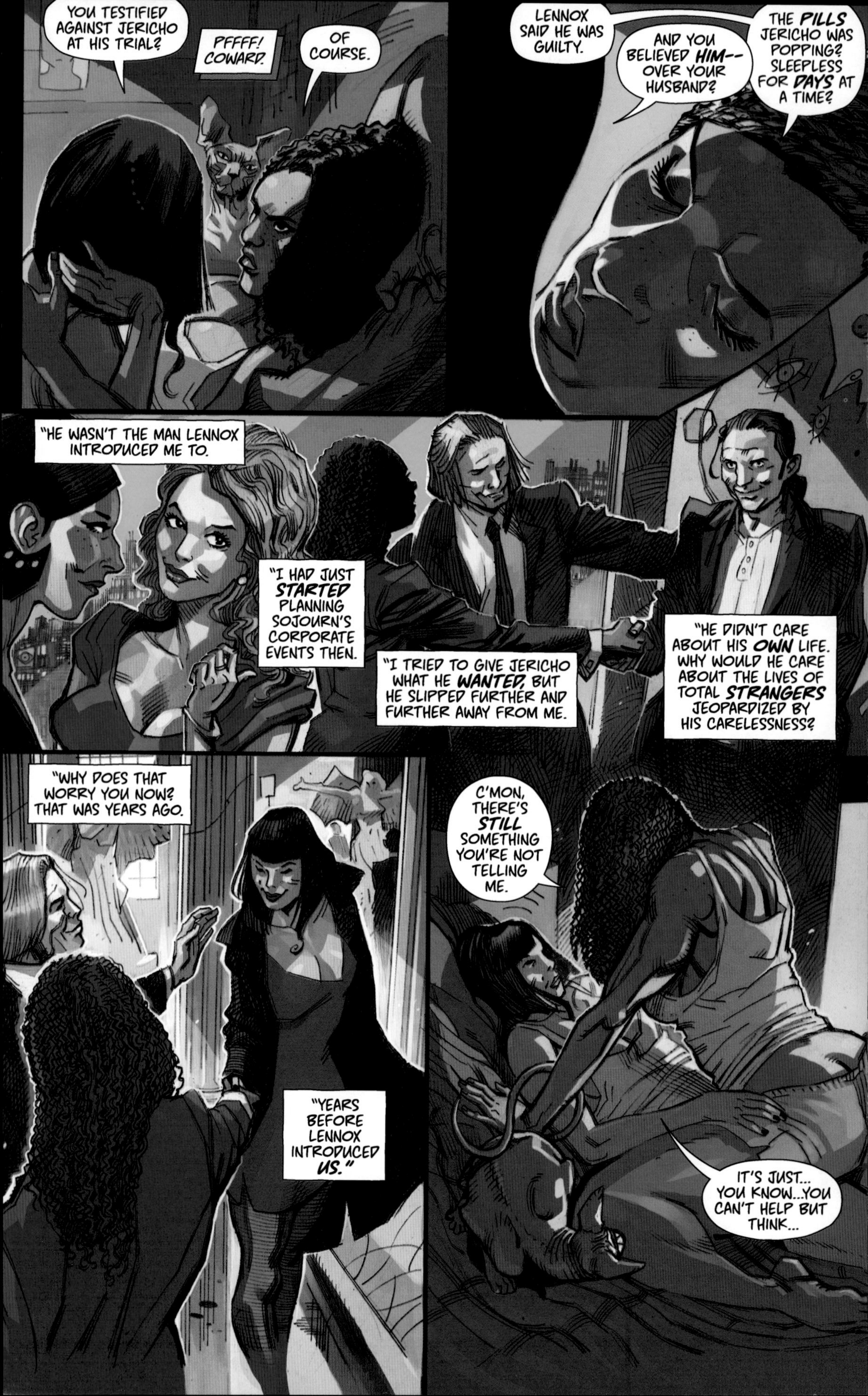
YOU TESTIFIED AGAINST JERICHO AT HIS TRIAL?
PFFFF! COWARD.
OF COURSE.
LENNOX SAID HE WAS GUILTY.
AND YOU BELIEVED HIM-- OVER YOUR HUSBAND?
THE PILLS JERICHO WAS POPPING? SLEEPLESS FOR DAYS AT A TIME?
"HE WASN'T THE MAN LENNOX INTRODUCED ME TO.
"I HAD JUST STARTED PLANNING SOJOURN'S CORPORATE EVENTS THEN.
"I TRIED TO GIVE JERICHO WHAT HE WANTED, BUT HE SLIPPED FURTHER AND FURTHER AWAY FROM ME.
"HE DIDN'T CARE ABOUT HIS OWN LIFE. WHY WOULD HE CARE ABOUT THE LIVES OF TOTAL STRANGERS JEOPARDIZED BY HIS CARELESSNESS?
"WHY DOES THAT WORRY YOU NOW? THAT WAS YEARS AGO.
"YEARS BEFORE LENNOX INTRODUCED US."
C'MON, THERE'S STILL SOMETHING YOU'RE NOT TELLING ME.
IT'S JUST... YOU KNOW...YOU CAN'T HELP BUT THINK...

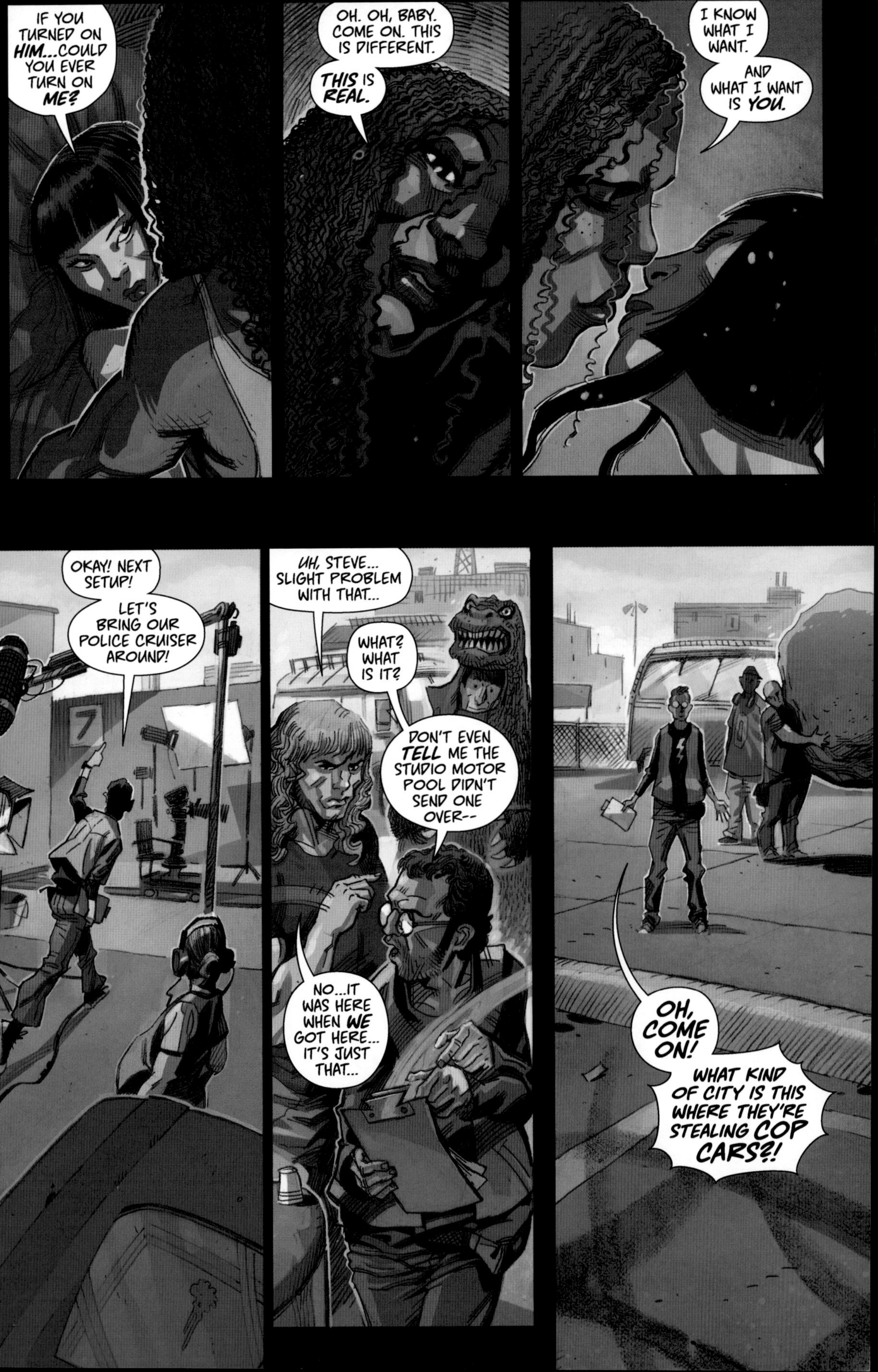
IF YOU TURNED ON HIM...COULD YOU EVER TURN ON ME?
OH. OH, BABY. COME ON. THIS IS DIFFERENT.
THIS IS REAL.
I KNOW WHAT I WANT.
AND WHAT I WANT IS YOU.
OKAY! NEXT SETUP!
LET'S BRING OUR POLICE CRUISER AROUND!
UH, STEVE... SLIGHT PROBLEM WITH THAT...
WHAT? WHAT IS IT?
DON'T EVEN TELL ME THE STUDIO MOTOR POOL DIDN'T SEND ONE OVER--
NO...IT WAS HERE WHEN WE GOT HERE... IT'S JUST THAT...
7
OH, COME ON!
WHAT KIND OF CITY IS THIS WHERE THEY'RE STEALING COP CARS?!

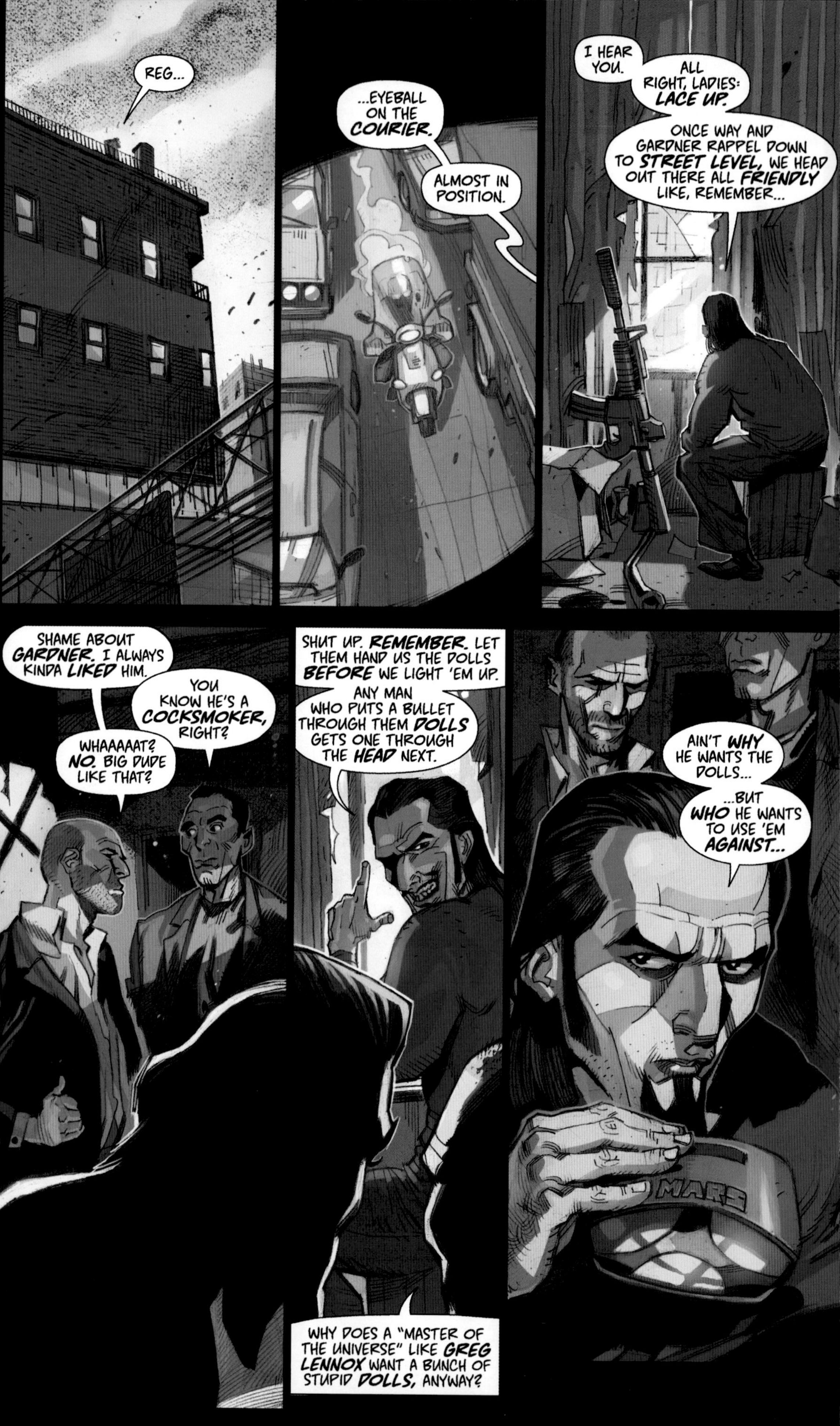
REG...
...EYEBALL ON THE COURIER.
ALMOST IN POSITION.
I HEAR YOU.
ALL RIGHT, LADIES: LACE UP.
ONCE WAY AND GARDNER RAPPEL DOWN TO STREET LEVEL, WE HEAD OUT THERE ALL FRIENDLY LIKE, REMEMBER...
SHAME ABOUT GARDNER. I ALWAYS KINDA LIKED HIM.
YOU KNOW HE'S A COCKSMOKER, RIGHT?
WHAAAAAT? NO. BIG DUDE LIKE THAT?
SHUT UP. REMEMBER. LET THEM HAND US THE DOLLS BEFORE WE LIGHT 'EM UP.
ANY MAN WHO PUTS A BULLET THROUGH THEM DOLLS GETS ONE THROUGH THE HEAD NEXT.
WHY DOES A "MASTER OF THE UNIVERSE" LIKE GREG LENNOX WANT A BUNCH OF STUPID DOLLS, ANYWAY?
AIN'T WHY HE WANTS THE DOLLS...
...BUT WHO HE WANTS TO USE 'EM AGAINST...
MARS

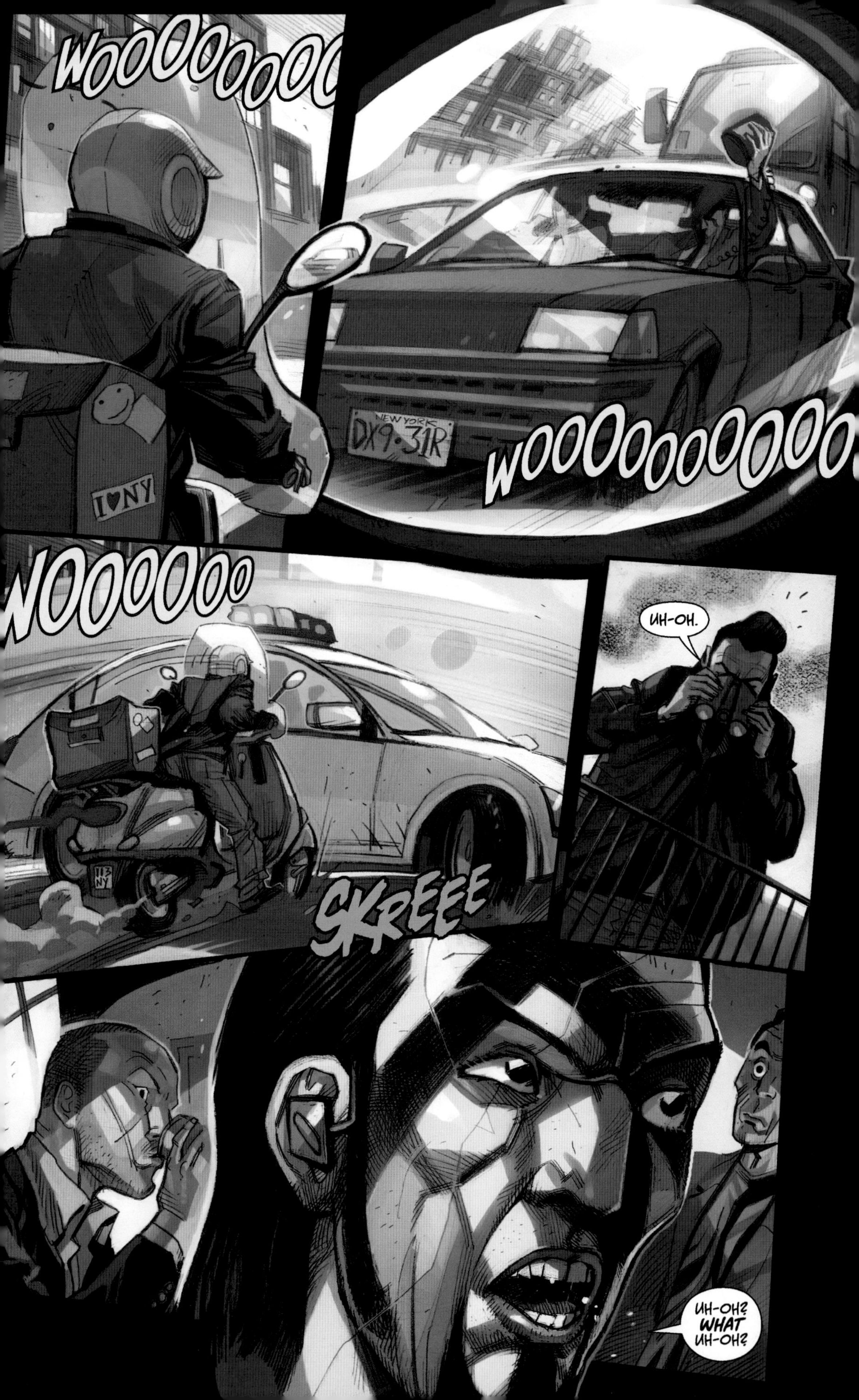
WOOOOOOOO
NEW YORK DX9·31R
WOOOOOOOOOOO
I ♥ NY
WOOOOOO
SKREEE
UH-OH.
UH-OH? WHAT UH-OH?

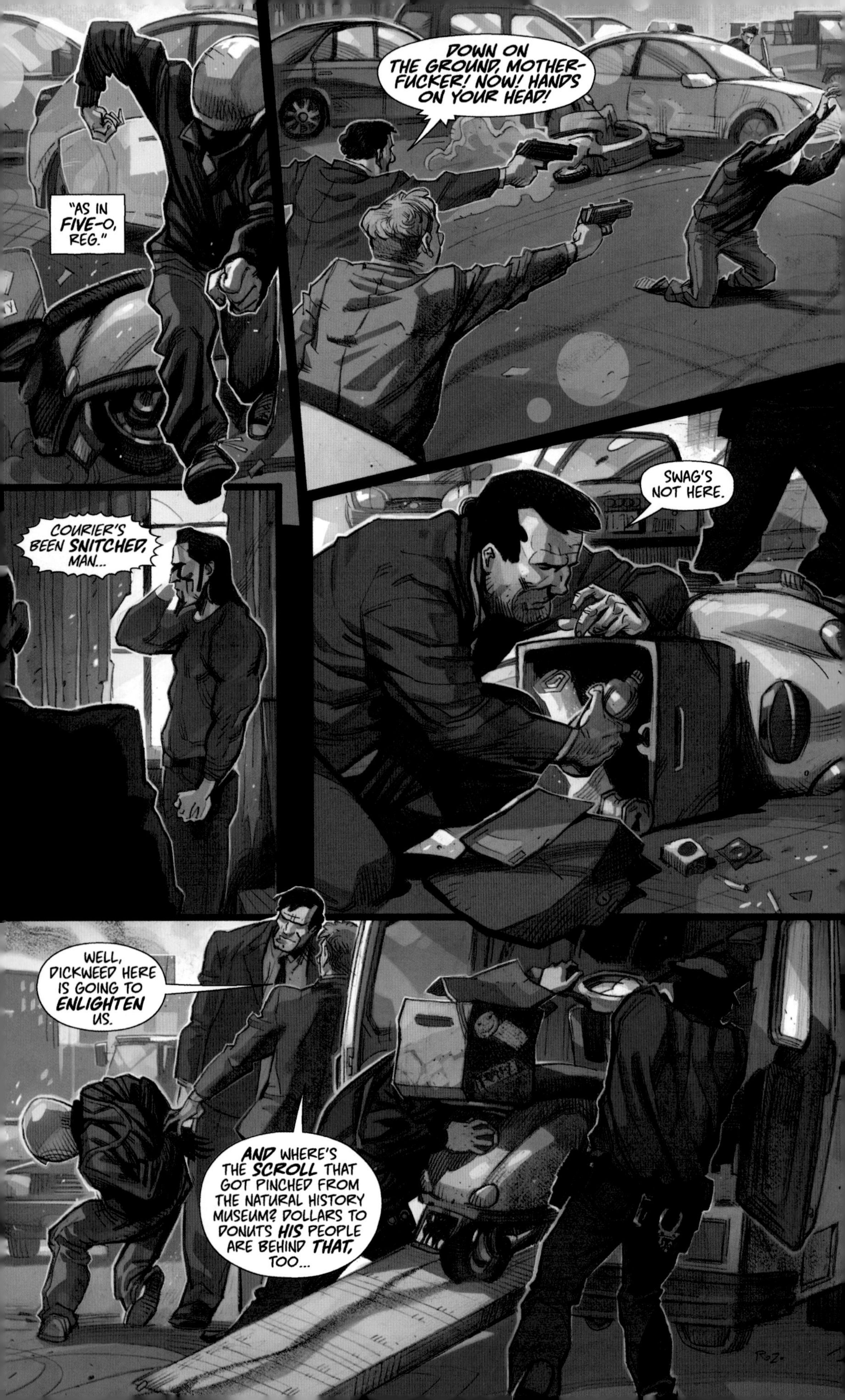
"AS IN FIVE-O, REG."
DOWN ON THE GROUND, MOTHER-FUCKER! NOW! HANDS ON YOUR HEAD!
COURIER'S BEEN SNITCHED, MAN...
SWAG'S NOT HERE.
WELL, DICKWEED HERE IS GOING TO ENLIGHTEN US.
AND WHERE'S THE SCROLL THAT GOT PINCHED FROM THE NATURAL HISTORY MUSEUM? DOLLARS TO DONUTS HIS PEOPLE ARE BEHIND THAT, TOO...

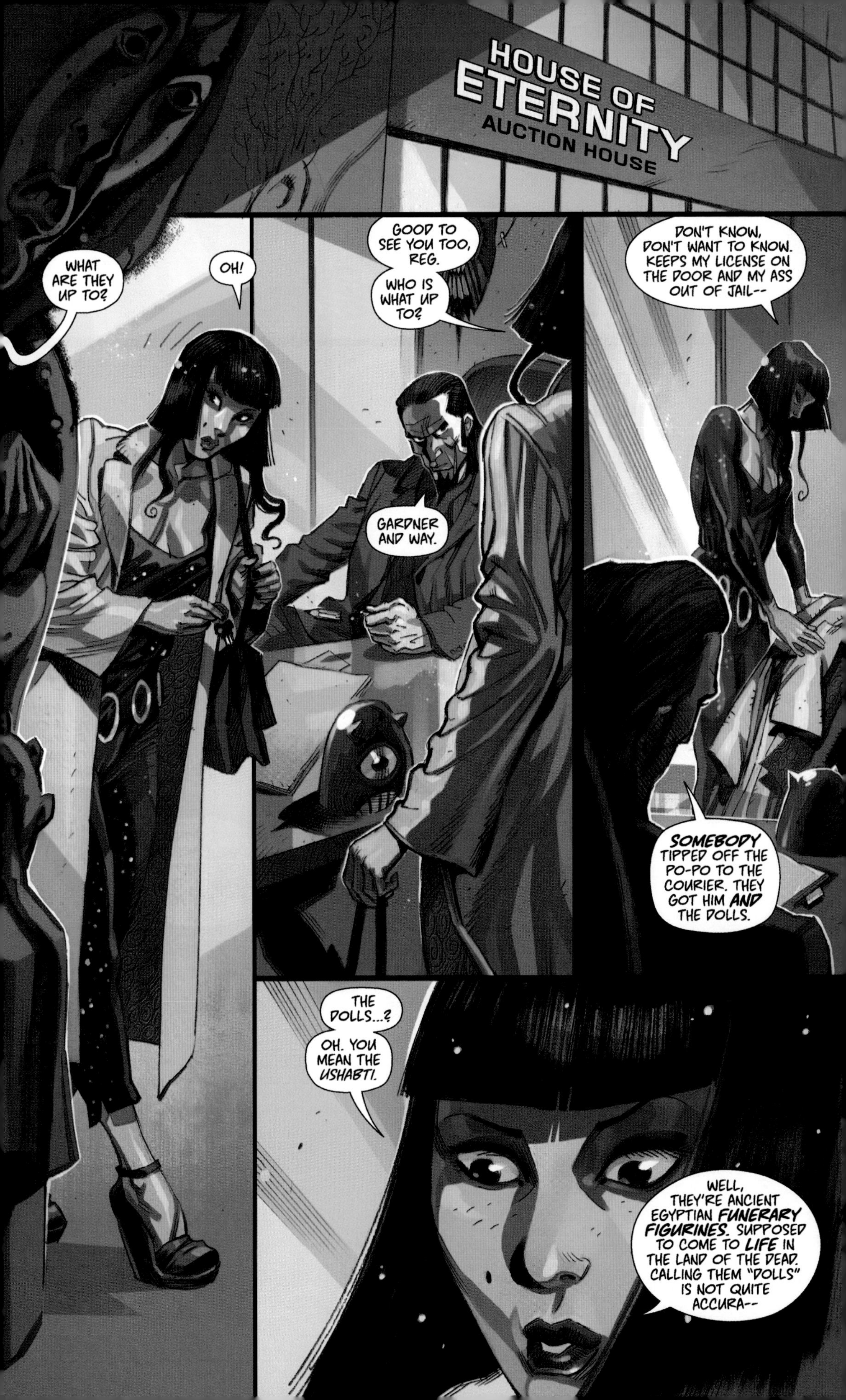
HOUSE OF ETERNITY AUCTION HOUSE
WHAT ARE THEY UP TO?
OH!
GOOD TO SEE YOU TOO, REG.
WHO IS WHAT UP TO?
GARDNER AND WAY.
DON'T KNOW, DON'T WANT TO KNOW. KEEPS MY LICENSE ON THE DOOR AND MY ASS OUT OF JAIL--
SOMEBODY TIPPED OFF THE PO-PO TO THE COURIER. THEY GOT HIM AND THE DOLLS.
THE DOLLS...?
OH. YOU MEAN THE USHABTI.
WELL, THEY'RE ANCIENT EGYPTIAN FUNERARY FIGURINES. SUPPOSED TO COME TO LIFE IN THE LAND OF THE DEAD. CALLING THEM "DOLLS" IS NOT QUITE ACCURA--

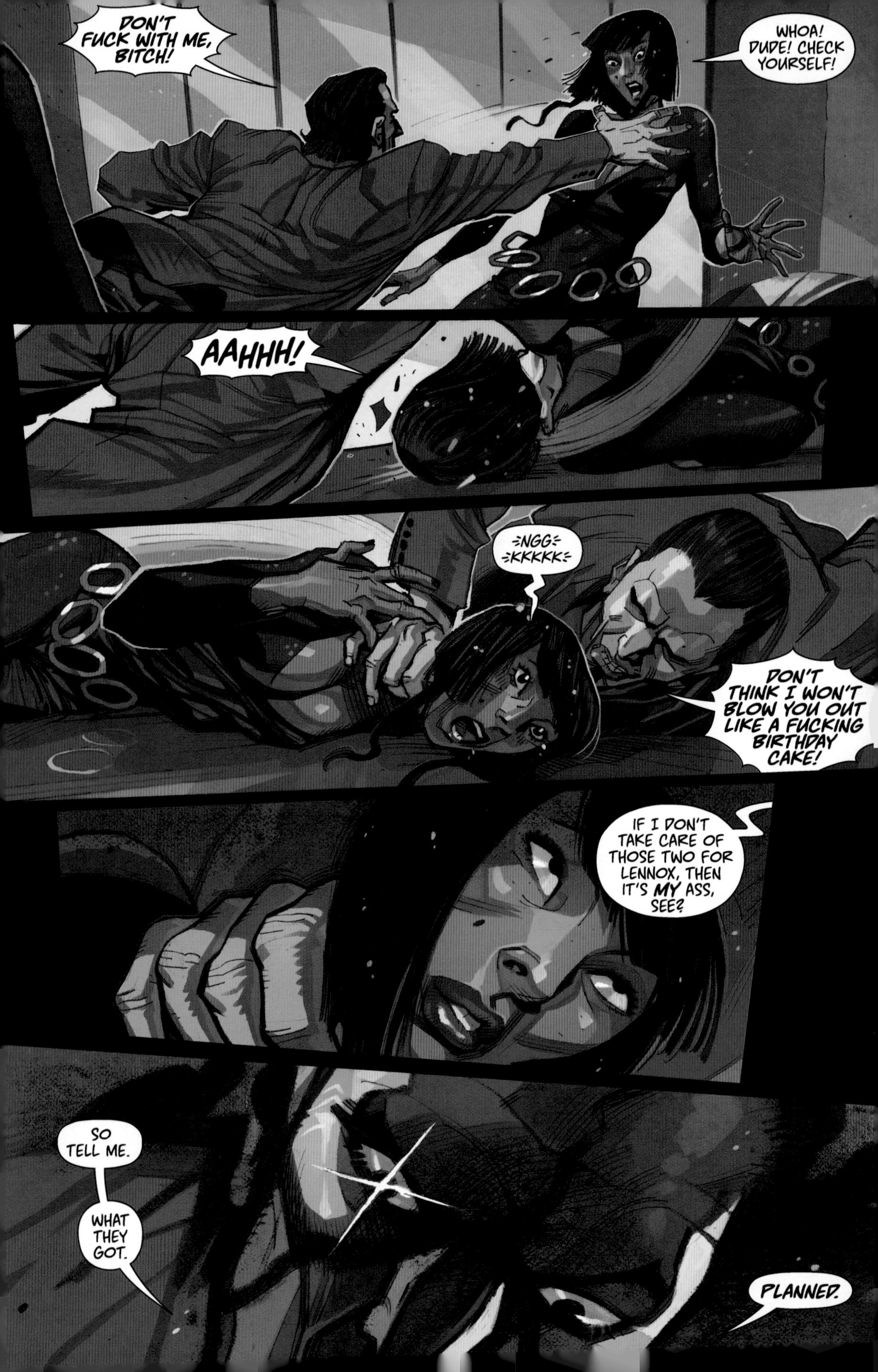
DON'T FUCK WITH ME, BITCH!
WHOA! DUDE! CHECK YOURSELF!
AAHHH!
NGG KKKKK
DON'T THINK I WON'T BLOW YOU OUT LIKE A FUCKING BIRTHDAY CAKE!
IF I DON'T TAKE CARE OF THOSE TWO FOR LENNOX, THEN IT'S MY ASS, SEE?
SO TELL ME.
WHAT THEY GOT.
PLANNED.

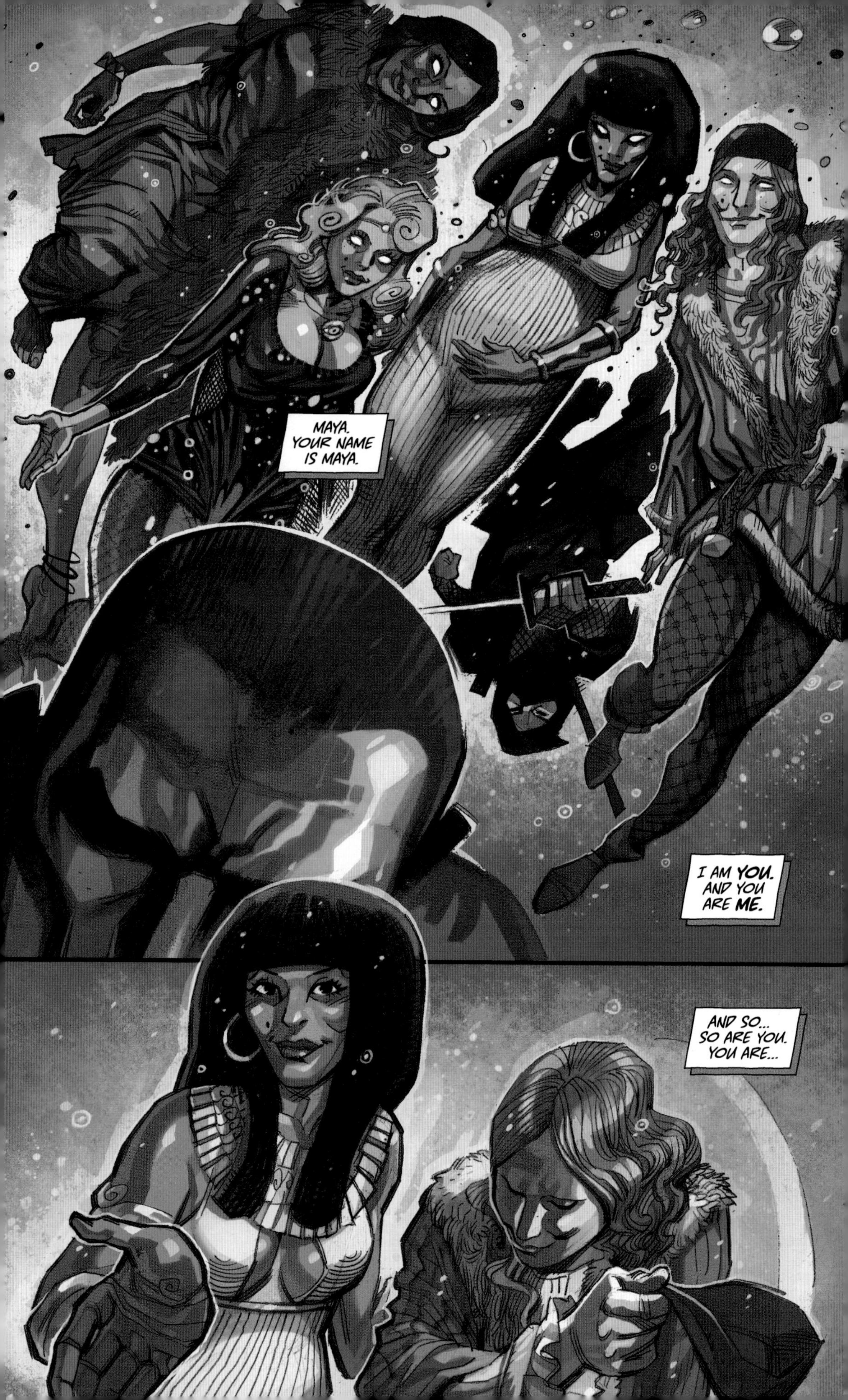
MAYA. YOUR NAME IS MAYA.
I AM YOU. AND YOU ARE ME.
AND SO... SO ARE YOU. YOU ARE...

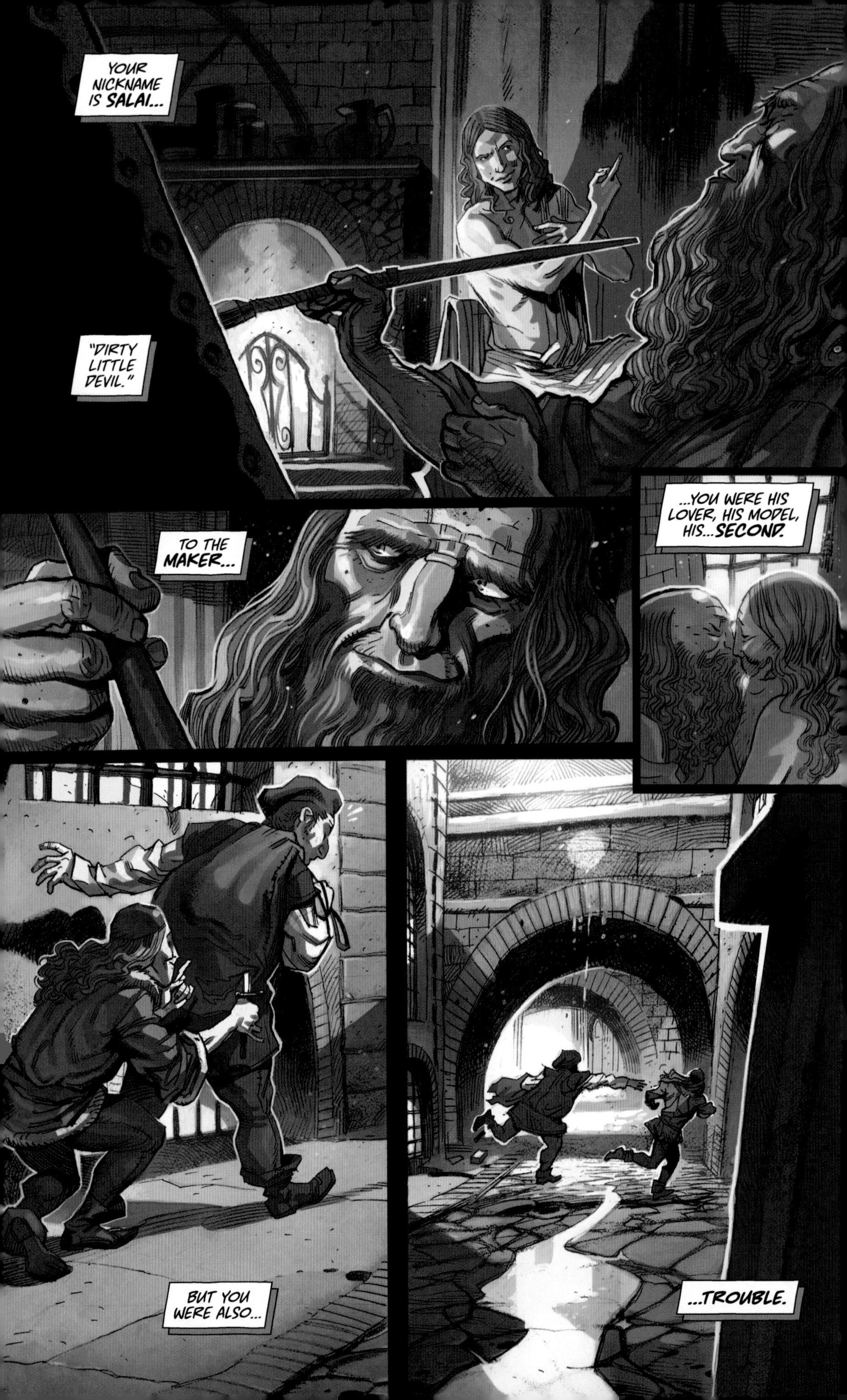
YOUR NICKNAME IS SALAI...
"DIRTY LITTLE DEVIL."
TO THE MAKER...
...YOU WERE HIS LOVER, HIS MODEL, HIS...SECOND.
BUT YOU WERE ALSO...
...TROUBLE.

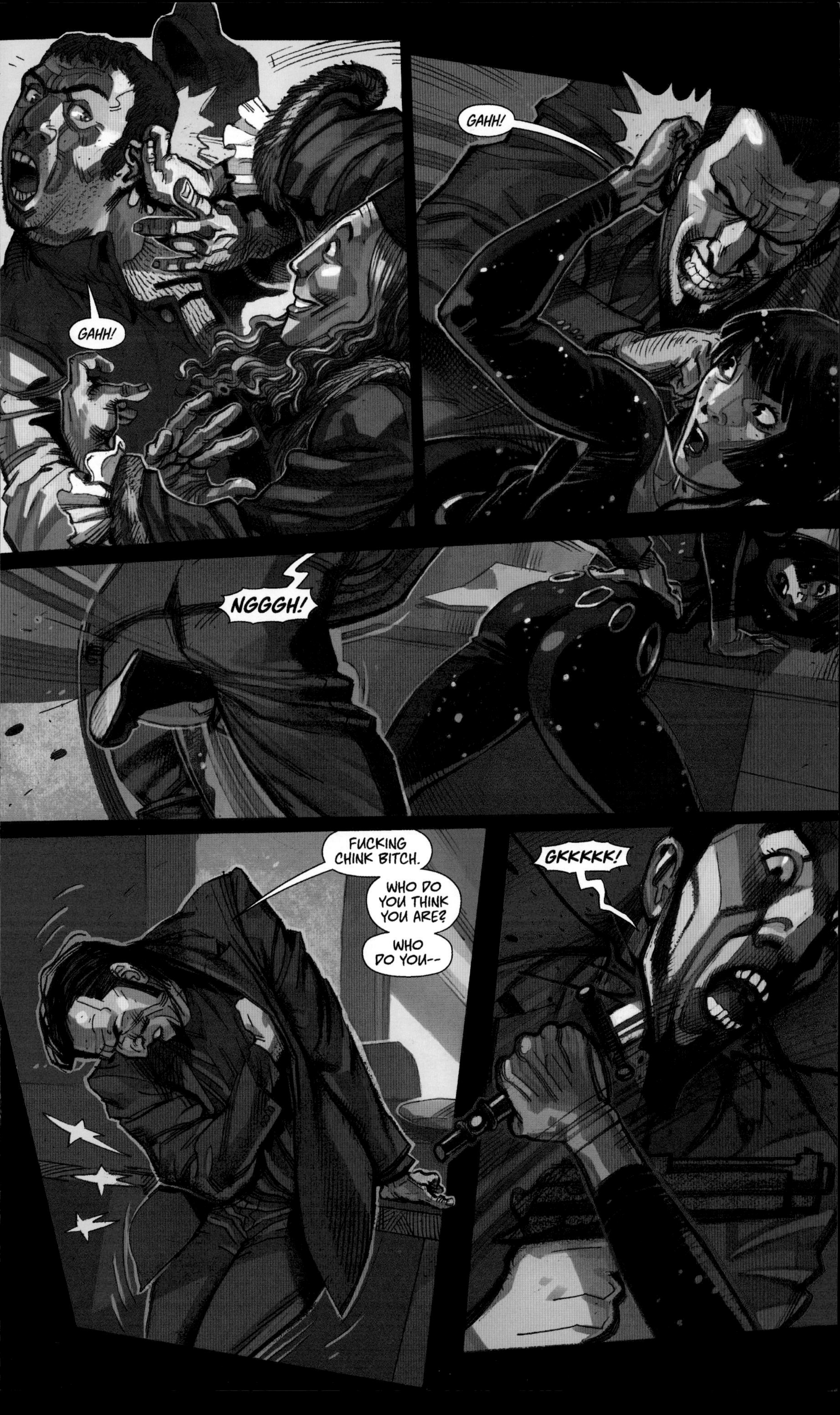
GAHH!
GAHH!
NGGGH!
FUCKING CHINK BITCH.
WHO DO YOU THINK YOU ARE?
WHO DO YOU--
GKKKKK!

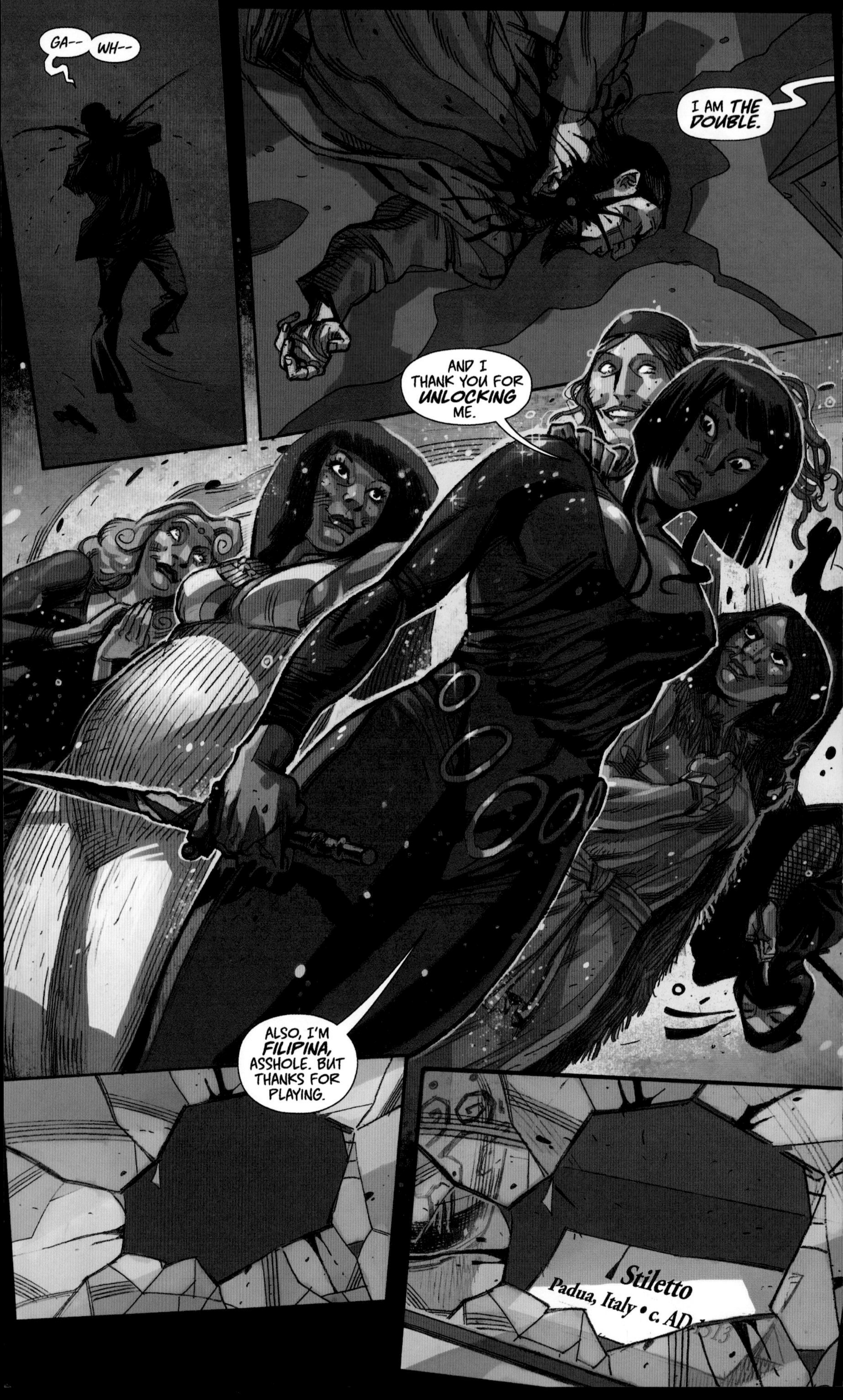
GA--
WH--
I AM THE DOUBLE.
AND I THANK YOU FOR UNLOCKING ME.
ALSO, I'M FILIPINA, ASSHOLE. BUT THANKS FOR PLAYING.
Stiletto
Padua, Italy • c. AD

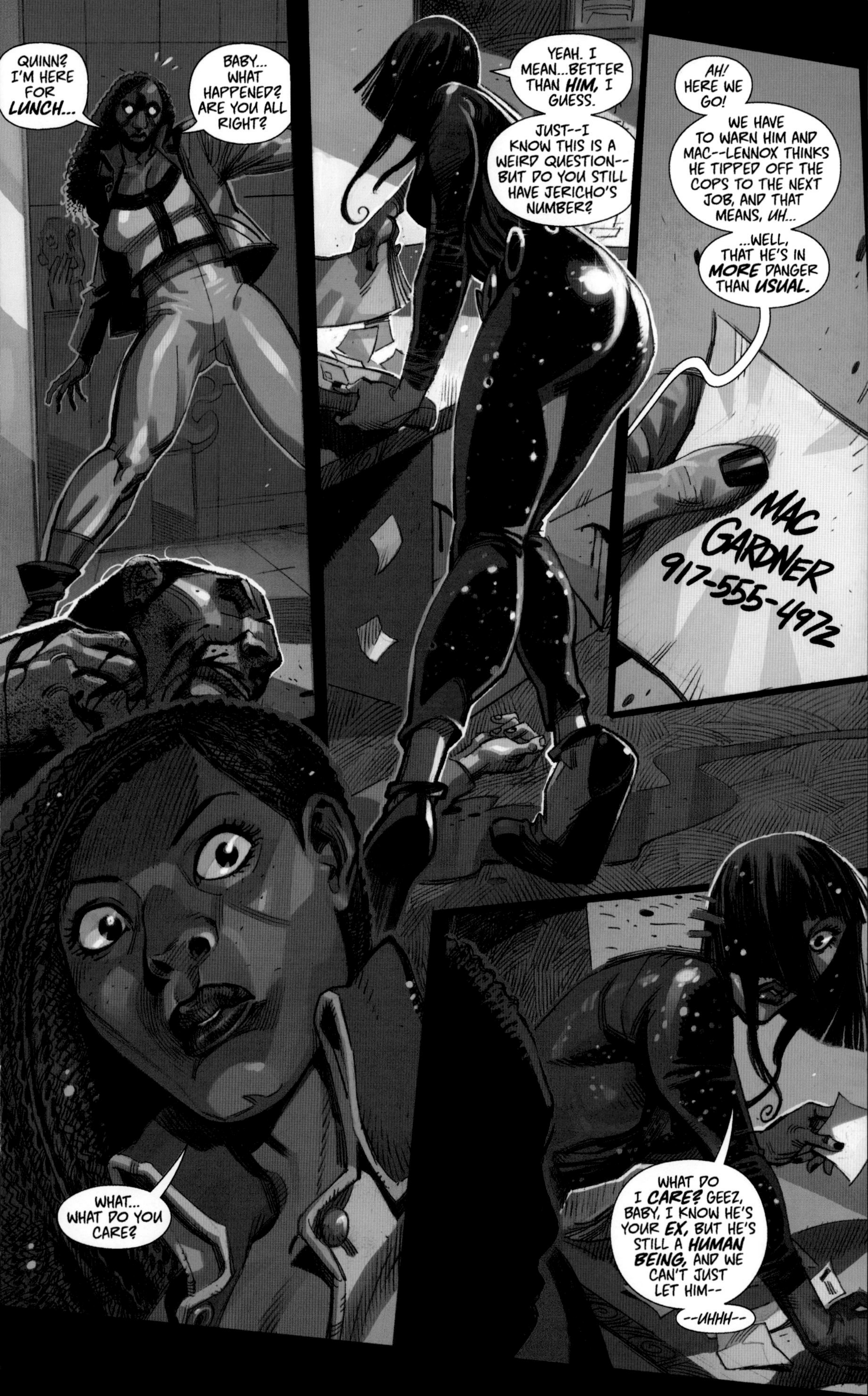
QUINN? I'M HERE FOR LUNCH...
BABY... WHAT HAPPENED? ARE YOU ALL RIGHT?
YEAH. I MEAN...BETTER THAN HIM, I GUESS.
JUST--I KNOW THIS IS A WEIRD QUESTION--BUT DO YOU STILL HAVE JERICHO'S NUMBER?
AH! HERE WE GO!
WE HAVE TO WARN HIM AND MAC--LENNOX THINKS HE TIPPED OFF THE COPS TO THE NEXT JOB, AND THAT MEANS, UH...
...WELL, THAT HE'S IN MORE DANGER THAN USUAL.
MAC GARDNER 917-555-4972
WHAT... WHAT DO YOU CARE?
WHAT DO I CARE? GEEZ, BABY, I KNOW HE'S YOUR EX, BUT HE'S STILL A HUMAN BEING, AND WE CAN'T JUST LET HIM--
--UHHH--

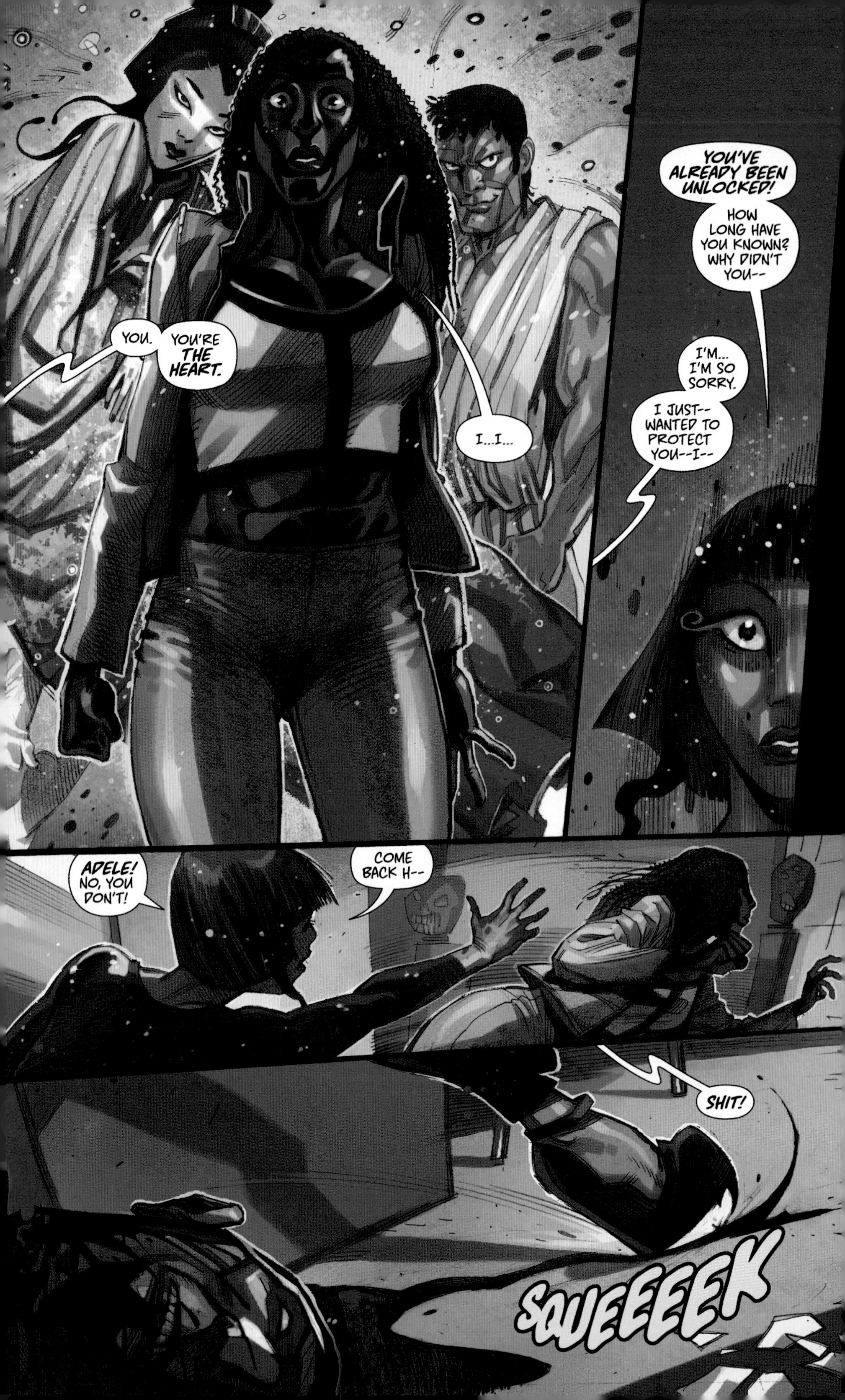
YOU.
YOU'RE THE HEART.
I...I...
YOU'VE ALREADY BEEN UNLOCKED!
HOW LONG HAVE YOU KNOWN? WHY DIDN'T YOU--
I'M... I'M SO SORRY.
I JUST-- WANTED TO PROTECT YOU--I--
ADELE! NO, YOU DON'T!
COME BACK H--
SHIT!
SQUEEEEEK

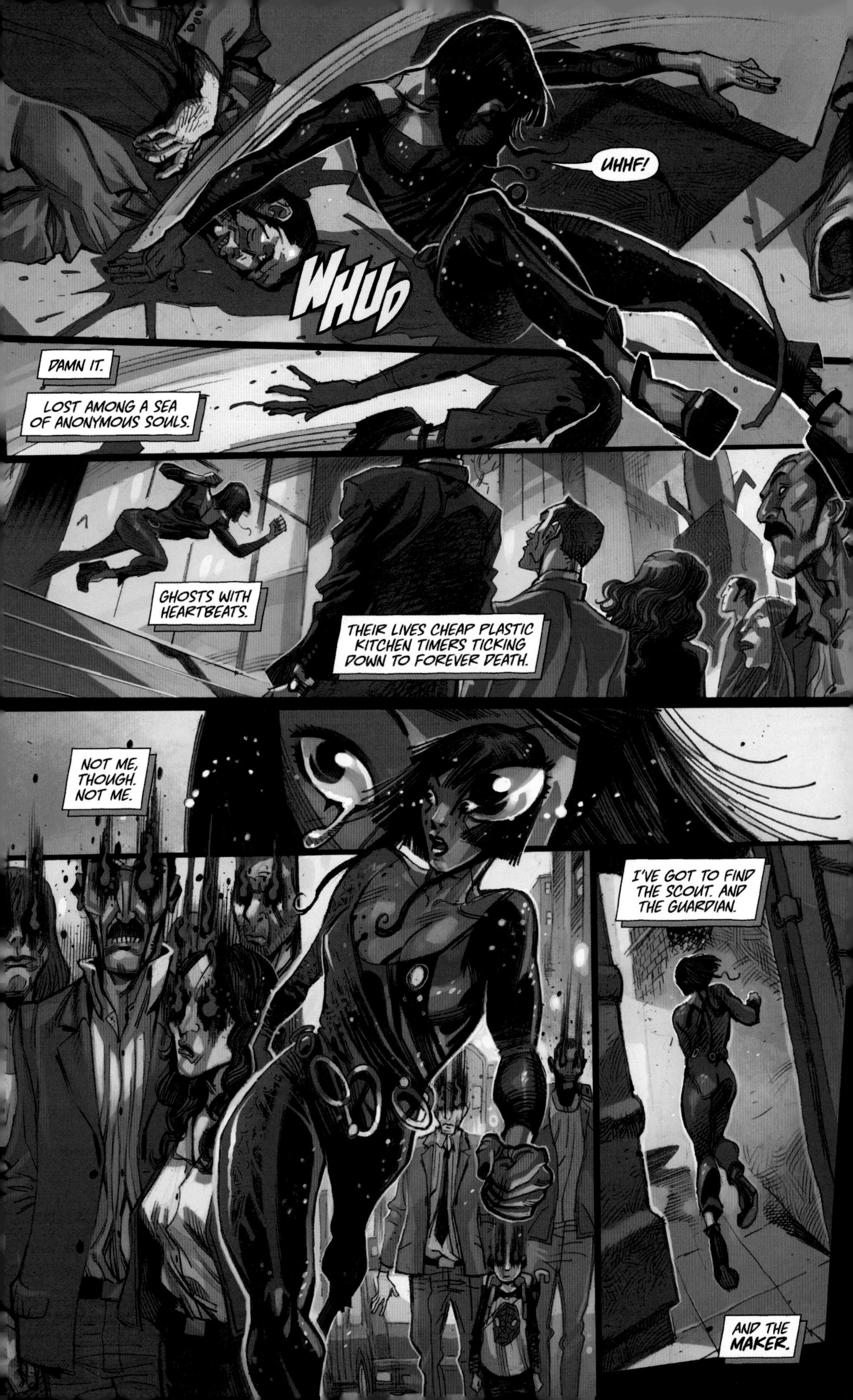
UHHF!
WHUD
DAMN IT.
LOST AMONG A SEA OF ANONYMOUS SOULS.
GHOSTS WITH HEARTBEATS.
THEIR LIVES CHEAP PLASTIC KITCHEN TIMERS TICKING DOWN TO FOREVER DEATH.
NOT ME, THOUGH. NOT ME.
I'VE GOT TO FIND THE SCOUT. AND THE GUARDIAN.
AND THE MAKER.

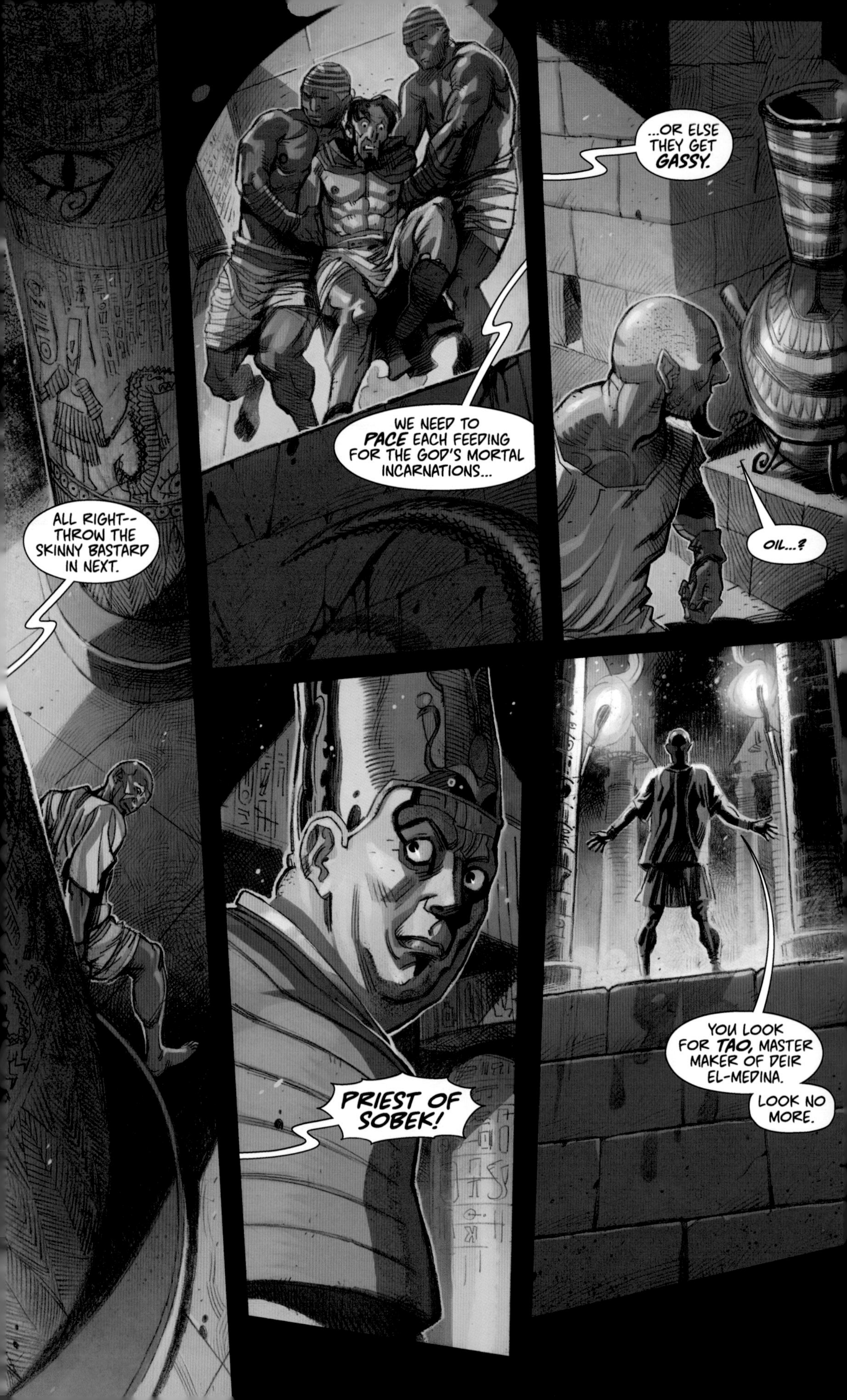
WE NEED TO PACE EACH FEEDING FOR THE GOD'S MORTAL INCARNATIONS...
...OR ELSE THEY GET GASSY.
OIL...?
ALL RIGHT-- THROW THE SKINNY BASTARD IN NEXT.
PRIEST OF SOBEK!
YOU LOOK FOR TAO, MASTER MAKER OF DEIR EL-MEDINA.
LOOK NO MORE.

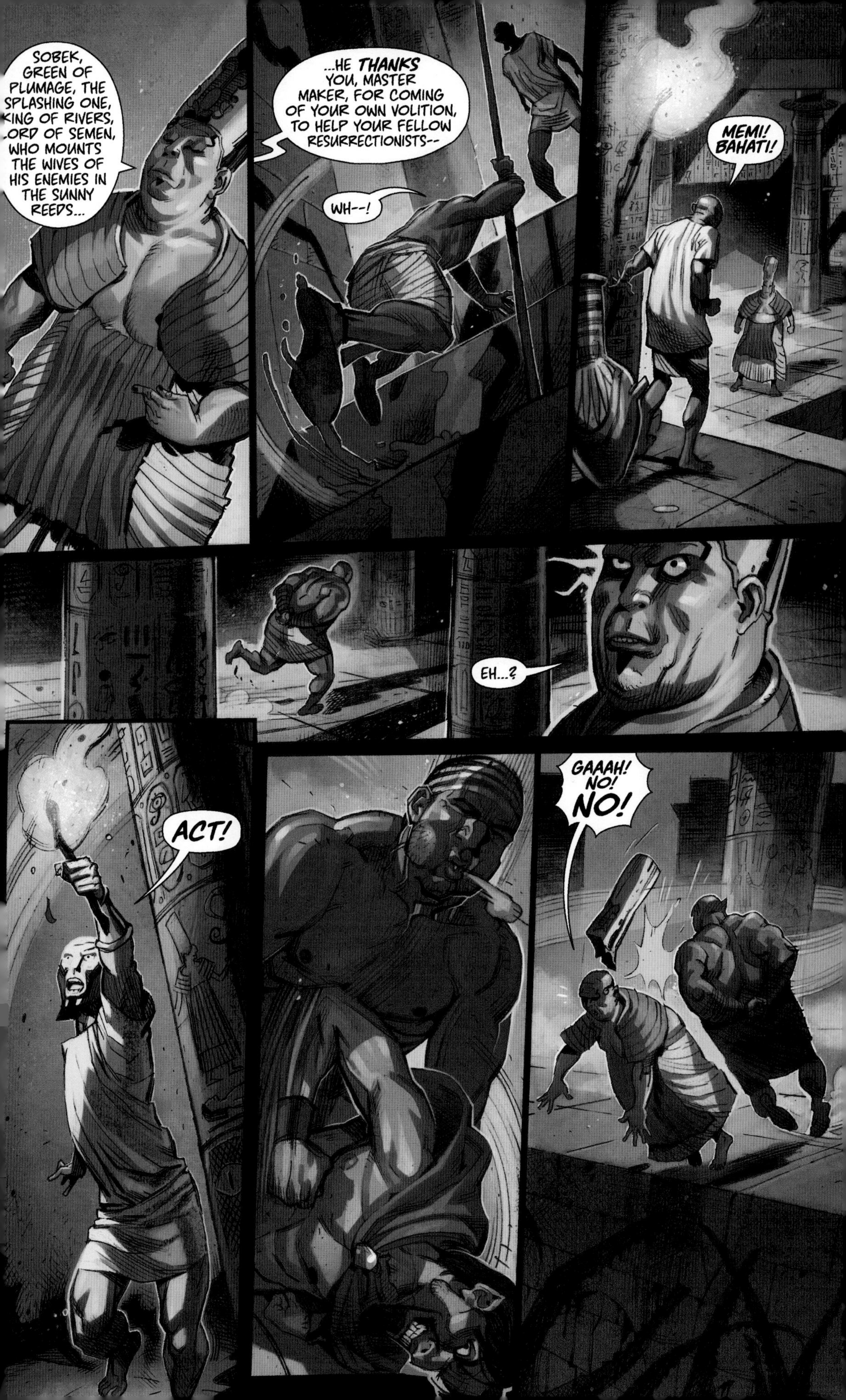
SOBEK, GREEN OF PLUMAGE, THE SPLASHING ONE, KING OF RIVERS, LORD OF SEMEN, WHO MOUNTS THE WIVES OF HIS ENEMIES IN THE SUNNY REEDS...
...HE THANKS YOU, MASTER MAKER, FOR COMING OF YOUR OWN VOLITION, TO HELP YOUR FELLOW RESURRECTIONISTS--
WH--!
MEMI! BAHATI!
EH...?
ACT!
GAAAH! NO! NO!

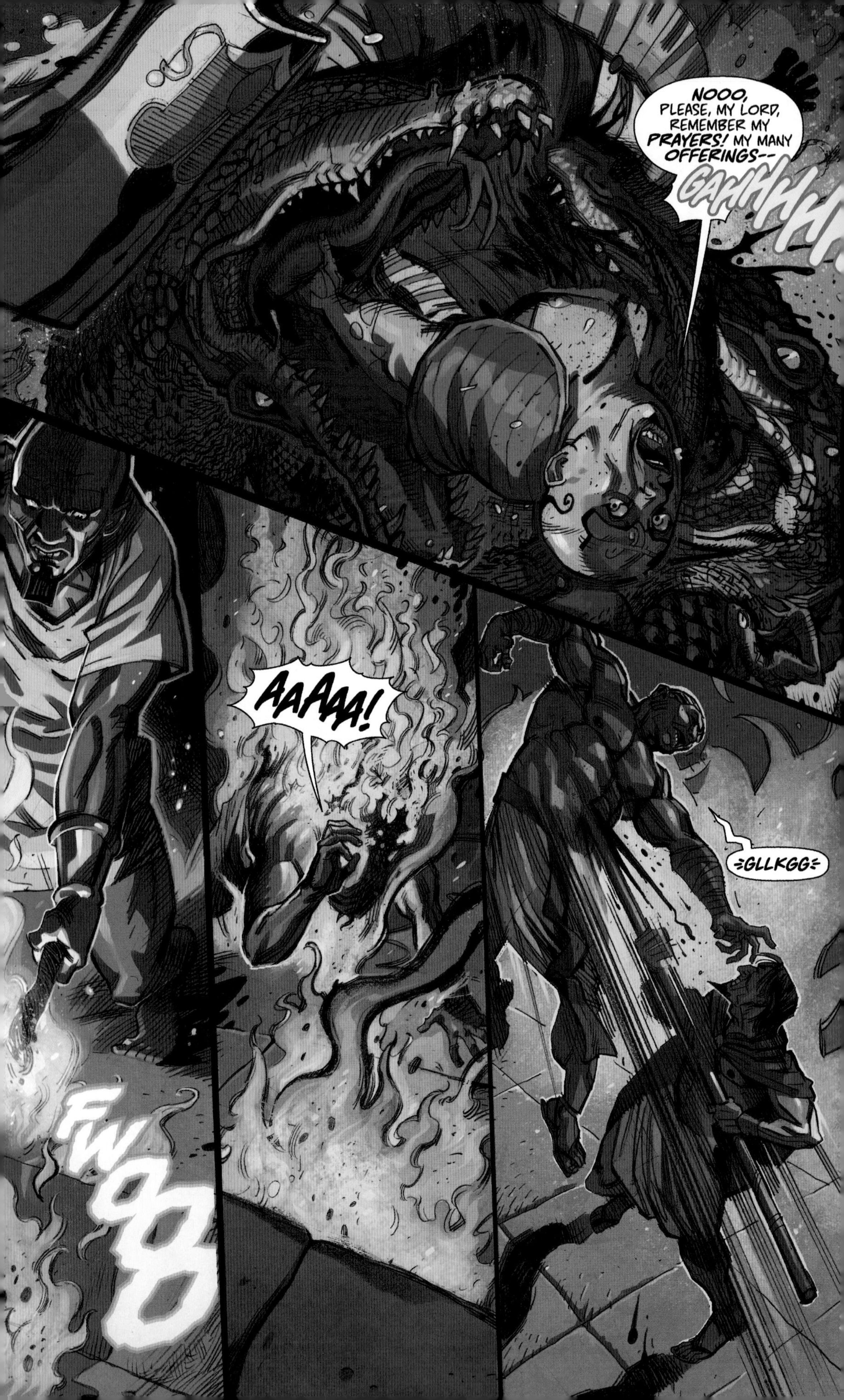
NOOO, PLEASE, MY LORD, REMEMBER MY PRAYERS! MY MANY OFFERINGS--
GAHHHH!
AAAAA!
GLLKGG
FWOOB

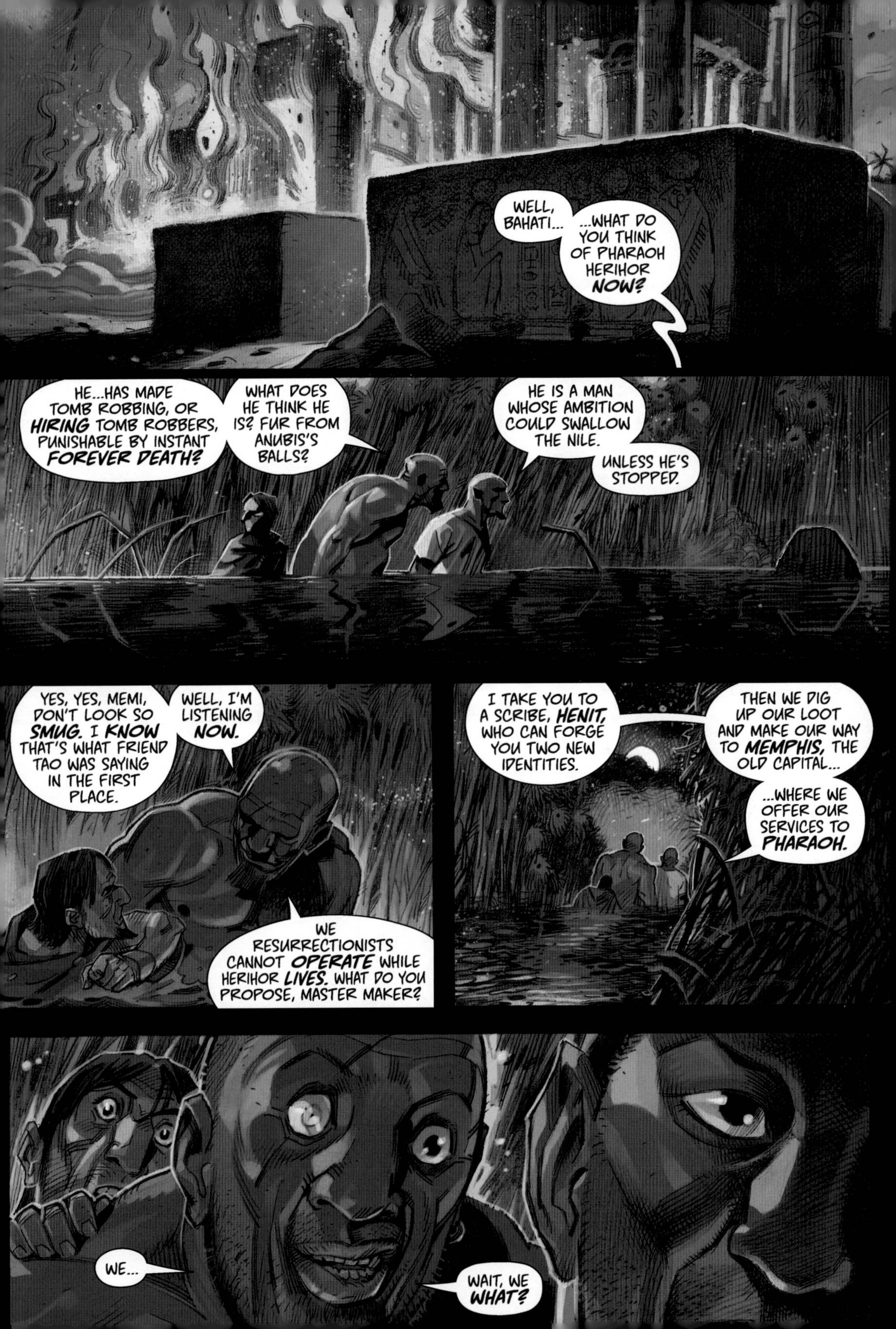
WELL, BAHATI...
...WHAT DO YOU THINK OF PHARAOH HERIHOR NOW?
HE...HAS MADE TOMB ROBBING, OR HIRING TOMB ROBBERS, PUNISHABLE BY INSTANT FOREVER DEATH?
WHAT DOES HE THINK HE IS? FUR FROM ANUBIS'S BALLS?
HE IS A MAN WHOSE AMBITION COULD SWALLOW THE NILE.
UNLESS HE'S STOPPED.
YES, YES, MEMI, DON'T LOOK SO SMUG. I KNOW THAT'S WHAT FRIEND TAO WAS SAYING IN THE FIRST PLACE.
WELL, I'M LISTENING NOW.
WE RESURRECTIONISTS CANNOT OPERATE WHILE HERIHOR LIVES. WHAT DO YOU PROPOSE, MASTER MAKER?
I TAKE YOU TO A SCRIBE, HENIT, WHO CAN FORGE YOU TWO NEW IDENTITIES.
THEN WE DIG UP OUR LOOT AND MAKE OUR WAY TO MEMPHIS, THE OLD CAPITAL...
...WHERE WE OFFER OUR SERVICES TO PHARAOH.
WE...
WAIT, WE WHAT?

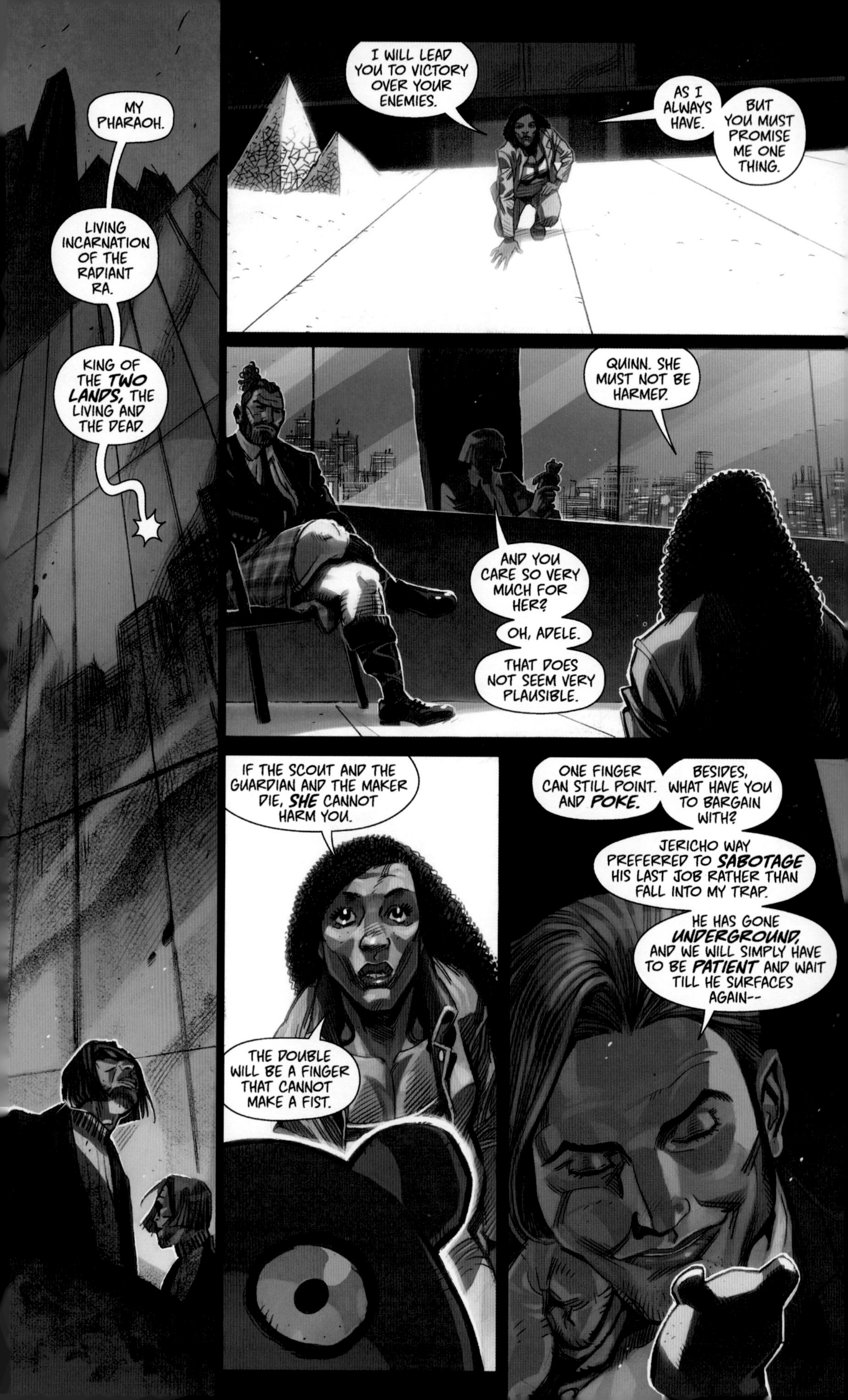
MY PHARAOH.
LIVING INCARNATION OF THE RADIANT RA.
KING OF THE TWO LANDS, THE LIVING AND THE DEAD.
I WILL LEAD YOU TO VICTORY OVER YOUR ENEMIES.
AS I ALWAYS HAVE.
BUT YOU MUST PROMISE ME ONE THING.
QUINN. SHE MUST NOT BE HARMED.
AND YOU CARE SO VERY MUCH FOR HER?
OH, ADELE.
THAT DOES NOT SEEM VERY PLAUSIBLE.
IF THE SCOUT AND THE GUARDIAN AND THE MAKER DIE, SHE CANNOT HARM YOU.
THE DOUBLE WILL BE A FINGER THAT CANNOT MAKE A FIST.
ONE FINGER CAN STILL POINT. AND POKE.
BESIDES, WHAT HAVE YOU TO BARGAIN WITH?
JERICHO WAY PREFERRED TO SABOTAGE HIS LAST JOB RATHER THAN FALL INTO MY TRAP.
HE HAS GONE UNDERGROUND, AND WE WILL SIMPLY HAVE TO BE PATIENT AND WAIT TILL HE SURFACES AGAIN--

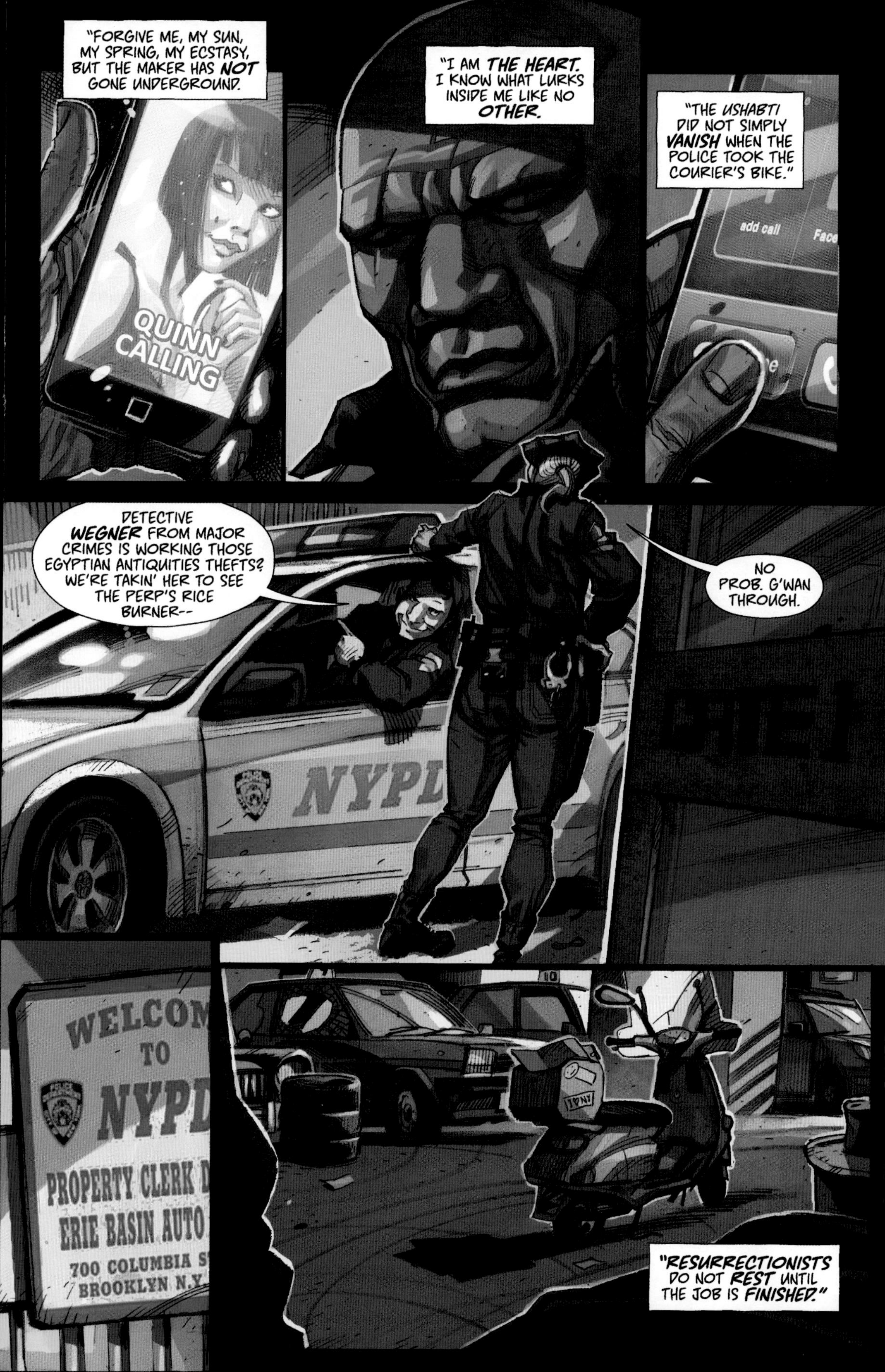
"FORGIVE ME, MY SUN, MY SPRING, MY ECSTASY, BUT THE MAKER HAS NOT GONE UNDERGROUND.
QUINN CALLING
"I AM THE HEART. I KNOW WHAT LURKS INSIDE ME LIKE NO OTHER.
"THE USHABTI DID NOT SIMPLY VANISH WHEN THE POLICE TOOK THE COURIER'S BIKE."
add call
DETECTIVE WEGNER FROM MAJOR CRIMES IS WORKING THOSE EGYPTIAN ANTIQUITIES THEFTS? WE'RE TAKIN' HER TO SEE THE PERP'S RICE BURNER--
NO PROB. G'WAN THROUGH.
NYPD
WELCOM TO NYPD
PROPERTY CLERK D
ERIE BASIN AUTO
700 COLUMBIA S
BROOKLYN N.Y
"RESURRECTIONISTS DO NOT REST UNTIL THE JOB IS FINISHED."

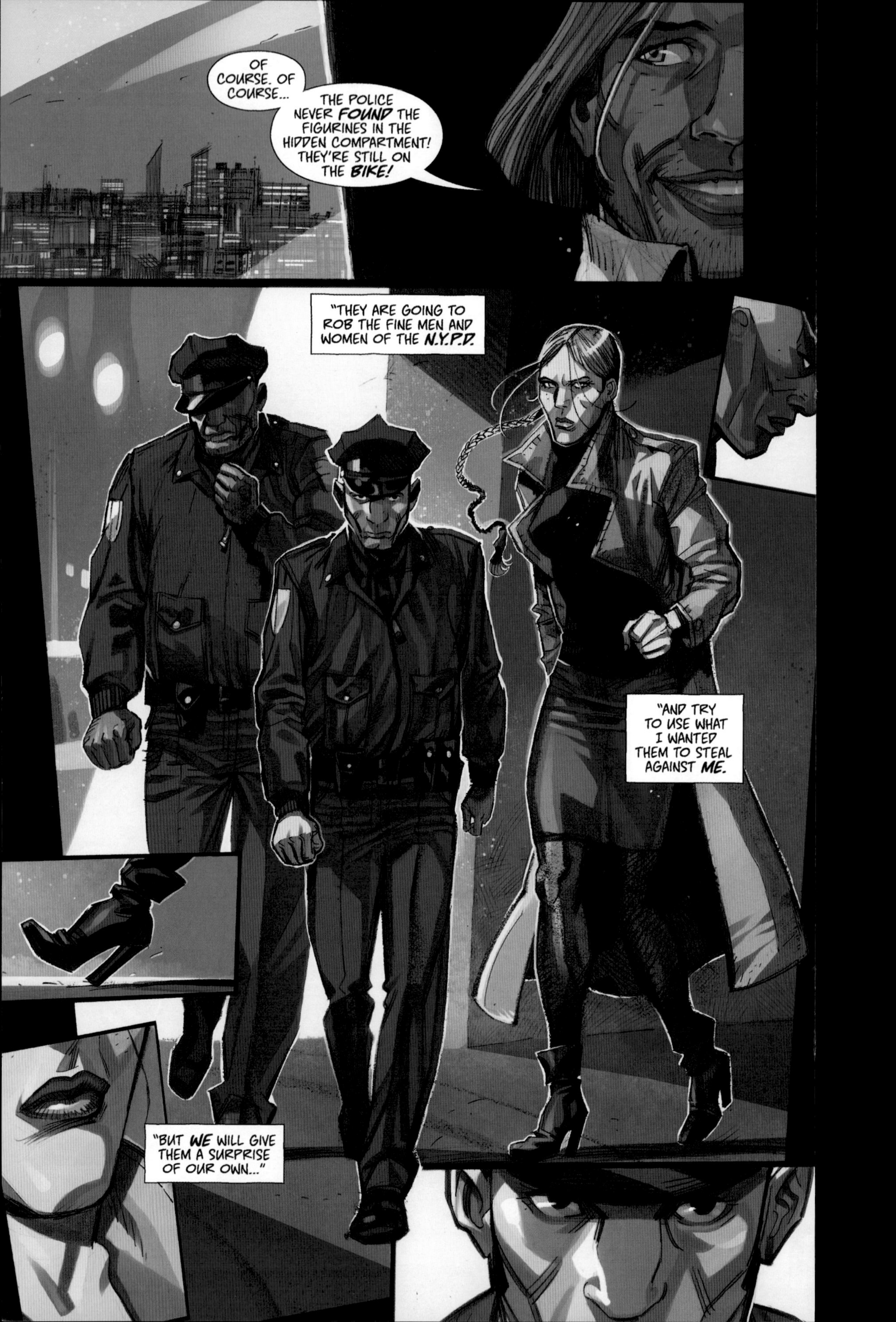
OF COURSE. OF COURSE...
THE POLICE NEVER FOUND THE FIGURINES IN THE HIDDEN COMPARTMENT! THEY'RE STILL ON THE BIKE!
"THEY ARE GOING TO ROB THE FINE MEN AND WOMEN OF THE N.Y.P.D.
"AND TRY TO USE WHAT I WANTED THEM TO STEAL AGAINST ME.
"BUT WE WILL GIVE THEM A SURPRISE OF OUR OWN..."

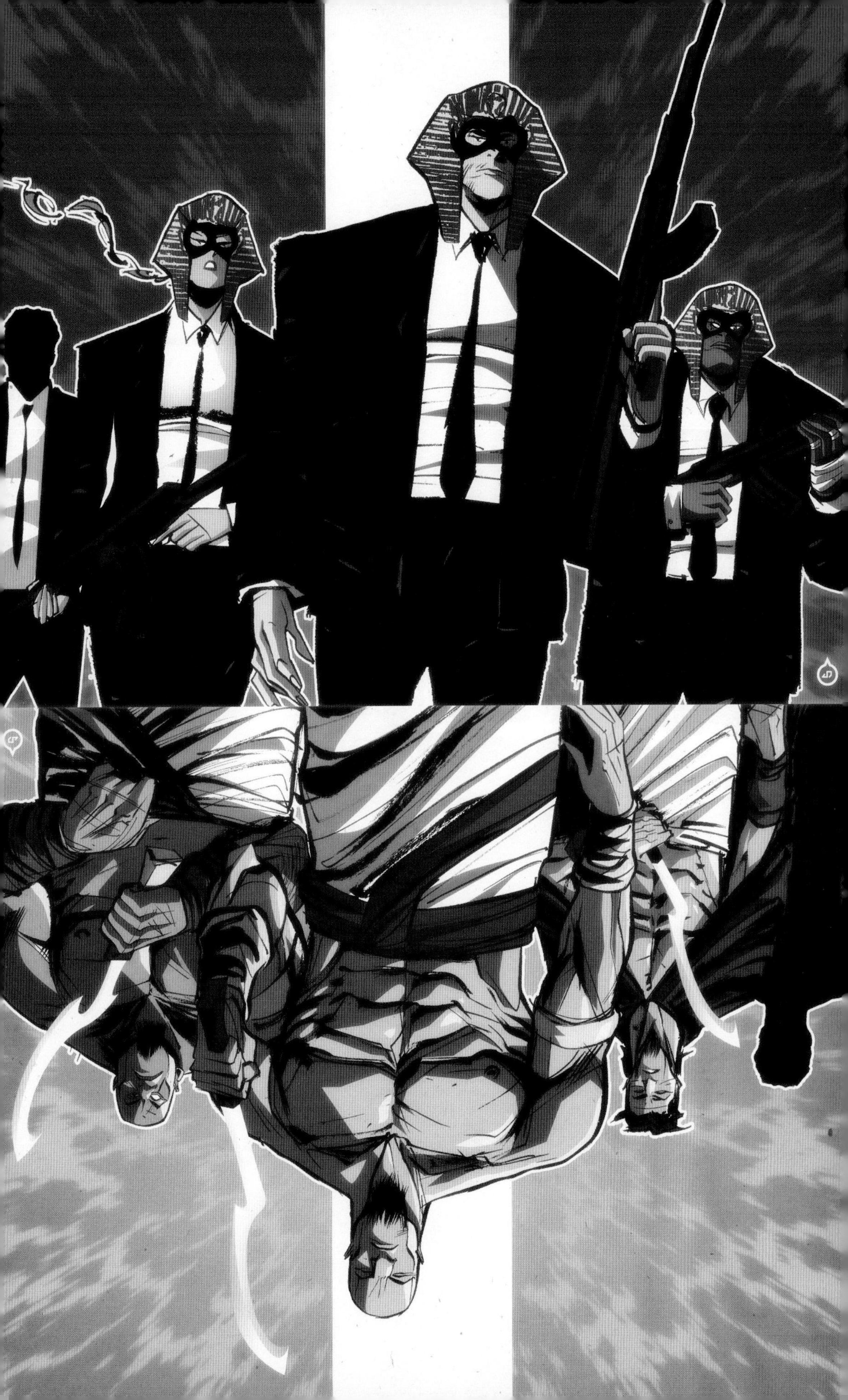

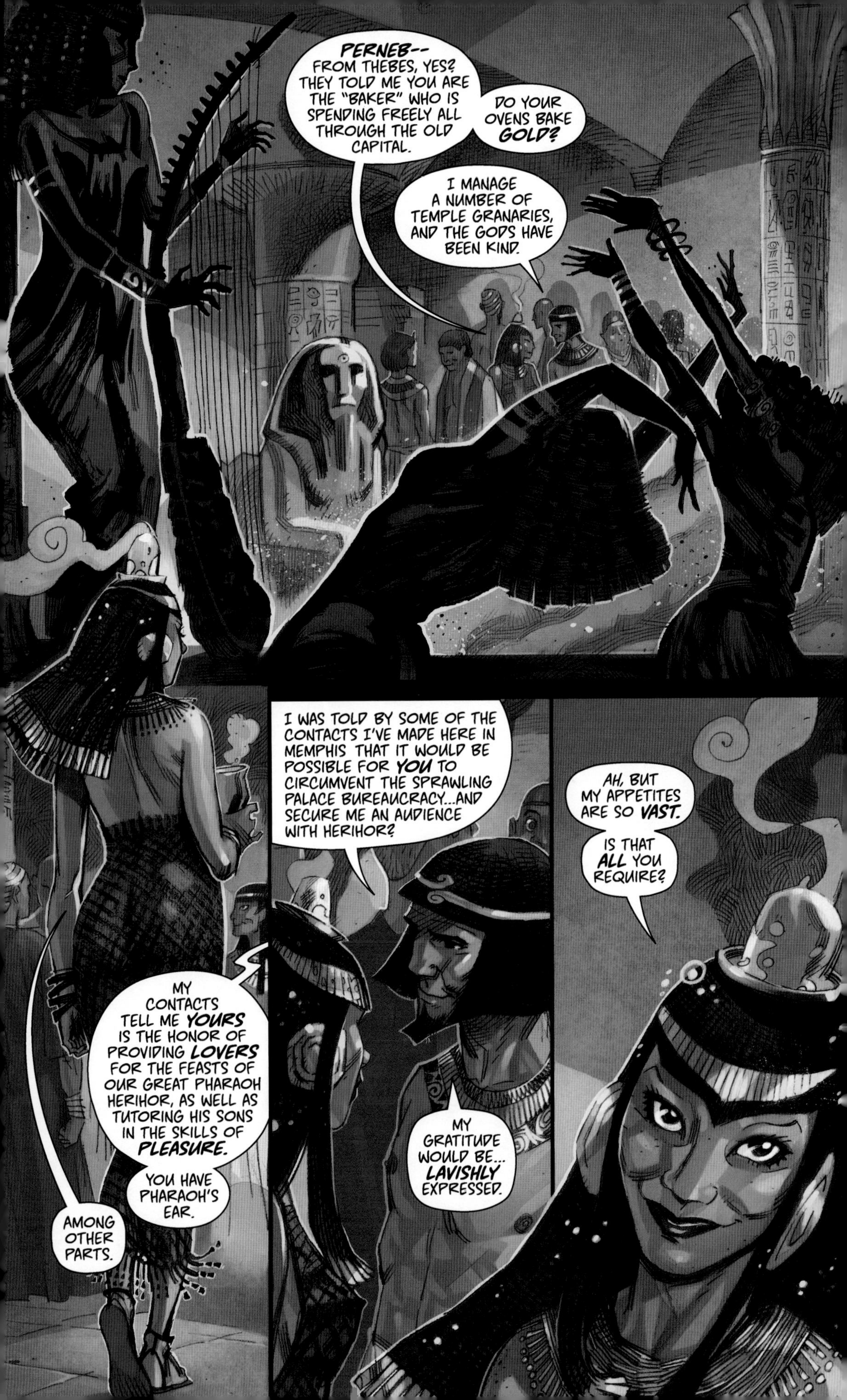
PERNEB-- FROM THEBES, YES? THEY TOLD ME YOU ARE THE "BAKER" WHO IS SPENDING FREELY ALL THROUGH THE OLD CAPITAL.
DO YOUR OVENS BAKE GOLD?
I MANAGE A NUMBER OF TEMPLE GRANARIES, AND THE GODS HAVE BEEN KIND.
MY CONTACTS TELL ME YOURS IS THE HONOR OF PROVIDING LOVERS FOR THE FEASTS OF OUR GREAT PHARAOH HERIHOR, AS WELL AS TUTORING HIS SONS IN THE SKILLS OF PLEASURE.
YOU HAVE PHARAOH'S EAR.
AMONG OTHER PARTS.
I WAS TOLD BY SOME OF THE CONTACTS I'VE MADE HERE IN MEMPHIS THAT IT WOULD BE POSSIBLE FOR YOU TO CIRCUMVENT THE SPRAWLING PALACE BUREAUCRACY...AND SECURE ME AN AUDIENCE WITH HERIHOR?
MY GRATITUDE WOULD BE... LAVISHLY EXPRESSED.
AH, BUT MY APPETITES ARE SO VAST.
IS THAT ALL YOU REQUIRE?

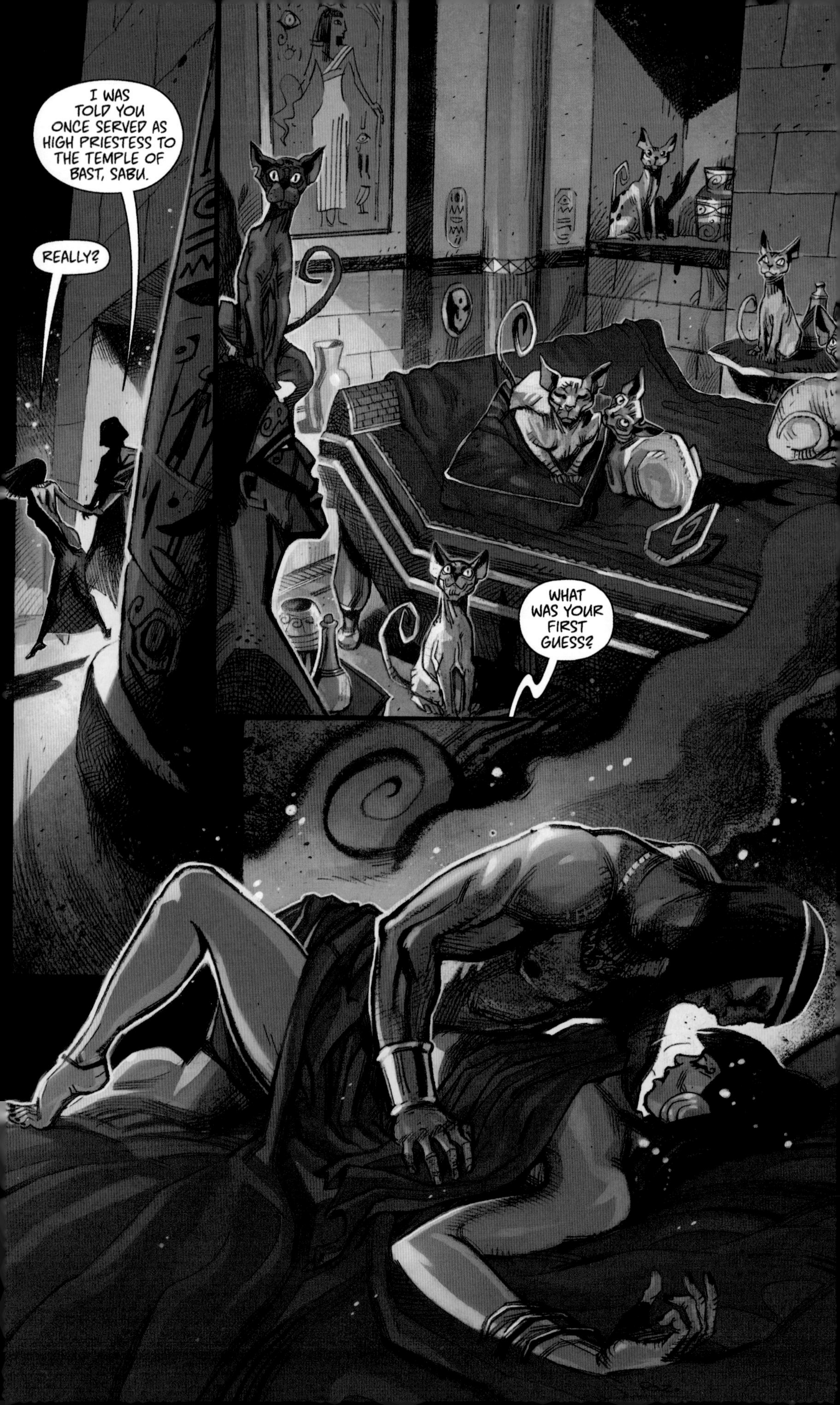
I WAS TOLD YOU ONCE SERVED AS HIGH PRIESTESS TO THE TEMPLE OF BAST, SABU.
REALLY?
WHAT WAS YOUR FIRST GUESS?

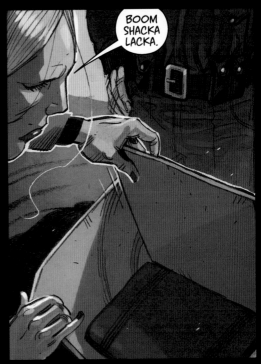

BOOM SHACKA LACKA.

BOOM.

GOTTA HAND IT TO YOU, JERICHO. CRAZY OR **NOT,** YOU OUTDID YOURSELF WITH THE PLAN *THIS* TI--

SKREEEEEEEEEEEE

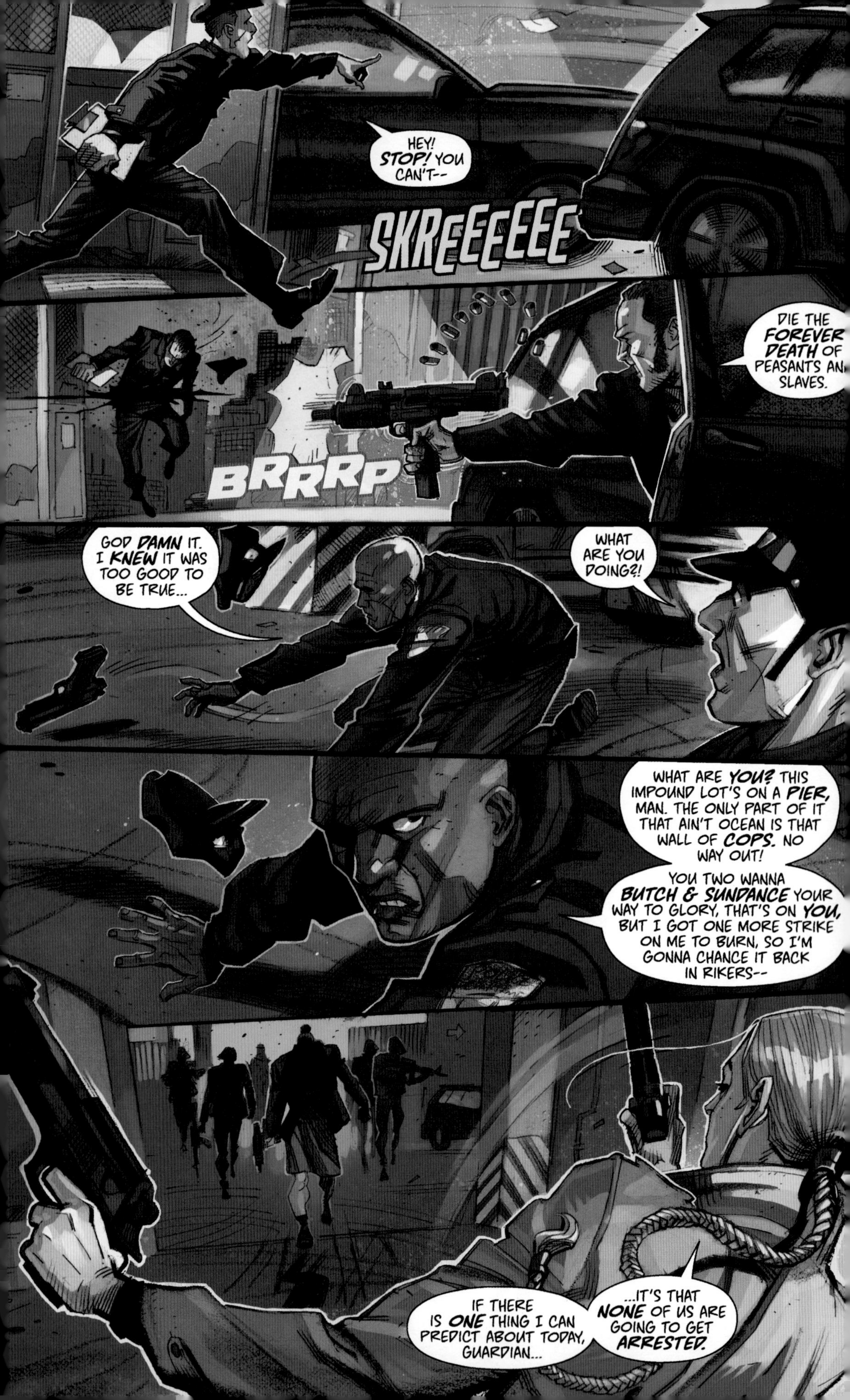

HEY! STOP! YOU CAN'T--
SKREEEEEE
DIE THE FOREVER DEATH OF PEASANTS AN SLAVES.
BRRRP
GOD DAMN IT. I KNEW IT WAS TOO GOOD TO BE TRUE...
WHAT ARE YOU DOING?!
WHAT ARE YOU? THIS IMPOUND LOT'S ON A PIER, MAN. THE ONLY PART OF IT THAT AIN'T OCEAN IS THAT WALL OF COPS. NO WAY OUT!
YOU TWO WANNA BUTCH & SUNDANCE YOUR WAY TO GLORY, THAT'S ON YOU, BUT I GOT ONE MORE STRIKE ON ME TO BURN, SO I'M GONNA CHANCE IT BACK IN RIKERS--
IF THERE IS ONE THING I CAN PREDICT ABOUT TODAY, GUARDIAN...
...IT'S THAT NONE OF US ARE GOING TO GET ARRESTED.

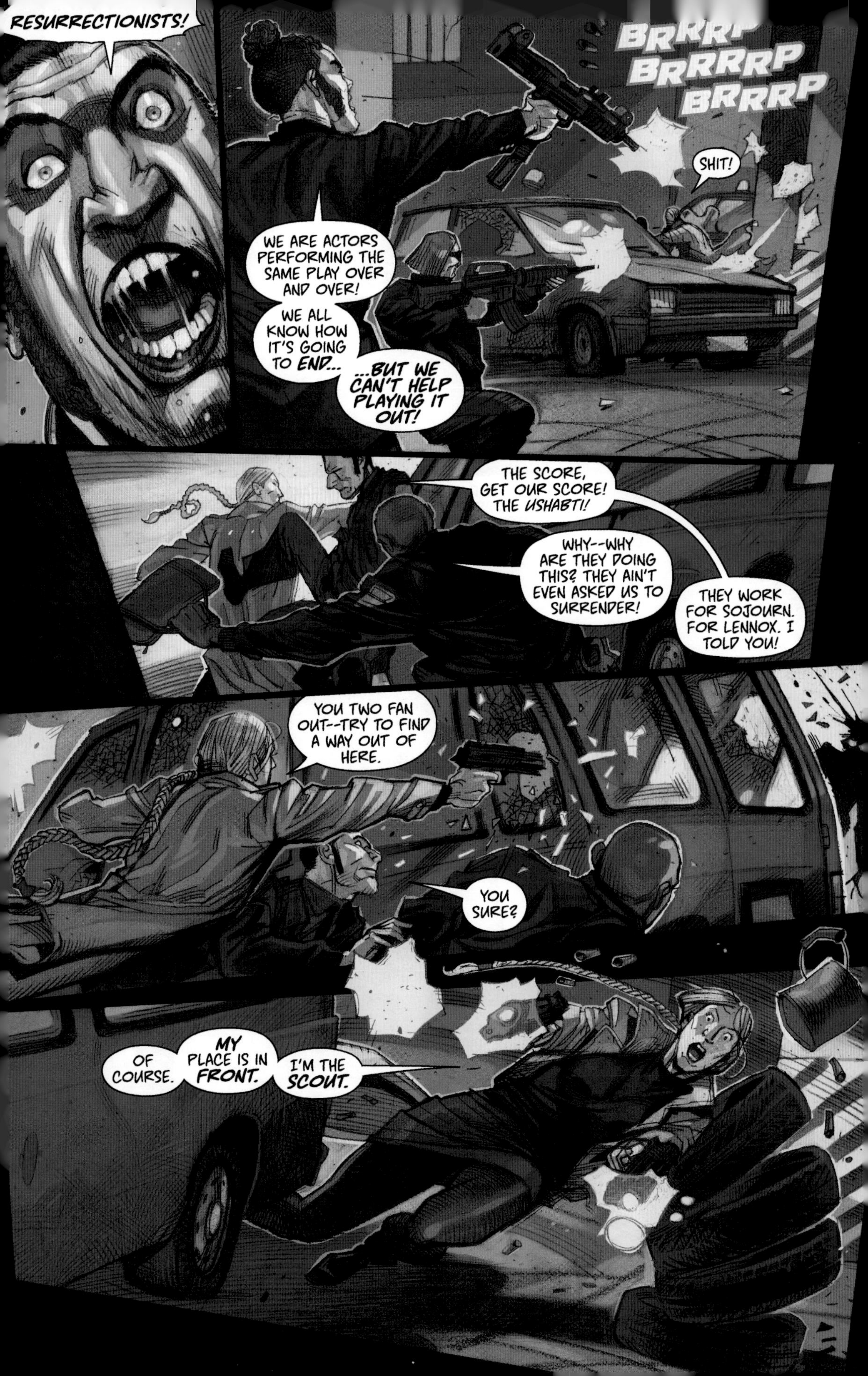
RESURRECTIONISTS!
BRRRP
BRRRRP
BRRRP
SHIT!
WE ARE ACTORS PERFORMING THE SAME PLAY OVER AND OVER!
WE ALL KNOW HOW IT'S GOING TO END...
...BUT WE CAN'T HELP PLAYING IT OUT!
THE SCORE, GET OUR SCORE! THE USHABTI!
WHY--WHY ARE THEY DOING THIS? THEY AIN'T EVEN ASKED US TO SURRENDER!
THEY WORK FOR SOJOURN. FOR LENNOX. I TOLD YOU!
YOU TWO FAN OUT--TRY TO FIND A WAY OUT OF HERE.
YOU SURE?
OF COURSE.
MY PLACE IS IN FRONT.
I'M THE SCOUT.

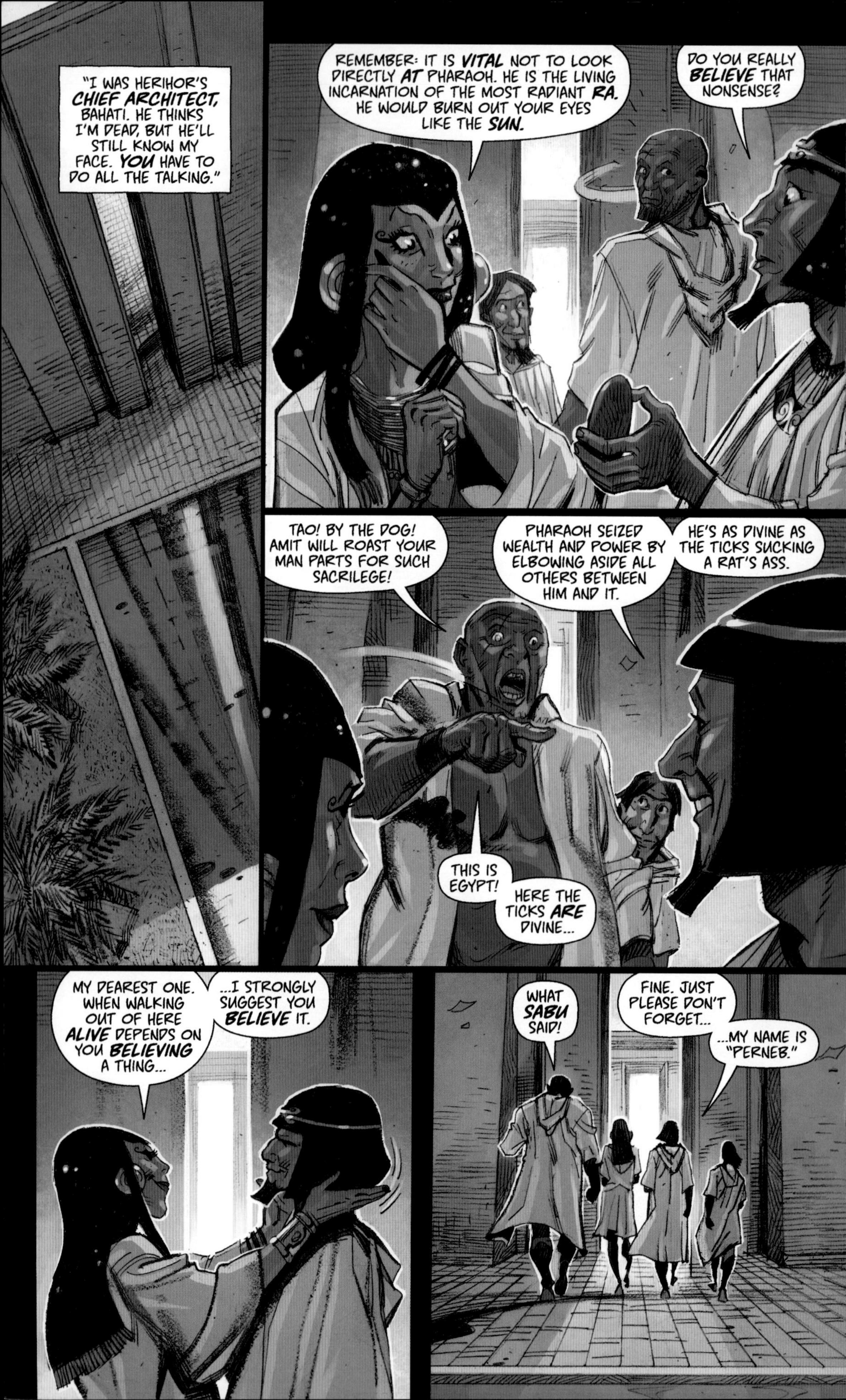
"I WAS HERIHOR'S CHIEF ARCHITECT, BAHATI. HE THINKS I'M DEAD, BUT HE'LL STILL KNOW MY FACE. YOU HAVE TO DO ALL THE TALKING."
REMEMBER: IT IS VITAL NOT TO LOOK DIRECTLY AT PHARAOH. HE IS THE LIVING INCARNATION OF THE MOST RADIANT RA. HE WOULD BURN OUT YOUR EYES LIKE THE SUN.
DO YOU REALLY BELIEVE THAT NONSENSE?
TAO! BY THE DOG! AMIT WILL ROAST YOUR MAN PARTS FOR SUCH SACRILEGE!
PHARAOH SEIZED WEALTH AND POWER BY ELBOWING ASIDE ALL OTHERS BETWEEN HIM AND IT.
HE'S AS DIVINE AS THE TICKS SUCKING A RAT'S ASS.
THIS IS EGYPT!
HERE THE TICKS ARE DIVINE...
MY DEAREST ONE. WHEN WALKING OUT OF HERE ALIVE DEPENDS ON YOU BELIEVING A THING...
...I STRONGLY SUGGEST YOU BELIEVE IT.
WHAT SABU SAID!
FINE. JUST PLEASE DON'T FORGET...
...MY NAME IS "PERNEB."

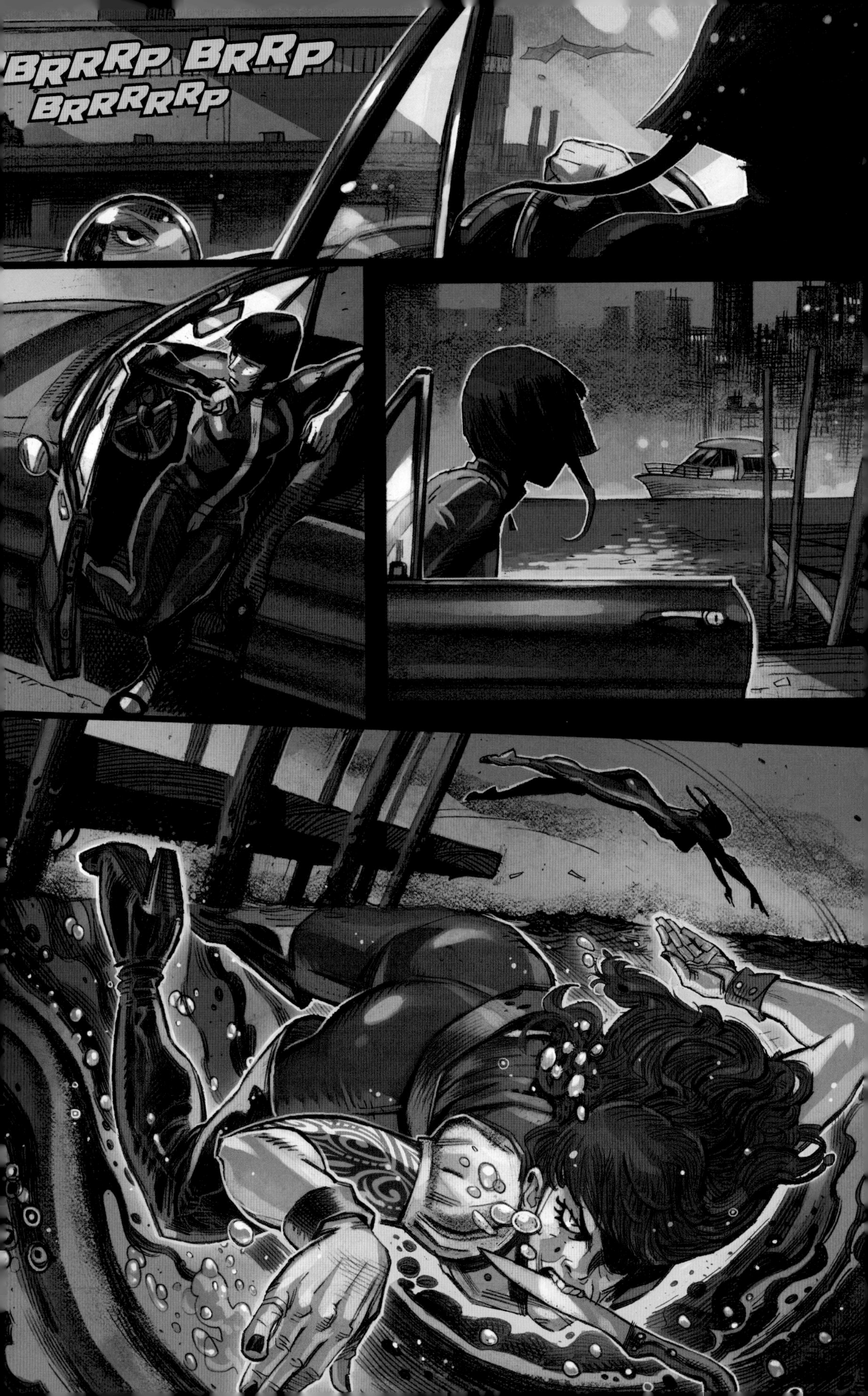
BRRRP BRRP
BRRRRRP

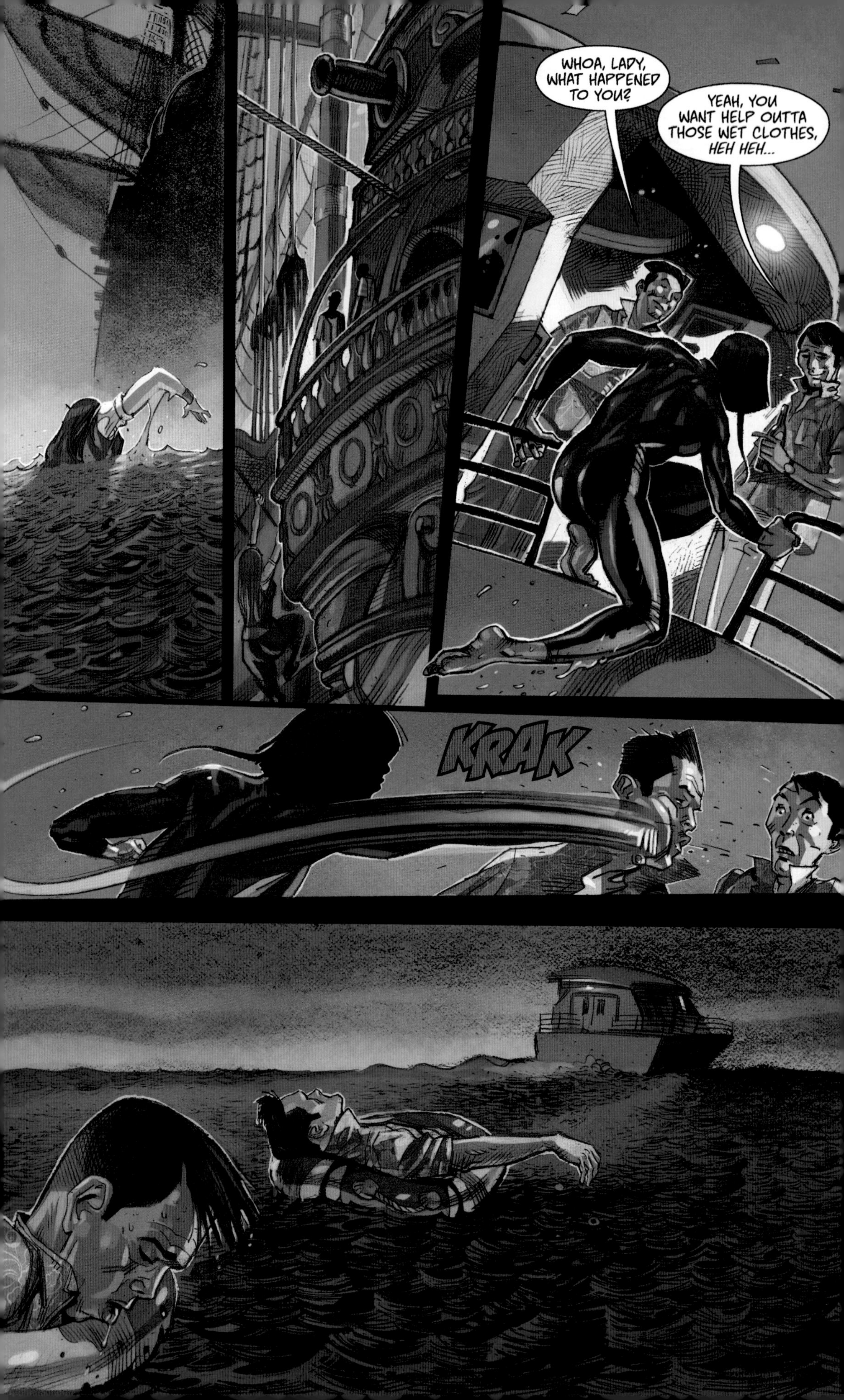
WHOA, LADY, WHAT HAPPENED TO YOU?
YEAH, YOU WANT HELP OUTTA THOSE WET CLOTHES, HEH HEH...
KRAK

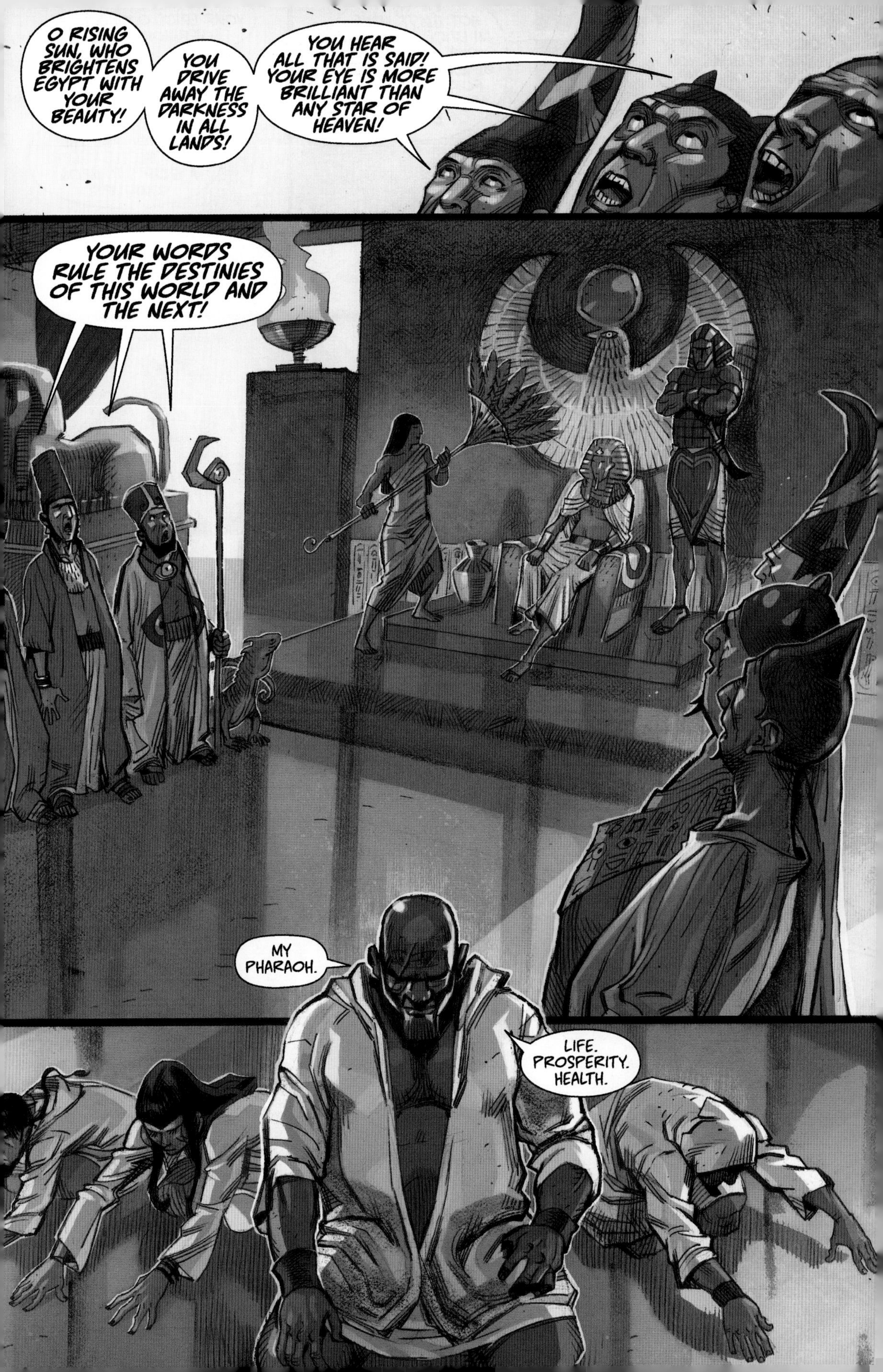
O RISING SUN, WHO BRIGHTENS EGYPT WITH YOUR BEAUTY!
YOU DRIVE AWAY THE DARKNESS IN ALL LANDS!
YOU HEAR ALL THAT IS SAID! YOUR EYE IS MORE BRILLIANT THAN ANY STAR OF HEAVEN!
YOUR WORDS RULE THE DESTINIES OF THIS WORLD AND THE NEXT!
MY PHARAOH.
LIFE. PROSPERITY. HEALTH.

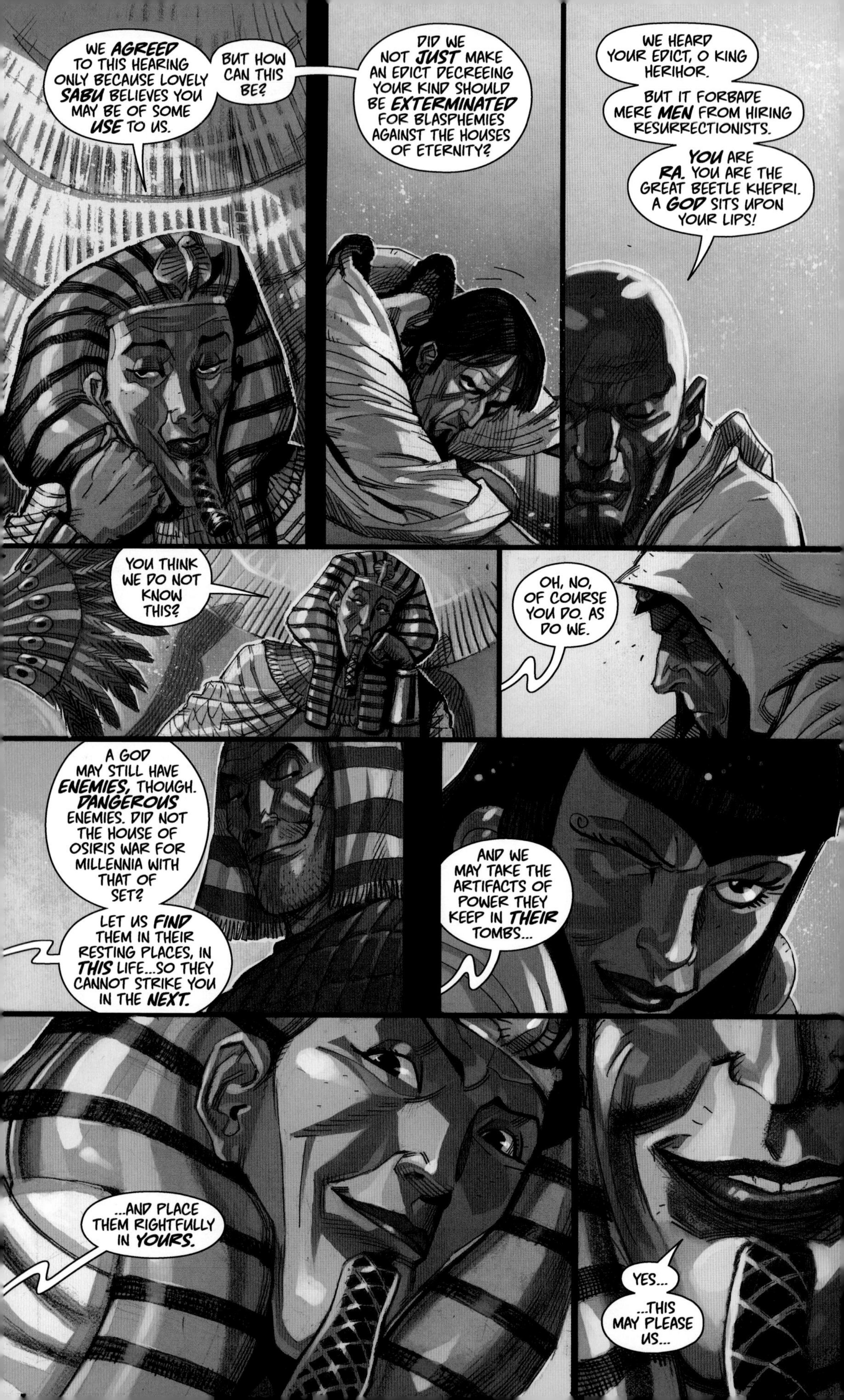
WE AGREED TO THIS HEARING ONLY BECAUSE LOVELY SABU BELIEVES YOU MAY BE OF SOME USE TO US.
BUT HOW CAN THIS BE?
DID WE NOT JUST MAKE AN EDICT DECREEING YOUR KIND SHOULD BE EXTERMINATED FOR BLASPHEMIES AGAINST THE HOUSES OF ETERNITY?
WE HEARD YOUR EDICT, O KING HERIHOR.
BUT IT FORBADE MERE MEN FROM HIRING RESURRECTIONISTS.
YOU ARE RA. YOU ARE THE GREAT BEETLE KHEPRI. A GOD SITS UPON YOUR LIPS!
YOU THINK WE DO NOT KNOW THIS?
OH, NO, OF COURSE YOU DO. AS DO WE.
A GOD MAY STILL HAVE ENEMIES, THOUGH. DANGEROUS ENEMIES. DID NOT THE HOUSE OF OSIRIS WAR FOR MILLENNIA WITH THAT OF SET?
LET US FIND THEM IN THEIR RESTING PLACES, IN THIS LIFE...SO THEY CANNOT STRIKE YOU IN THE NEXT.
AND WE MAY TAKE THE ARTIFACTS OF POWER THEY KEEP IN THEIR TOMBS...
...AND PLACE THEM RIGHTFULLY IN YOURS.
YES...
...THIS MAY PLEASE US...

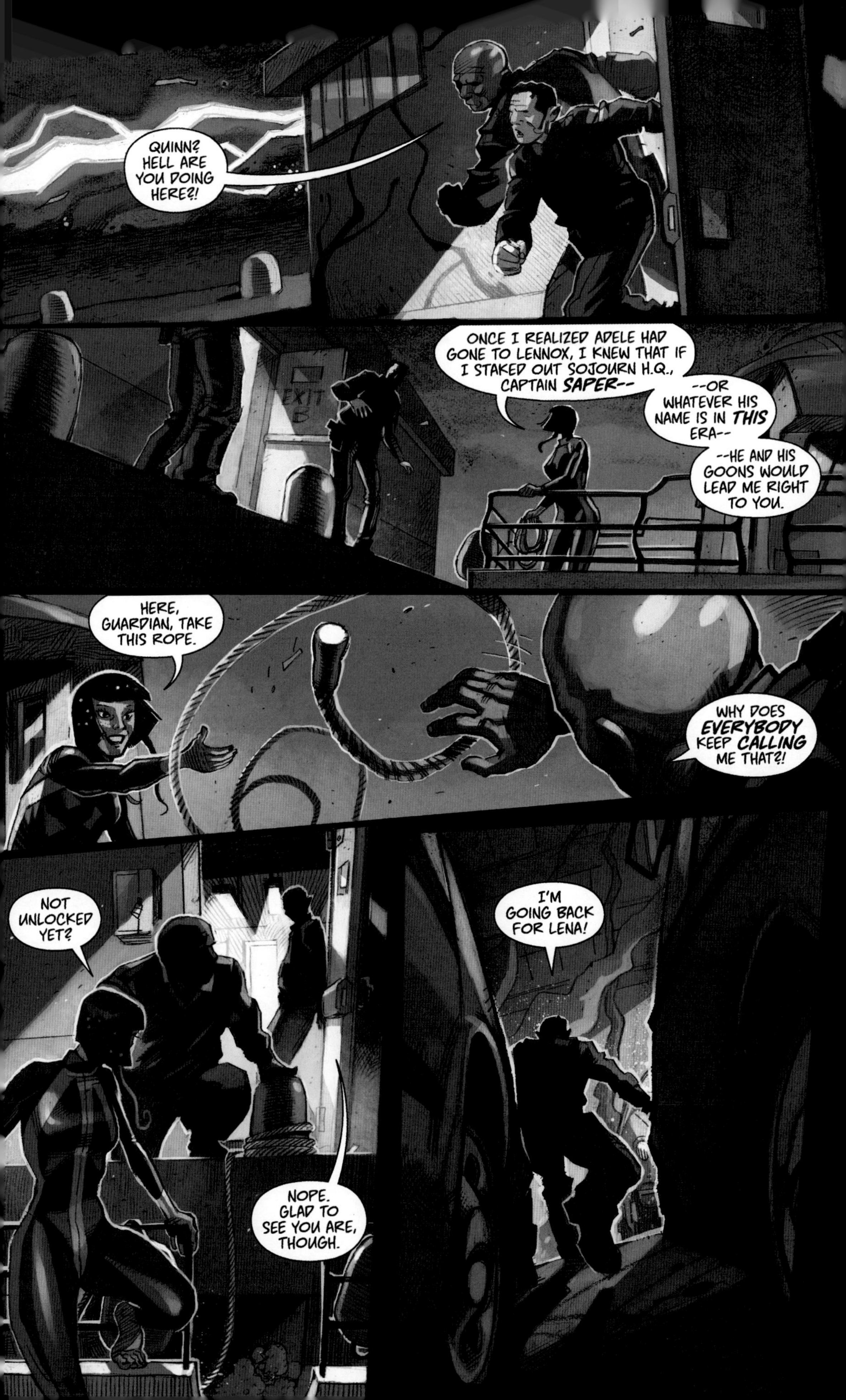
QUINN? HELL ARE YOU DOING HERE?!
ONCE I REALIZED ADELE HAD GONE TO LENNOX, I KNEW THAT IF I STAKED OUT SOJOURN H.Q., CAPTAIN SAPER--
--OR WHATEVER HIS NAME IS IN THIS ERA--
--HE AND HIS GOONS WOULD LEAD ME RIGHT TO YOU.
EXIT
HERE, GUARDIAN, TAKE THIS ROPE.
WHY DOES EVERYBODY KEEP CALLING ME THAT?!
NOT UNLOCKED YET?
NOPE. GLAD TO SEE YOU ARE, THOUGH.
I'M GOING BACK FOR LENA!

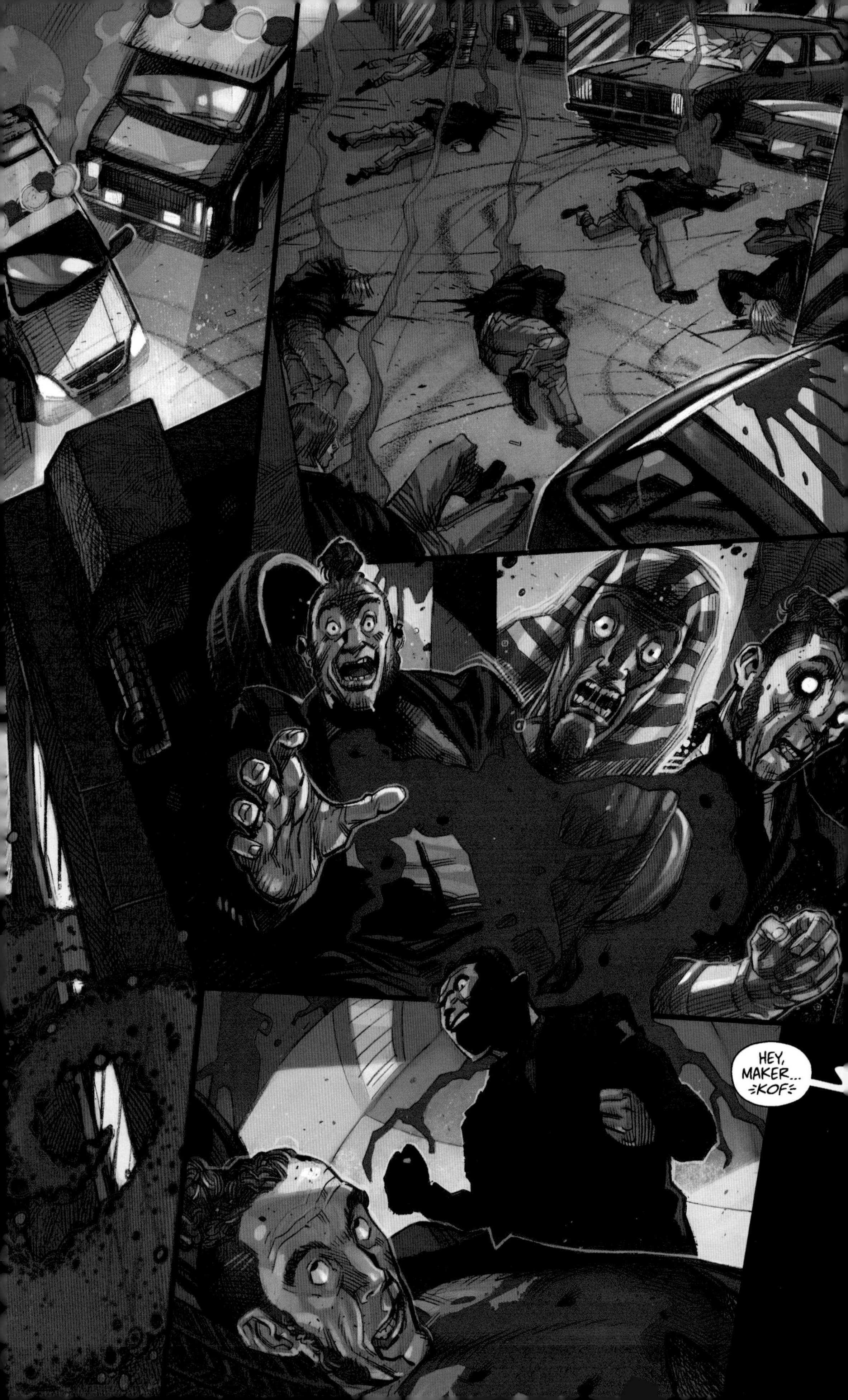
HEY, MAKER... =KOF=

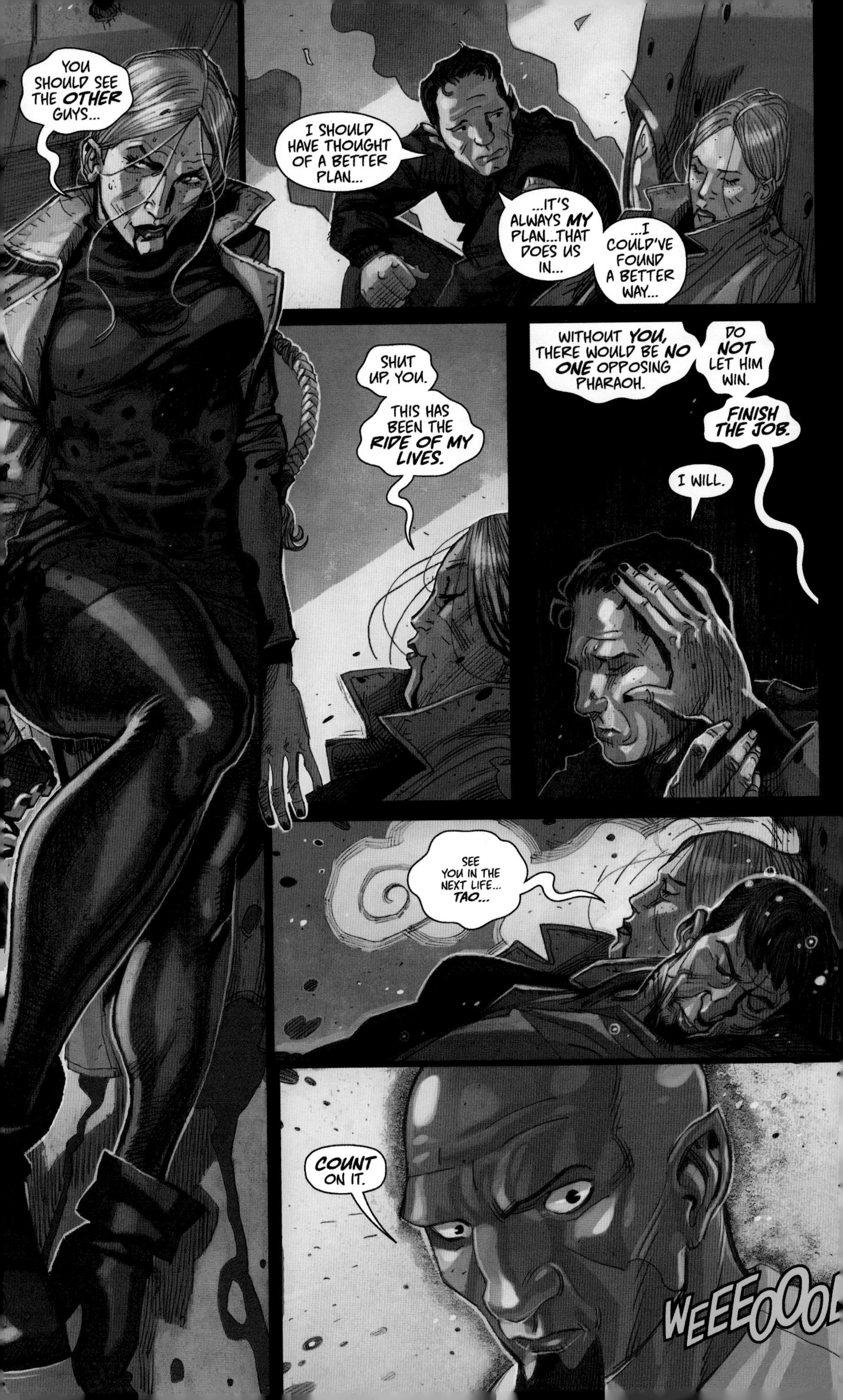
YOU SHOULD SEE THE **OTHER** GUYS...
I SHOULD HAVE THOUGHT OF A BETTER PLAN...
...IT'S ALWAYS **MY** PLAN...THAT DOES US IN...
...I COULD'VE FOUND A BETTER WAY...
SHUT UP, YOU.
THIS HAS BEEN THE **RIDE OF MY LIVES.**
WITHOUT **YOU,** THERE WOULD BE **NO ONE** OPPOSING PHARAOH.
DO **NOT** LET HIM WIN.
FINISH THE JOB.
I WILL.
SEE YOU IN THE NEXT LIFE... **TAO...**
COUNT ON IT.
WEEEOOOL

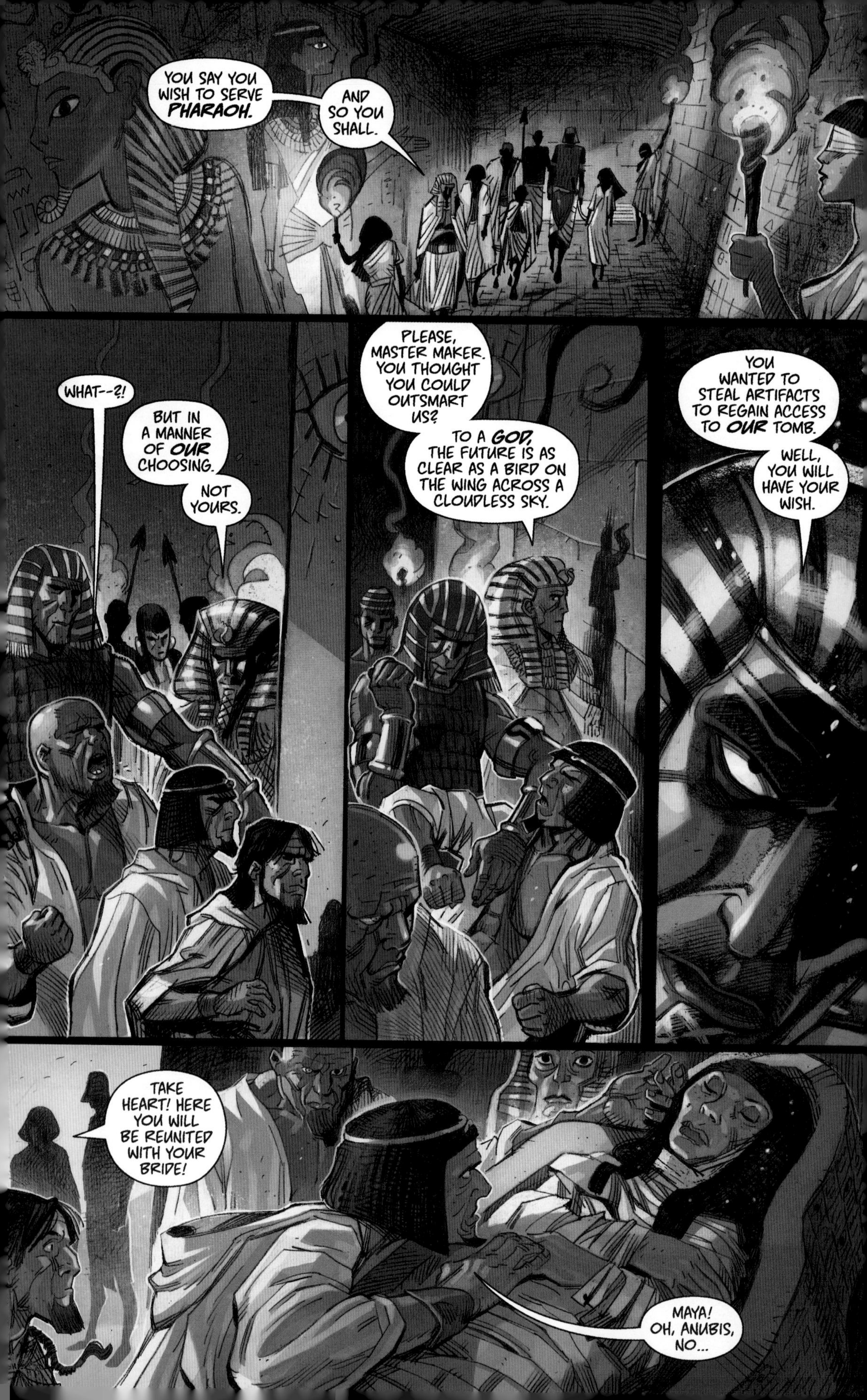
YOU SAY YOU WISH TO SERVE PHARAOH.
AND SO YOU SHALL.
WHAT--?!
BUT IN A MANNER OF OUR CHOOSING.
NOT YOURS.
PLEASE, MASTER MAKER. YOU THOUGHT YOU COULD OUTSMART US?
TO A GOD, THE FUTURE IS AS CLEAR AS A BIRD ON THE WING ACROSS A CLOUDLESS SKY.
YOU WANTED TO STEAL ARTIFACTS TO REGAIN ACCESS TO OUR TOMB.
WELL, YOU WILL HAVE YOUR WISH.
TAKE HEART! HERE YOU WILL BE REUNITED WITH YOUR BRIDE!
MAYA! OH, ANUBIS, NO...

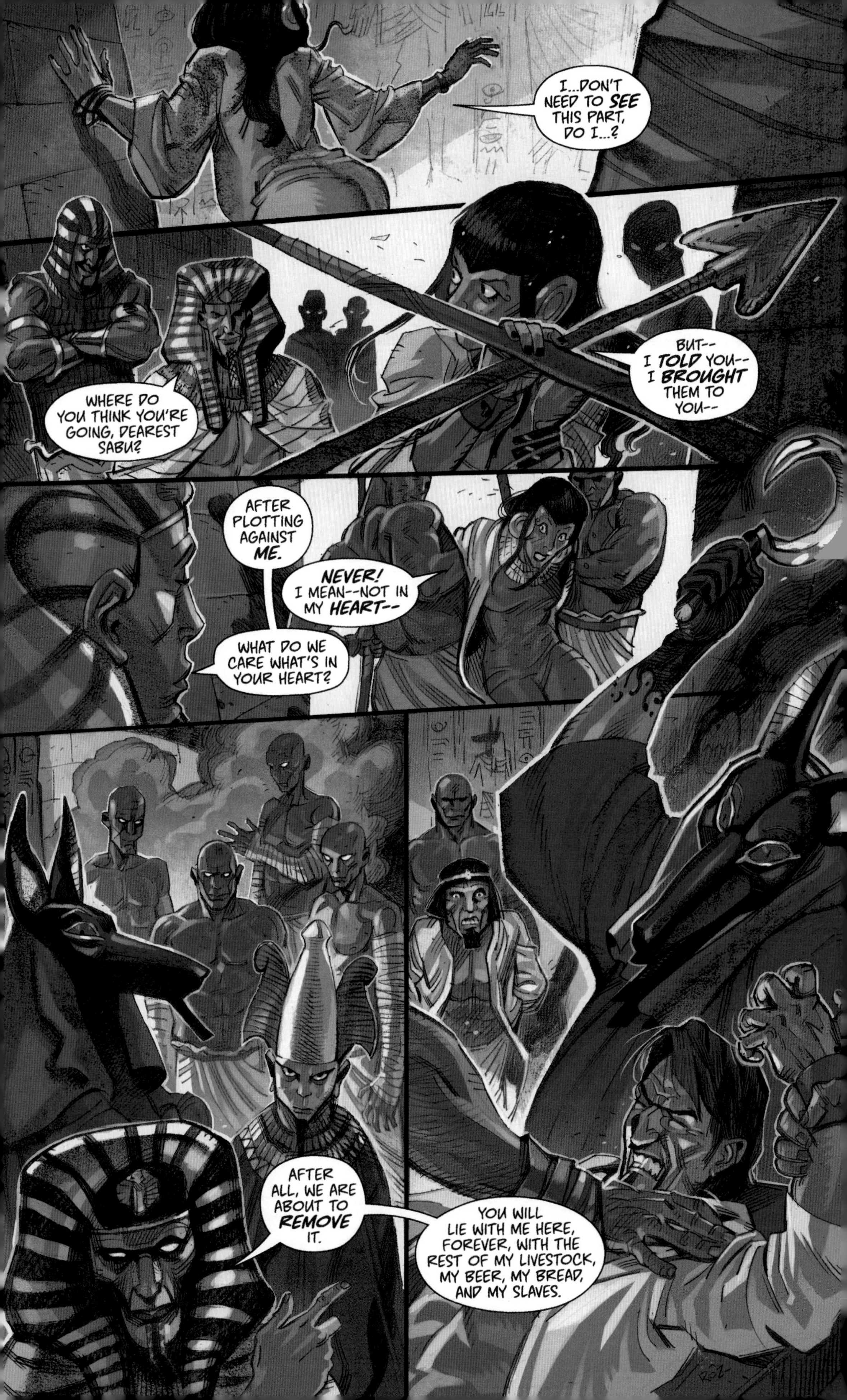
I...DON'T NEED TO SEE THIS PART, DO I...?
WHERE DO YOU THINK YOU'RE GOING, DEAREST SABU?
BUT-- I TOLD YOU-- I BROUGHT THEM TO YOU--
AFTER PLOTTING AGAINST ME.
NEVER! I MEAN--NOT IN MY HEART--
WHAT DO WE CARE WHAT'S IN YOUR HEART?
AFTER ALL, WE ARE ABOUT TO REMOVE IT.
YOU WILL LIE WITH ME HERE, FOREVER, WITH THE REST OF MY LIVESTOCK, MY BEER, MY BREAD, AND MY SLAVES.

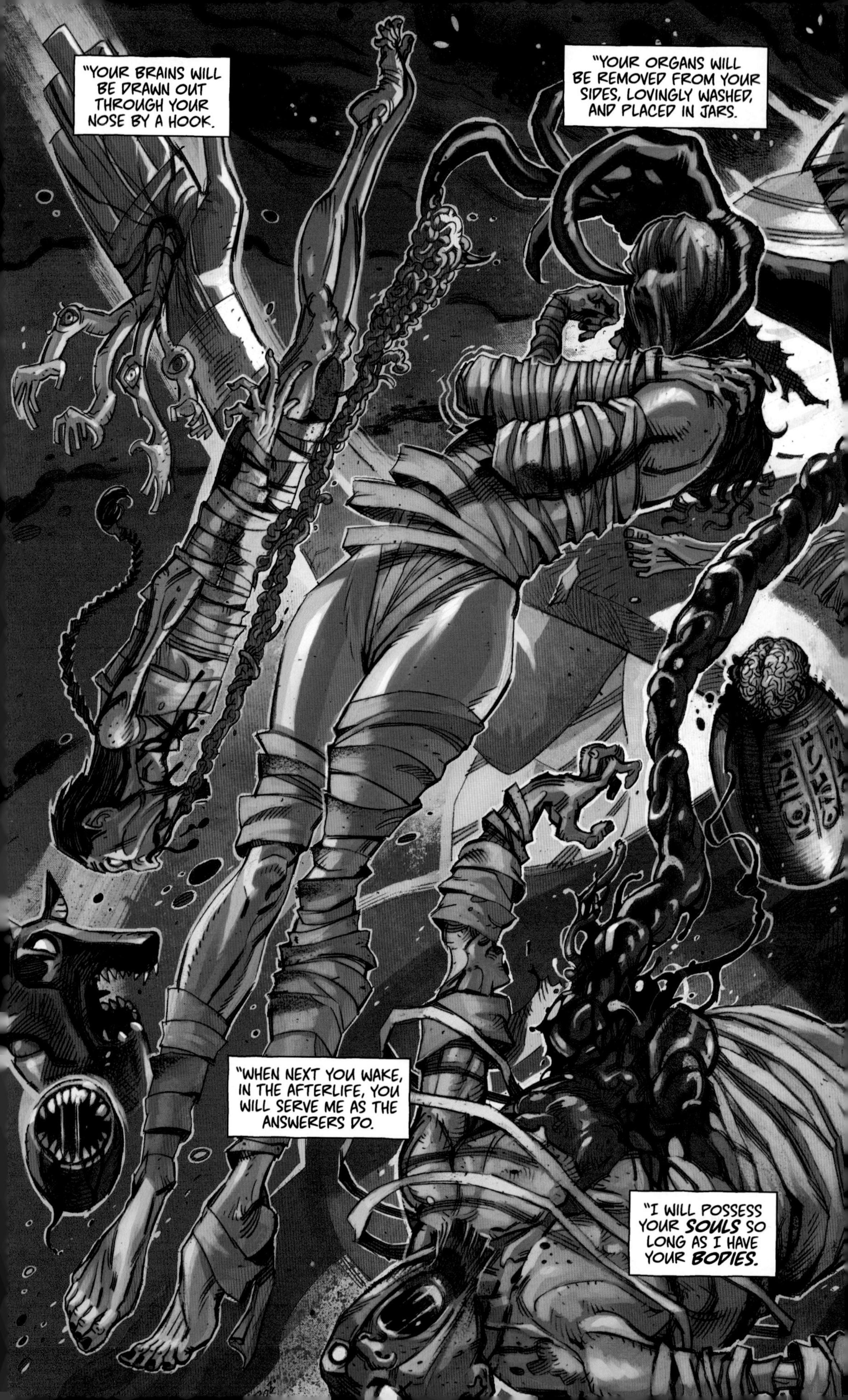
"YOUR BRAINS WILL BE DRAWN OUT THROUGH YOUR NOSE BY A HOOK.
"YOUR ORGANS WILL BE REMOVED FROM YOUR SIDES, LOVINGLY WASHED, AND PLACED IN JARS.
"WHEN NEXT YOU WAKE, IN THE AFTERLIFE, YOU WILL SERVE ME AS THE ANSWERERS DO.
"I WILL POSSESS YOUR **SOULS** SO LONG AS I HAVE YOUR **BODIES.**

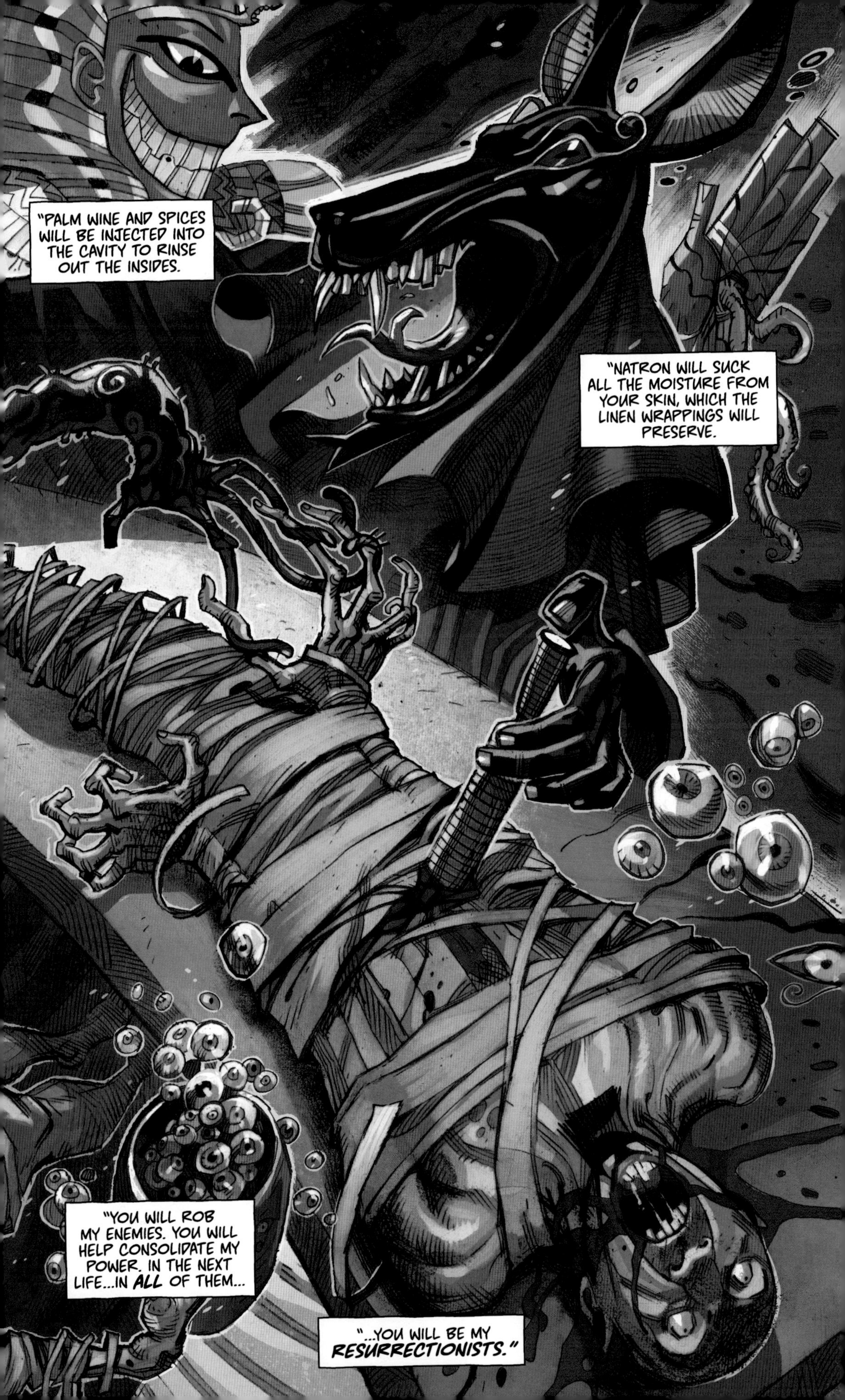
"PALM WINE AND SPICES WILL BE INJECTED INTO THE CAVITY TO RINSE OUT THE INSIDES.
"NATRON WILL SUCK ALL THE MOISTURE FROM YOUR SKIN, WHICH THE LINEN WRAPPINGS WILL PRESERVE.
"YOU WILL ROB MY ENEMIES. YOU WILL HELP CONSOLIDATE MY POWER. IN THE NEXT LIFE...IN ALL OF THEM...
"...YOU WILL BE MY RESURRECTIONISTS."

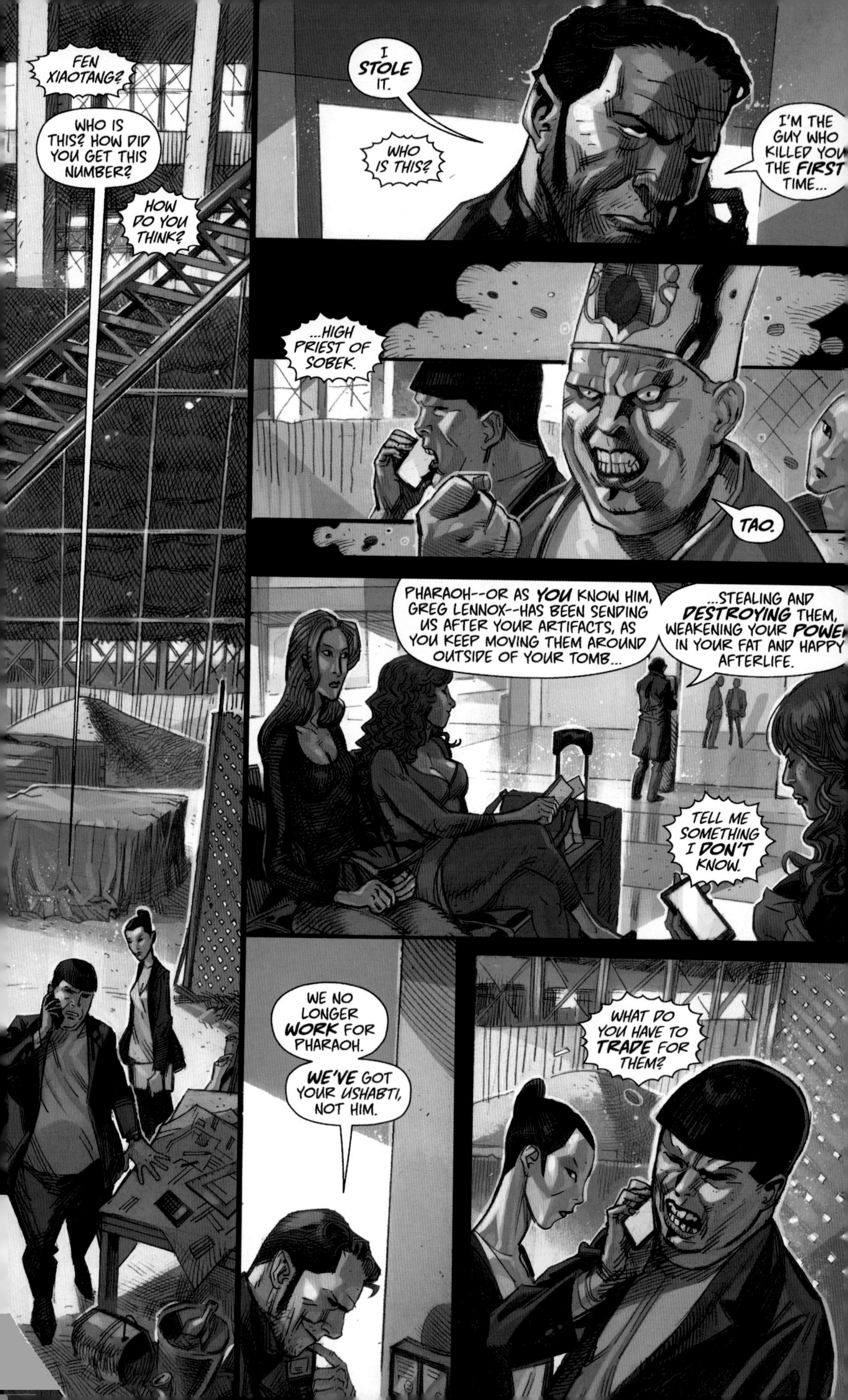
FEN XIAOTANG?
WHO IS THIS? HOW DID YOU GET THIS NUMBER?
HOW DO YOU THINK?
I STOLE IT.
WHO IS THIS?
I'M THE GUY WHO KILLED YOU THE FIRST TIME...
...HIGH PRIEST OF SOBEK.
TAO.
PHARAOH--OR AS YOU KNOW HIM, GREG LENNOX--HAS BEEN SENDING US AFTER YOUR ARTIFACTS, AS YOU KEEP MOVING THEM AROUND OUTSIDE OF YOUR TOMB...
...STEALING AND DESTROYING THEM, WEAKENING YOUR POWER IN YOUR FAT AND HAPPY AFTERLIFE.
TELL ME SOMETHING I DON'T KNOW.
WE NO LONGER WORK FOR PHARAOH.
WE'VE GOT YOUR USHABTI, NOT HIM.
WHAT DO YOU HAVE TO TRADE FOR THEM?

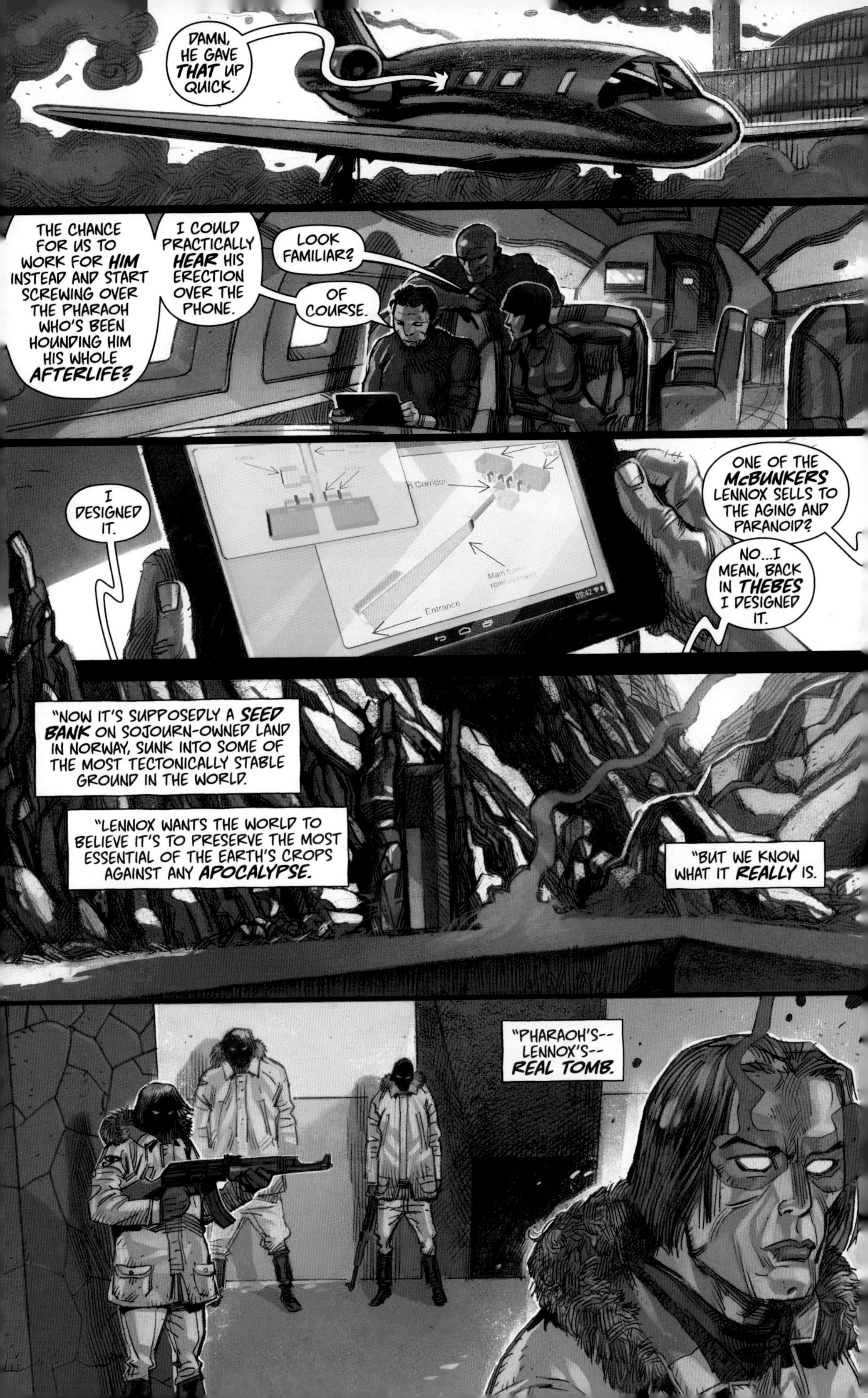

DAMN, HE GAVE THAT UP QUICK.
THE CHANCE FOR US TO WORK FOR HIM INSTEAD AND START SCREWING OVER THE PHARAOH WHO'S BEEN HOUNDING HIM HIS WHOLE AFTERLIFE?
I COULD PRACTICALLY HEAR HIS ERECTION OVER THE PHONE.
LOOK FAMILIAR?
OF COURSE.
Seed Vault
Main tunnel reinforcement
Entrance
09:42
I DESIGNED IT.
ONE OF THE McBUNKERS LENNOX SELLS TO THE AGING AND PARANOID?
NO...I MEAN, BACK IN THEBES I DESIGNED IT.
"NOW IT'S SUPPOSEDLY A SEED BANK ON SOJOURN-OWNED LAND IN NORWAY, SUNK INTO SOME OF THE MOST TECTONICALLY STABLE GROUND IN THE WORLD.
"LENNOX WANTS THE WORLD TO BELIEVE IT'S TO PRESERVE THE MOST ESSENTIAL OF THE EARTH'S CROPS AGAINST ANY APOCALYPSE.
"BUT WE KNOW WHAT IT REALLY IS.
"PHARAOH'S-- LENNOX'S-- REAL TOMB.

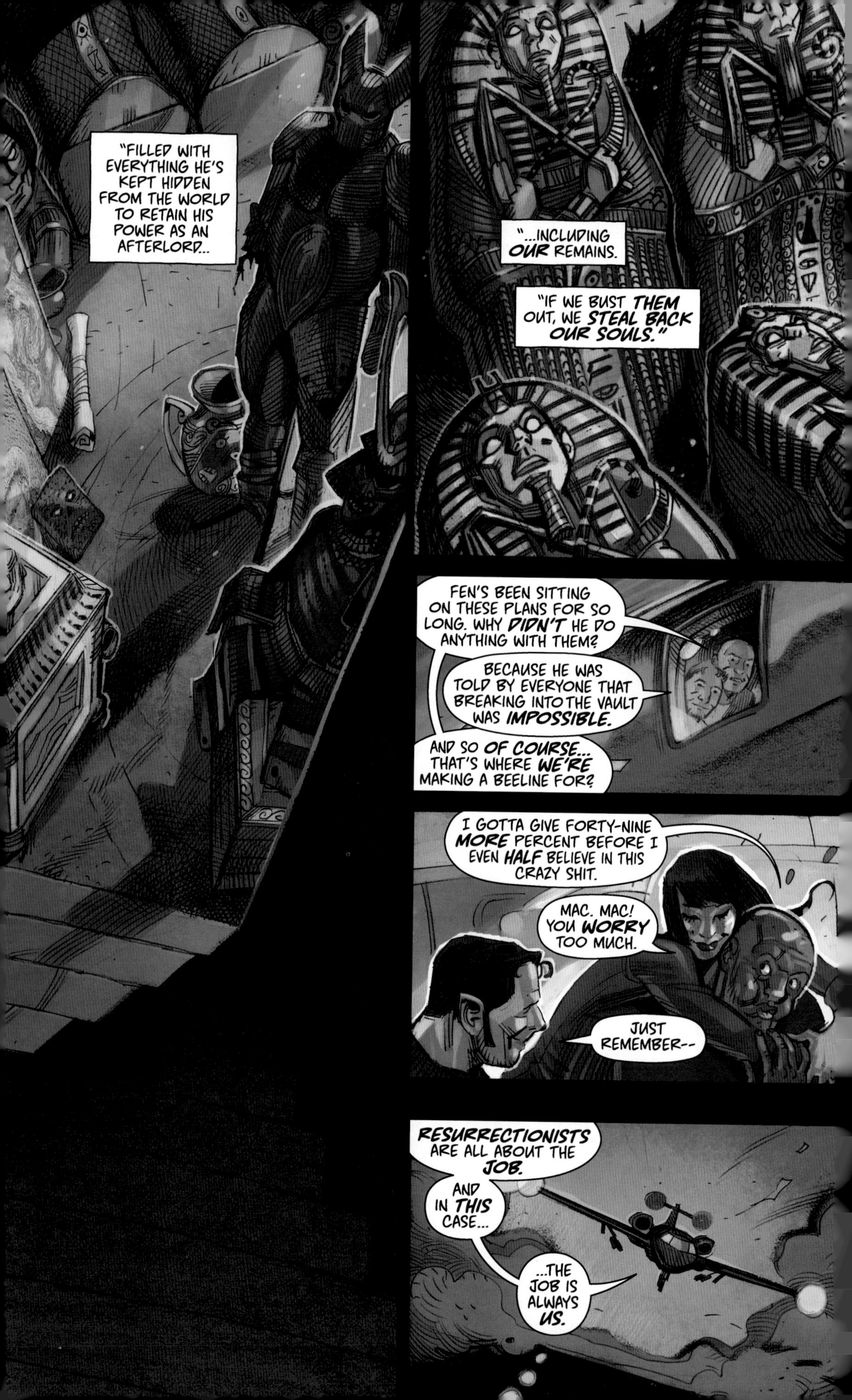
"FILLED WITH EVERYTHING HE'S KEPT HIDDEN FROM THE WORLD TO RETAIN HIS POWER AS AN AFTERLORD...
"...INCLUDING OUR REMAINS.
"IF WE BUST THEM OUT, WE STEAL BACK OUR SOULS."
FEN'S BEEN SITTING ON THESE PLANS FOR SO LONG. WHY DIDN'T HE DO ANYTHING WITH THEM?
BECAUSE HE WAS TOLD BY EVERYONE THAT BREAKING INTO THE VAULT WAS IMPOSSIBLE.
AND SO OF COURSE... THAT'S WHERE WE'RE MAKING A BEELINE FOR?
I GOTTA GIVE FORTY-NINE MORE PERCENT BEFORE I EVEN HALF BELIEVE IN THIS CRAZY SHIT.
MAC. MAC! YOU WORRY TOO MUCH.
JUST REMEMBER--
RESURRECTIONISTS ARE ALL ABOUT THE JOB.
AND IN THIS CASE...
...THE JOB IS ALWAYS US.

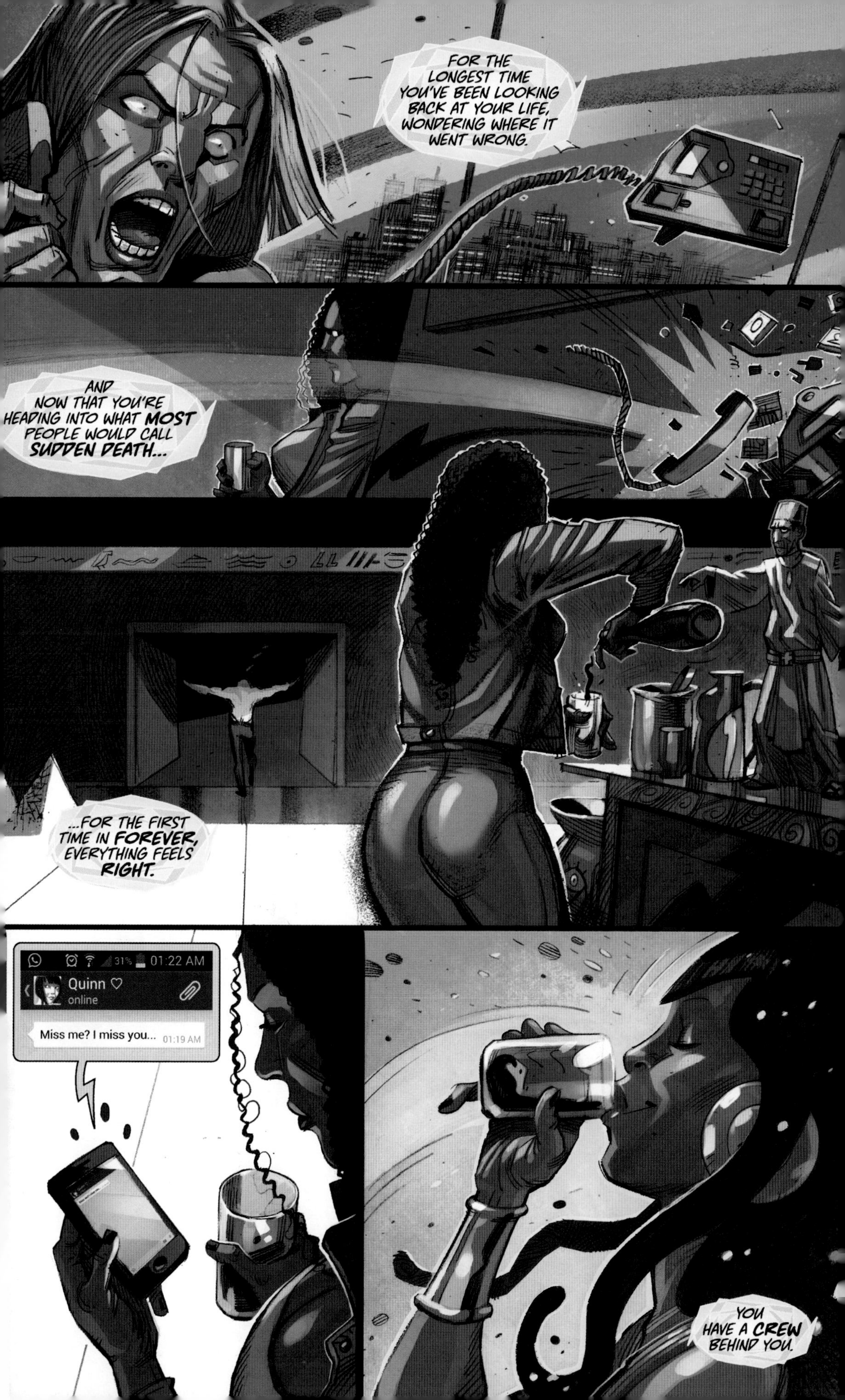

FOR THE LONGEST TIME YOU'VE BEEN LOOKING BACK AT YOUR LIFE, WONDERING WHERE IT WENT WRONG.
AND NOW THAT YOU'RE HEADING INTO WHAT MOST PEOPLE WOULD CALL SUDDEN DEATH...
...FOR THE FIRST TIME IN FOREVER, EVERYTHING FEELS RIGHT.
31% 01:22 AM
Quinn ♡
online
Miss me? I miss you... 01:19 AM
YOU HAVE A CREW BEHIND YOU.

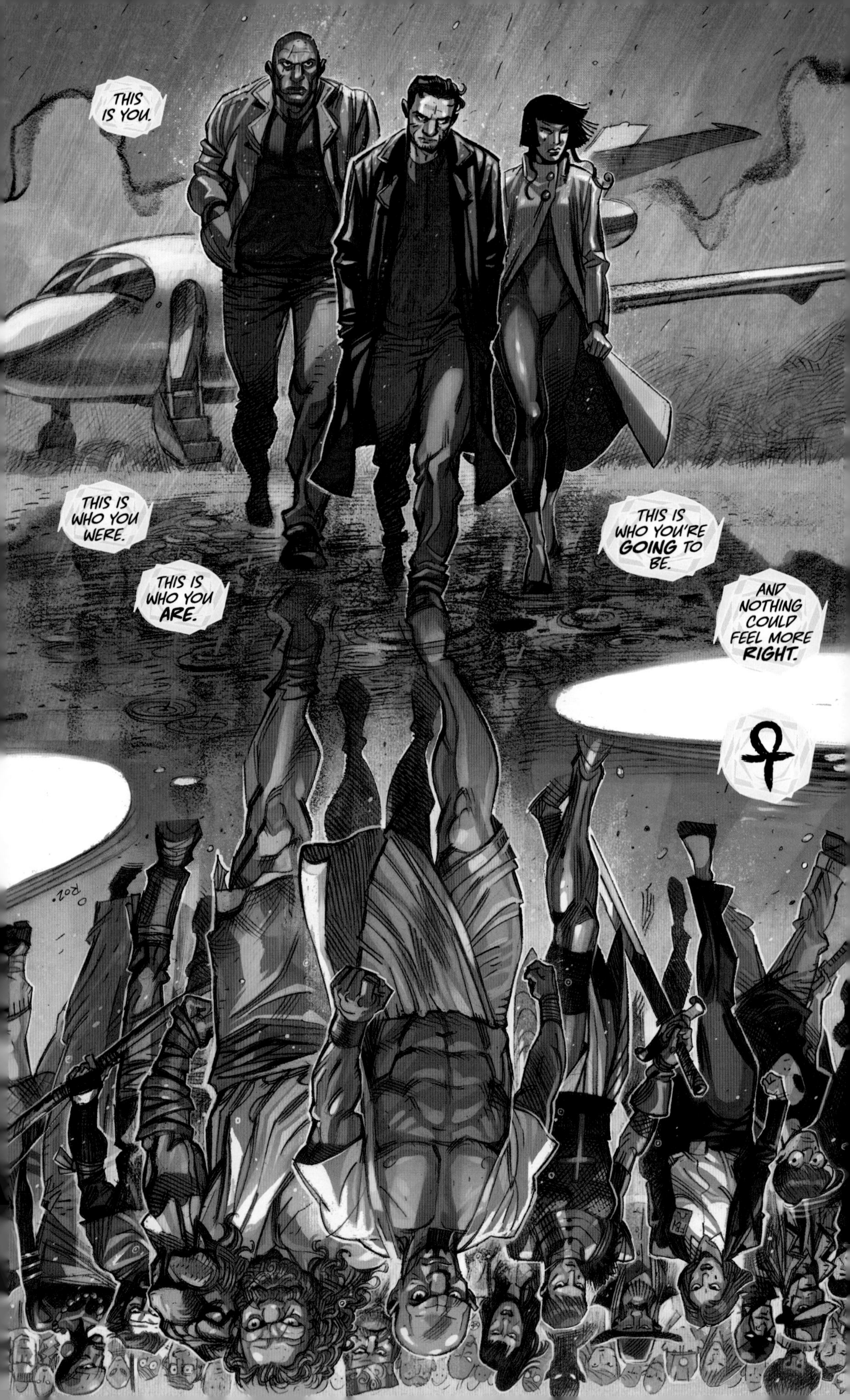
THIS IS YOU.
THIS IS WHO YOU WERE.
THIS IS WHO YOU ARE.
THIS IS WHO YOU'RE GOING TO BE.
AND NOTHING COULD FEEL MORE RIGHT.

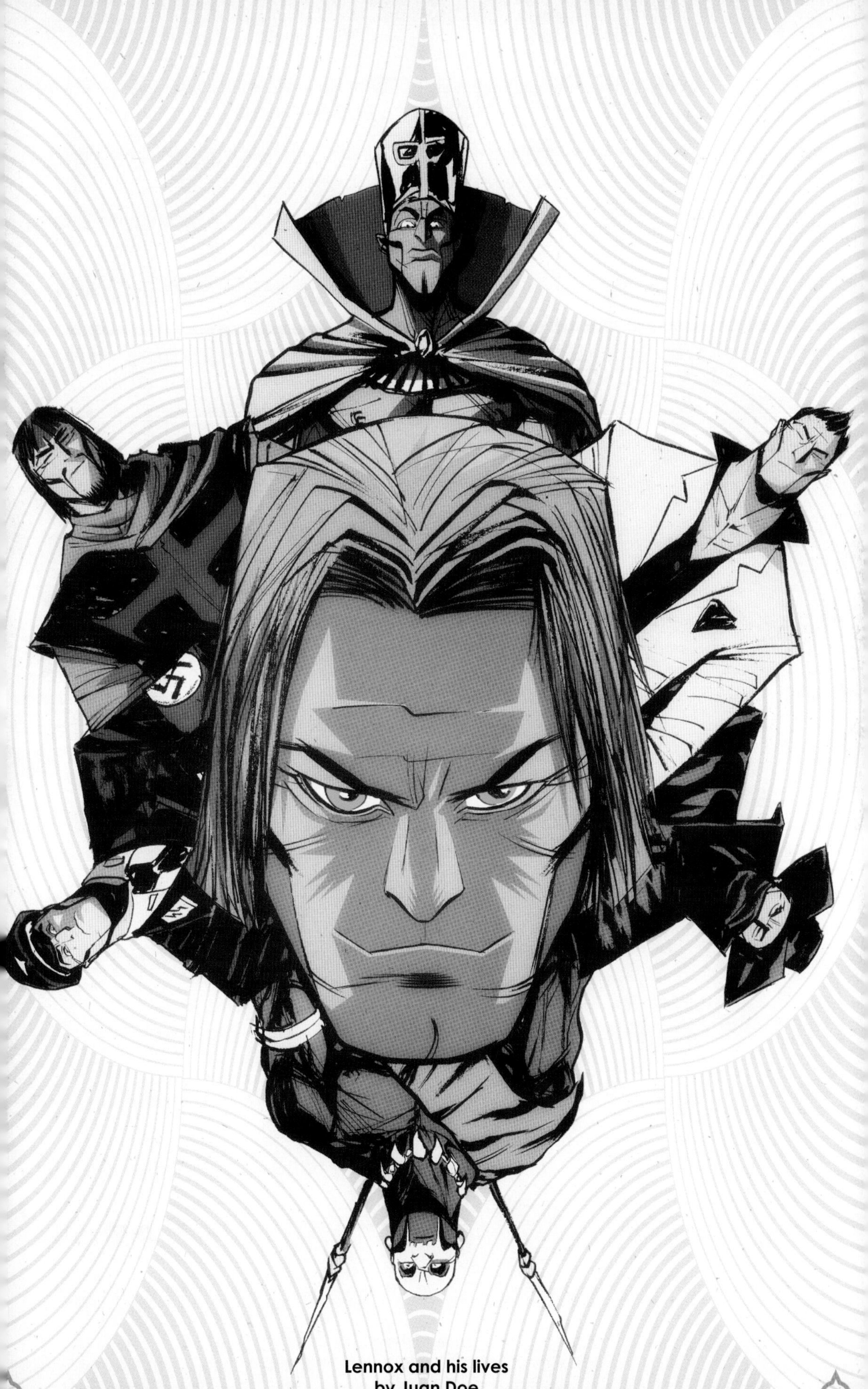

Lennox and his lives
by Juan Doe

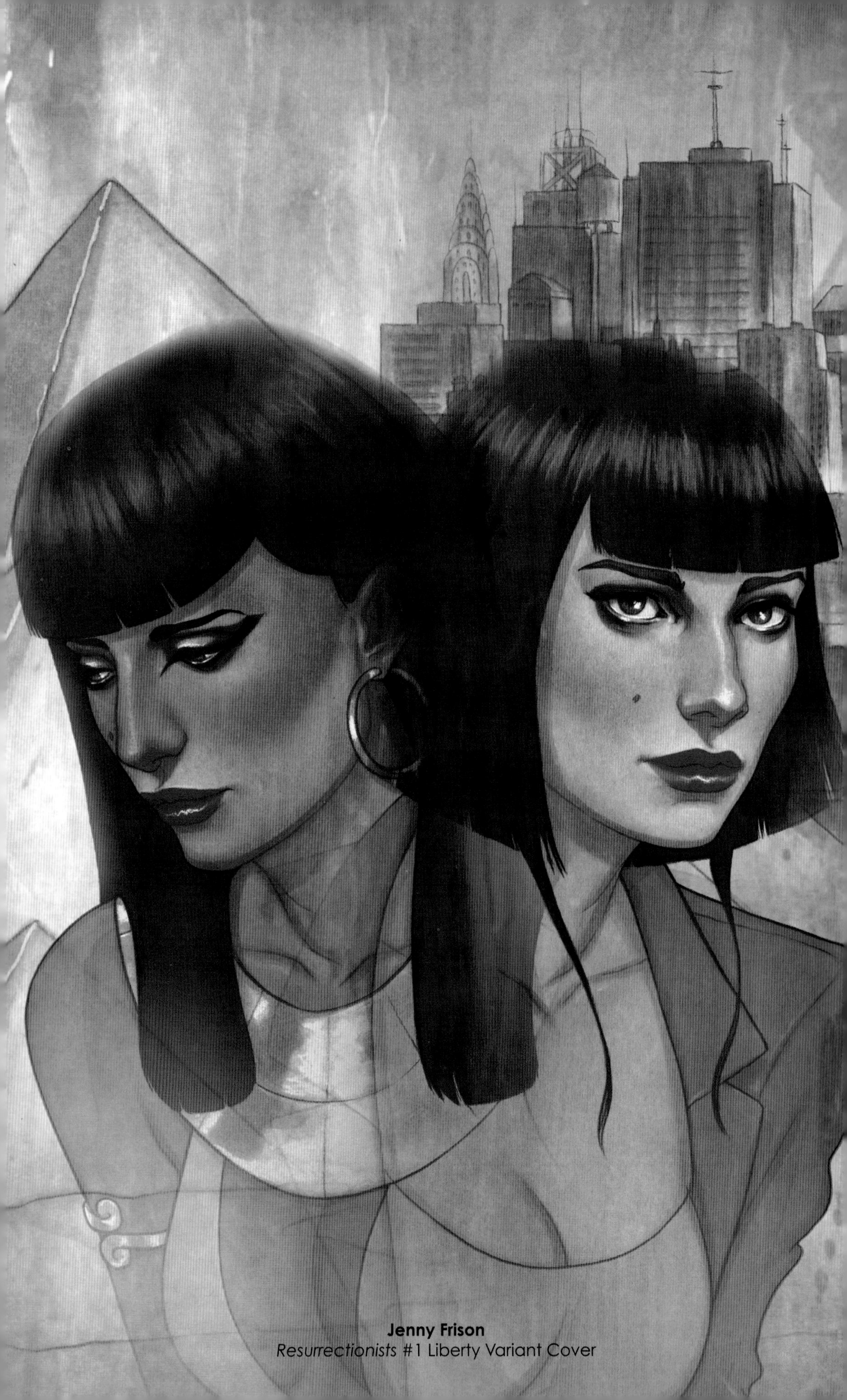

Jenny Frison
Resurrectionists #1 Liberty Variant Cover

The Making of
RESURRECTIONISTS

People are trapped in history and history is trapped in them.

Maurizio Rosenzweig provided incredibly detailed pencils for this series. Here's a look at page 1 before Moreno Dinisio's inking and coloring magic. Check out page 157 for more examples of Maurizio's pencils. And please note the cat by Jericho Way—more on that on the next page.

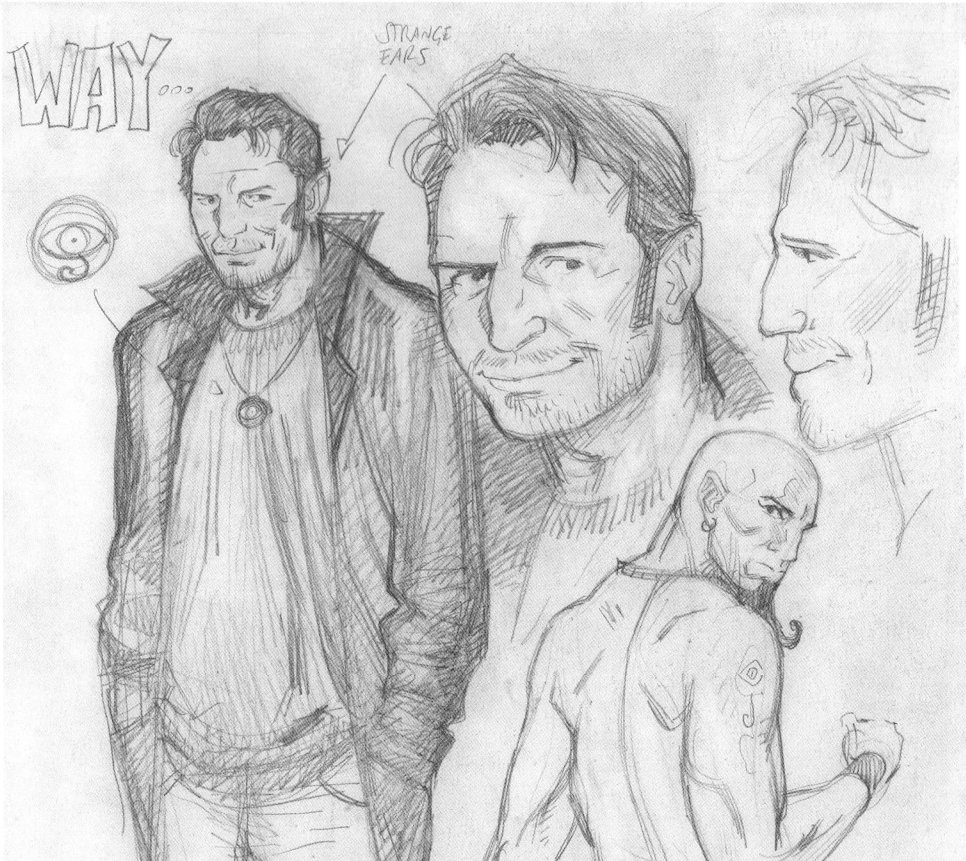

WAY...
STRANGE EARS
HIS NICKNAME IS SPHYNX!
HE HAS SIMILAR LINES
I THINK IT'S A

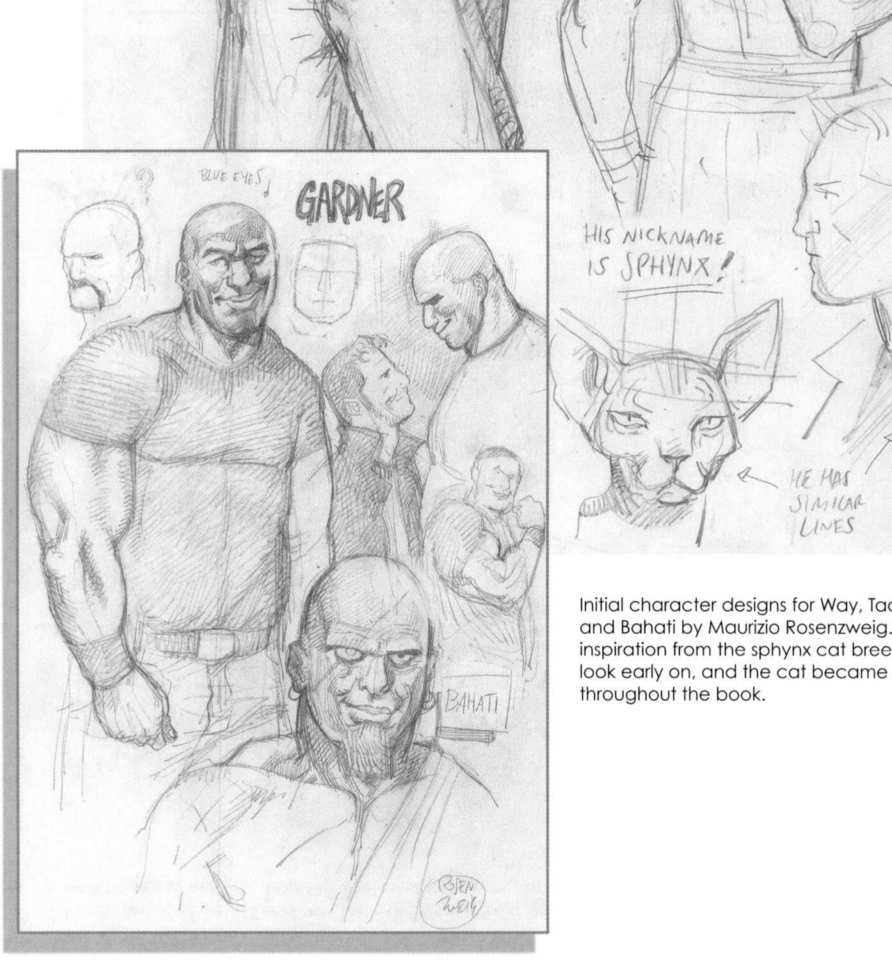

BLUE EYES
GARDNER
BAHATI
ROSEN ZWEIG

Initial character designs for Way, Tao, Gardner, and Bahati by Maurizio Rosenzweig. Maurizio drew inspiration from the sphynx cat breed for Way's look early on, and the cat became a running motif throughout the book.

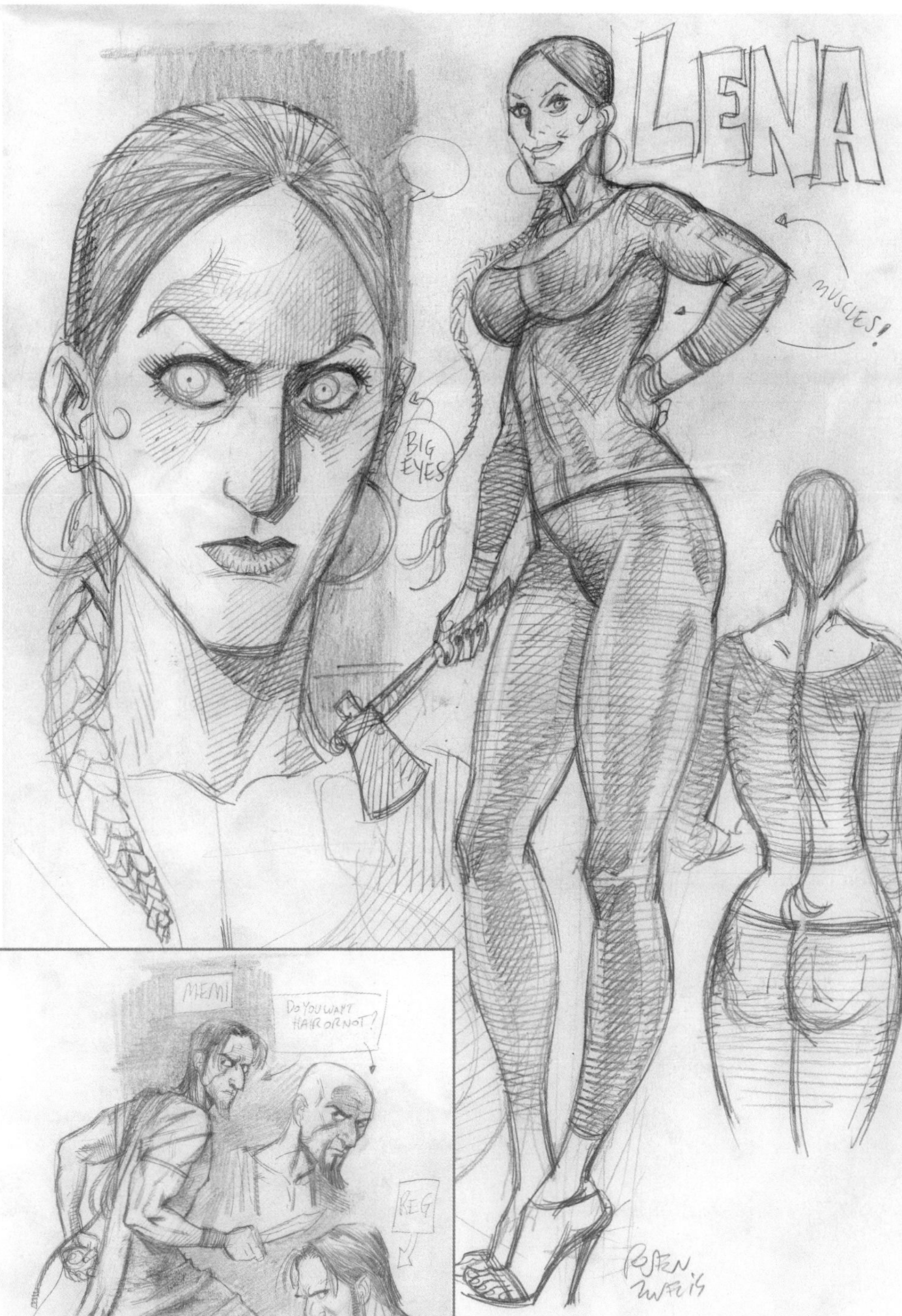
LENA
MUSCLES!
BIG EYES

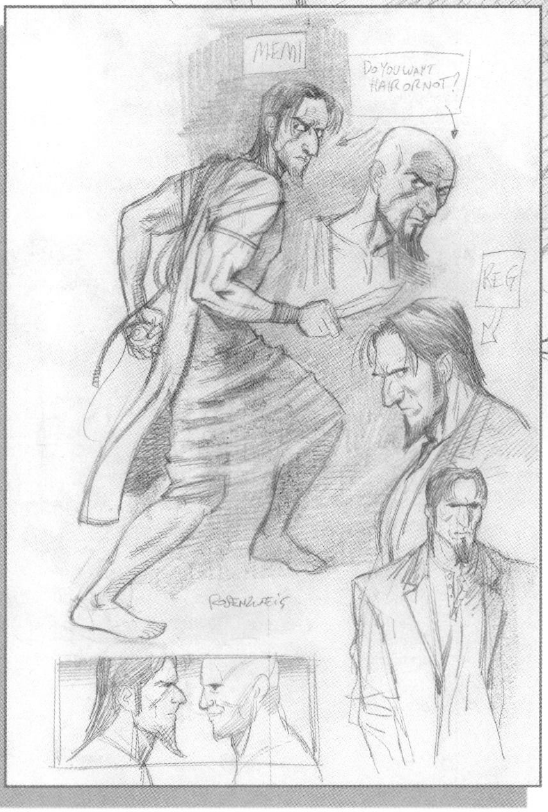
MEMI
DO YOU WANT HAIR OR NOT?
REG

Lena, Memi, and Reg concepts. Maurizio originally believed that Memi was the ancient-Egyptian version of Reg, an early misdirection from Fred's script that showed up even as far back as the character-design phase of the book.

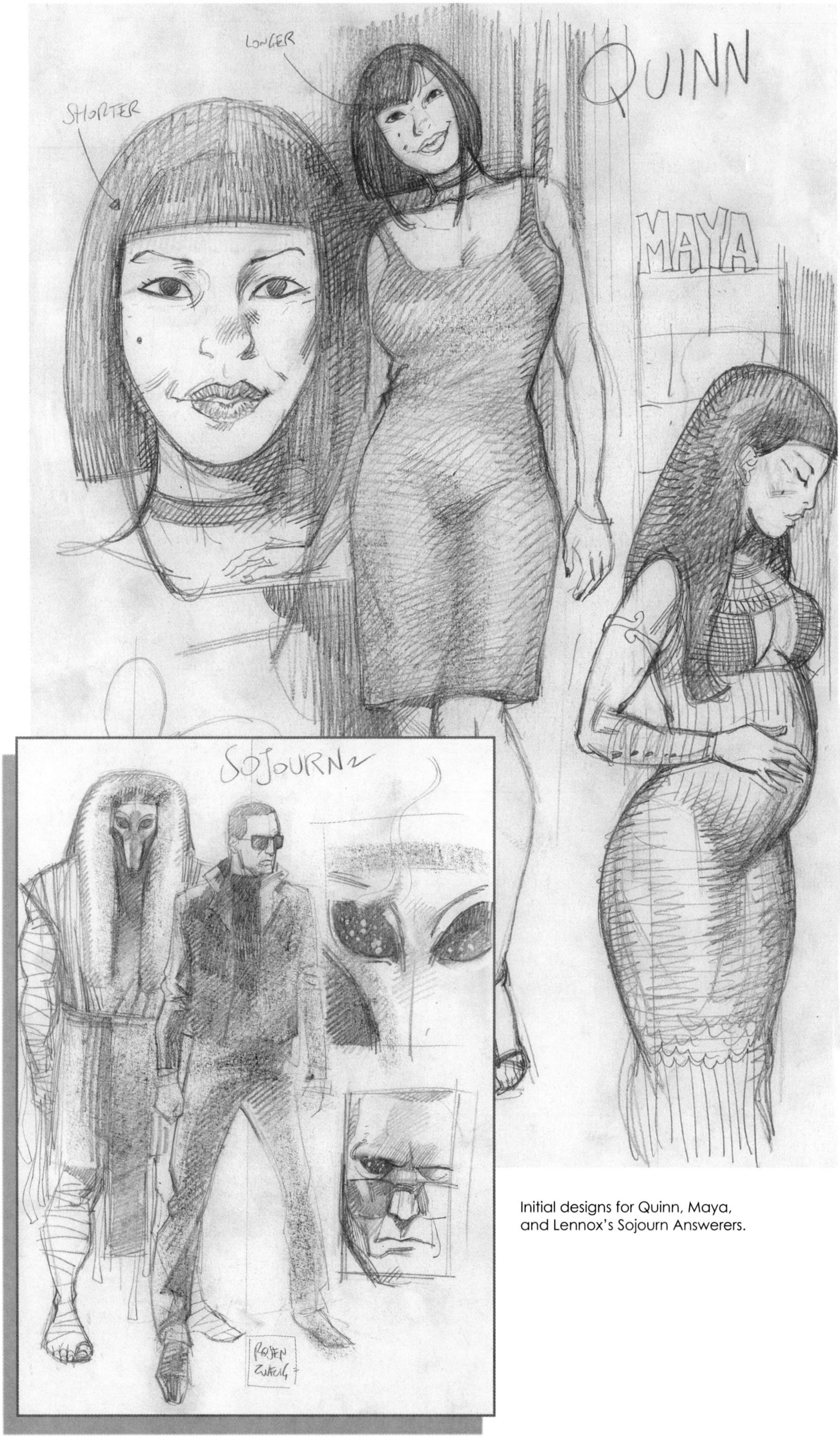
LONGER
SHORTER
QUINN
MAYA
SOJOURN

Initial designs for Quinn, Maya,
and Lennox's Sojourn Answerers.

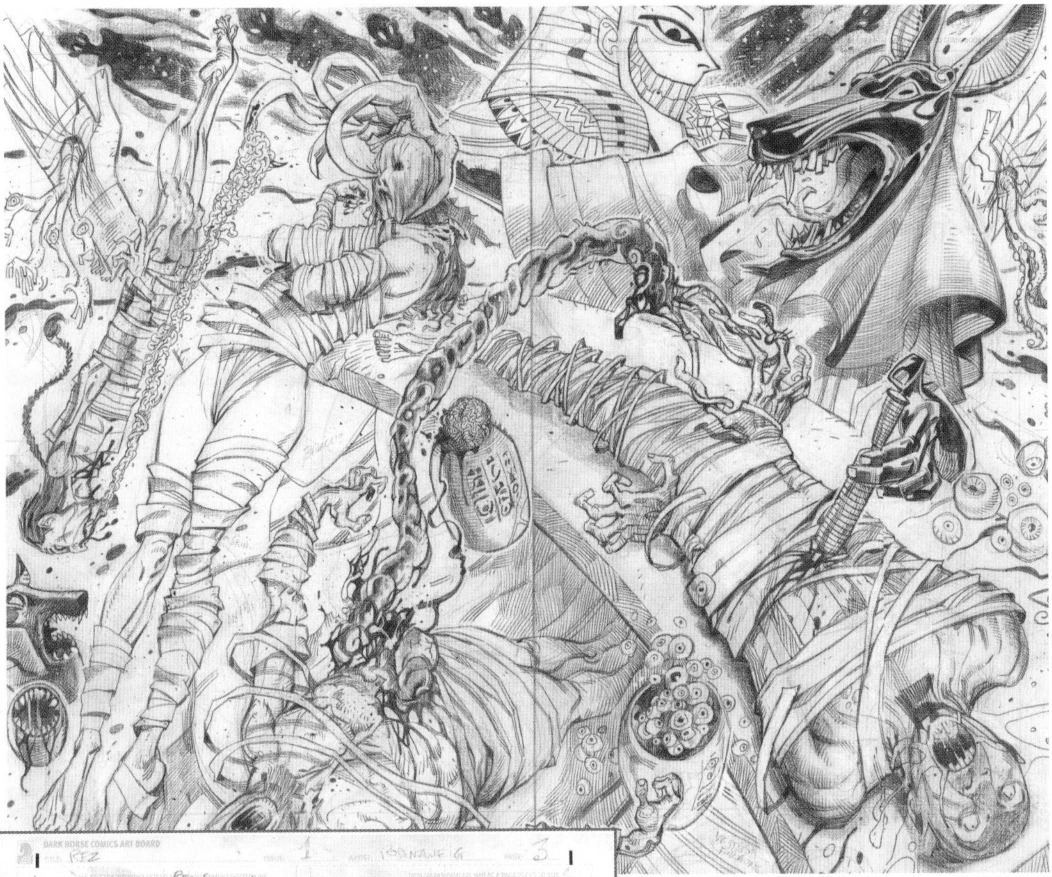

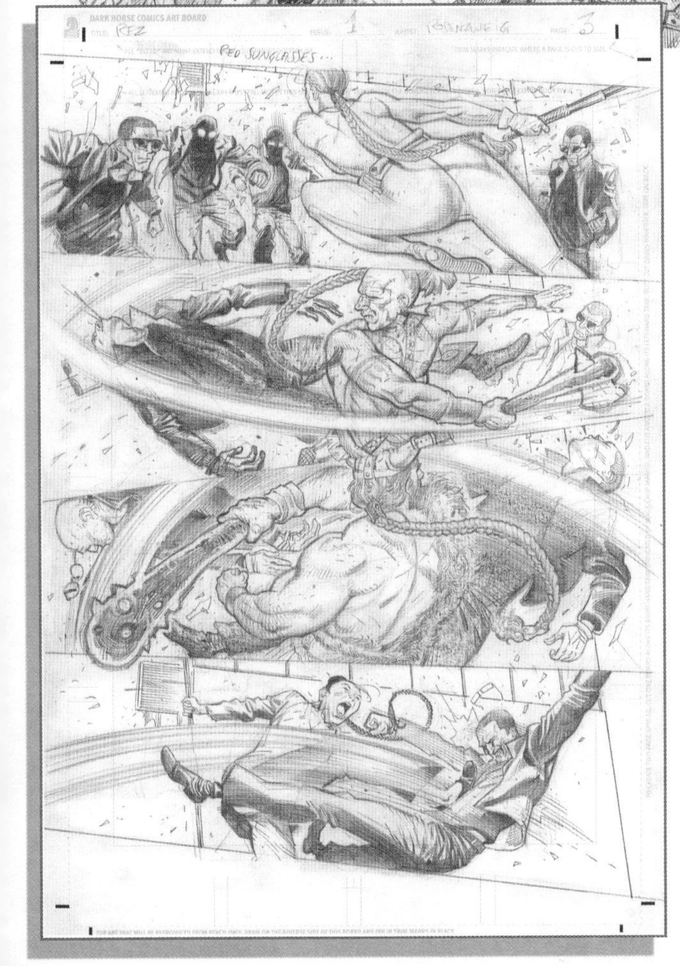
DARK HORSE COMICS ART BOARD
TITLE: REZ
ISSUE: 1
PAGE: 3
RED SUNGLASSES...

A look at Maurizio's incredibly detailed pencils. On page 3 of issue #1, it was Maurizio's clever idea to give each incarnation of Lena a ponytail to tie them together visually.

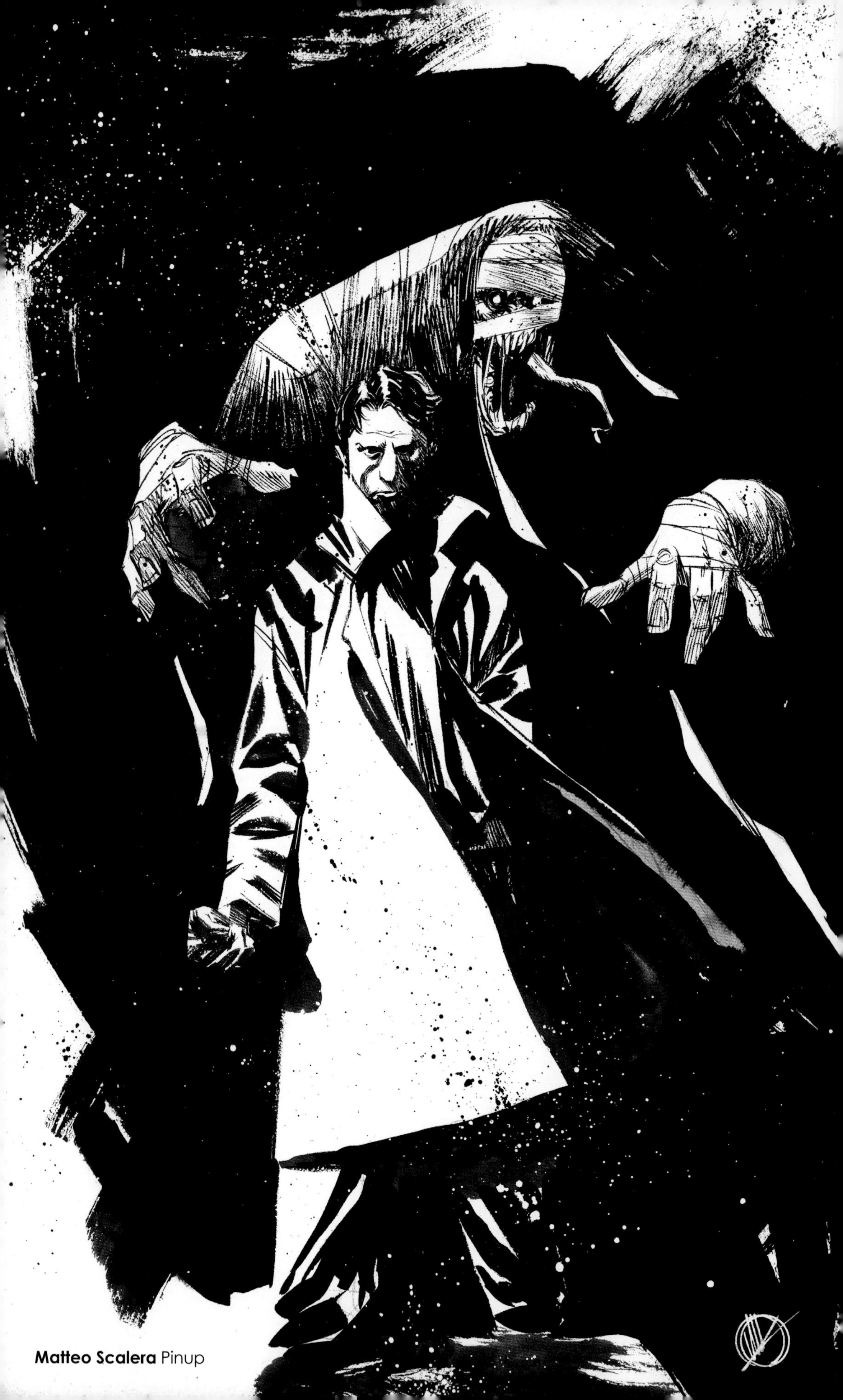

Matteo Scalera Pinup

FROM *NEW YORK TIMES* BEST-SELLING AUTHOR

FRED VAN LENTE

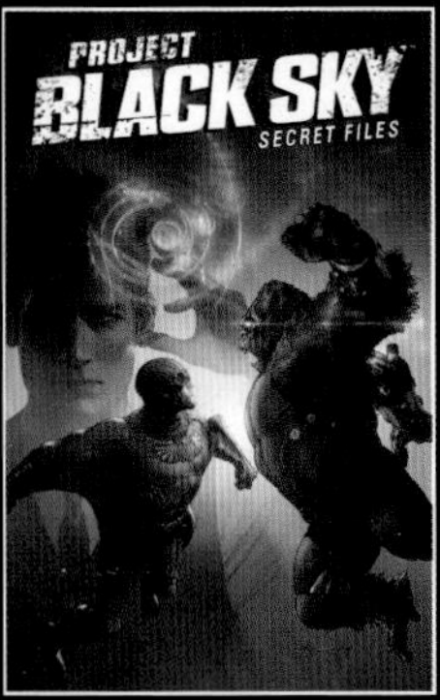
PROJECT
BLACK SKY
SECRET FILES

PROJECT BLACK SKY: SECRET FILES

Art by Michael Broussard, Steve Ellis, and Guiu Vilanova

In the late 1930s, a covert government agency was established to protect Earth from potential extraterrestrial threats. These brave men and women were called Project Black Sky, and what they discovered would change the course of human history.

ISBN 978-1-61655-604-4 | $14.99

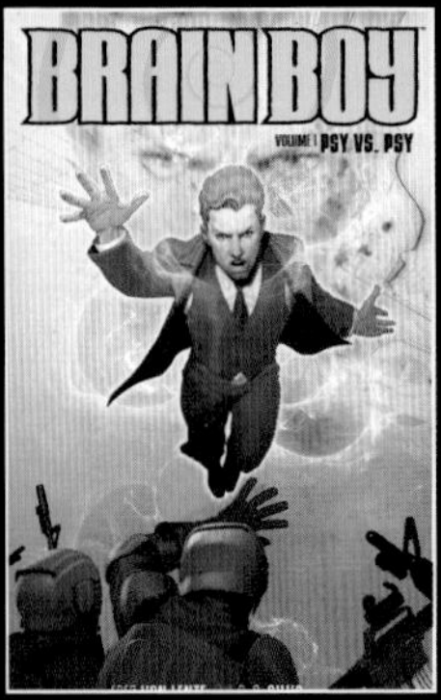
BRAIN BOY
PSY VS. PSY

BRAIN BOY VOLUME 1: PSY VS. PSY

Art by Freddie Williams II, R. B. Silva, and Rob Lean

When the United States Secret Service needs to stop an assassination before the killer's even decided to buy a gun, they call the world's most powerful telepath: Matt Price, a.k.a. Brain Boy. But when the secret agent that can read anyone's mind finds that a powerful psychic network has been hidden from him, Brain Boy begins to wonder whether he knows everything or nothing at all!

ISBN 978-1-61655-317-3 | $14.99

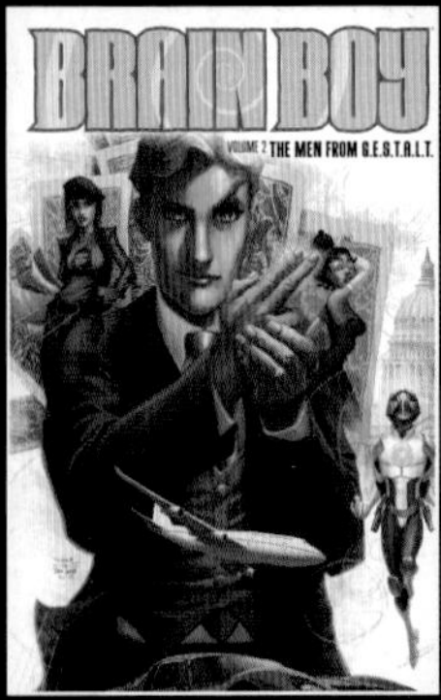
BRAIN BOY
THE MEN FROM G.E.S.T.A.L.T.

BRAIN BOY VOLUME 2: THE MEN FROM G.E.S.T.A.L.T.

Art by Freddie Williams II and Jeremy Colwell

Agent Price's new mission pits him against a doomsday-cult leader with a political agenda that poses a direct threat to the president. But a mysterious hive mind has more menacing plans for Brain Boy. He'll have no choice but to go head to head—brain to brain—with the mysterious Men from G.E.S.T.A.L.T.!

ISBN 978-1-61655-506-1 | $14.99

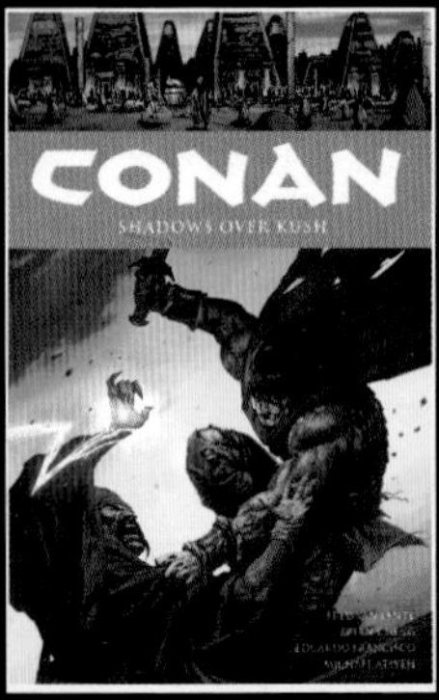
CONAN
SHADOWS OVER KUSH

CONAN VOLUME 17: SHADOWS OVER KUSH

Art by Brian Ching and Eduardo Francisco

Conan drinks himself into a stupor while in the city of Shumballa—until an act of thievery propels him into a witch hunt full of adventure, demons, and rebellion! "By Crom! Now this is how a Conan story should read!" —Geeks of Doom

TPB: ISBN 978-1-61655-659-4 | $19.99
HC: ISBN 978-1-61655-522-1 | $24.99